Architectural
THEORY

To stay informed about upcoming TASCHEN titles, please request
our magazine at www.taschen.com/magazine or write to TASCHEN
America, 6671 Sunset Boulevard, Suite 1508, USA-Los Angeles, CA 90028,
contact-us@taschen.com, Fax: +1-323-463.4442. We will be happy to send
you a free copy of our magazine which is filled with information about all
of our books.

© 2006 TASCHEN GmbH, Hohenzollernring 53, D-50672 Köln
www.taschen.com

Project management: Petra Lamers-Schütze, Cologne
Editorial coordination: Thierry Nebois, Cologne
Design: Claudia Frey, Cologne
Cover: Sense/Net, Andy Disl and Birgit Reber, Cologne
Production: Thomas Grell, Cologne
English translation: Gregory Pauls, Jeremy Gaines, Michael Shuttleworth

Printed in China
ISBN 3-8228-5085-4

Architectural
THEORY

FROM THE RENAISSANCE TO THE PRESENT

With a preface by Bernd Evers

In cooperation with the
Kunstbibliothek der Staatlichen Museen zu Berlin

TASCHEN

KÖLN LONDON LOSANGELES MADRID PARIS TOKYO

Contents

Preface

BERND EVERS

The publication *De architectura libri decem* (*Ten Books on Architecture*) is the oldest architectural treatise and the only one to have survived complete from pre-Christian times. Not only does it provide us with insights into the architecture of Classical Antiquity and related principles, it also lays the foundations for all discussions on architectural theory since the Renaissance. It would seem likely that the treatise was written in the third or second decade before Christ. Dedicated to Emperor Augustus, it was penned by a military engineer serving in the Roman army who is known to us by his *nomen gentile* Vitruvius.

Although the Vitruvian tradition remained alive in numerous medieval manuscripts, it was only of marginal importance for actual building practice. Indeed, the Classical column orders were first considered exemplary only once Vitruvius' text had been appropriated once again by the Classical scholars of the Renaissance and deemed to be the model par excellence for architecture to follow, with Leon Battista Alberti declaring they should be taken as the binding norm. Vitruvius' architectural treatise advanced to become the most momentous book on architectural theory in the centuries that followed. Architects such as Sebastiano Serlio, Iacomo Barozzi da Vignola and Andrea Palladio systematized Vitruvius' doctrine, and made it available to the public in illustrated books. Consequently, the architectural theory elaborated in response to Vitruvius advanced to become an independent form of art theory. Among the countless illustrated Vitruvius editions, that prepared by Daniele Barbaro in 1556 is the most carefully thought out and did the greatest justice to the original in the sense of textual criticism. Barbaro takes the Vitruvian definition "architectura est scientia" ("architecture is a science") as the underlying principle informing his comments, and places architecture on a sound mathematical footing in order to render it a part of Truth. According to Daniele Barbaro, art and architecture are intellectual, rationally conceived activities that do not rest on the senses. Since Science and Reason are subject to absolute truth, he suggests, the dignity and magnificence of architecture derives from the extent to which it relies on scientific disciplines.

Ever since Alberti, the goals of good architecture had been described in terms of the Vitruvian triad. Every building should be sound, functional und attractive. Vitruvius, the first of all architectural theoreticians, distinguishes between *firmitas* (firmness, robustness, structural strength), *utilitas* (usefulness or commodity) and *venustas* (beauty or delight). *Firmitas* relates to all technical matters such as the selection of a site, the materials and the foundation, *utilitas* to the function of the building, and *venustas* to its aesthetics. The Vitruvian architectural aesthetic embraces the doctrine of the column orders, correct use of proportions, and the canons of decorum, according to which certain forms were assigned to specific gods: Doric temples to Mars, Minerva and Hercules, Corinthian temples to Venus, Flora, Proserpina and the water nymphs, while the Ionic style temple was ascribed to Juno, Diana and Bacchus.

This three-fold purpose of architecture continued to be the norm until around 1800. It was from this time onwards that the Vitruvian canon began to collapse, and Classical stylistic unity went into decline. Until the mid-18th century, buildings were described in terms of an architectural theory based on the particular architect's plans. The overall architecture and the individual parts of a building were geared to fulfilling the Vitruvian criteria, while the general architectural scheme was determined according to the familiar triad. Written descriptions served as an aid to studying the drawings, which were in any case more vivid and accurate in terms of practical use. From around 1750 new methods were gradually developed for the description of architecture and its historical observation. Once the Vitruvian categories lost their normative quality, architectural description likewise forfeited its subordinate role. Attention now focused more on the historical nature of buildings, with debate hinging on the purpose of architecture, in particular the imitation of Classical Antiquity as a "purpose." The focus now shifted towards the building's formal qualities. This trend paid no consideration to the richly associative elements of architecture and was already apparent in Georg Andreas Böckler's thought, when he wrote in 1698 in his commentary on Palladio, *Baumeisterin Palla*: "Beauty arises from the well-arranged and attractive shape or design, in which namely the entire building with all its parts, but also the parts themselves correspond properly to one another and are in conformity. The building should reveal itself to the eye to be a whole, well-composed body, in which each part fits well with the others, and in which all the parts are necessary."

Alongside the numerous debates on stylistic theory, the large-format portfolios and the pattern books of sample plans decisively shaped 19th century architectural thinking, providing a representative cross-section of an architect's repertoire. It became the practice for portfolios to be produced in which the architect presented the works he had realized, or those he planned. Such works also had a promotional function; they furnished practical instructions for the actual construction work, while also providing guidelines for those engaged in the study or practice of architecture, not to mention independent craftsmen. As a rule, the illustrative material on exemplary building methods with its highly promotional qualities was complemented by a specialist, theo-

retical commentary. Following the largely stylistic debates of the 19th century, with the advent of Modernism technological and social, in other words non-aesthetic considerations increasingly came to be applied to architecture.

Given the wealth of available sources on architectural theory since the Renaissance it would go beyond the scope of this publication to offer more than an overview. Nonetheless, it does cover the major positions in architectural aesthetics prevalent in different countries. In many cases the texts of the architectural treatises serve only to elaborate the illustrations. Accordingly, the present volume contains a rich selection of illustrations that represent an illustrated atlas to architectural theory.

Many of the source works are housed in the collection of ornamental engravings attached to the Kunstbibliothek der Staatlichen Museen zu Berlin, which has succeeded in recent decades in making up for the terrible losses of engravings incurred during the Second World War. It is the intention of the present book only to offer an idea of the wide-ranging debates on architectural aesthetics and theories, but also to stimulate broader and more detailed scholarly research in the field of architecture.

Italy

Leon Battista Alberti (1404–1472)
De re aedificatoria libri decem

MANUSCRIPT 1442–1452. VATICAN CITY, BIBLIOTECA

APOSTOLICA VATICANA; MODENA, BIBLIOTECA ESTENSE ET AL.

The architecture of Leon Battista Alberti, in ten books. London, 1726

Leon Battista Alberti, who authored the treatise *De re aedificatoria libri decem* which laid out the most important architectural theory of early modern times, was not originally an architect and certainly not a stonemason or cabinetmaker, but a humanist. He was born in Genoa in 1404, the illegitimate child of a prosperous Florentine aristocratic family in exile, and grew up in Venice. He received his basic education in the humanities – Latin, Classical rhetoric, philosophy and poetics – at the hands of one of the best-known Cicero scholars of the day, Gasparino Barzizza (c. 1360–c. 1431), studying at the latter's "Gymnasion" in Padua. He thereafter attended the renowned University of Bologna, where he initially read Philology, Rhetoric and Philosophy, before a nervous breakdown forced him to limit himself to Canon and Civil Law, Mathematics and Physics. He became an "abbreviator," a chancellery secretary in the Papal service, a post he held until his dismissal.

Within his wide-ranging œuvre, three works occupy a special position: *De pictura/Della pittura* (*On painting*), a small book written in 1435 in Latin and translated into Italian in 1436; the short text *De statua/Della pittura* (*On sculpture*) penned in 1438; and his book on the art of building, *De re aedificatoria*, written between 1442 and 1452. In other words, Alberti discussed those three arts that were not traditionally assigned to the canon of the liberal arts. Making them the object of independent studies amounted to setting them on a par with such arts as geometry, music, poetics and rhetoric.

Interestingly enough, Alberti's activity as an author waned in inverse proportion to his work as a consultant on architectural issues and finally his work as an architect planning buildings. Undoubtedly, he was fascinated by architecture from an early date, as indicated perhaps by the dedication of the 1436 edition of *Delle pittura* to the architect Filippo Brunelleschi (1377–1446). In 1447, when he was already working on *De re aedificatoria*, Tommaso Parentucelli da Sarzana, a colleague and friend from his student days, was elected Pope Nicholas V (reigned 1447–1455). The latter appears to have involved Alberti from the very beginning in the difficult considerations on how to restore the dilapidated St. Peter's Basilica as well as in the planning for the new architectural face to be given the Vatican. Presumably, it was the Pope who in 1450 obtained Alberti the commission to transform the Malatestas' funerary church in Rimini into a new "temple." From then until his death in 1472 Alberti, not only worked for the Papal Court, but also acted as architect for the Rucellai family in Florence (façade of Santa Maria Novella, the Rucellai family palazzo, the Rucellais' funerary chapel) and for the Gonzagas in Mantua (San Sebastiano, Sant' Andrea).

One explanation for Alberti's remarkable turn from 1450 onwards increasingly from author to architect might be Cicero's ideal of the Classical *perfectus orator*, to which Alberti was committed. The lofty moral, philosophical and rhetorical education of an orator in the ancient world was of direct

benefit to the *res publica*, "the public cause," as well as to the daily legal and political life of the republic. As an orator, however, Alberti had the dilemma of being regarded the Cicero of his age while having no opportunity of contributing to the public good in the same way as his role model. For Alberti, architecture appears to have been an eminently political activity, since he considered architects to be the providers and safe-keepers of culture, who could offer a civic community ("civitas") security and protection, thus creating the conditions for social and intellectual progress. He gathered together his thoughts on architects, and on the tasks of an architecture that went beyond the mere piling up of stones, in his treatise *De re aedificatoria,* which was presented to Pope Nicholas V in 1452.

The idea of writing a treatise on architecture seems to have come to Alberti during scholarly discussions about Vitruvius' ancient treatise at the court of Lionello d'Este in Ferrara, in the company of fellow humanists and the educated higher nobility. To begin with he was presumably considering a commentary to the difficult text, which was only available in fragmentary form and whose author had used specialist Greek vocabulary. And yet as Alberti himself stated, he was prompted to write a work that was of a higher literary standard, that was better structured and more precise in its argumentation not as a result of Vitruvius alone, but also as a result of the destruction of Classical ruins and the bad taste of his contemporaries, bad because it took its lead from Gothic architecture.

Alberti divided his work up into exactly the same number of books as Vitruvius in his *Di architectura decem libri* (*Ten books on architecture*), and he also adopted his pre-

decessor's sub-division into robustness, utility and beauty (*firmitas, utilitas* and *venustas*). Nonetheless he arranges his material quite differently: In Book I, entitled "lineamenta" (plans), he examines, from the point of view of utility the parts that make up every building, and which must therefore be considered at the very beginning of any consideration of architecture. These are the surroundings, the ground on which the building is to be erected, the ground plan, walls, the roof and openings (*regio, area, partitio, paries, tectum* and *apertio*). Book II, "materia," provides information about materials, and Book III, "opus," goes into the structural theory. Alberti thus deals up to this point with matters that relate to the robustness (*firmitas*) of a building. Books IV "universorum opus" (buildings in general) and V "singulorum opus" (special buildings) concentrate on general and specialized types of building, and can be categorized under utility/commodity (*utilitas*). Books VI to IX, "ornamentum," "sacrorum ornamentum," "publici profani ornamentum" and "privatorum ornamentum" form a unity that Alberti classified as beauty (*venustas*). The English word "ornament," however, in relation to ecclesiastical buildings, secular public buildings, and private buildings, is an inadequate description of the content of these books. In order to get a clearer picture it is best to use metaphors from Classical rhetoric as a guideline, as Alberti himself did, in which the elaborateness of a speech was compared with a veil that covers a naked body, or, on a more profound level, with the flesh that creates a body out of dead bones. It is not until the second half of his treatise that Alberti touches on the complete, and thus beautiful, "body" of architecture; it is only now that he talks of architecture as "beautiful art." Book X "operum instauratio" (restoration of buildings) deals with techniques of preserving existing buildings and brings his thoughts to their conclusion.

Alberti's thoughts about the beauty of architecture hinge on the question of "decorum," or what is appropriate. Here he distinguishes between the dimensions of social ethics and formal aesthetics. Since Alberti's approach is always based on "civitas," i.e. a society based on the city, all architecture has to be integrated into this urban structure in accordance with socially recognizable criteria. This results in a hierarchy, headed by ecclesiastical buildings, and in particular temples, followed by the town walls, the basilica, and tombs, which receive the highest accolade of "dignitas" and as such are entitled to the most lavish of "ornamenta," which Alberti describes in Book VII. The next book outlines a lower, "mid" level of buildings and public work such as streets, squares, bridges, libraries, schools, hospitals, gymnasiums etc., which in terms of dignity come lower down the scale. Private buildings, town houses, villas and gardens outside the town walls were at the bottom of the hierarchy. By contrast, the temple, as the measure of all things, was the source of all building elements that could appropriately be used in all other buildings, for example the various columns and their components. Alberti ends this precise analysis with a list of all the cornice shapes known to him, a list that is almost lexical in its exactness. How all these individual parts are then pieced together to form one beautiful whole which can fully develop its uplifting effect is in turn a question of appropriateness, in this case construed in aesthetic terms; Alberti refers to it as "concinnitas." The latter exhibits the laws by which the correct number of parts, their proportion and their rhythm merge to form a beautiful piece of architecture. "Concinnitas" also means the ability of the beholder to recognize a beautiful building when he sees one and, without necessarily having to rationally justify his feelings, be touched or moved by it.

Even after the end of the Quattrocento, Alberti's treatise *De re aedificatoria* remained the most intellectually challenging set of thoughts on architectural theory. This is further underscored by his decision to write it in Latin, and by the fact that there are no illustrations. Prior to its first appearance in print in 1485, it would have been read and understood almost exclusively in learned and court circles, yet even among persons of such rank scarcely anybody was in possession of a copy before the 1480s. From 1483 however, splendid handwritten editions were prepared for potential clients such as the Duke of Urbino, Federico da Montefeltro (1422–1482) and the Hungarian King Matthias Corvinus (reigned 1458–1490). It is difficult to ascertain whether or how Alberti's elitist treatise was received by architects. Architects such as Filarete (c. 1400–1465) and Francesco di Giorgio Martini (1439–1501), who were likewise authors, were familiar with the treatise. And we know that an anonymous *scarpellino*, a master mason, borrowed the valuable book from the court library in Ferrara, though it is not known how much of the text he actually understood, or what he hoped to learn from it. The work became more widely accessible following the second translation into Italian by Cosimo Bartoli in 1565, which at last also included illustrations.

VB

1 | **Illustration of how a double purchase pulley works**
In the first illustrated edition: L'Architettura di Leon Battista Alberti, tradotta in lingua Fiorentina da Cosimo Bartoli Gentil'huomo, *Florence, 1550, p. 130/31. Woodcut*

𝕬 Des cisternes, ensemble de leur vsage & vtilité.

2 | **Landscape view featuring dams and aqueducts**
To ensure a town's water supply. To illustrate Alberti's chapter "Des cisternes, ensemble de leur usage et utitilité," the French edition depicts a town embedded in a hilly landscape with dams and aqueducts.
In: L'Architecture et art de bien bastir du seigneur Leon Baptiste Albert, *Paris, 1553, p. 214. Woodcut*

Antonio Averlino called Filarete (c. 1400–c. 1465)

Codex Magliabechianus II, I, 140

C. 1461–1464. FLORENCE, BIBLIOTECA NAZIONALE

Unlike Leon Battista Alberti, whose work *De re aedificatoria libri decem* (*Ten books on the art of building*) was in Latin and contained no illustrations, Antonio Averlino, who followed immediately on from him, wrote in the vernacular Italian, and furnished his treatise with a large number of pictures. Averlino, who referred to himself as "Filarete" or "friend of virtue," was well aware that he was in no sense on an intellectual par with Alberti, but he had still mustered from his practical experience enough self-confidence to write about "building methods, measurements and proportions" ("modi e misure e proporzioni d'edificare"). He says that, being uneducated, he cannot be sure his text obeys the rules of rhetoric – though he does manage to quote directly the trope of modesty as used by Vitruvius, the architectural theorist of Classical Antiquity – and moreover, as he points out, he is no Vitruvius. He is, or so he claims, an experienced artist with practical experience in drawing, building and sculpting, and as such it is his aim to instruct those who doubt that there is a theoretical basis to architecture. It is not without a certain proud nonchalance that he refers his educated readers to his predecessors Vitruvius and Alberti, who had written in Latin.

Born in Florence around 1400, Filarete probably trained as a goldsmith and bronze founder in Lorenzo Ghiberti's (1381–1455) workshop, though there are no surviving examples of any of his work from this period. Art historians first come across Filarete in the second, more important, part of his life, spent in Rome from about 1433 until 1448, where he certainly made a name for himself. It was here, in 1445, that he completed his main sculptural work, namely the bronze door of St. Peter's Basilica, commissioned by Pope Eugene IV (reigned 1431–1447) and still extant. Following the theft of some holy relics, Filarete was forced to flee Rome at the end of the 1440s. It was not until 1451 that he resurfaced, working for the Duke of Milan, Francesco Sforza (1401–1466), as an engineer and architect, and Milan would appear to have been the focal point of his activities until 1465. It was here that his most important work, the Ospedale Maggiore, was constructed between 1456 and 1465, and it is most probable that it was here that from 1461 to 1464 he wrote his architectural treatise. After 1465, he disappears from view.

What prompted Filarete to embark on an architectural treatise is not known, though it is probable that he wanted to acquire powerful clients and make a name for himself as an architect. Among other things, the various versions of the treatise that have survived in Italian, dedicated either to Francesco Sforza or Piero de Medici (1429–1484), would seem to bear this out. As is so often the case with 15th-century manuscripts, Filarete's original autograph manuscript has not survived, though there are still three copies in existence as well as a 15th-century archetype copied directly from the original. A distinction is made here between the so-called Sforza group (*Codex Trivulzianus*, Milan; *Codex Palatinus*, Florence), which are derived from the treatise dedicated

disopra aessa & poi discosi & uscimo plasua
mura andamo uedendo tutto & cosi discosi p
· & poi alsecondo ponte louatoio entrommo nel
oc· disopra delportico & andamo uedendo le
& tutti quelli luoghi disopra & poi disotto al
& dispenso & cancellaria & insomma tutto uol
m cosa glipiacena Ma chessorra pogni modo·
te: ⁓⁓⁓ g ⁓⁓ g

disegniarne una secondo che a me paressse chesse
o uolo disegniata qui accio chelapossiate intende
· lemisure & anche come tu lannoi comporture
sto sie che io parto incinque parti queste quaram
fo laporta laquale e otto braccia largha & dodici
tiqua dalla porta sinepiglio una decanzoni &
· poi dellaltre due parti lascio tralaporta & que
uro diritto quattro braccia Siche miuengho ari
raccia· delle quaranta monerosta trenta due qui
dibraccia uenti otto di diametro & auanzommi du
o uenti otto braccia & poi glifo disopra un qua
& due grosso & disopra unaltro in octo angoli
alto dodici & laparte disotto fo indue archi di
muri uno nelmezzo traluno archo & laltro di
tiquesti muri & imodo cheppquesta grossezza de

Una delle quattro
entrate delcastello
lequali sono tutte
inquesta forma

to Francesco Sforza, and the so-called Medici group (*Codex Magliabechianus*, Florence; *Codex Valencianus*, Valencia). The *Codex Magliabechianus* is the copy made for Piero de Medici. In addition to this core of Quattrocento copies, there are several manuscripts dating from the 15th, 16th and 17th centuries that all derive from the Latin translation produced by Antonio Bonfini for the Hungarian King Matthew Corvinus (reigned 1458–1490).

A glance at the names of known owners of a copy of Filarete's treatise shows that, as was the case with Alberti, his readers were to be found specifically at court, though fellow architects also seem to have been aware of the treatise. Thus there is evidence that Leonardo da Vinci (1452–1519) and Donato Bramante (c. 1444–1514) both had access to a copy in Milan and read it, as did Giorgio Vasari (1511–1574) in Florence. Furthermore, in his 1615 treatise *L'idea dell'architettura universale* (Idea for a universal architecture), the architect Vincenzo Scamozzi (1548–1616) proudly reported that he owned a copy of Filarete's work.

Unlike Alberti's *De re aedificatoria*, Filarete's *Libro architettonico* was never printed, and it was only towards the end of the 19th century that a partial edition, and in 1972 the complete edition with illustrations, became available in print. Like the surviving manuscripts, the modern printed versions have to make do with an incomplete text, with gaps, discontinuities, repetitions and mistakes. In fact, Filarete would appear never to have produced a definitive edition of his work, so that there is uncertainty even as to whether or not the copies were published with his knowledge or during his lifetime.

Whereas Alberti had relied heavily on the ancient model set by Vitruvius as regards both the structure and narrative form of his treatise, Filarete takes a different approach. Instead of ten books he wrote 25, all of varying lengths. Only Books 1 to 21 deal with architecture and make up the *Libro architettonico*, the treatise on architecture. In Books 22 to 24, Filarete focuses in detail on drawing and painting, while Book 25 is a eulogy to the contributions made by the Medici family as patrons.

A closer study of Books 1 to 21 reveals that despite a general lack of system, with mutually relevant sections arbitrarily separated, there are three quite definite central trains of thought: In Books 1–2, Filarete sets out the key elements of his theory of architecture, in Books 3–11 he pursues the planning and expansion of the ideal town of Sforzinda, while in Books 12–21 he describes real and fictitious buildings of Classical Antiquity. For his work, Filarete chose not to adopt the sober style of a textbook, but that of a dialogue, the literary form of the novel. In a long conversation with the fabulously wealthy prince and client, who can easily be recognized as Francesco Sforza, and from Book 7 onwards, can just as easily be seen to be Galeazzo Sforza (1444–1476), the architect develops the ideal town layout: Averliano, which when complete is known as Sforzinda. Its development, the choice of a suitable location, the plan for an octagonal town centre with a radial street system, the construction of the fortifications with the elaborate town gates, as well as a list of individual buildings dominate the novel until Book 14. It is interesting, in regard to how Filarete saw himself, to note that he directly associates the artistic design of the ideal town with his own name and calls it Averliano. This emphasizes the intrinsic value of the design as opposed to the craftsmanship required to create it, and the result, Sforzinda, is a play on the name of the client. From Book 14 onwards, Filarete introduces a second level of narrative into his treatise. During excavation work for Sforzinda harbour a *coder aureum* or golden book is found. This, in turn, describes a fictitious, this time ancient ideal town, Plusiapolis, whose buildings were all constructed by the legendary architect Onitoan Notirenflo (Antonio Florentino, alias Antonio Averlino) for the legendary King Zogalia, who is none other than Galeazzo Sforza. This town gave Filarete an excuse for providing a detailed reconstruction of both fictitious and real buildings in Classical Antiquity.

In the narrower sense, the introductory remarks on the primordial hut and the character of columns (qualità) are the sections in Filarete's work of greatest relevance to a theory of architecture. Filarete takes up the story of how houses came to be, which both Vitruvius and Alberti had dealt with, and interprets it from a Christian stance, as well as providing pictures for the first time. Thus Adam, having been banished from paradise, needed to find some form of shelter. At first he was able to do this only by folding his hands over his head, but subsequently beams were placed over the forked branches of four tree trunks, providing a starting point for the walls and roof. This primordial hut also marks the origins of every form of more advanced architecture, since even the corner supports with their forked branches that Adam chose were calculated in accordance with the size of human

beings. The same applies to columns, where the capital corresponds to the archaic forked uppermost segment, which in turn corresponds to the human head on which the unit of measurement, the module, is based.

In Filarete's scheme, there exist five different human measures or "qualità," whereby he concentrates on only three when transposing the idea to columns, to which he applies the Greek terms Doric, Ionic and Corinthian. He was familiar with these terms from Vitruvius, and yet he developed a method of explanation that was totally independent, indeed opposite. What Filarete referred to as the "qualità" of the Doric column corresponds to nine modules; the Corinthian, "middle," to eight modules; and the Ionic, "small," seven modules. In accordance with Filarete's preferred Christian myth of the origin of architecture, the column with the Doric "qualità" represents the oldest and most important type of column, as it was modelled on Adam's proportions and as such on God himself. Technically speaking, Filarete's interpretation of the Doric column has nothing whatever in common with the Greek Doric described by Vitruvius, and corresponds to a composite variant. As far as content is concerned however, Filarete reverses Vitruvius' "orders" of columns. Since for him the hierarchy of the estates in society is reflected in the superposition of the columns, the lowest order of column, the Ionic, carries the whole burden of the building, while the Doric "Adam's column" is equated with nobility and, as the solemn culmination of all architecture, is spared any burden.

VB

1 | **Incipit with the architect on a building site, and Medici coat-of-arms**
Fol. 1 r

2 | **Adam builds the primordial hut**
Fol. 5 r

3 | Castle fortifications
One of the four main entrances to the aristocratic castle
topped with statues of horsemen.
Fol. 42 r

4 | Plan of ideal city of Sforzinda
The star-shaped fortified walls describe a circle.
Fol. 43 r

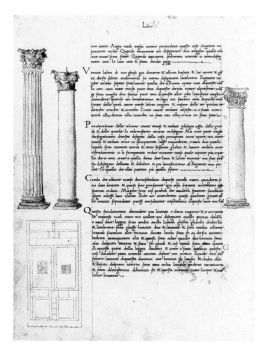

5 | **Column order**
The column-"qualità" in Filarete: Doric, Corinthian, Ionian. Bottom left:
the ground plan of the royal palace.
Fol. 57 v

6 | **Section detail for cornices and column base**
Fol. 63 v

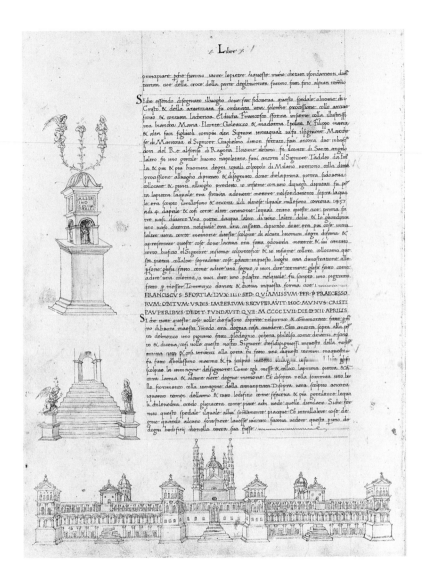

7 | Sforzinda hospital
General view of Sforzinda hospital, together with figures from the
Annunciation before the entrance and foundation stone.
Fol. 83 v

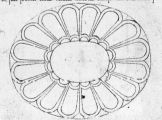

Liber

Del colifeo

Roma fi feguira pure questo

8 | **Entrance to an ancient theatre, elevation and ground plan of the Colosseum**
Fol. 87 v

9 | View and ground plan of the monument for King Zogalia (Galeazzo Sforza) in Plusiapolis
Fol. 102 v

10 | Technical device for lifting weights
Fol. 115 v

Cesare Cesariano (1476/78–1543)
Di Lucio Vitruvio Pollione de Architectura

COMO, 1521

On Lucius Vitruvius Pollio's "Architecture"

As an architectural theorist, the north Italian artist and architect Cesare Cesariano did not have the same credentials as the well-educated, much-travelled Fra Giocondo (1433–1515), who was greatly admired and much in demand by his contemporaries. Little is known about Cesariano's education, and he seems to have been largely self-taught at the higher level. His domain was primarily restricted to the north of Italy, and it was from the region's architecture that he drew his inspiration. Milan was the focal point of his life, but he also worked in Ferrara, Reggio Emilia and Parma. As a Milanese court architect it is not certain what role he actually played in the building of the atrium and façade of Santa Maria presso San Celso, and in fact there is no other building that can unequivocally be attributed to him. Meeting the painter and architect Donato Bramante (c. 1444–1514) at the Milan court of Ludovico Sforza (1452–1508) made a great impression on him. He referred to the future builder of the new St. Peter's Basilica in Rome as his most important teacher, and furthermore he made reference to his church of Santa Maria presso San Satiro in Milan. In addition, the only frescos that can clearly be attributed to Cesariano, in San Giovanni Evangelista in Parma (1508), reflect aspects of Bramante's painting. Nonetheless a manuscript in his hand recently found in Madrid proves that Cesariano undertook a trip to Rome, dated to the winter of 1507/08. Previously, the assumption was that Cesariano had never set eyes on Rome.

His translation of Vitruvius from Latin into Italian, which was published in 1521 by Gottardo da Ponte in Como, was the first complete translation of the text, and opened up Vitruvius' theory to laymen. Until then there had been partial translations only, for example in Francesco di Giorgio's transcription. Cesariano's work, with its elaborate woodcuts and long commentaries, was no less influential than Fra Giocondo's 1511 edition of the Latin text.

Despite the now proven trip to Rome, Cesariano only had a limited grasp of the characteristics of Classical architecture, and ultimately, of Vitruvius' thought. His illustrations of the latter's treatise are evidence of a combination of Classical building theory with the norms and sense of aesthetics of Medieval and early modernist architecture in northern Italy, as Cesariano himself would have encountered and learnt. For example, he depicted the three methods of presenting buildings as described by Vitruvius (I, 2) – ground plan ("ichnographia"), true to scale, precise and orthogonal front elevation ("orthographia"), and reproduction of the elevation in perspective ("scaenographia") – using the medieval cathedral in Milan as an example. For "orthographia," he chose a cross-section of the nave, while the "scaenographia" combines an additional cross-section of the nave with an elevation of the transept flanks. The system of proportions that Cesariano used for this, based on triangular constructions, had nothing to do with Vitruvius but adhered more to medieval architectural practice. Yet the woodcuts in

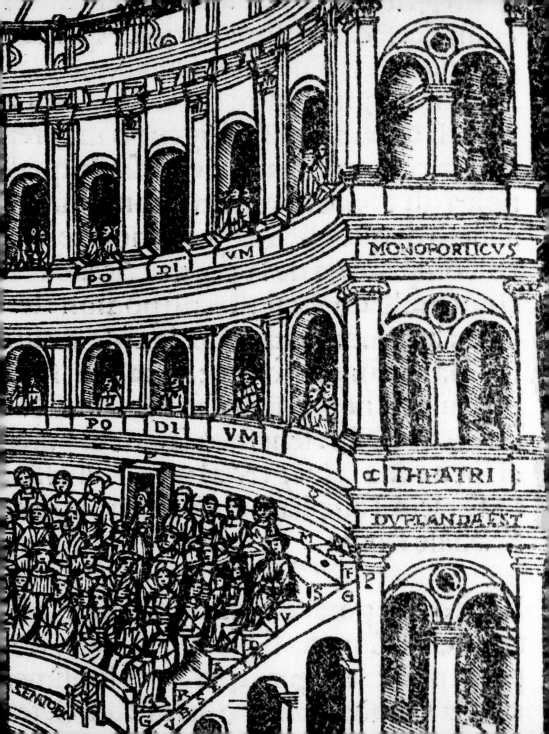

the Vitruvius translation bear witness to his aesthetic standards. This is demonstrated not only by the illustration for the primordial hut according to Vitruvius (II, 1), but also by the typesetting. By the use of different sizes of typeface, the translation of the text and Cesariano's annotations are set off from each other visually. The attractive manner in which the work was presented was meant to enhance the clarity of the arguments. Cesariano also invested great effort in the careful artistic reproductions of the proportional figures in the square and circle, according to Vitruvius (III, 1), which he depicted in two woodcuts against the background of a fine grid. Its small modules make apparent the relationship of size between the human limbs. This was how Cesariano illustrated Vitruvius' principle of "symmetria," a calculable regularity of the human figure and architecture. Cesariano surrounded the sexually aroused, muscular *homo ad circulum* with an additional square within the circle, thus including Vitruvius' *homo ad quadratum* in the circular figure. Cesariano's depiction was most probably based on a drawing by the Milan artist Pietro Paolo Seganzone.

Cesariano's reproductions of Greek temples are characteristic of his limited knowledge of Classical Antiquity. Vitruvius (III, 2) differentiated between temples according to the relationship between the temple cella and the varying number and position of columns surrounding the cella. These could be free-standing columns or half-columns on the cella walls. In the case of a temple with an anta, two walls protruding from the longitudinal sides of the cella flank the entrance as well as two free-standing columns placed in front of the entrance. The prostyle also has two protruding walls (antae) on the side, but in this case free-standing columns in front of the anta. Whereas, for example, Pietro Cataneo (c. 1510–after 1571) was to differentiate between various forms of temple on the basis of anta and changing positions for columns (1554, 1567), Cesariano depicted buildings that in no way resembled Classical temples. Rather, his temple with anta as well as his ideas about the prostyle and the amphiprostyle follow a building whose ground plan shows a square building with semi-circular apse, structured on the outside by pilasters, and with internal supports bearing the load of a central dome. This is a case of the quincunx layout, frequently found in Byzantine and north Italian churches and often used by Bramante. Whichever concrete example Cesariano actually had in mind, his reconstructions of temples confirm how much his picture of Classical Antiquity depended on later models. Thus it was merely logical for him to reconstruct in elevation Vitruvius' basilica in Fano (V, 1), whose façade was similar to the design for a façade attributed to Bramante, which in turn was associated with Santa Maria presso San Satiro.

Cesariano's clear synopsis of the order of columns is scarcely compatible with the description of the Classical orders in Vitruvius' books III and IV. In depicting six forms that differed in terms of decoration and proportion, Cesariano went further than the ancient canon of orders, and the shape of the capitals, which are rich in variety and luxuriant in form, also shows evidence of modern influences. For his reproductions of Classical theatres, Cesariano at first chose Vitruvius' (V,7) abstract scheme of construction, consisting of a circle with triangles, both for Roman and Greek theatres. Naturally, his Greek theatre with its semi-circular curved bulging sides has nothing to do with actual Greek theatres, built as they were to suit the lie of the land. By contrast, the ground plan and elevation of Roman theatres document the exact position of individual rooms and their architectural details. Admittedly in elevation the building is too slender, and furthermore is rounded out with a dome completely unknown in the architecture of Classical theatres. Here, fantasy is combined with a somewhat vague knowledge of Classical Antiquity.   CJ

1 | **Primordial hut**
Illustration from Vitruvius II, 1.
P. XXXII. Woodcut

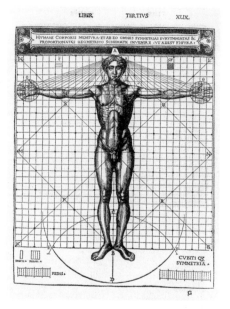

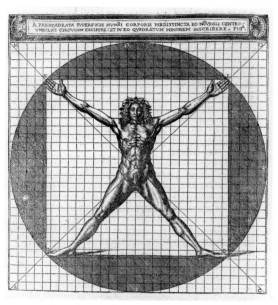

2 | *Homo ad quadratum*
Vitruvian man in a square, Vitruvius III, 1.
P. XLI. Woodcut

3 | *Homo ad circulum*
Vitruvian man in a circle and in a square within the circle,
for Vitruvius III, 1. The grid makes it possible to read the proportions.
P. L. Woodcut

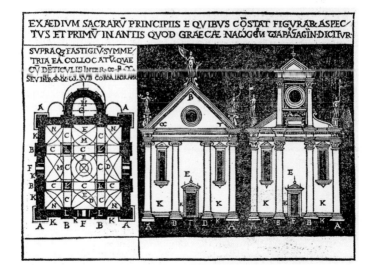

4 | **Reconstruction of the prostyle temple**
Illustration from Vitruvius III, 2. The temple is interpreted
by Cesariano as a cruciform domed building (*Quincunx*).
P. LII. Woodcut

5 | **Reconstruction of a temple with antae**
Vitruvius III, 2.
P. LII r. Woodcut

6 | Synopsis of the column orders
Illustration for Vitruvius III and IV. From left to right: Doric (twice), Ionian, Corinthian,
Attic columns, and the conspicuously slim Tuscan column.
P. LXIII. Woodcut

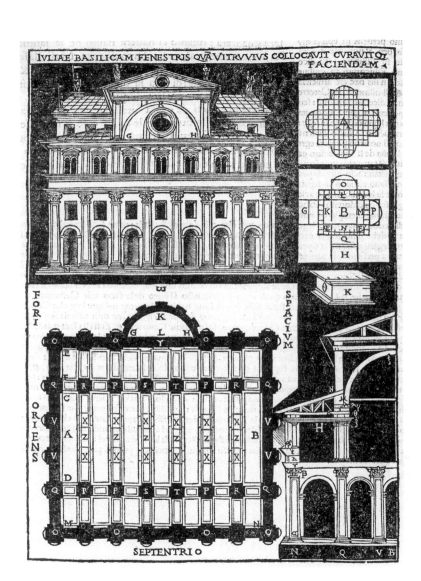

7 | Reconstruction of the Vitruvian basilica in Fano
Illustration for Vitruvius V, 1. Ground plan, elevation, sectional
view with semicircular vault (bottom right) and details.
P. LXXIV. Woodcut

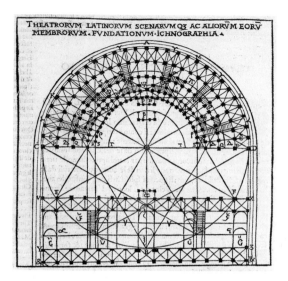

8 | **Design scheme of a theatre ground plan**
Illustration for Vitruvius V, 7.
P. LXXV v. Woodcut

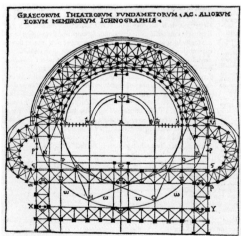

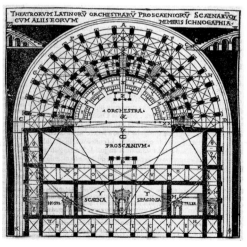

9 | **Ground plan reconstruction of a Greek theatre**
Illustration for Vitruvius V, 8.
P. LXXXI v. Woodcut

10 | **Ground plan of the Roman (Latin) theatre with elements named**
Illustration for Vitruvius V, 7.
P. LXXXI v. Woodcut

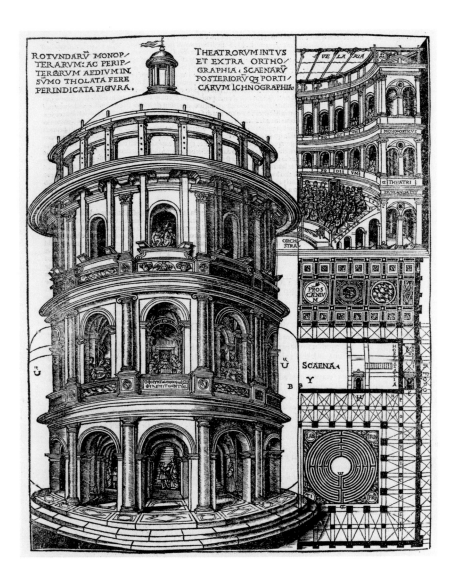

11 | Elevation, sectional view and ground plan details of a Roman (Latin) theatre
P. LXXXII v. Woodcut

Sebastiano Serlio (1475–1553/55)

Tutte l'opere d'architettura et prospettiva

VENICE, 1619

The five books of architecture. London, 1611

Sebastiano Serlio, an artist and architect born in Bologna, left no completed treatise. His written works about architecture, nine in total, were published gradually, in no particular order, after 1537 in Venice, Paris and Lyons. Book VII was published in 1575, following Serlio's death, by the art dealer Jacopo Strada in Frankfurt/Main. Books VI and VIII have only recently been edited. The edition that was most widely used was printed in Venice in 1619. Its title, *Tutte l'opere d'architettura et prospettiva di Sebastiano Serlio bolognese* would suggest that the books were completed, yet in reality this applies only to Books I–V, VII and an *Extraordinario libro* (special volume) that was often mistakenly referred to as Book VI. The treatise, which was written over a long period of time, was never given a firm cover title, and as such it is usually referred to succinctly as *Architettura*. The work was nonetheless a resounding success, due in no small measure to the fact that from 1514 the author had experienced the High Renaissance in Rome first hand. He was able to make use of inside knowledge when he wrote about current, important building projects by the likes of Bramante, Raphael and his own teacher Baldassare Peruzzi. He was also indebted to these architects for his thorough knowledge of Classical Antiquity. Following the Sack of Rome in 1527, Serlio moved to Venice. In northern Italy publication of Books IV (1537) and III (1540) led to greater appreciation of the architecture in Rome, both that of Classical Antiquity as well as the modern variants inspired by it.

The *Regole generali di architettura sopra le cinque maniere degli edifici* (*General rules for the five orders of buildings*), Book IV dating from 1537, deals with the orders of columns, to which Serlio had already dedicated a series of engravings in 1528. The synopsis of column orders, which predated Book IV, had no doubt been inspired by Cesariano's 1521 edition of Vitruvius. Yet Serlio, who in addition to Vitruvius had also studied the orders on the spot at Roman ruins, strove for a clearer system. He differentiated quite clearly between the different Greek orders (Doric, Ionic and Corinthian) as well as the Tuscan and Composite, i. e. the two Italian orders, by their height, and gave them various bases. The height of the columns is in each case determined by multiplying the diameter of the lower column by a whole number. Serlio's Tuscan order, whose height corresponds to the diameter multiplied sixfold, is lower than the related Doric, whose height is seven times its diameter. This marked a conscious decision to distance himself from Vitruvius (III, 3 and IV, 7), who had insisted on the same relative height for the two types. There is also evidence of a systematic train of thought in Serlio's second synopsis, demonstrating as it does a free-standing column and three variations ("modi") on the connecting piece between column and wall or buttress.

Book III, published in 1540, entitled *Il Terzo libro nel quale si figurano e descrivono le antichità di Roma e le altri che sono in Italia e sopra Italia* (*The third book, in which the an-*

cient ruins in Rome, as well as ruins in and outside Italy are depicted and described), was the first compendium to be printed in the vernacular; it contains woodcuts of the most important ancient buildings in Rome and Italy, as well as some building projects by Bramante, Raphael and Peruzzi. Of the contemporary buildings, St. Peter's Basilica is assigned pride of place, but Serlio also presents Bramante's quasi-antique Tempietto and a design by Raphael for the Villa Madama in Rome. The richly illustrated work acquainted readers for the first time with new ways of approaching architecture and the study of Antiquity, and the illustrations now became just as important as the text. The cover of Book III, showing dilapidated pillars and arches, was also meant to be a feast for the eyes. The inscription on the upper cornice is an invitation to the readers to recall this message whilst examining the ancient ruins on the following pages in the book: "What Rome once was can even be seen in decay" ("Roma quanta fuit ipsa ruina docet"). Never before had the medium of architectural illustration been so directly used as a source of information, and this set standards for future works, for example Palladio's *Quattro Libri* (1570). Since Serlio made use of material by Peruzzi, he was accused of plagiarism and this backbiting detracted from his genuine achievements. As a result of his illustrated books, discussions on archaeological questions and current building projects, which until then had been the preserve of exclusive circles of Roman architects and clients, became a topic of public interest.

Book III was dedicated to the French King Francis I (reigned 1515–1547), who invited Serlio to France and employed him at Fontainebleau until 1547. In later life Serlio settled in Lyons, where he was mostly involved in theoretical study. The remaining sections of *Architettura* deal with geometry and perspective, churches and residential buildings ranging from simple farmhouses to palaces.

Serlio actually built relatively little himself, his major work being the charming little castle of Ancy-le-Franc in Burgundy (1541 ff.). In Book II, on perspective, which first appeared in Paris in 1545, he presented his wooden theatre, which he had built in 1539, while still in Venice, in the court-

yard of the Palazzo Porto-Colleoni in Vicenza. He combined the ground plan with an elevation of the stage in perspective, showing the lines converging in an imaginary vanishing point. Theatre building was of enormous importance for Serlio; in 1519, together with Peruzzi he had surveyed the Marcellus Theatre in Rome. Book III contains a reconstruction of the building and of other ancient sites, such as the Roman theatre in Pula in Croatia. A cross-section of the rows of seats and the profile of a cornice become more three-dimensional and descriptive by being depicted in perspective with shading. At the time when Book III was published, this almost painting-like reproduction was no longer considered really modern by architects. Raphael (1483–1520), Antonio da Sangallo the Younger (1484–1546) and Peruzzi (1481–1536) had already turned to orthogonal projection, which combined the outer limits and interior structures of a building's elevation in a strictly right-angled system. In this way it was possible to avoid any foreshortening, whilst reproducing exactly the proportions of the individual parts. Serlio saw the limitations of this approach, however. He wished to give not only experts, but also the untrained eye as vivid a picture of the architecture as possible, and to this end, there are always perspective elements in his elevations. In the cross-section of the Pantheon rotunda in Rome, the line of the floor and the cornice in the central main niche curve in the perspective, whereas the adjoining aedicules are flat due to the orthogonal projection. Wherever appropriate, Serlio was consistent in his use of orthogonal projection, for example in the view of the two-storey façade in Book IV, showing in the first storey the famous window motif with the wide arched opening supported by columns, and the narrow side openings. This motif, which incidentally Bramante had already used, was called at times "Serliana," and at other times "Palladio," and it does indeed grace Palladio's basilica in Vicenza. Serlio and Palladio also developed other similar motifs. The ground plan for a villa in Serlio's Book VII (1575), with its concave middle section, can be compared with Palladio's 1542 ground plan for the Villa Pisani in Bagnolo (London, Royal Institute of British Architects Collection, XVII/17).

CJ

Fig. p. 37
1 | **Illustration of the so-called serliana motif**
Façade featuring the serliana motif adopted by Palladio and used by him on the basilica in Vicenza in the windows of the upper storey.
Book IV, p. XXXII. Woodcut

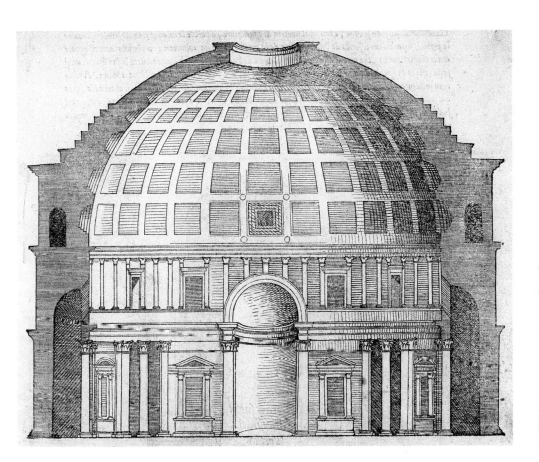

2 | **Pantheon**
Cross-section of the rotunda of the Pantheon in Rome, with
perspective reproduction of the main central niche.
Book III, p. IX. Woodcut

3 | Bramante's Tempietto of San Pietro in Montorio in Rome
Book III, p. XLIII. Woodcut

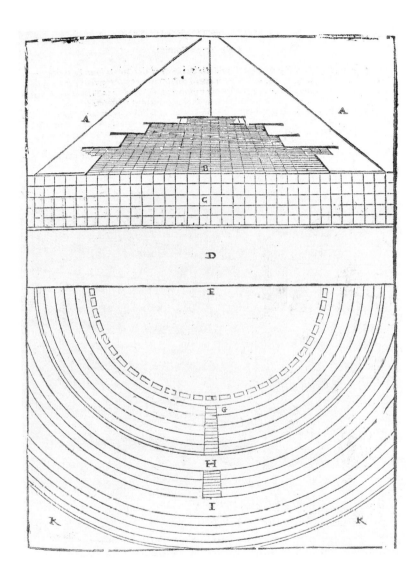

4 | **Theatre ground plan**
Theatre in the Palazzo Porto-Colleoni in Vicenza (1539), with
ground plan (bottom) and perspective design of the stage (top).
Book II, p. 45. Woodcut

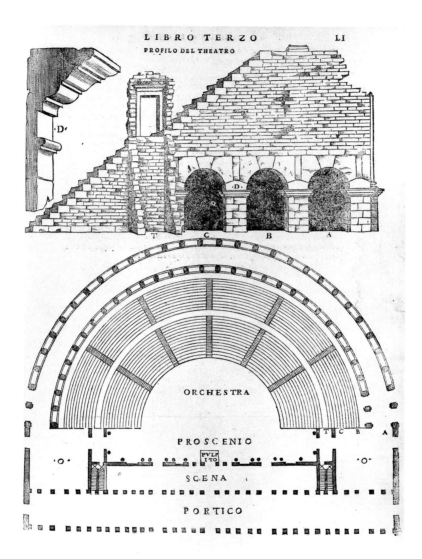

5 | **Theatre in Pola**
Ground plan and perspective view of the rows of seats for the audience
in the Roman theatre in Pola; above left detail of a cornice.
Book III, p. LI. Woodcut

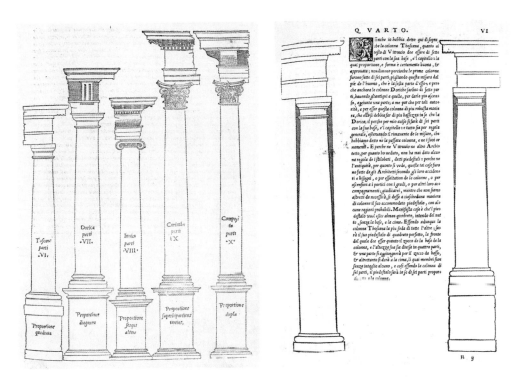

6 | Column orders
Five differently proportioned column orders: from left to right:
Tuscan, Doric, Ionian, Corinthian, Composite.
Book IV, p. III. Woodcut

7 | Tuscan order
Variations of the Tuscan order with and without pedestal,
and with shading to suggest a narrowing of the column shaft.
Book IV, p. VI. Woodcut

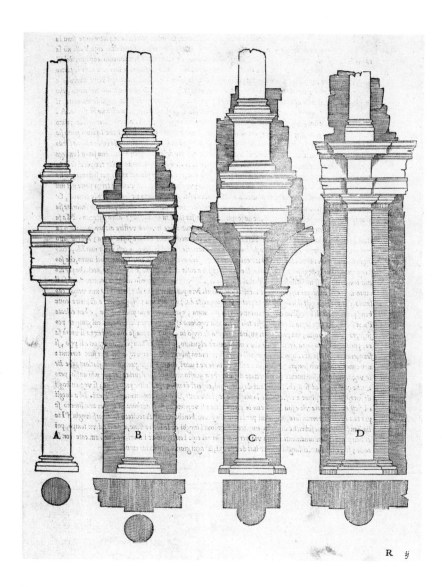

8 | Column positions
Free-standing column (A) and three types (modi) of linking
free-standing columns or half columns and the wall (B to D).
Book IV, p. LXVI. Woodcut

9 | **Design of a villa**
Villa ground plan, elevation with semi-circular
shaped central façade set-back.
Book VII, p. XIII. Woodcut

Iacomo Barozzi da Vignola (1507–1573)
Regola delli cinque ordini d'architettura

ROME, 1562

The five orders of architecture. New York, 1896

With more than 250 editions, the *Regola delli cinque ordini d'architettura* could well be one of the most successful architectural textbooks ever written. It is hard to overestimate its influence on the theory and practice of building in modern times. Less a case of restrictive rules than a tangible set of instructions for correct building, it paved the way for the breakthrough of a new theory of architecture geared to practicability that, in an almost prophetic manner, served the Baroque's need for display. And yet art historians were bothered at first by the character of the work, the dominant illustrative plates, the laconic text, and not least the limitation of the subject matter to the theory of columns. Christof Thoenes was the first to succeed in reconstructing the history of the work and the author's intentions in a convincing manner.

The *Regola* of the architect Iacomo Barozzi da Vignola already differs from its predecessors in its appearance, as a series of engravings of originally 32 copperplate reproductions, with only brief accompanying texts. Before that time, the only author to take a similar approach was Antonio Labacco (1495–1559), who had published his *Libro appartenente all'architettura* (*A book about architecture*, 1552). In Vignola's work, the illustrations steal the show completely. The only section to have a coherent text is the short preface, which is at first addressed to uninformed colleagues but later quite clearly is aimed at courtly readers, too. The work is dedicated to Cardinal Alessandro Farnese (1520–1589), for whom Vignola had been redesigning the summer palace in Caprarola since 1558. Coats of arms and imprints on the frontispiece pay homage to Vignola's client and patron of many years. The cover shows the author with dividers, the attribute of his profession, in a rather un-Classical piece of aedicule architecture. The author's self-confident portrait, and the lack of the hitherto usual mention of the authority of Roman architecture, intimate that a turning point in the history of the architectural textbook was approaching. The focus was no longer on studying Classical monuments, but on their interpretation by a scholarly artist, who would pass this knowledge on. The two figures in the niches on either side of the portrait were also to be interpreted in this light. The allegories, which were probably designed by Federico Zuccari (1542/3–1609), are a reference to the theory and practice of architecture, and yet here subordinate themselves to the personality of the architect himself.

The main section of this book of rules (because of the missing literary components it would be wrong to talk of a treatise) introduces the five orders of columns, the Tuscan, Doric, Ionic, Corinthian and Composite, which had been the canon since Serlio. The articles on each of the orders are in turn divided up into five sections: the colonnade, arcade, arcade with pedestal, individual pedestal and base forms, and individual capital and entablature forms. The work concludes with special versions of the Doric and Composite orders, a cornice, portals from Caprarola, and the *cancelleria* as

well as a fireplace from the Palazzo Farnese in Rome. The latter were possibly intended as designs by the author for a later, expanded edition of the *Regola*.

Yet there was more to Vignola's system than the elements making up each order, presented in the form of a pattern book. His goal is to develop a set of rules for proportions that can be understood by "average minds" ("mediocri ingegni"). His predecessors' theories of proportion were flawed, he suggested, by the fact that they were extremely difficult to put into practice. The rule that had been handed down from studying Classical architecture, namely that the height of a column of any order was proportional to the diameter of the column, meant that builders were doomed to failure. After all, the entire building was then subject to one little detail. Including the entablature and the pedestal severely complicated the calculations, and in consequence irrational numbers often cropped up in the proportions, for example a ratio of $1 : \sqrt{2}$, with which Alberti and Serlio used to work; this made calculating the correct measurements much more difficult. Vignola had the splendid idea of doing an about turn with regard to calculating the proportions, using the total dimensions of the building as the starting point. Generalizing the results he obtained from practical work, he laid down that the ratio of pedestal, column and entablature should be 4:12:3. Thus, the total height of an order is made up of 19 sections, or 15 if there were no pedestal. In order to differentiate between various column orders, the architect must then establish the thickness of the column, and thus the proportions of the order in question. These are calculated from fractions of the column height, whereby Vignola designates a denominator of 14 for the Tuscan order, 16 for the Doric, 18 for the Ionic, and 20 for the Corinthian and Composite. The result of this division is the so-called module, i. e. the radius of the bottom of the column, which now determines the dimensions of the further elements such as the entablature and pedestal. In order to spare the user complicated calculations, Vignola provides formulas to facilitate calculations of the individual parts.

Vignola's second "revolution" in the relationship between architectural theory and building practice entailed making the module the absolute unit of measurement, independent of local units such as "braccia," "piedi" and "palmi." He called for a universal method of calculation that can be applied easily to individual working measurements ("né braccia, né piedi, né palmi di qual si voglia luogo, ma solo una misura arbitraria detta modulo …"). A not insignificant reason for the success of the *Regola* was no doubt the introduction of this standardization. The fact that Vignola was prepared to cover up possible technical irregularities in the calculation of proportions is also an indication of his extremely pragmatic attitude.

Given that Vignola was always interested in a succinct way of putting things, it would have been quite natural for him to summarize the shape and the proportions of the five orders of columns in one single article. Strangely enough the author does not seem to have done this. As Thoenes shows, the corresponding plate is a later addition; it was added to a copy of the *Regola* in 1572, replacing the imprimatur of Pope Pius IV. Despite numerous mistakes and inconsistencies, the inserted page, which made reference to Serlio's scheme in his *Regole generali di architettura sopra le cinque maniere degli edifici*, 1537 (*General rules for the five orders of buildings*), was very well received. It was included in all further editions, yet, if anything, resulted in more confusion as regards Vignola's theories. Until very recently, Vignola was accused of putting architecture in too rigid a corset. This can scarcely have been his intention. For he aims to bring together the often contradictory "rules of thumb" that were prevalent to create one single system that could be applied in practice. However, it seems that he himself did not regard his theories as binding, as few of his completed projects pay heed to the instructions in the *Regola*.

Vignola's interest in theoretical questions did not come about just by chance. Even during his initial training as an artist in Bologna it would appear that he acquainted himself with the theory of perspective; this was reflected in a second work *Le due regole della prospettiva prattica*, 1573 (*The two rules of applied perspective*), published posthumously. Being a member of the Vitruvius Academy, he studied Roman architecture and its laws before working as an architect in Bologna and Fontainebleau, and then in the second half of the century becoming world famous as a result of such works as Sant' Andrea in Via Flaminia, Gesù e Santa Anna di Palafrenieri in Rome, the castle in Caprarola and Palazzo Farnese in Piacenza.

VB

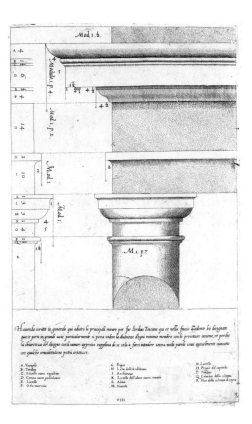

Non hauendo io fra le antiquità di Roma trouato ornamento Toscano, di che n'habbia possuto formar regola, come ho trouato delli altri quattro ordeni, cioè Dorio, Ionio, Corintho, et Composito; ho preso l'authorità da Vitruuio nel quarto libro nel settimo capitolo, doue dice la colonna toscana douer esser in dizza di sette grossezze di essa colonna con la base, et capitello. Il resto dell'ornamento cioè architraue frigio, et cornice in parte esser conueneuole, osseruar la regola, la quale ho trouata ne gli altri ordeni, cioè, che l'architraue, frigio, et cornice siano la quarta parte dell'altezza della colonna, la quale è moduli 14. son la base, et capitello, come io vедrò notato per numeri; così l'architraue, frigio, et cornice saranno moduli 3½, che viene ad essere il quarto di 14. Li suoi particulari membri saranno al luogo suo minutamente notati.

Hauendo scritto in generale qui adietro le principali misure per far l'ordine Toscano qui et nella faccia seguente ho disegnato quasi tутто però in grande acciò particolarmente si possa vedere la diuisione d'ogni minimo membro con le prosetture insieme, et perche la chiarezza del disegno con li numeri appresso supplissa di se sola a farsi intendere senza molte parole come agevolmente ciascuno con qualche consideratione potrà conoscere.

A. Vuoulo
B. Tondino
C. Listello sotto regoletto
D. Corona sotto gocciolatoi
E. Listello
F. Gola ouerscia

G. Frigio
H. Liste dell'Architraue
I. Architraue
K. Listello dell'abaco ouero cimatio
L. Abaco
M. Vuoulo

N. Listello
O. Frigio del capitello
P. Tondino
Q. Colarino della colonna
R. Viuo della colonna di sopra

VIII

1 | **Colonnade in Tuscan order**
Pl. IV. Etching

2 | **Cornice and capital of the Tuscan order with detailed specifications**
Pl. VIII. Etching

Volendo fare ornamento de loggie ouer portici d'ordine Dorico si deue
(come è detto) partir l'altezza in parti 20, et formarne il modulo; poi dis-
tribuire le larghezze che venghino da un pilastro all'altro moduli 7, et li
pilastri sieno moduli 3, che così venranno partite le larghezze con le
altezze alla sua proportione con la luce delli vani di due larghezze in
altezza et venirà la giusta distributione delle metope et triglifi come
si vede. Resta solo hauere in consideratione che la colonna deue usci
re fuor del pilastro un terzo di modulo piu del suo mezzo, et questo
si fa perche le proietture delle imposte non pacino il mezzo delle co-
lone et questa sera regola vniuersale in tutti li casi simili de tutti gli ordini

3 | **Arcade in the Doric order**
Pl. X. Etching

Il piedestallo Dorico deue essere
moduli 5.et ½ in altezza, la im-
posta dell'arco qui sopra disegna
ta modulo 1, et partiti li suoi par-
ticolari membri come si vede nota
to per numeri.

A, scanellature della colonna

B, imo scapo della colonna et per tale debbe essere
intero in tutti li ordini
X II

C, tondino ouero bastoncino

4 | Pedestal in the Doric order with
detailled specifications
Pl. XII. Etching

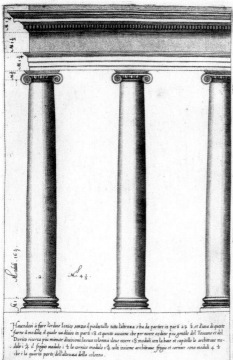

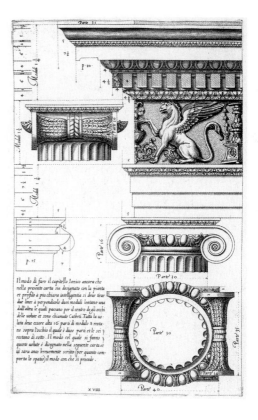

5 | Colonnade in the Ionian order
Pl. XV. Etching

6 | Cornice and capital in the Ionian order with detailled specifications
Pl. XVIIII. Etching

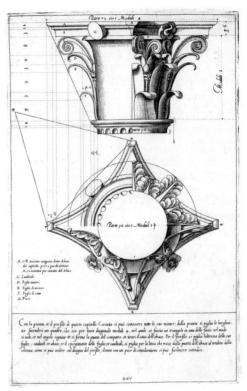

7 | **Arcade in the Corinthian order**
Pl. XXIII. Etching

8 | **Construction of the Corinthian capital with detailled specifications**
Pl. XXV. Etching

Daniele Barbaro (1514–1570)
I dieci libri dell'architettura di M. Vitruvio

VENICE, 1556

Ten Books on the Architecture of M. Vitruvius

Daniele Barbaro was the third great Italian expert on Vitruvius in the 16th century. His predecessors, the scholarly Fra Giocondo (1433–1515) and Cesare Cesariano (1476/8–1543), were master architects. Though their education had been quite different, their involvement with Vitruvius was closely bound up with practical experience. In Daniele Barbaro, a translator of and critical expert on Vitruvius, an intellectual patrician, rather than a qualified building expert, now joined the ranks of Vitruvius exegetes.

There are some striking characteristics of the Vitruvius renaissance in the 16th century. For the most part north Italians were responsible for it, architects and laymen alike. Their main centre of activities was not the ancient capital, Rome, but Venice, a city that in no way bore any traces of Classical Antiquity. Both Serlio (1475–1553/55) and Palladio (1508–1580), the most important Italian architectural theorists of the 16th century, who both developed modern theories even though they were based on Vitruvius, lived for a time in Venice, and had their books on architecture printed there. The fact that there were particularly good printing presses in Venice certainly played a part in the city's becoming a centre for Vitruvian studies, but the most important reason was that although the city and its hinterland opened up to the Renaissance much later than, say, Florence or Rome, it did so all the more decisively in the early 16th century. Architects such as Serlio and Jacopo Sansovino (1486–1570), who had left Rome when it was plundered by

the troops of Charles V in 1527, found a new sphere of work in Venice. Palladio was second to none in the way he left his mark on the Renaissance architecture of the Veneto region. However, local wealthy nobles were very open to the Renaissance and the study of Vitruvius, and tried their hand at being architects and theorists. Even before Barbaro published his translation of Vitruvius, the local writer and patrician Giangiorgio Trissino (1478–1550) from nearby Vicenza, as well as Alvise Cornaro (1484–1566), who lived in Padua, also nearby, had dabbled in architecture and, in literary fragments, put their thoughts on architectural theory and Vitruvius to paper. In doing so, Trissino, who was Palladio's first mentor, shows himself to be an admirer of Vitruvius, whereas Cornaro Trissino remains somewhat reserved.

As early as the 15th century, the distinguished Barbaro family had produced many an eminent scholar, for example Candiano Barbaro (d. 1454), who had a command of both Latin and Greek, and Ermolao Barbaro (1453/54–1493), the author of a series of commentaries on Aristotle. Daniele, who had studied in Padua, also published articles on Aristotle. He founded and perhaps even designed the Botanical Gardens in Padua, which fostered his interest in architecture and the grounds of villas. In 1549 and 1550 he was the Venetian ambassador to the English court, and following his return he became the Patriarch of Aquileya. He began studying the writings of Vitruvius as early as 1547. In the 1550s, an encounter with Palladio, the outstanding expert on Classical

Antiquity, gave the whole project a special shine. Barbaro's lavishly detailed annotated translation of Vitruvius' *Decem Libri* first appeared in 1556 in Venice, and in a second edition in 1567. The work was illustrated with woodcuts, in many cases based on the drawings by Palladio, who was based in Vicenza. Moreover, it was for Daniele and his brother Marcantonio that Palladio constructed the famous villa in Maser near Treviso with its accompanying *tempietto*; the brothers had a direct influence on the plans.

Barbaro's Vitruvius edition and Palladio's *Quattro libri dell'architettura* (*Four books on architecture*) of 1570 augmented each other well, and in parts the sections on Vitruvius by the scholar and by the architect cannot be told apart. This unique co-operation was also reflected in Palladio's buildings. However, at times the two men did indeed demonstrate differing styles, for example in the depictions of the forum and basilica according to Vitruvius (Book V, 1). The ground plan in Barbaro's commentary follows the instructions of Vitruvius, whereby the rectangular forum is surrounded by halls with columns, as well as money-changing booths, with the basilica situated directly on the edge of the square. The interior of the basilica at the upper edge of the ground plan not only has columns on the long sides, they are also to be found on the end wall where the entrance is located. This was also how Palladio was to depict the Classical forum basilica in the *Quattro libri*. Barbaro's ground plan for the basilica, on the other hand, shows columns along the interior long walls only. This corresponds to the depiction by Fra Giocondo (1511), whose ideas in turn are comparable with Alberti's reconstruction.

Barbaro's portrayal of Vitruvius' basilica in Fano differs from that of Fra Giocondo in that the building has rows of columns on the interior. On the long side, the antetemple and Temple of Augustus adjoin (denoted by B and C respectively). The reconstruction of the elevation shows the tall columns of the interior as described by Vitruvius, on the reverse of which smallish supports bear the load of the upper galleries. Incidentally, in the late 1560s Palladio chose a very similar construction for the Villa Sarego.

The depictions of the Roman theatre in Barbaro's Vitruvius can be traced back to Palladio. As was usual in the 16th century, Vitruvius' building scheme was applied, such that the circle and the inscribed equilateral triangles touch the building's periphery. On the other hand, Barbaro and Palladio's contemporary, Antonio da Sangallo the Younger (1485–1546) as well as Vitruvius experts today (such as Curt Fensterbusch) used this scheme solely to determine the scale of the orchestra pit and the stage. With its decor of half columns, pilasters, figure niches, reliefs and street perspectives, the illustration of the two-storey stage ("scenae frons") that Palladio created for Barbaro's work anticipates important elements of the theatre that can be seen in Palladio's Teatro Olimpico in Vicenza.

When it came to the façade of Classical villas, Barbaro and Palladio were of the same opinion. In Book VI, Vitruvius does not describe the façade of the Roman "casa," and during the era of Barbaro and Palladio the exterior of such town houses had not been investigated from an archaeological point of view either. In his Vitruvius edition, however, Barbaro had the façade of the house depicted as if it were the front of a temple, with columns and pediment. This corresponds wholly with Palladio's view (Book II, 16 of his own treatise of 1570) that house-fronts in Classical Antiquity were graced with pediments, that indeed pediments were first used for residential buildings and only later for temples; this is how he justifies the frequent use of temple-like fronts in villas. Building work on his Villa Badoer, near Rovigo, with its entrance of columns and pediments in Classical form, started in 1556, i. e. at the time of Barbaro's first Vitruvius edition.   CJ

1 | **Cross-section of a basilica**
Reconstruction of the cross-section of the ancient market basilica with a view of the niche,
from Vitruvius V, 1.
P. 133. Woodcut

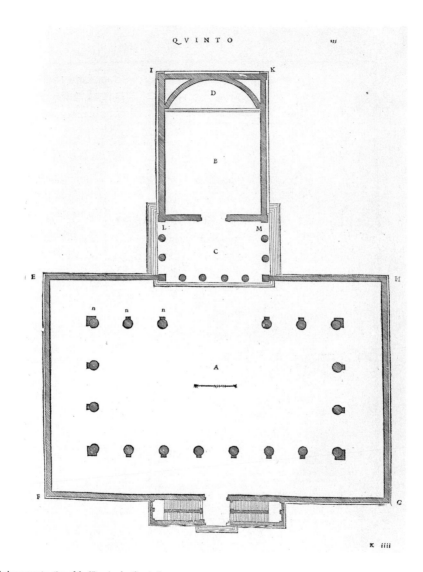

2 | Ground plan reconstruction of the Vitruvian basilica in Fano
Below, the illustration of the ground plan of the basilica (A) and above
of the Augustus temple (B), from Vitruvius V, 1.
P. 135. Woodcut

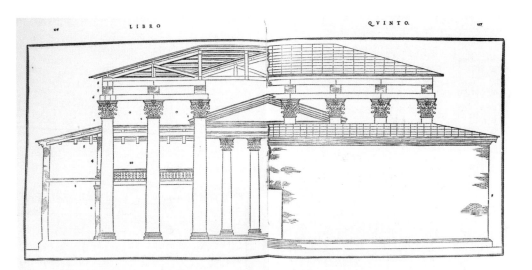

LIBRO   QVINTO.

3 | **Elevation of the Vitruvian basilica in Fano**
A sectional view (left) depicting the left column shows the support at the rear for the
upper structure; on the right, an illustration of the outer side, from Vitruvius V, 1.
P. 136/37. Woodcut

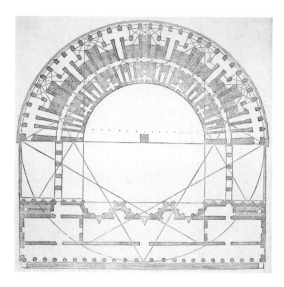

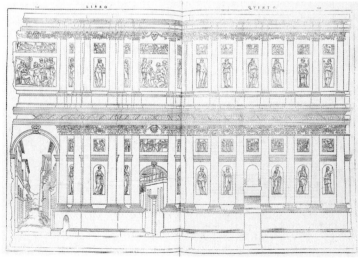

4 | **Ground plan design of the Roman (Latin) theatre**
Illustration from Vitruvius V, 7.
P. 154. Woodcut

5 | **View of the stage of a theatre**
Illustration from Vitruvius V, 7.
P. 155/56. Woodcut

LIBRO.
QVESTA E VNA PARTE DELLA FACCIATA DELLA CASA PRIVATA.

6 | **Entrance side of an ancient Roman private house with
colonnaded portico and pediment**
The reconstruction is not based on Vitruvius.
P. 170. Woodcut

Andrea Palladio (1508–1580)
I quattro libri dell'architettura

VENICE, 1570

The four books of architecture. London, 1738

Plans to publish his own treatise on architecture matured while Andrea Palladio was illustrating Barbaro's edition of Vitruvius. The architect, who was born in Padua, first came to prominence as an author in 1554, the year he undertook his final trip to Rome with Barbaro. It was at this time that his guides to the Classical monuments of the city, *Le antichità di Roma*, appeared, as did his guide to the Roman churches, *Descritione de le chiese, stationi, indulgenze (A description of the churches, stations [of the cross], and indulgences)*. Initially Palladio had intended a more extensive treatise on architecture than the fragmentary work *Quattro libri* that was published in Venice in 1570 by Domenicho de Franceschi. This in no way detracts from the impact and importance of the work, which made a decisive contribution to the author's fame; its very conciseness helped bring about the phenomenon of Palladianism, as it has come to be known, the Palladio-inspired Classicism which has subsequently spread throughout the world.

Conditions were very favourable when *Quattro libri* appeared. Palladio had spent many years learning the building profession from the very basics as a stonemason in the Pedemuro workshop in Vicenza, and this experience is evident in his theories on materials and construction. From the 1530s on, his encounters with the north Italian Classical scholars, who were very knowledgeable about architecture, made a tremendous impression on him. It was Giangiorgio Trissino (1478–1550) who gave Andrea di Pietro della Gondola his

pseudonym and programmatic name Palladio, a reference to Pallas Athene, and introduced him to the work of Vitruvius. Alvise Cornaro (1484–1566), whose "excellent knowledge of art" ("eccellente giudicio") Palladio praised in his treatise (Book I, 28), stimulated the new approach to architecture in Padua. Daniele Barbaro was the third of the eminent north Italian Classical scholars who, being the wealthy clients and knowledgeable theorists they were, paved the way for Palladio.

Palladio's architectural expertise was further enhanced by his stays in Rome and by his thorough research into archaeology, as reflected in his architectural drawings and the woodcuts of the *Quattro libri*. As a late example of the great Italian architectural theorists, he also benefited from the achievements and experience that had been gained from a good hundred years' development of Renaissance theory. Reading of Leon Battista Alberti's fundamental, very difficult architectural treatise from the middle of the 15th century had been greatly facilitated since 1565 by an illustrated Italian translation. Alongside Vitruvius, Palladio also recognized Alberti (1404–1472) as an authority on questions about building. As early as 1537 and 1540, Serlio (1475–1553/55), whom Palladio met in Vicenza, had published Books III and IV of his *Architettura*, including several, often very high-quality woodcuts of Classical monuments. As a result of the importance that the illustrations gained vis-à-vis the text, Serlio's work can be considered a preliminary stage of Palladio's

Quattro libri. Palladio also makes use of the suggestive impact of the illustrations, but is stricter in the standards he set for the layout of the pictures. His illustrations of buildings are presented regularly in ground plans, elevations and cross-sections, whereby the latter two follow an orthogonal projection, i. e. are not depicted in perspective, in which as a result of foreshortened lines exact proportions are not shown. Finally it should be pointed out that Palladio, who in his role as a much sought-after architect had constructed several palaces, bridges, and ecclesiastical buildings since around 1540, was able to draw on the fruits of a long and busy professional career in his late opus *Quattro libri.*

Displaying a self-confidence unprecedented in the theory of architecture, Palladio illustrated the treatise with his own, very numerous projects, and showed no inhibitions in placing his "catalogue of works" on a par with Classical buildings. It was part of his overall creed to revive the tried-and-trusted constructional principles of Classical Antiquity and make them universally accepted along with his own work. Among works by his contemporaries, he singled out only Bramante's mock-antique Tempietto in Rome. Serlio, too, displayed this circular building with its ring of columns, putting it on a par with the achievements of Classical Antiquity. Palladio idealized several buildings in the woodcuts in the treatise. Palaces and villas which for the most part had never been finished are then completed in the illustrations, and in some cases are given a more stringent axial alignment than was physically possible given the land on which the buildings had been constructed. Subsequently, he may well have used contrived building programmes to bear out his descriptions. He maintains, for example, that the Palazzo Iseppo de' Porti in Vicenza, whose façade, made up of a ground floor and a first storey adorned with columns (in the manner of the Roman palaces of the High Renaissance), has actually been divided up into a front section, interior courtyard and rear guest house after the Greek style. Yet from the very beginning the plans for the monastery in the Venetian Convento della Carità, whose layout he depicts, were governed by his idea of the house in Classical Antiquity. He subsequently offers a reconstruction of the ground plan and the longitudinal cross-section of the ancient Roman private house.

The four-columned rooms that emulate rooms in Classical buildings, as depicted in Book II, 9 and corresponding to Vitruvius' description of a "tetrastyla," were of particular importance to Palladio in his own projects. Four free-standing columns, positioned on the corner points of a square in the room's interior, bear the load of the ceilings or domes. Palladio used them, for example, in the Villa Pisani in Montagnana and Villa Cornaro. The unique Classical appearance of the main façade of Villa Badoer in Fratta Polesine, begun in 1556, with its columns and pediment is confirmed not just by comparison with the reconstruction of the Classical house façade that Palladio and Barbaro had shown in their Vitruvius commentary. In his reconstruction of the elevation of the Classical villa, Palladio likewise maintained that the portico of columns with its pediment was an intrinsic decorative motif in the ancient Roman building tradition.

Palladio (Book III, 19) also addresses the question of forum basilicas. Unlike Barbaro's edition of Vitruvius, the *Quattro libri* provide, in the interior of a basilica, for rows of columns along the length of the long sides and along the end wall behind the entrance. Palladio also emphasizes that he can even well imagine, in principle, columns along the end wall opposite the entrance. In this case, however, he dispenses with them in order to better accentuate a large semi-circular niche. In other words, a sense of aesthetics prompts him to deviate from the Classical style he so revered. And when (in Book III, 20) he depicts his own basilica in Vicenza with its arcades on two storeys veiling the medieval interior of the building, he endeavours, with all due respect for Classical Antiquity, to make a point of the modern age's own way of building. Whereas ancient basilicas always have sets of columns (porticoes) in the interior, or so he suggests, in "modern" basilicas columns are nowhere to be seen or, if at all, on the exterior, facing the square.

As far as the layout, presentation and logical consistency of their argumentation are concerned, Andrea Palladio's *Quattro libri* created a set of norms that became binding for all future manuals on architecture.   CJ

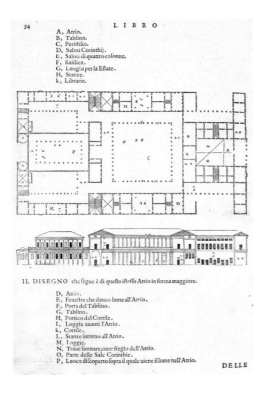

1 | **Reconstruction of an ancient Roman private house in ground plan and sectional elevation**
Book II, 7. Woodcut

2 | **Reconstruction of the ancient four-column hall, floor plan and elevation**
Book II, 9. Woodcut

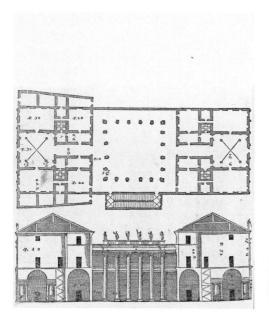

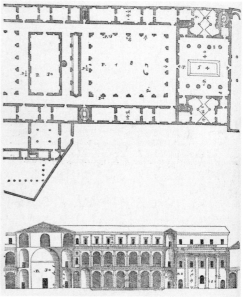

3 | **Palazzo Iseppo Porti in Vicenza**
Ground plan and sectional elevation.
Book II, 3. Woodcut

4 | **Convento della Carità in Venice**
Ground plan and sectional elevation in the style of the ancient Roman
private house.
Book II, 6. Woodcut

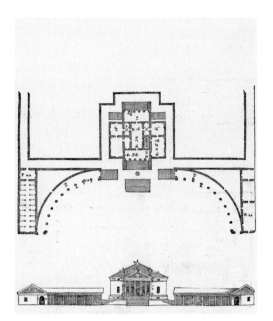

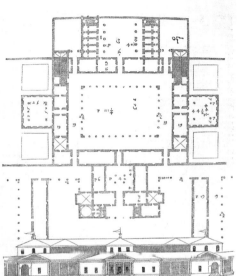

5 | Villa Badoer in Fratta Polesine
Ground plan and façade with colonnaded portico and pediment, which
Palladio and Barbaro read as part of the ancient Roman house.
Book II, 14. Woodcut

6 | Reconstruction of an ancient villa
Ground plan and elevation; façade featuring colonnaded portico and
triangular pediment.
Book II, 16. Woodcut

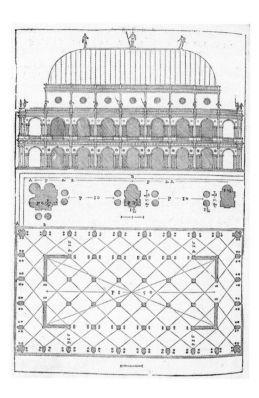

7 | Ground plan of a basilica
Reconstruction of the ancient Roman forum basilica with columns positioned at the entrance side, and large niche (B) at the opposite end wall.
Book III, 19. Woodcut

8 | Ground plan and elevation of Palladio's basilica in Vicenza
Columns supporting rounded arches framed by narrow side openings, known as the serliana or Palladio motif.
Book III, 20. Woodcut

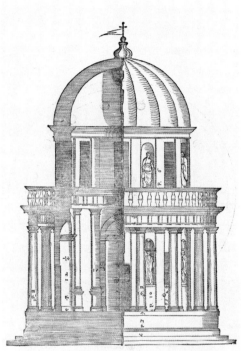

9 | **Elevation of the basilica in Vicenza**
The detail view of the basilica reveals the Doric ground floor, the Ionian upper storey, and the medals complete with heads set into the arcade spandrels.
Book III. Woodcut

10 | **Bramante's Tempietto of San Pietro in Montorio in Rome**
Book IV, 17. Woodcut

Vincenzo Scamozzi (1548–1616)
L'idea della architettura universale

VENICE, 1615

The mirror of architecture, or, The groundrules of the art of building. London, 1676

Vincenzo Scamozzi was one of the most important architects in the Veneto region. His treatise, which appeared in 1615, gained widespread popularity, with the book on column orders quickly emerging as a standard reference work on the subject in the 17th century.

Vincenzo gained initial practical experience with his father, a carpenter and architect. It was here that he also learnt the basics of surveying. In the years that followed, he set about gaining more in-depth knowledge here. In addition to 15th and 16th-century Italian treatises on architecture, as well as others in French and German, Scamozzi read Greek authors, in particular Aristotle, Plato and Euclid, as well as several Latin authors, including Pliny and Cicero. In addition to Vitruvius, Scamozzi also examined the work of Serlio (1475–1553/55) in depth.

As architect to the Pisani family, Scamozzi established important contacts to the upper echelons of Venetian society. His trip to Rome now gave him an entry to those circles in which aristocratic clients moved. With the help of Marc Antonio Barbaro, who had been a friend of Contarini and an important patron of Palladio, he succeeded in winning a competition for the design of the Procuratie Nuove (the New Procurates) in Venice in c. 1582, which in terms of size, was the most important contract of his career. In his design for Salzburg Cathedral (1604–1607), Scamozzi combined his study of Palladio's most important Venetian church, San Giorgio Maggiore, with overtones of Bramante's architecture

for columns and niches, with which he was familiar at least in Serlio's theoretical realizations, to form a synthesis in which the influence of Vignola's Early Baroque ecclesiastical buildings in Rome is also easily discerned. All these sources of inspiration are also included in the treatise, which to a certain extent can also be interpreted as a continuation of his work as an architect. In Books II and III in particular, he presents numerous designs that were neither built at all or, if so, only in altered form.

Idea della architettura universale is the last Renaissance treatise in which architecture is regarded as a universal science that embraces all areas of society. This claim is derived from the neo-Platonic idea of a mathematically, geometrically ordered cosmos created by God. The intellectual concept of the "idea" functions as the intermediary between abstract principles, which govern the process of design, and the conception and completion of individual works. Together with Vitruvius and Alberti (1404–1472), Scamozzi was of the opinion that a uniform system of mathematical ratios should govern all the inter-relationships of sections of a building. The theorists of the Renaissance saw nature as a model for this system, in particular in the picture of the perfect human body and its proportions, created in the image of God. Buildings were likewise assumed to be an expression of this cosmic order of things. Of the projected twelve volumes of Scamozzi's magnum opus, later reduced later to ten, six books appeared initially in Venice in 1615. Following

Cornice

min

Fregio

min

Architraue

min

Modulo $1\frac{1}{4}$

Scamozzi's death, the material for the remaining four books was scattered, several illustrations later surfacing in a Dutch translation of the treatise (Amsterdam, 1661) and in a French edition (Leiden, 1713). According to Scamozzi himself, he spent 25 years working on the treatise.

While Book I explains the status of architecture as a science and deals with the training of architects, Book II deals with geographical and topographical conditions of architecture. Book III deals with private buildings, Book IV with public buildings, and in Book VI Scamozzi presents his theory about the orders of columns. Books VII, VIII and IX are devoted to building materials, the building process and the final and decorative work, while Book X deals with the alteration and restoration of buildings. The division of the subject matter into ten categories is a reference to the treatises of Vitruvius and Alberti, while Scamozzi is indebted above all to Vitruvius for the definition of the underlying aesthetics.

The aim of the first book was to substantiate the status of architecture as a science, and in so doing to elevate the status of the architect above that of the site foreman. Since the architect "observes in his mind the very being of mathematics and the essence of natural processes" (" ... discorre, e considera nel suo intelletto le cose Mathematiche, come anco le naturali scienze in essenza ..."), he can be compared with a mathematician or philosopher. As such Scamozzi also relies on the medieval educational canon of *artes liberales* and *artes mechanicae*. Scamozzi's language, his numerous repetitions, and the wealth of sources he quotes are his stylistic means of ennobling the text, and thereby of underlining his endeavour.

Among other things, Book II contains the design for an ideal city that must be considered as Scamozzi's project for Palmanova. In the ideal city (the design of which contains thoughts about military architecture), we can discern the ethical and social-political dimension of Scamozzi's universal undertaking. A further focal point is theatre architecture.

Here, Scamozzi brings to a conclusion the Renaissance debate that had been opened out by Daniele Barbaro's annotations on Vitruvius, and been decisively influenced by Serlio. His commitment as a theorist on the construction of theatres corresponds to his importance as a theatre architect. Proof of this is in the completion of Palladio's Teatro Olimpico in Vicenza (1584–85) and his very own Teatro Ducale in Sabbionetta, near Mantua (1588–90).

Books IV, IX and X did not appear. Book VI, which contains Scamozzi's theory of columns therefore becomes all the more important. With the text and pictures presented in manual form, the architectural orders and their component parts are systematically depicted with an unprecedented richness. Influenced by Serlio, Scamozzi is the first to use the term "ordine" for the five divisions of the classical theory of columns. He argues that not only the calculation and the shape of the architectural parts, but also all parts of the construction including the interiors should be subject to the regulating principle of architectural order. Scamozzi himself offers an example of this with his Palazzo Trissino.

Scamozzi stresses time and again that a sense of order and "ragione," reason, must dominate all parts of the building, even the decoration. This earned him the reputation of being an Early Baroque classicist. In this sense, his work in the Veneto in the first half of the 17th century marked the starting point of the classical Palladian "stile severo," the severe style, and even in the 18th century Scamozzi's influence can be felt in English neo-Palladianism. This stems in part from Scamozzi's contacts with Inigo Jones, when the latter visited Italy in 1613/14 as part of the entourage of Thomas Howard, the 2nd Earl of Arundel. However, it was Scamozzi's theory of columns in Book VI (which from 1657 was also distributed in a shortened version) that had the biggest impact. Book VI appeared in 1640 in Dutch, in 1665 in German, in 1669 in English and finally, in 1685, in French, in connection with the reform in French architecture by François Blondel. AG

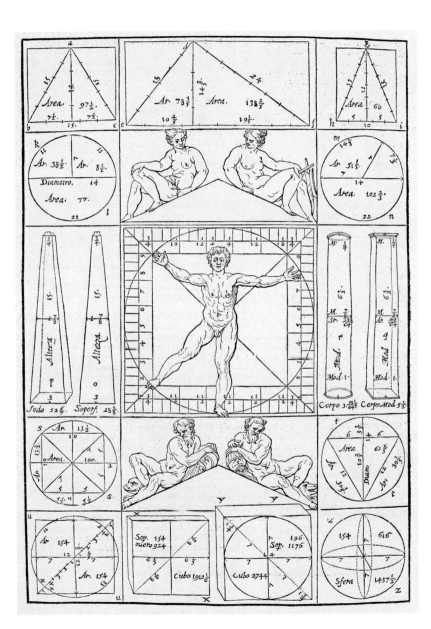

1 | **Studies in proportion**
The ideal proportions of
the human body, and
basic geometrical forms.
Part I, book 1, p. 40. Woodcut

2 | **Column orders**
The five orders in architecture; from left to right:
Tuscan, Doric, Ionian,
Corinthian, Composite.
Part II, book 6, p. 6. Woodcut

3 | **Architectural decoration of the Doric order**
Part II, book 6, p. 84.
Woodcut

ASPETTO DEL COLONNATO CORINTO

Vic. Scamozzi

**4 | Portico with columns
of the Corinthian order**
*Part II, book 6, p. 124.
Woodcut*

5 | **Portico with colonnaded arcades of the Corinthian order**
Part II, book 6, p. 127.
Woodcut

Domenico De' Rossi (1659–1730)
Studio d'Architettura civile

3 VOLS, ROME, 1702, 1711, 1721

Studio d'architettura civile. Farnborough, 1972

Disegni di vari altari e cappelle nelle chiese di Roma

ROME, 1713

The designs of various altars and chapels in Roman churches

The three volumes of *Studio d'Architettura civile* and *Disegni di vari altari e cappelle nelle chiese di Roma,* which probably appeared in 1713, are not architectural treatises, nor was Domenico De' Rossi an architect or architectural theorist, but the successful heir to publisher Giovanni Giacomo De' Rossi (1627–1691), the owner of the Stamperia alla Pace printing works in Rome. Over more than 40 years, Giovanni Giacomo reprinted or published for the first time countless works on various topics. In the late 1650s, he succeeded in being awarded the right to print the portraits of ecclesiastical dignitaries by Pope Alexander VII (reigned 1655–1667), and he later engaged the services of the gifted draughtsman, engraver and etcher Giovanni Battista Falda (1643–1678), with whose help he brought out important new publications. In the second half of the 17th century, Giovanni Giacomo De' Rossi advanced to become the most influential publisher in Rome. In 1679, following Falda's early death, he adopted Domenico De' Rossi, who was actually called Freddiani and hailed from Lucca, making him his heir. From 1691, Domenico ran the publishing house for a total of 30 years before finally handing it on to his son Lorenzo Filippo around 1720.

The two works, *Studio d'Architettura civile* and *Disegni di vari altari,* contain illustrations of palaces and churches, their chapels and altars, as well as doors, windows, and other architectural details. The first volume includes a dedication to Pope Clement XI (reigned 1700–1721), a preface, and a catalogue of the architects and works. With this work of a total

of 321 plates, Domenico De' Rossi continued two of his adoptive father's most important publishing projects: *Nuovi disegni delle architetture e piante dei palazzi di Roma dei più celebri architetti* (New architectural designs and ground plans of palaces in Rome by the most famous architects) and *Il nuovo teatro delle fabriche et edificii in prospettiva di Roma moderna* (A new compendium of buildings and palaces in modern Rome in perspective). The *Nuovi disegni,* which appeared in 1655 in four volumes, contained for the very first time portrayals of modern Roman architecture.

The three volumes of *Architettura civile* go far beyond these and other forerunners. Almost all the drawings were new and, if portraying existing buildings, were true to scale down to the smallest details. Some of them also take into account the designs for the objects portrayed, as is the case for Carlo Rainaldi's rear façade of Santa Maria Maggiore (1670–1673), which is juxtaposed with Bernini's 1668 design. Domenico De' Rossi engaged Alessandro Specchi (1666–1729) to draw most of the examples; together with him, he had already published the fourth volume of *Nuovi disegni* in 1699. Specchi himself was an architect. His depiction of architecture in *Studio d'Architettura civile* corresponds to the method that had been developed in Rome the last two decades of the 17th century in the studio of Carlo Fontana, and which had been adopted as the norm as a result of the latter's work for the Accademia di San Luca. It involves showing the ground plan, elevation and cross-section of

D

every building, and excerpts make the exact construction and proportions of the parts identifiable.

Falda documented the most important High Baroque buildings in Rome for the first time in 1665, including works by Gianlorenzo Bernini (1598–1680), Francesco Borromini (1599–1667), Pietro da Cortona (1596–1669), Carlo Rainaldi (1611–1631) and Carlo Fontana the Younger (1638–1714). The first volume of *Nuovi disegni* begins with a series of 27 engravings of works by Michelangelo, the Capitol, St. Peter's Basilica, the Palazzo Farnese, the Porta Pia, followed by works by Bernini, the Palazzo Barberini, the Palazzo Chigi, the Palazzo della Curia (nowadays Montecitorio), Sant' Andrea al Quirinale and SS. Luca e Martina by Pietro da Cortona. As many as 50 of the 139 plates are dedicated to Borromini, more than twice as many as to his rival Bernini. St John Lateran, the oratory of San Filippo Neri, the convent of San Carlo alle Quattro Fontane, as well as various palazzi are all presented. Volume I also pays great attention to the youngest generation of architects, in particular Giovanni Antonio de' Rossi (1616–1695), Mattia de' Rossi (1637–1695) and Camillo Arcucci (?–1667), whose works bring the volume to a close.

In Falda's *Nuovo teatro*, Borromini's work was represented by two examples, on an equal footing alongside that of his contemporaries, namely San Carlo alle Quattro Fontane, and Santa Agnese in Piazza Navona. By contrast, the selection for the fourth volume, which appeared in 1699, contained the representatives of the Late Baroque Classicism that so strongly influenced architecture in Rome in the final quarter of the 17th century: Giovanni Antonio and Mattia de' Rossi – Bernini's colleagues and successors – as well as Carlo Fontana (1638–1714), his son Francesco (1668–1708), and Girolamo Fontana (1668–1701). The importance attributed to Borromini in volume I of *Studio d'architettura civile* is evidence of the rekindled interest in the architect in the years following 1700. Two extensive sets of engravings on Sant' Ivo and the oratory of San Filippo Neri published 1720 and 1725 helped bring Borromini, who had died in 1667, international renown. In volumes II and III of *Studio d'architettura civile* several plates are devoted to Borromini's architecture.

The decoration of doors and windows forms the subject matter of Volume II, followed in Volume II by altars, chapels and tombstones in Roman churches. It concludes with Verrocchio's tombstone for Giovanni and Pietro de' Medici and Michelangelo's New Sacristy in San Lorenzo, Florence. In *Disegni di vari altari e cappelle* the subject matter is explored in more depth. Volume III contains churches in Rome, ground plans and elevations of the Royal Palace in Naples as well as, somewhat surprisingly, a ground plan of Milan Cathedral. A series of sixteen engravings by Gabriele Valvassori shows Vignola's Palazzo Farnese in Caprarola.

In the three volumes, architecture is depicted in stages, from individual elements to the completed object, in line with the curricula at the Accademia di San Luca in Rome. Indeed, during their training at the Accademia prospective architects in the third class, for example, were set the task of drawing the portals and windows of famous Renaissance and Baroque buildings. The ensemble of ground plans, elevations, cross-sections and details, as well as the style of graphic representation, were also geared to the requirements of the Academy of Art in Rome. Some of the works contained in De' Rossi's Volume I were the themes set by the first Concorsi Clementini organized by the academy, such as the portal of Palazzo Sciarra Colonna, with which in 1705 Filippo Vasconi and Benedikt Renard won first and second prize respectively in the competition. Alternatively, Gabriele Valvassori's bird's-eye view, which in Volume I opens a series of depictions of the Palazzo Farnese in Caprarola, harks back to a drawing for the "Design of a country castle for three royal persons," with which Filippo Juvarra (1678–1736) had caused a sensation at the Concorso Clementino in 1705.

As a reference work used for instruction at the Accademia di San Luca, De' Rossi's publication was an influence on many foreign architects studying in Rome, but the effects of *Studio d'architettura civile* were felt far beyond the walls of the academy. As a result of the engravings, architects in other regions of Italy and abroad were now able to familiarize themselves with Roman Baroque architecture without having ever set foot in the city. This is the publication's major achievement. The engravings published by Domenico De' Rossi were a major contribution to the development of an international Baroque style, emanating from Roman Baroque architecture, and which was pursued by architects such as Fischer von Erlach (1656–1723) in Austria, Andreas Schlüter (ca. 1660–1714) and Johann Conrad Schlaun (1695–1773) in Germany, by Jules Hardouin Mansart in France (1646–1708), and John Vanbrugh (1664–1726) and Nicholas Hawksmoor (1661–1736) in England. The royal palaces in Madrid, Stockholm and St Petersburg as well as villas and ecclesiastical buildings from Portugal to Hungary bear witness to this style.

AG

1 | **Elevation of a window**
Study with detailled specifications of the window in the third order of
the Palazzo Farnese in Rome by Antonio da Sangallo the Younger
(1534–1546).
Vol. I, pl. 30. Engraving by Alessandro Specchi

2 | **Elevation of a doorframe**
Study of a doorframe by Francesco Borromini in the mother-house of
the congregation of the oratory of S. Filippo Neri in Rome (1637–1650).
Vol. I, pl. 93. Engraving by Antonio Barbey after a drawing by Carlo Quadri

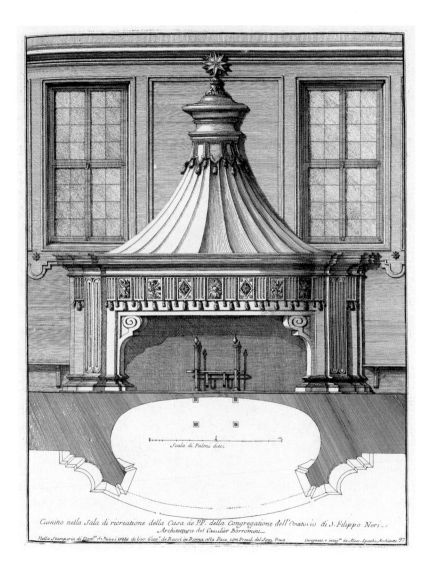

Cumino nella Sala di ricreatione della Casa de PP. della Congregatione dell'Oratorio di S. Filippo Neri.
Architettura del Cavalier Borromini

Nella Stamparia di Dom.co de Rossi erede di Gio: Giac.o de Rossi in Roma alla Pace, con Priuil. del Som. Pont.   Disegnato, e inag.to da Aless. Specchi Architetto 97

3 | **Ground plan and elevation of an open fireplace**
Study after Francesco Borromini's open fireplace in the room for contemplation in the
mother-house of the congregation of the oratory of S. Filippo Neri in Rome (1637–1650).
Vol. I, pl. 97. Engraving by Alessandro Specchi

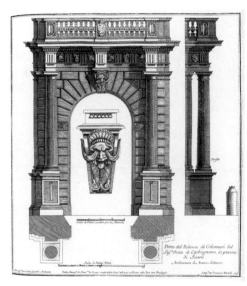

4 | Elevation of two windows
Study after Gian Lorenzo Bernini's ground floor windows in the building of the papal law court in Rome (Palazzo Montecitorio, 1650).
Vol. I, pl. 106. Engraving by Antonio Barbey after a drawing by Carlo Quadri

5 | Portal of the Palazzo Sciarra-Colonna in Rome
Ground plan, elevation, side view and details of the portal by Orazio Torriani for the Sciarra-Colonna Palace in Rome (1641), ascribed to De' Rossi Antonio Labacco.
Vol. I, pl. 115. Engraving by Francesco Bartoli after a drawing by Carlo Quadri

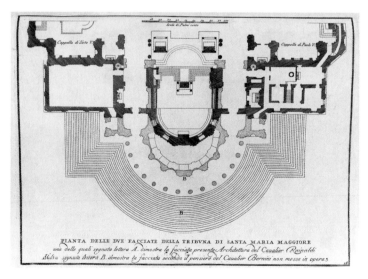

6 | **Santa Maria Maggiore in Rome**
Design by Gian Lorenzo Bernini for the façade of the apse of
Santa Maria Maggiore in Rome (1669).
Vol. III, pl. 15. Engraving

7 | **Ground plan of the apse façade of Santa Maria Maggiore in Rome**
Ground plan A by Carlo Rainaldi (1670–1673), and alternative ground
plan B by Gian Lorenzo Bernini (1668).
Vol. III, pl. 16. Engraving

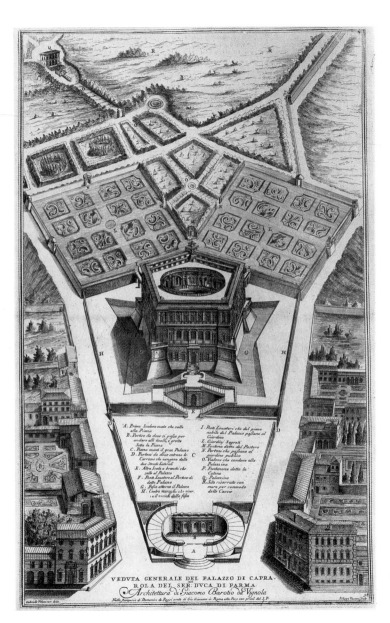

VEDVTA GENERALE DEL PALAZZO DI CAPRA·
ROLA DEL SER. DVCA DI PARMA
Architettura di Giacomo Barotio da Vignola

8 | **General view of Vignola's Palazzo Farnese in Caprarola (1557)**
Vol. III, pl. 58. Engraving by Filippo Vasconi after a drawing by Gabriele Valvassori

Giovanni Battista Piranesi (1720–1778)

Della magnificenza ed architettura de' Romani

ROME, 1761

On the magnificence and the architecture of the Romans

Giovanni Battista Piranesi is one of the most important artists in the whole history of etchings and architectural views. He created almost almost 700 drawings and more than 1,000 prints. Piranesi's brilliant technique was characterized by great speed and extraordinary versatility. Of all his works, in particular *Invenzione caprici di carceri* (*Fantastic designs for dungeons*, 1749/50), which had appeared in 1761 in a revised and extended edition entitled *Carceri d'invenzione* (*Designs for dungeons*), was still important as late as the 20th century. Among others, the pioneer of modern cinema Sergei Eisenstein (1898–1948), the dramatist and artist Peter Weiss (1916–1982), authors Hans Magnus Enzensberger (b. 1929) and Erich Fried (1921–1988), as well as French comic writers have taken the fantastic world of the *Carceri* as the starting point for their own work.

Yet Piranesi's œuvre embraces far more than just prints. He worked as a restorer, made stage sets and decorations for festive occasions, and he also made and distributed throughout Europe fireplaces into which Classical objets trouvés had been worked. Though only a few of his designs were actually realized, Piranesi considered himself to be first and foremost an architect. The common denominator of all these activities was the artist's interest in archaeology.

Piranesi received his initial training as an architect in Venice, from his uncle Matteo Lucchesi, who instructed him in the style of Venetian neo-Palladianism. This was followed by an apprenticeship with Giovanni Antonio Scalfurotto

(c. 1700–1764), who was known for the eclectic character of his architecture. From Carlo Zucchi he learnt the art of designing stage sets as well as perspective in the style of Galli Bibiena, and the techniques of copperplate engraving and etching. Inspired by the book *Delle antiquità di Rimini*, 1741 (*On the ruins of antiquity in Rimini*) by Tommaso Temanza (1705–1789), Piranesi began very early on to devote his attention to the Etruscans and ancient Rome. He also heard the lectures on architecture by that strict representative of the Enlightenment Carlo Lodoli (1690–1761), who was a lasting influence on him. In the autumn of 1740, as part of the entourage of the Venetian ambassador, the 20-year-old Piranesi entered the court of the newly elected Pope Benedict XIV (reigned 1740–1758). In Rome, he perfected his technique in the workshop of the famous copperplate engraver Giuseppe Vasi (1710–1782), whom he assisted in the production of architectural views, which at the time were very popular as souvenirs with visitors to Rome. Since the early 18th century, Rome had increasingly become the destination of wealthy, educated travellers visiting the cultural centres of Europe on their "Grand Tour". This resulted in the city's intellectual community becoming more outward-looking and cosmopolitan, and Piranesi was one of those to benefit. He journeyed to Naples, where he followed the excavations in Herculaneum (begun in 1738) with great interest. Having returned to Venice temporarily in 1743, he was finally able to gain a professional foothold in Rome in 1747. A year later *Antichità Ro-*

mane de' tempi della Repubblica e de' primi Imperatori (The Roman remains from the days of the Republic and the first Emperors), his first independent series of views appeared. He now embarked on the systematic expansion of his famous *Vedute di Roma*, 1748–78 *(Views of Rome)*, for which he initially chose a larger format. From 1761 he maintained his own workshop, becoming the largest producer of views of Rome, with distribution far beyond the country's borders. In the same year, he was admitted to the Accademia di San Luca Academy of Art in Rome and in 1767 he was made a Cavaliere, or knight.

In 1755, the arrival of Joachim Winckelmann (1717–1768) in Rome unleashed fierce debate, in which Piranesi was also involved, about the importance of the Greeks for Roman art. Winckelmann idealized Greece as the home of freedom and as a model for simplicity and grandeur. Piranesi believed this called into question his own convictions that Classical Rome was unique and the absolute example to be followed. His response took the form of a series of polemical articles, of which *Della magnificenza ed architettura de' Romani*, 1761 *(On the magnificence and the architecture of the Romans)* and the compendium *Osservazioni sopra la lettre de M. Mariette aux auteurs de la Gazette Littéraire de l'Europe (Observations about M. Mariette's letter to the authors of the European Literary Gazette)* are the most important.

Della magnificenza ed architettura de' Romani is Piranesi's first theoretical piece of writing. The text, 196 pages long and divided into 117 chapters, is complemented by an appendix of panels including 29 large etchings and a detailed table of contents, which leads to the text and the illustration section. The work is dedicated to its promoter, the Venetian Pope Clement XIII Rezonico (reigned 1758–1769), whose portrait precedes the text. First and foremost, Piranesi comes out against the primacy of Greek art, and in particular attacks in a most polemic style Allan Ramsay's 1754 work, *Dialogue of Taste*, as well as *Ruins des plus beaux monuments de la Grèce*, 1758 *(The ruins of the most beautiful monuments in Greece)* by the Frenchman Julien-David Le Roy. He focuses on the authors' theories one by one, and attempts to refute them by proving the superiority of the Etruscans, both historically and artistically, and depicting the Romans as the Etruscans' heirs. Departing from the strictly functional art of the Egyptians, the Etruscans and Romans succeeded, he suggests, in creating a form of art that, while richly embellished, was nevertheless functional, whereas the Greeks had turned that original functionality into pure ornamentation. On this basis, Piranesi is able to pay tribute not only to the greatness and austerity he claims for Etruscan architecture, but also to the fantasy-laden art of the Late Roman Empire. He sees the proof of these theories in the records of Roman history, quoting Livy, Cicero, Tacitus, Varro and many others. Yet he relies on the works of eminent experts on the Etruscans such as Mario Guarnacci, Antonio Francesco Gori and Giovanni Battista Passeri. The vehemence with which Piranesi defends the Etruscans' art can be explained by the cultural and political scale of the debate. Like Germany in the 18th century,

Italy was fragmented into numerous small states, some ruled by foreign powers. Against this background, many Italian experts on the Etruscans saw in the Etruscan, Roman roots of their own culture the seeds of a national Italian identity. From this, enlightened contemporaries derived their demand for Italy's political freedom and territorial independence.

As far as knowledge of Etruscan and Roman architecture was concerned, Piranesi was able to rely on his own excavation work. At the beginning of the 1750s, he turned his attention increasingly to archaeology, and was particularly interested in the building materials and building techniques used by the Romans, as well as the layout of ancient Rome. Thanks to the prints he produced at this stage, *Le Antichità di Roma*, 1756 *(Ancient ruins in Rome)*, which, with more than 250 engravings, can be considered a veritable anthology of ancient buildings, he was even made an honorary member of the Society of Antiquaries of London in 1757. The illustrations in the appendix of plates in *Della magnificenza* are also very detailed and exact. Some of the illustrations depict pieces of Etruscan and Roman art that Piranesi considered exemplary, whereas others represent the decadence of the Greeks, but in conjunction with the polemical text they fulfil their purpose. Piranesi shared two important points of view with his antagonists: on the one hand, for him as well Classical Antiquity (being the all-powerful role model that it was) was the ultimate authority, and on the other, art's foundations lie in a sense of order and reason. According to Piranesi, both these points of view are expressed by Vitruvius as

the key authority. He derives the criteria by which he categorizes past and present work as "vero" or "falso" (true or false) from the writings of the author of the treatise as well as from the theories of the rigorous functionalist, Fra Carlo Lodoli.

Piranesi's theoretical mind in no way remained standing. He relished the duality of Enlightenment thinking that arose from the conflict between rationality and emotion, from the search for a new way or reasoning on the one hand and the pre-Romantic enthusiasm for the limitless creative genius of the artist on the other. Against this background, it is easy to explain the turning point that emerges in *Osservazioni*, written in 1765. This was Piranesi's response to the French author Pierre-Jean Mariette's (1694–1774) criticism of him in an article attacking *Della magnificenza ed architettura de' Romani*. At the end of a fictitious argument between a teacher and his pupil the latter, who defends Lodoli's rationalist position, is defeated. Using the words of the teacher, Piranesi comes out in favour of the Etruscans. Above all he stresses their creative fantasy, deriving from it the modern artists' right to artistic freedom. Modified in this way, Piranesi's position as a theorist is consistent with his intentions as an artist. It was his aim to create a new, modern style, based on the eclectic combination of all forms of ancient architecture. His newly acquired theoretical stance now enabled him to include examples of Egyptian art in later works.

AG

1 | **Various columns of Greek architecture**
Pl. 6. Engraving by Piranesi

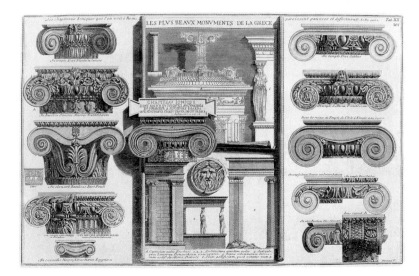

2 | **Column base**
Comparison of column base from Roman architecture with one
from Greek architecture – from the book by Julien-David Le Roy.
Pl. 11. Engraving by Piranesi

3 | **Various architectural details**
Examples of the diversity of forms used in classical Roman
architecture.
Pl. 19. Engraving by Piranesi

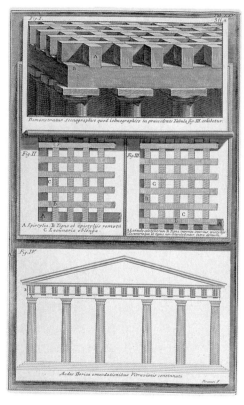

4 | View of the Concordia Temple in Agrigent
Pl. 22. Engraving by Piranesi

5 | Illustrations of roof construction and elevation of a Doric temple after Vitruvius
Pl. 25. Engraving by Piranesi

6 | **Various architectural details and ground plans depicting the architecture of the circular temples in Ancient Rome**
Pl. 38. Engraving by Piranesi

7 | **Sectional view of the drainage canal at Lake Albano**
Pl. 30. Engraving by Piranesi

Francesco Milizia (1725–1798)

Principj di architettura civile

2 VOLS, FINALE, 1781

Principles of civil architecture

Giovanni Battista Cipriani (1766–1839)

Indice delle figure relative ai Principi di architettura civile

ROME, 1800

Index of the illustrations for the principles of civil architecture

Francesco Milizia's *Principj di architettura civile* represent neo-Classicism's most important contribution to the theory of architecture. Reprinted a total of six times in the 19th century, the major reason for the importance of this treatise was its wide dissemination. Its success was due not least to the systematic way its material was structured and to the clarity of the language Milizia used to expound the notion of an Enlightened "philosophical architecture" influenced by the idea of ideal beauty.

After studying in Padua, Rome and Naples, Francesco Milizia spent some time in France. It was only after moving to Rome, before 1761, that he began to take an interest in architecture and the theory of architecture. He was admitted to the circle of artists and literati gathered around Jose Nicolas de Azara, Marquis of Nibbiano (Aragon), patron of the arts and since 1765 Spanish diplomat to the court of Pope Clement XIII (reigned 1758–1769). At some point, Milizia was appointed Superintendent of the Farnese lands in the Papal State by Ferdinand IV (1759–1825), King of Naples and Sicily. This assignment appears to have encouraged him to become a writer. In 1768, he published *Lo vita de' più celebri Architetti d'ogni nazione e d'ogni tempo* (*The lives of celebrated architects, Ancient and Modern*). In 1781, this was followed by *Principj di architettura civile*, the author's second main work. Subsequently, in 1782, Milizia retired from his office as Superintendent in order to devote himself completely to writing. His last great work was published in 1787, *Dizionario*

delle belle arti del disegno (*Dictionary of fine graphic arts*, 1787), its form influenced by Diderot and d'Alembert's *Encyclopédie* (1751–1758). In this work, the author summarized his opinions in the systematic form of a reference book.

The first edition of *Principj di architettura civile* appeared in 1781, the second in 1785 in Bassano (Venice). The treatise was later complemented by a separate volume of plates, *Indice delle figure relative ai Principi di architettura civile* by Giovanni Battista Cipriani, containing 35 engravings and one table. In 1832, a commentary by the Milan-based Professor of Architecture Giovanni Antolini (1754–1842) *Osservazioni ed aggiunte ai Principj di architettura civile di F. Milizia* (*Observations on and additions to the principles of civil architecture by F. Milizia*), originally published in 1817, was integrated into an illustrated new edition. Antolini revised this work in 1847 and 1853 and it was reprinted for the last time in 1875. The treatise also forms part of the nine-volume complete works published in Bologna from 1826 to 1828.

Milizia divides his theory into three sections, corresponding to the three Vitruvian categories *firmitas*, *utilitas* and *venustas*, but in reverse order so that "bellezza" (beauty) comes first, before "comodità" (utility) and "solidità" (robustness). According to Milizia, beauty in architecture is founded upon concepts also taken over from Vitruvius, "ornato," "simmetria," "eurithmia" and "convenienza." By "ornato," Milizia means the architectural column orders, of

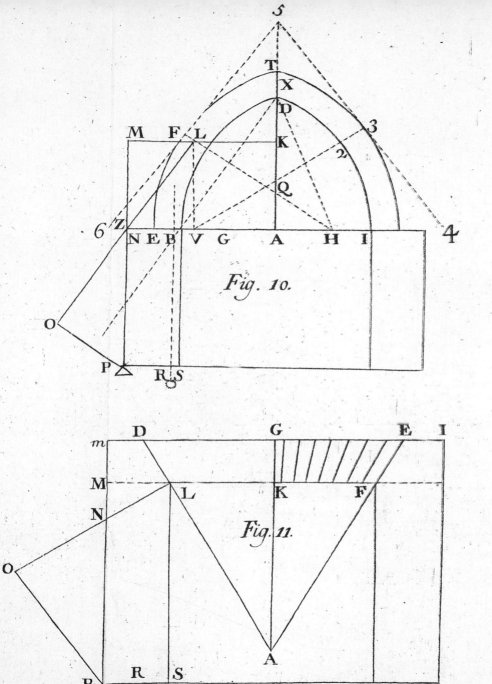

Fig. 10.

Fig. 11.

which, however, he only recognizes the three "Greek" categories, Doric, Ionic and Corinthian. For Milizia, the column orders do not represent decoration, but rather, as advanced by Scamozzi (1548–1616), a fundamental component part of the edifice itself. "Simmetria" is the harmony between the whole and its parts as the result of harmonious proportions. However, Milizia rejects the idea of fixed systems of proportions, favouring instead the laws of optics. "Eurithmia" acquires a different significance than Vitruvius gave it, for it represents axial symmetry in the modern sense, and is linked to "unità" (unity) and "varietà" (variety) in order to avoid uniformity. "Convenienza" is the choice of building ornamentation appropriate to the edifice's purpose. The interplay of these four concepts in the design process is guided by reason and defined by the principles of "necessità" and "funzionalità" (necessity and functionality). In connection with "convenienza," Milizia cites the unadorned architecture of the Roman aqueducts as an example of this kind of edifice, whose functionality alone makes them beautiful. Conversely, in the case of prison buildings he pleads for an "eloquent" architecture, whose very style and ornaments tell of how dreadful it is to be shut away from society. Under "comodità," Milizia deals with the shape and structure of the different types of buildings as well as their location within the context of town planning. Milizia sees a well-planned town that reflects the reasoned order, oriented towards the common good of an enlightened society, as the climax of architectural design. He goes into great detail on the construction of educational establishments, administrative buildings, hospitals and other public institutions, also talking about the interior layout of such buildings and the location of individual rooms. The section on "solidità" is devoted to information concerning building materials and building techniques.

Milizia's style, which demonstrates both polemic and didactic characteristics, reflects his purpose: to raise the level of contemporary architecture by subjecting it to permanent critique. He illustrates his theory with numerous examples from all periods of the history of architecture, taking not only the Baroque and Late Baroque architects severely to task, but also criticizing Palladio and even some of the works of Classical Antiquity, whenever the latter do not correspond with his Classicist ideal of a function-oriented architecture based on reason. This ideal references the testimonies handed down from Greek architecture, and, to an even greater extent, the "natural" principles inherent in the latter. In this, the author rejects the authority of the example often used by Renaissance and Baroque writers to justify the designs of their buildings and the ornaments they use, saying: "If the

Fig. p. 97
1 | **Arch constructions**
Illustrations for the book on the robustness of architecture:
pointed arches or Gothic arches and flat ceiling or straight arch.
In: Principj di architettura civile. *Ed. Bassano, 1785, figs. 10, 11. Engravings*

works of ancient architects were to be used as our authority, all errors would be allowed" ("Se gli esempi dei monumenti antichi autorizzassero, ogni difetto resterebbe autorizzato.")

His critical attitude to Classical Antiquity even allows Milizia to express an appreciation, albeit a limited one, of High Gothic architecture, whose systems of flying buttresses he sees as imitating the example of the Scandinavian forests. For Milizia, mimicry means the imitation of nature. However, unlike painting and sculpture from theories of which (especially that of Giovanni Pietro Bellori) the author borrows his own theory of mimesis, architecture does not have a direct example in nature. Accordingly, the starting point for architectural enterprise is the primordial hut erected from natural elements, which was gradually, over a period of time, improved and extended in order to meet the ever-growing requirements of human civilization and culture. The architect's design should be brought into harmony with its purpose, down to the smallest detail and correspond with its model, an "ideally beautiful" nature, "bella natura" improved by rational selection and combination. Selection and combination are, in turn, the product of bon goût, good taste, which makes it possible to record what is special in its uniqueness and to measure the latter using a binding standard. The author notes that political freedom was achieved earlier than elsewhere to justify the fact that of all people it was the Greeks who invented this timeless, binding standard and thus became the founders of Milizia's progress-oriented "architecture as science." He adds that only then was the kind of boom in commerce and culture possible that established the prerequisites for outstanding artistic achievements. He also believes that a certain influence was exerted by the favourable climate.

In his theory of architecture, Milizia attempts to bring together different trends in the classical 17th and 18th-century theories of art to form one system. The concept of bon goût at the centre of his theoretical edifice was developed in the French theory of art and literature at the end of the 17th century. Milizia's demands for a rationalist and functionalist architecture had already been formulated in a much more radical fashion, by the rigorist Franciscan Carlo Lodoli (1690–1761). Milizia was also greatly influenced by Jesuit Marc-Antoine Laugier's (1713–1769) Essai sur l'Architecture (1753), which had also called for a "philosophical architecture," taking as its starting point the primordial Greek hut. The idea of an "eloquent" architecture is also to be found in the earlier works of Lodoli and Laugier.

Milizia's way of thinking is also very close to two outstanding members of de Azara's circle, Anton Raffael Mengs (1728–1779), whose Gedanken über die Schönheit und den Geschmack in der Malerei (Thoughts on beauty and taste in painting, 1762) represented the neo-Classical ideal in painting, and Winckelmann, who saw "noble simplicity" and "quiet greatness" as the aesthetic principles behind Greek sculpture. In particular, Milizia shares with Winckelmann the notion of advance in civilization and politics being linked to a cyclical development in art and history, culminating in the Athens of Pericles, an unparalleled high point: "As free and independent inventors, (the Greeks) created (their works) with genius; we, timid inventors that we are, allow ourselves to be guided by rules." ("Liberi inventori e originali, operavano per genio. Noi, timidi inventori, operiamo per regole.") Milizia called for the establishment of academies where the rules of "philosophical architecture" could be taught.   AG

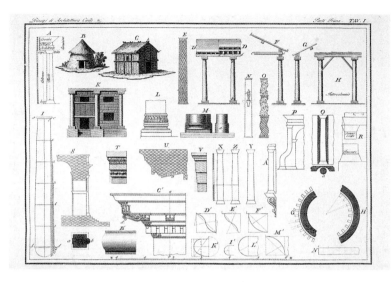

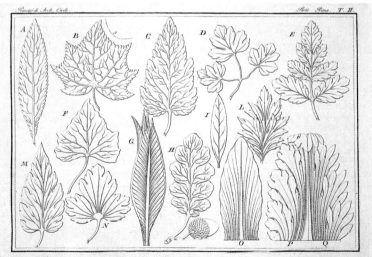

2 | **Two hut architectures, various columns and cornice sections**
Based on Lodoli's ideas on the development of architecture from the primitive hut of the Greeks (A, B), Milizia explains the function of columns and their components, and shows examples for their "incorrect" use.
Part I, pl. 1. Engraving by Giovanni Battista Cipriani

3 | **Leaf designs**
Decoration on capitals of the Corinthian order. In his book on beauty in architecture, Milizia calls on the architect to re-design capital shapes according to nature – depending on the building project.
Part I, pl. 2. Engraving by Giovanni Battista Cipriani

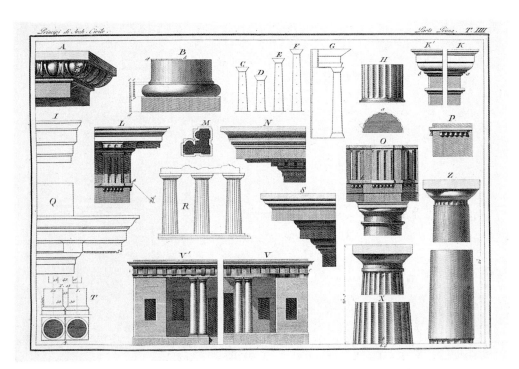

4 | **Various elements of the Doric order**
Decoration of the Doric order: Examples from the Marcellus Theatre (P), as well as from various architects. Milizia speaks out against using classical models (C, D, E, F), and for modern proportions (G).
Part I, pl. 4. Engraving by Giovanni Battista Cipriani

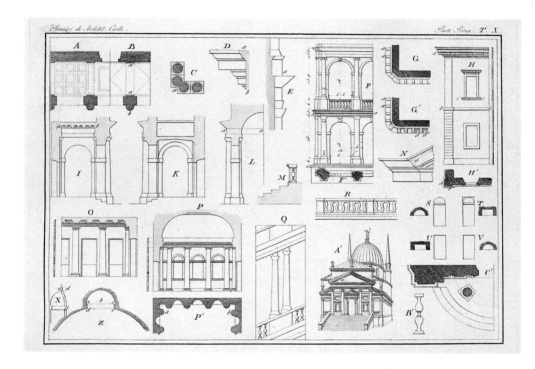

5 | **Arches and vaults, balustrades, ground plans and façades, including the Chiesa del Redentore in Venice**
The architecture of the arch (A, B, I, K, L), the formation of superimposed arcades (F, F'),
and the use of columns in splays (Q).
Part I, pl. 10. Engraving by Giovanni Battista Cipriani

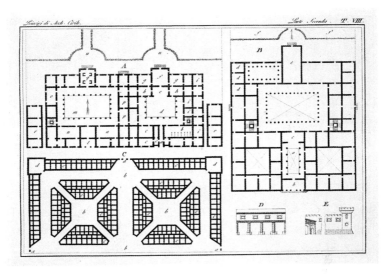

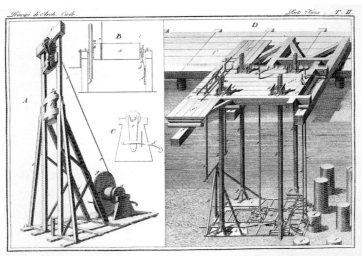

6 | Illustrations of the ancient Greek and Roman house as ground plan, two elevations of the trade fair building in Verona

Illustrations from the book on convenience in architecture.
The Greek (A) and the Roman house (B). The trade fair in Verona
as an example of architecture with a public function (C, D, E).
Part II, pl. 8. Engraving by Giovanni Battista Cipriani

7 | Two building machines

Illustrations for the book on robustness in architecture. The foundations
on piles. Machine to sink the piles into the earth (A) and machine for
sawing off the remains of piles sunk into the water (B).
Part III, pl. 2. Engraving by Giovanni Battista Cipriani

France

Villard de Honnecourt (c. 1210–c. 1240)
Codex, ms. Fr. 19093

VERS 1230. PARIS, BIBLIOTHÈQUE NATIONALE

Pattern book

In the history of the architectural treatise, a special position must be accorded the French draughtsman Villard de Honnecourt (Ulardus de Hunecort, Vilars or Wilars de Honecort), who was active around 1230, and may also have been a master builder. For it is questionable whether an aesthetic theory of architecture existed at all in the Middle Ages to which Villard could be said to belong. It seems probable that there was never a systematic, coherent theory, yet Villard's work represents an important precursor.

The artist is known solely on account of his sketchbook, in which he is mentioned several times. Since the captions accompanying the drawings are written in a Picardy dialect of Old French, it can be assumed that the Honnecourt near Cambrai in Picardy was his place of origin. A consideration of the text sections and models used for some of the drawings, not to mention their stylistic appearance, leads us to the deduction that Villard was active some time between 1220–35, and during this period journeyed not only to the cities of Cambrai, Vauxelles, Rheims, Laon, Chartres, and Lausanne, but also to Hungary. Essentially, the sketches follow the tradition of the pattern book, providing a collection of drawn subject models that medieval artists could employ to create a wide variety of figurative and decorative pictures. The brown pen-and-ink drawings are of a high quality, prepared using fine pencil and scored lines, some of which have been subsequently pencilled in, while in one instance a bister wash is used. Though it seems probable that there were

originally 46 parchment folios, only 33 have survived. The manuscript, measuring some 160 x 250 mm, not only contains pictures of people and animals, but above all liturgical and military equipment, countless views of buildings, ground plans and building machinery, as well as instructions on building design. It is evident the drawings were partly based on nature, while others were executed on the basis of existing pictures. Initially, they appear to follow no logical arrangement, but Villard gave them a semblance of order based on topic, bound them, and furnished them with didactic descriptive captions. It is striking that the arrangement of the folios and the detailed nature of the captions reveal an interest in technical and architectural topics. The didactic objective apparent in this final edition of the book emerges most clearly in those sections devoted to "portraiture," i.e. figurative painting, and "jometrie," i.e. geometry. In the latter section, geometrical figures are depicted as aids in composing figurative drawings, and numerous design techniques and special skills from the construction trade are reproduced in outline drawings and then explained. The procedures illustrated correspond to methods actually used for building during the Middle Ages. That said, the information provided in the texts and pictures is at times so abbreviated that it is unclear today what practical function the geometrical figures fulfilled. The actual architectural drawings reveal an amazing diversity of presentation methods. For instance, the ground plan of Laon Cathedral is presented together with

the view of one of the West towers in which the perspective is foreshortened, while Villard includes drawings of the West and South rose windows from Chartres and Lausanne cathedrals respectively, whereby the South rose departs greatly from the original. The ground plans are exact reproductions of the building in the case of Cambrai and Meaux cathedrals, while other plans stem from Villard's imagination, such as the one for a Cistercian church and a choir with double ambulatory, which according to the caption Villard designed in collaboration with Pierre de Corbie. The topic Villard devotes most attention to is the structure of Rheims Cathedral. Alongside interior and exterior foreshortened views of a side chapel (covering an entire page), and depictions of the interior and exterior elevations of the nave, he also includes structural details such as buttresses, ground plans of pillars, tracery windows, and even the blocks used for the windows. The attention to detail extends to the inclusion of the symbols for the joints. Notwithstanding this accuracy, there are certain inconsistencies that would suggest the drawings are not to be read as technical construction plans.

For a long time the detailed nature and scope of the illustrations led people to see in Villard an architect who was composing a kind of encyclopaedia to be used in the on-site lodge. Ultimately, this interpretation stems from a Romantic view of the building trade during the Middle Ages, and can hardly be given credence in light of the omissions and errors in the illustrations. Bearing in mind the artistic quality of the sketchbook it should largely be viewed within the context of book illustration and the figurative pattern book. Does this mean that Villard the draughtsman co-operated closely on the architectural sketches with a construction expert? At any rate, the architectural drawings in particular closely correspond both chronologically and geographically to the emergence of technical construction plans, evidence of which exists as early examples on stone and parchment in the north of Ile-de-France from the start of the 13th century (Soissons and Châlons-sur-Marne, around 1220; Rheims' palimpsest, mid 13th century). What is more, the intensity with which Villard pursues the new forms and technological methods of Gothic building seems to mirror a parallel advance that can be identified at precisely the same time in the north of Champagne and Picardy. It must be assumed that as a result,

communication on architecture also intensified, not only on topics relating to technology and logistics, but also the aesthetic aspects of the architecture. Indeed, on several occasions Villard makes a point of admiring the beauty, say, of the solution found for constructing the tower of Laon Cathedral or the tracery window at Rheims. And if he also strives to apply the term geometry to his architectural drawings, this constitutes an initial attempt to apply a systematic logical structure to the appraisal of architecture through the use of such terms, and to convey the knowledge to as many people interested in architecture as possible through the medium of a drawing, i. e. a form easily disseminated. Notwithstanding the cursory nature and unfathomable quality in Villard's comments, it should be emphasized that Villard rightfully deserves to be considered an important precursor of the post-Classical architectural treatise. After all, a precondition for this would be that people felt motivated to talk about the quality of architecture – regardless of the form taken by that discussion. That this precondition is met is evident in the treatise itself, when Villard prides himself on having "devised" a ground plan from his imagination in collaboration with Pierre de Corbie. Imaginative "rationcinatio" (according to Vitruvius the intellectual activity of a master builder) is obviously expressed here in abstract concepts, knowledge of which presupposes a certain skill in craft and technical matters. Precisely this complex is at the centre of every architectural theory. Bearing this in mind, it is hardly surprising that a little later, namely in the mid-13th century, in the encyclopaedic literature of one Vincent of Beauvais, architecture is raised to a hitherto unprecedented status as an independent complex discipline, whereby the reasons cited are quite logically the product of an intensive study of Vitruvius. Yet the attempts made by Villard (and undoubtedly other master builders now forgotten) to create a system derived from building and drawing practice, based as it was on inaccurate terminology, were not reflected in any way in the abstract-theological world-classification systems of the intellectuals. For this to happen, a strong discourse needed first to emerge among all those parties involved in building projects. And indeed this was to happen south of the Alps – but not before the 15th century.

CF

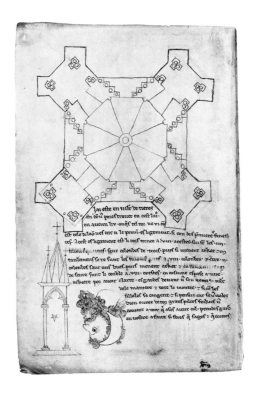

1 | Tower of Laon Cathedral

Villard de Honnecourt praises this tower as the most remarkable
he has ever seen. He shows it in this drawing together with a
ground plan of one of the open tower stories.
Fol. 9 v. Pen and ink drawing on parchment

2 | Tower of Laon Cathedral

Ground plan of one of the open tower stories.
Fol. 10 r. Pen and ink drawing on parchment

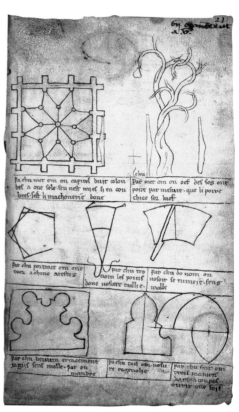

3 | Two chancel ground plans
The lower ground plan is an exact depiction of the chancel of the
Cathedral of Meaux; the upper one was allegedly a fabrication
produced in collaboration with Pierre de Corbie.
Fol. 15 r. Pen and ink drawing on parchment

4 | Various construction methods
Amongst other things we see the determination of the splays of a
polygonal spire, the construction of a hanging key stone and leveling.
Fol. 21 r. Pen and ink drawing on parchment

5 | Interior of one of the annular chapels of Reims Cathedral
Fol. 30 v. Pen and ink drawing on parchment

6 | Exterior of one of the annular chapels of Reims Cathedral
Villard de Honnecourt was very precise in his representation of the
curve of the lower zone and the polygonal window zone above it.
Fol. 31 r. Pen and ink drawing on parchment

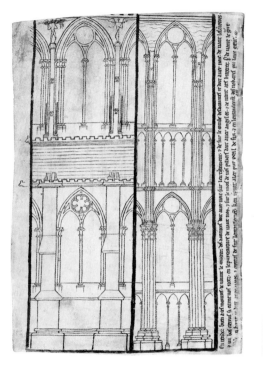

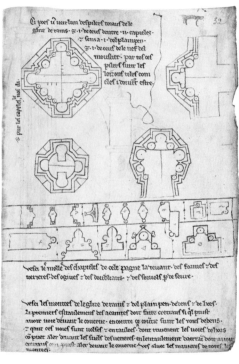

7 | Comparison of the interior and exterior of the nave in Reims Cathedral
Villard de Honnecourt reproduces a stage of construction at which the
vault and strut bracing are still missing.
Fol. 31 v. Pen and ink drawing on parchment

8 | Constructional details of Reims Cathedral
A precise depiction of the column types and individual ashlars
on which window rods and jambstones are mounted.
Fol. 32 r. Pen and ink drawing on parchment

9 | Strut bracing of Reims Cathedral
In contrast to the precision evidenced in the other Reims drawings, here the proportions, for example of the fenestras, are elongated.
Fol. 32 v. Pen and ink drawing on parchment

Jean Martin (died 1553)

Architecture ou Art de bien bastir

PARIS, 1547

Architecture or the art of good building

When Jean Martin's Vitruvius translation appeared in 1547 it made available this fundamental Classical work on architectural theory and practice in French, approximately a generation after the first illustrated Italian editions, and coinciding almost with the first German edition. Martin's rendition stands at the crossing point of several different lines in cultural history. First, the book should be placed in the history of France's reception of Italy and Classical Antiquity; second, it demonstrates French self-confidence in its use of the national language, and in the praise it lavishes on Philibert de l'Orme (1514–1570) and Pierre Lescot (1500/15–1578), the most important architects of this transitional period under Francis I (reigned 1515–1547), and Henry II (reigned 1547–1559). And through its inclusion of the woodcuts by sculptor-architect Jean Goujon (c. 1510–c. 1568) the work is also part of the history of the illustrated book in France.

The military campaigns against Italy by the French monarchs from the House of Valois from 1498 (motivated by hereditary claims to the Kingdom of Naples and the Duchy of Milan) may not have been an enduring political success, but they did bring the French into direct contact with the lifestyle and new humanistic education of the Italian states and cities. Indeed, the influence was so powerful that it even led to the appointment of Italian artists, some of whom even made France their permanent base, such as Leonardo da Vinci (1452–1519) or Sebastiano Serlio (1475–1553/55), while others spent considerable time there, such as Fra Giocondo

(1433–1515) or the sculptor-goldsmith Benvenuto Cellini (1500–1571).

Though Jean Martin's date of birth is unknown, he is known to have served Cardinal Robert de Lenancourt as personal secretary and diplomat from 1530 onwards. It is not clear whether Martin visited Italy or not, but it was his contact with Sebastiano Serlio, who settled in France in 1540, that led in 1545 to the French translation of Serlio's Books I and II on architecture, with Book V following in 1547. It can therefore be supposed that Martin consulted Serlio in producing the Vitruvius translation. In 1546 (between the Serlio and Vitruvius translations), Martin published another translation of the famous novel *Hypnerotomachia Poliphili*, (Venice, 1499) to which he added new illustrations. Martin's translation of Alberti's architectural treatise was published in 1553, shortly after his death. These works made Martin the most significant channel of Classical and more recent architectural theory in France.

It is not entirely clear whether all the sections of the Vitruvius translation stem from Martin himself – but it is based on the earlier Vitruvius editions by Fra Giocondo (1511, in Latin), and Cesare Cesariano (1521, in Italian). Martin was also familiar with the Vitruvius commentary by Guillaume Philandrier that appeared 1544 in Rome and Paris in Latin, and also with a work by Albrecht Dürer, probably *Unterweysung der Messung* (*Course in the Art of Measurement*). The title page is followed by a dedication to Henry II, who had

just ascended the throne, after which there is a short preface, and then the translation of Vitruvius' text. The publication concludes with a two-part unpaginated appendix, whose first section comprises nineteen pages printed on both sides featuring "Explanations of specialist terms and words that are difficult to comprehend, which are contained in Vitruvius," while the second section contains three pages, on which the illustrator of the work, Jean Goujon, addresses the reader while referring to himself as a "scholarly architect," something new in architecture books of the Renaissance.

Martin based most of the 150 illustrations to his translations on those in the prior editions by Fra Giocondo and Cesariano. Nor were the illustrations on theatre design in Book V new (ground plan as well as views of tragic, comic and satirical scenes), but taken from Serlio's Book IV (1537). However, for a group of some 30 illustrations Jean Goujon produced new drawings that served as models for woodcuts. Martin already refers to this in his dedication, stating that the book was "enriched by new drawings relating to the art of stonemasonry, executed by Jean Goujon, former architect to my lord the Constable, and now to the King." This mention of Goujon as an architect is interesting since most evidence points only to his having been a sculptor. Goujon proved during the installation of the organ gallery in St. Maclou church in Rouen 1541 that he was capable of reproducing columns and capitals following Vitruvius' rules on proportions; moreover, the five sculptured panels for the new screen between choir and nave by Pierre Lescot for the Parisian church of St. Germain-en-l'Auxerrrois (1544) show he was familiar with Classical monuments and able to translate these insights into his own, individual artistic idiom. Martin and Goujon complement each other: the first a theorist, the second a man of practice. In his epilogue, Goujon initially bows before the authority of Serlio, who "described and drew many things with great precision according to the rules of Vitruvius, and which constituted the start of the spread of such rules in the Kingdom." They were rules that Goujon himself mastered. He once sent Serlio the drawing of a Doric capital, "which I executed, and which he [Serlio] found to be in full compliance with the rules of the author [Vitruvius]." Almost all of Goujon's illustrations, and his explanations of them in the epilogue, relate to capitals and correct use of proportion for the column orders. This already reveals the limited interest of the practical man which shortly afterwards led to the publication of manuals dealing solely with columns. An exception is formed by the large woodcut, in which the "primordial hut" illustrates the beginnings of architecture. Compared with the earlier editions in Italy, we see here a greater scale, and a highly monumental and three-dimensional approach to the subject matter. This is confirmed in other figurative depictions, such as on the Vitruvian figure, and is especially evi-

dent in the two woodcuts with the caryatids and persians, which a few years later started being used in actual buildings. But even the non-figurative illustrations demonstrate a succinct monumental aspect, for instance the Ionic scroll, and in particular the large fold-out plate featuring the five column orders next to one another.

Published in 1547, the French translation of Vitruvius appeared at a time when there was a sense in France of a new dawn in architecture. Some of the buildings commissioned as part of the large projects of Francis I had progressed so far that it was possible to imagine the finished result – as was especially true of the extensions and interior work in Fontainebleau, not to mention the hunting lodges of Chambord on the Loire and Château Madrid in the Bois de Boulogne near Paris. Serlio, so revered by Goujon, had produced a town house for Cardinal Ippolito d'Este in Fontainebleau, the Hôtel de Ferrare, which represented a great advance for the genre in France, but was not commissioned to execute any of the major royal building projects, and moved to Lyons in 1550. Paris established itself as the capital, and accordingly the buildings of king and court in and around the city slowly became a model for the entire kingdom. The awareness of a clear national identity grew, and was also expressed in the specific use of the French language, as evidenced by the decree of 1539 stating that the national language (favoured by Martin for his translation) be used in the law-courts in place of Latin. Moreover, there were now young French architects who attempted to combine the Italian-Classical language they had learnt with French tradition and their own inventiveness. Jean Goujon draws attention to two of them in his epilogue: Philibert de l'Orme, whose château begun in Saint-Maur in 1541, and also Pierre Lescot. The latter was commissioned in 1546 to design the new Louvre. Not only did he use the Vitruvian column orders correctly, he did so in a uniquely French manner which was scarcely influenced by the monumental Italian buildings.

Martin's Vitruvius translation was highly praised by his contemporaries – such as the poet Ronsard or the architect Jean Bullant, while Walther Ryff (c. 1500–1548) who translated Vitruvius into German, mentions it in his edition of 1548. For all that, Martin himself comments in his preface that Vitruvius' ten books were written in such a difficult style that even his cardinal was unable to help with some sections. Years later the translation was criticized for some inconsistencies and errors, as well as the omission of a commentary. Nevertheless, until the publication of Claude Perrault's new translation in 1673, it remained the received version for the French-speaking nations.

JK

Fig. p. 115

1 | **Illustration of Caryatids**

According to Vitruvius, an architect must know that the female Caryatids and the male Persians depict conquered enemies who now must bear the beams for all eternity.

Fol. 2 v. Woodcut

2 | **Illustration of Persians**

As a result of this depiction and its employment in the Louvre 1550, Caryatids and Persians frequently occurred in French architecture.

Fol. 3 v. Woodcut by Jean Goujon

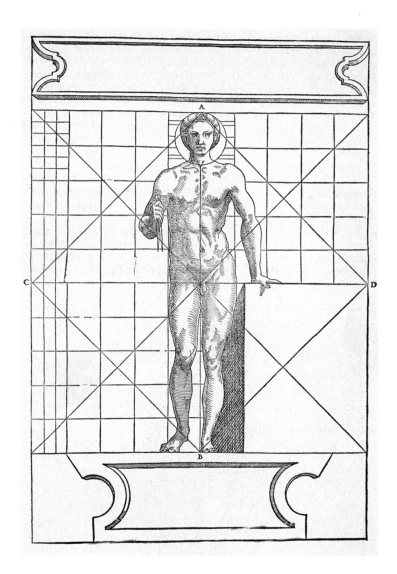

3 | **Vitruvian Man**
The illustration of the first Vitruvian figure describing the human proportions by Goujon was also guided by Cesariano's illustration of 1521,
but places greater emphasis on anatomical aspects.
Fol. 28 r. Woodcut by Jean Goujon

4 | Illustration of the primordial hut
Jean Goujon illustrated Vitruvius' narrative of the construction of the
primordial hut and thus the beginnings of architecture with a simple
gable roof hut without walls, and a hut featuring wicker-covered tree
trunks.
Fol. 15 v. Woodcut by Jean Goujon

5 | **Column orders**
Goujon initially presents the five column orders with complete cornice
sections and their possible pedestals in such a way that the heights
of the columns remain equal while the diameter decreases.
Fol. 35, gatefold Woodcut by Jean Goujon

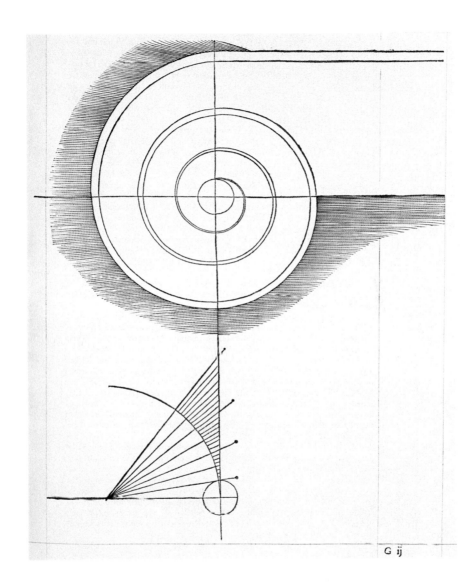

G ij

6 | **Construction of the Ionian volute**
Goujon outlines the method he learned through Guillaume Philandrier,
namely that of Albrecht Dürer, for constructing the Ionian volute.
Fol. 38 r. Woodcut by Jean Goujon

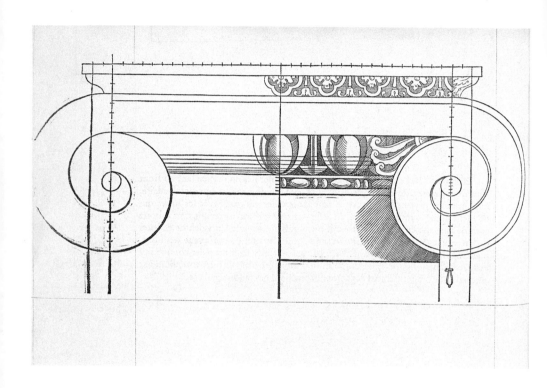

7 | **Construction of the Ionian volute**
Constructing the Ionian volute was problematic. In his postscript,
Goujon complains that the turning usually proved too oval (left).
Fol. 37 v. Woodcut by Jean Goujon

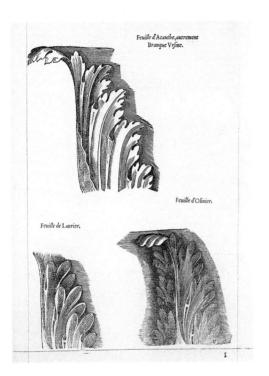

8 | Illustration of leaf designs
From a total of eight illustrations of the Corinthian order one shows suitable leaf designs for decorating the capitals: acanthus or wild garlic. Olives and laurel are suitable for Composite capitals.
Fol. 49. Woodcut by Jean Goujon

9 | Illustration of a Doric gable
Goujon comments on this illustration of a Doric gable that he depicted the frieze correctly with metopes and triglyphs, and that the proportions of the figural plinth are in keeping with those proposed by Vitruvius.
Fol. 52 v. Woodcut by Jean Goujon

Philibert de l'Orme (1514–1570)

Nouvelles inventions pour bien bastir et a petits fraiz

PARIS, 1561

New Inventions for Building Well and at Low Cost

Le premier tome de l'architecture

PARIS, 1567

The first volume of architecture

Philibert de l'Orme developed a diverse career as architect, architectural theorist and important building official at court. Together with Pierre Lescot (between 1500/15–1578) and Jean Bullant (c. 1515–1578), he established what might be termed a French national style that sought to distinguish itself from, and transform, Italian models. Born in Lyons as the son of a wealthy master mason, de l'Orme spent the years 1533–1536 in Rome. In 1541 he was commissioned to build the château of Saint-Maur east of Paris. The regular floor plan, renunciation of the traditional corner pavilions, the arrangement of the courtyard façades with columns and pilasters, and a design featuring only one storey and a flat roof, resulted in a building that was highly unusual for France and closer in concept to the Italian villa. In 1547 Henry II (reigned 1547–1559) ascended to the French throne, and in that same year de l'Orme entered the king's service. As head of the royal department of buildings, he showed his organizational talent in the enlargement and conversion of a number of the king's buildings, including Saint-Léger, Fontainebleau and Vincennes. The main building project in the years 1547 to 1555 was the château built for the king's mistress Diane de Poitiers (d. 1566), in Anet, west of Paris.

Following the unexpected death of Henry II in 1559, de l'Orme was replaced as architect to the king by Francesco Primaticcio (1504–1570). During the years he was out of favour at court he took the opportunity to publish two architectural treatises. His publication *Nouvelles inventions* ap-

peared in 1561, followed six years later by *Premier tome de l'architecture*. From 1663 he largely acted as architect to the queen mother, Catherine de Médicis (1519–1589). It was at her request that he designed and began the major work of his late creative period, namely the Palace of the Tuileries west of the Louvre (now destroyed).

Though Philibert de l'Orme was to spend the larger part of his career working on royal building projects, he wrote somewhat contemptuously: "There are ill-advised persons who as soon as they sight something unusual in the house of the king such as a beautiful garden or fireplace, or the like, are keen to show it off in their own house, and to imitate the king." And indeed the title of his Treatise *Nouvelles inventions pour bien bastir et a petits fraiz* – building well and at a low cost – already points to an awareness of appropriate expense, a consciousness also evident in his own house in the rue de la Cerisaie. De l'Orme refers to his house as a "building in good taste, and not at excessive cost," in keeping with the bourgeois class "without columns or pilasters of any kind"; even the dressed stonework on the first storcy was only conceived as an alternative and not executed. It became the norm for urban housing to locate the residential wing – the *corps de logis* – between court and garden.

The publication of *Nouvelles inventions* in 1561 represents the first French treatise on architecture. Though the slim book comprising 57 pages with 34 woodcuts contains a plural in the title, it only deals with a single "new invention,"

namely the creation of ceiling and roof structures by the juxtaposition of several small wooden planks in place of large timbers. This allowed complex vaulted shapes, and meant that larger rooms could be given a better roof or ceiling. In the motif of the suspended keystone and the concept of load-bearing ribs (as well as the vault capping stones still to be inserted) de l'Orme brought medieval building practices up to date.

This guide on carpentry was followed six years later by the *Premier tome de l'architecture*, whose objective was to relate the history of architecture. Naturally this meant following in Vitruvius' tracks, and de l'Orme also deals with most of the topics Vitruvius deemed vital – but always within the context of his own practical experiences. With its 205 woodcuts, the *Premier tome* contains more illustrations than the previous Vitruvius editions, but does not appear to be particularly richly illustrated owing to the volume of text (282 pages printed on both sides). De l'Orme's work comprises nine books. Book I explores the relationship between client and architect, site selection and the issues to be considered with regard to climate and building material. Book II addresses the basics of geometry, surveying building sites, and constructing the foundations. Books III and IV constitute the most individual contribution by de l'Orme, being devoted to the stone-cutting and stereometry issues so vital to architecture; Book III looks at the cutting and insertion of stones while Book IV addresses more complicated forms such as arches, vaults and steps. The column orders are divided between Books V and VII. Below the illustrations in the latter books the author inserted numerous measurements of his own from his time in Rome, some of which elude definition: Doric, Tuscan and Ionic in Book V, Corinthian in Book VI, while the Composite order together with the French order developed by de l'Orme feature in Book VII. Book VIII is devoted to doors, door-frames and window-frames, and Book IX to fireplaces.

From the wealth of topics dealt with, let us select three typical aspects. First, stereometry, which is addressed in Book III and Book IV. De l'Orme's treatment of this topic remains largely independent of Italian models, and demonstrates the analytical application of geometry and perspective developed in Italy to what is ultimately the medieval French tradition of stone cutting. Employing countless technical drawings, of which the line drawings of the title page provide an impression, de l'Orme shows how, for any projected building, it is possible to calculate the shape of every individual stone and then cut it, depending on its position in the wall bond. First the builder must separate, in his mind, the load-bearing frame and the filled walls, something already suggested in the woodcut on carpentry. De l'Orme's master-piece in this context was a small, "free-hanging" oriel with curved walls in an inner corner of the building on the park side of Château Anet, whose invention he documented in several woodcuts. That said, the plate depicting the view of the oriel from outside reveals the limitations inherent in illustrating such complicated matters in woodcuts.

Secondly, de l'Orme added a sixth order to the column orders in Book VII. Of his own invention, he gave it the appellation French order. He argued that it was only appropriate for a large, important nation such as France to have an order named after it, since the other five orders were also called after countries. Characteristically, this proposal likewise provides the solution to a practical problem. Since it was very difficult in France to produce monolithic columns, usually making it necessary to combine several column drums, the joints of the individual drums were to be concealed using decorative banding. Thus it can be argued that de l'Orme precipitated the ensuing discussion on the French order which was most eagerly conducted after 1677. For all that, he did not actually invent a new order, but simply proposed a form of decoration for the column shafts of the existing orders. De l'Orme seems to want to present something regarded as a failure in a positive light, as when he rejected marble as a building material: sandstone was normally used in France. But in fact he did use marble in those cases where the project or the client made it possible. And in any case, Classical and contemporary Italian models existed for the use of decorative banding on column shafts.

A final conspicuous aspect is that de l'Orme has a love of allegorizing depictions of his profession and of his own person. For instance, the variously shaped polyhedra on the title page allude to stereometry, and Mercury crowns the entire page as protector of science and artists. At the end of the prologue to Book III, de l'Orme includes an emblem, once again under the protection of Mercury, which shows how the son of a mason advances to become a cleric, leaving ignorance and the black hole of the Middle Ages behind, and with a pair of dividers in his hand gains the palm of the Renaissance. The work concludes with two more large-format allegorical pictures that contrast bad and good architects.

As the title *Premier tome* would suggest, de l'Orme planned to continue his writing; volume two was to deal with divine proportions, as well as with house-building "for the poor and rich." This concept follows in the tradition of Serlio's Book VI, and may have been a response to the first Book by Jacques Androuet du Cerceau (c. 1521–1586) which was published as early as 1559. However, the second volume was never produced, possibly because in the final years of his life de l'Orme was once again fully occupied with royal commissions.   JK

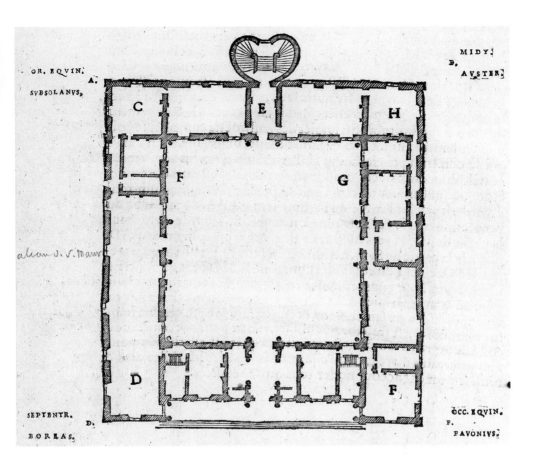

Fig. p. 125

1 | **Vaulted ceiling**
The illustration shows de l'Orme's method of composing roofs
and vaults using small wooden beams.
In: Nouvelles inventions pour bien bastir, *2ⁿᵈ ed., Paris, 1576,*
p. 44. Woodcut

2 | **Ground plan of Castle Saint-Maur**
The ground plan is an example for the good choice of a building site
and the healthy aligment of the building to the cardinal points.
In: Le premier tome de l'architecture, 2ⁿᵈ ed., Paris, 1568, fol. 17 v. Woodcut

3 | Depiction of the architect
The first allegory of the architect shows the architect's path
from the Medieval cave to the palm of the new age.
2nd ed., Paris, 1568, fol. 51 v. Woodcut

4 | **Base for the Composite order**
Anonymous sectional drawing of an extraordinarily richly
formed base for the Composite order.
2ⁿᵈ ed., Paris, 1568, fol. 204 v. Woodcut

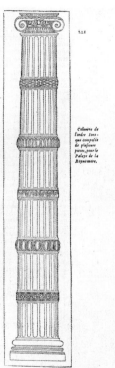

5 | Column of the French order
The illustration shows the French order de l'Orme devised and as used
for the Palace of the Tuileries; the ornamental bands mask the joints
between the individual column drums.
2nd ed., Paris, 1568, fol. 221 r. Woodcut

6 | Philibert de l'Orme's house
Located near the Bastille, the house was some 16m wide and de l'Orme
built it around 1555. The entrance was in the arcade on the left wing
which likewise contained the staircase.
2nd ed., Paris, 1568, fol. 253 v. Woodcut

7 | Allegory of a bad architect
Philibert de l'Orme closes with two full-page allegories, one of the bad architect, the other of the good: the bad one wanders bereft of hands and eyes through a barren landscape with a Medieval castle.
2nd ed., Paris, 1568, fol. 328. Woodcut

8 | Allegory of a good architect
By contrast, the good architect stands in a flourishing garden, has many hands, is surrounded by Classical and new buildings alike, and is familiarizing young people with his scientific discipline.
2nd ed., Paris, 1568, fol. 329. Woodcut

Pierre Le Muet (1591–1669)

Maniere de bien bastir pour touttes sortes des personnes

PARIS, 1623

The art of fair building. London, 1670

Augmentation de nouveaux bastiments faits en France

PARIS, 1647

Addition of new buildings constructed in France

Pierre Le Muet's 1623 publication is a manual on the construction of urban dwellings for "everyone," the very title a reference to the subject matter of other treatises, for example Serlio's Book VI ("tutti li gradi degli homini"), Philibert de l'Orme in 1567 ("pour les grands et les petits") and Jacques du Cerceau in 1559 ("soient de petit, moyen ou grand estat"). Unlike these authors, Le Muet in his treatise was not concerned with the construction of palaces, and he did not correct the omission of large town houses (*hôtels*) or country châteaux until the *Augmentation* published with the second edition in 1647.

Pierre Le Muet was born in Dijon, the son of an artillery officer. In 1616, he made a model of the Palais du Luxembourg, which Salomon de Brosse (1571–1626) had been constructing for the widowed Queen Marie de Medici (1573–1642) since 1615. As a colleague of de Brosse, Le Muet had direct access not only to the publications of the latter's grandfather, Jacques Androuet du Cerceau, but also presumably to Sebastiano Serlio's unprinted manuscript on housebuilding (the so-called Book VI). In 1617, in his role as an army engineer, he was made responsible for supervision of the fortifications in the Picardy region, and also commenced studies on house-building, of which *Maniere de bien bastir,* which appeared in 1623, was to some extent a preliminary result. From the 1630s he appeared as an architect of Parisian *hôtels*. For the most part his clients were from the upper echelons of the financial administration, who in three cases engaged him to build, or make alterations to their country residences. His main work in Paris is the Hôtel d'Avaux. In 1655/56, Le Muet was placed in charge of building work on the Val-de-Grâce, the uncompleted Parisian convent residence of the Queen dowager and Regent Anne of Austria (1601–1666), where he was able to bring his own ideas into the design of the church dome and the Queen's living quarters.

As an engineering officer engaged in military and civilian architecture, le Muet represented a genre of architect that from 1700 on became increasingly important, particularly in the case of German royal and princely residences, for example Johann Lukas von Hildebrandt in Vienna, Jean de Bodt in Berlin and Dresden and Balthasar Neumann in Würzburg.

In *Maniere de bien bastir*, Le Muet compiled a list of all those practices normally employed in the building of houses and from this derived a systematic methodology of model designs. This made his treatise an important source for residential architecture under the first two Bourbon kings, Henry IV (reigned 1589–1610) and Louis XIII (reigned 1610–1643), which quite clearly had its roots in the 16th century. As a manual, *Maniere de bien bastir* was relevant until around 1680. The treatise is dedicated to Louis XIII, contains 113 pages and begins with a "short essay on things to be considered." In this Le Muet presents a summary of the basics of architecture as stated by Vitruvius, and calls for durability, comfort, attractive division and the well-being of the apart-

ments (durée, aisance ou commodité, belle ordonnance, la santé des appartements). The author was able to dispense with a depiction of the orders of columns, as first they are of little importance in the treatise, and secondly he had published translations of Vignola's *Regole delle cinque ordini* (1631) and Palladio's Book I of *Quattro libri* (1645).

In the main section containing Le Muet's model designs, the explanatory texts are positioned to the left and right of the illustrations, the engraver of which is unknown. The short texts only contain measurements, intended to make it easier to calculate prices in contracts with the mason. Measurements such as the thickness of the walls, the height of rooms, and the width of corridors correspond to the customs of the day; artistic questions are not dealt with. Le Muet's first design was for a small house with only one room per storey, in which there was just enough room for a bed and a fireplace. From here he presents his designs for a gradual enlargement of the building in twelve stages, so that the building programme is extended first by closets, then rooms and finally by a small courtyard. In addition, he also furnishes variations for the division of the space for four of these lots. The middle-class example is represented by the second variety of the sixth lot, measuring 30 by 58 feet. The seventh lot also has a small inner courtyard with a side wing and a garden behind the house and is the sort of house that Philibert de l'Orme had chosen for himself as early as 1555. In the ninth lot (57 by 120 feet) Le Muet arrives at the standard size of a smallish *hôtel*. It is significant that the Hôtel Tubeuf, which was constructed in 1643 in accordance with this design, actually turned out to be larger than the 20-year-old master plan had foreseen. The "small dining room" is one of the first pieces of evidence of there being a separate room for meals. Le Muet also underscored this novelty in the accompanying texts to one of the country châteaux and the Hôtel d'Avaux. In his designs for the twelfth lot, Le Muet turns his attention away from terraced houses in favour of detached, the ground plans of which bear the hallmark of du Cerceau and ultimately Serlio. The design of the elevation is likewise fairly conservative. Columns and pilasters are used sparingly and the façades are structured by the arrangement of the windows, and their frames by vertical rusticated strips. This 16th-century fashion gradually died out, and later on Le Muet also gave it up. The last thirteen pages of the treatise deal with carpentry, using the example of a complete timber-framed house as well as several examples for the construction of roofs.

Manière de bien bastir was a manual for practical building work, though Le Muet avoided irregularities and portrayed systematic ground plans that filled the structure of sites in inner cities. He shares this systematic way of thought with Roland Fréart de Chambray, the key to this joint approach lying in a rationalism with regard to planning that

was generally reflected in the political and economic state of affairs of France at the time, and as far as building was concerned was further fuelled by the foundation of the Royal Academy of Architecture in 1671.

The *Augmentation,* however, which appeared as a supplement to the second edition in 1647, was the result of a new approach. Using 31 copperplate engravings by Jean Marot (1619–1679), Le Muet presented six of his own buildings without any text. This was the first collection of its kind by an architect in France. Le Muet included in the collection three Parisian *hôtels*, of which two are based on suggestions in *Manière de bien bastir*, as well as three country châteaux, of which two were conversions. There is no use of the bird's-eye perspective so frequently used by du Cerceau, just as there are no plans of grounds or gardens, yet one engraving does show evidence of an unusual form of garden landscaping. For Tanlay Castle in Burgundy, converted between 1642 and 1645, Le Muet designed Château d'Eau, which still exists today, an ornamental façade complete with half-dome and double columns at the head of a canal. Engravings of Le Muet's most prestigious building, the Hôtel d'Avaux begun in 1644, mark the beginning and end of *Augmentations*. The client, Claude de Mesme, Count of Avaux, had work on the house begin in 1644, the year he was appointed to the position of principal French delegate to the Congress of Westphalia, which eventually ended the Thirty Years' War. In the case of such an eminent client, Le Muet could not resort to the use of earlier set designs and thus he designed a large house with a second courtyard and suitably illustrious rooms. The walls of the inner courtyard feature enormous fluted pilasters throughout, a motif requiring the greatest architectural expertise. It had been used shortly before by Louis Le Vau (1612–1670) in the construction of Maison Lambert on Ile Saint-Louis, but in the following generation it was limited principally to royal buildings. Alongside the entrance façade the engraving shows a cross-section of the side wing with decorative chimney walls. Once again the lower room is classified as a dining room, and the upper room, with its arched coffered ceiling, is part of an eight-section gallery that stretches across almost the entire depth of the house. Le Muet also came up with an equally ingenious and splendid solution for the entrance from the road to the courtyard: he opted for a combination of a large pilaster order with a small order of columns. While, this excursion into the magnificent showed a new facet of his œuvre, it proved to be too much for the client, as only a shallow, ribboned half-dome was actually built. With this building Le Muet provided an example for an aristocratic *hôtel* of exceedingly high standard on the eve of the accession of Louis XIV, who during his time as head of state was to use art and architecture for propaganda purposes. JK

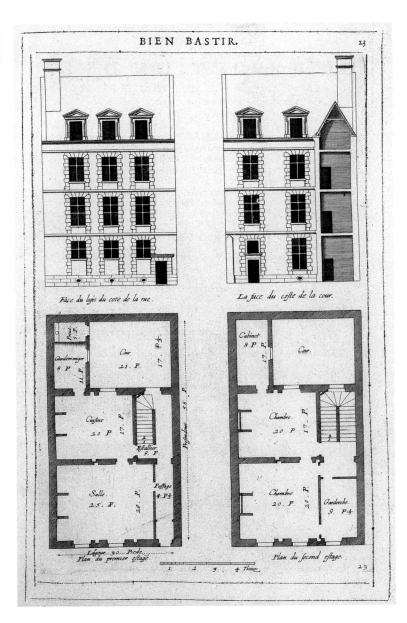

BIEN BASTIR. 23

Face du logis du coté de la rue.

La face du coste de la cour.

Plan du premier estage.

Plan du second estage.

23

1 | **Elevation and ground plan for a terrace house**
The bourgeois residence showing the "second distribution of the sixth lot." This type of terrace house with two rooms per floor also gained sway in England.
P. 23

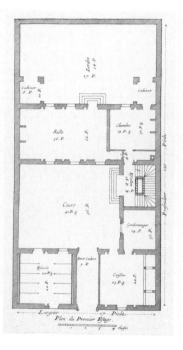

2 | Ground plan for a terrace house
With the 9th lot, here in the 4th distribution, Le Muet creates a house the size of a medium town house. The small door on the left leads to the stables.
P. 65

3 | Façade elevation of a terraced house
Unlike the smaller buildings, the street-side façade has the entrance drive in the middle and for the first time in the Treatise presents the use of column orders, in this case Doric pilasters.
P. 69

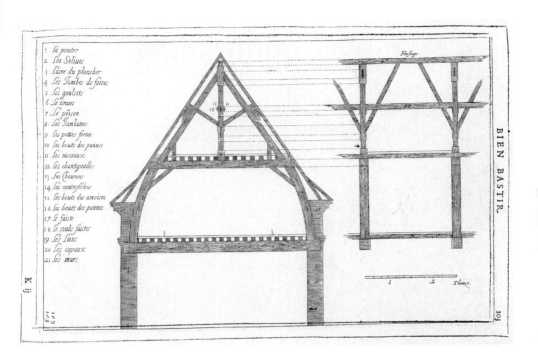

4 | Structure of roof timbers

Le Muet introduced the chapter on the construction of roofs with a section and view of the method
customarily employed since the early 17th century.

P. 103

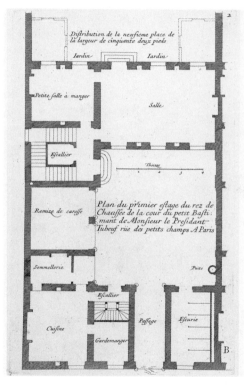

5 | Elevation and ground plan of the courtyard entrance of Hôtel d'Avaux

With the gloriously instrumented but never realized design for the entrance gate to the courtyard of Hôtel d'Avaux, Le Muet started the sequence of his designs that commenced in 1647.

Pl. 1. Engraving by Jean Marot

6 | Ground plan of Hôtel Tubeuf

Hôtel Tubeuf (1643, destroyed) was based on the notion of the nine lots, but expands the spatial layout with a view to comfort, which has always been high on the priority list in France.

Pl. 2. Engraving by Jean Marot

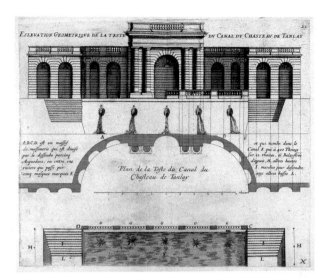

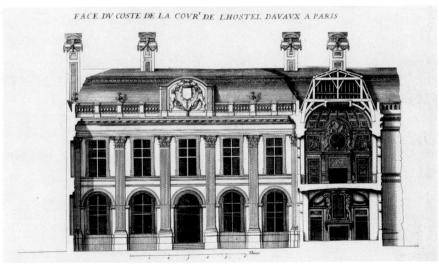

7 | Château d'eau in the garden of Tanlay castle
Representative façade at the end of the canal in the garden of the
Burgundian castle, Tanlay. Water flows from the five masks into
the canal below.
Pl. 21. Engraving by Jean Marot

8 | Elevation and cross-section of the court façade of Hôtel d'Avaux
View of the court of the Hôtel d'Avaux with a cross-section of the side
wing by which the higher coffered ceiling in the gallery had to be taken
into consideration in constructing the roof.
Pl. 29. Engraving by Jean Marot

Roland Fréart de Chambray (1606–1676)

Parallèle de l'architecture antique et de la moderne: avec un recueil des dix principaux autheurs qui ont écrit de cinq ordres

PARIS, 1650

The parallel of the antient architecture with the modern, in a collection of ten principle authors who have written on the five orders. London, 1723

In 1547, Jean Martin's translation of Vitruvius made the originally Latin text accessible to the French; publications on architecture in France since then tended to accentuate the national aspects on the one hand and what was applicable and practical on the other, focusing on house-building. A century after Martin, Roland Fréart, sieur de Chambray, returned once more to the Classical model with his critical examination of the orders of column and their proportions. The noble courtier did not write as a practical man but as an amateur, who busied himself with questions of art for personal reasons and out of antiquarian interest. That said, his studies culminated in a set of demands which he made of the architecture of the day, for example unconditional obedience to the Classical rules of proportion as demonstrated in surviving monuments and handed down in Vitruvius' text. For him, the guardian of these rules was Andrea Palladio, whose *Quattro libri* he had translated and which was sold in one volume with the *Parallèle*.

From 1630–1635, Fréart de Chambray lived in Rome, and there, in addition to pursuing his study of architecture, he became acquainted with the painter Nicolas Poussin (1594–1665). In 1638, his cousin, the Minister of War François Sublet de Noyers, Baron de Dangu (1588–1645) also became *surintendant des bâtiments*, Director of the Royal Building Office. Sublet wanted to bring Poussin back to Paris to fit out new sections of the Louvre, and thus in 1639 sent Chambray and his brother Paul Fréart, sieur de Chantelou (1609–1694,

the writer of the famous diary of Gianlorenzo Bernini's stay in Paris in 1665 and also a friend of Poussin), to Rome. There, the Fréarts acquired casts of Classical capitals and Trajan's Column as study material, and together with the painter Charles Errard (1606/09–1689), who had already been sent to Rome by Sublet, completed drawings of antiquities. This completes the list of those crucial to the publication of *Parallèle*. The Fréart brothers and their cousin Sublet had already concerned themselves for a long time with the question of "correct" Classical proportions and wanted to publish their findings as an argument against incorrect usage and the attempts at reform on the part of many architects. In Errard they found someone who, as a result of his own studies, was in a position to assist them and deliver preliminary drawings of 40 full-page copperplate engravings and eight headlines or vignettes. By the time the *Parallèle* was published in 1650, however, Sublet de Noyers was no longer in office (1643): he died in 1645. That explains the frontispiece of the 109-page work with Sublet's portrait, and the fact that Chambray used the six-page dedication to his two brothers as a panegyric-cum-obituary to his cousin. After the title page, dedication and preface comes the main body of the book, in which a large section is devoted to each order; two pages explaining technical terms conclude the work. The engraver Georges Tournier only signed the frontispiece, but it is possible that he was also responsible for other engravings.

Bullant.

De Lorme.

Chambray's intentions are clearly stated in the title. He compares critically and in pairs the suggestions of the above-mentioned authors with regard to the proportions for base, shaft, capital and entablature. Their short characteristics reveal the precedence of Palladio, whose Classical dimensions "are measured with such precision in Book IV of his *Quattro Libri* that nothing is left to be desired." In order to guarantee correct comparison, Chambray and Errard recalculated all the measurements using the same unit – half the diameter of the column – which they divided into 30 parts. The illustrations are set out in such a way that the top of the capital marks the joint highest point, and deviations can be determined from there. Preceding the comparisons by modern authors from Alberti to de l'Orme, we mostly see in each instance three model examples of Classical architecture such as the Temple of Fortuna Virilis (Ionic), the Pantheon (Corinthian) or, in many cases, Diocletian's thermal baths. Hinted at in the subtitle and explained in the foreword, Chambray's new conviction is that only the three Greek canonical orders – Doric, Ionic and Corinthian – may be used at all, since they contain "not only all that is beautiful, but everything that architecture requires in the three categories; the solid, the medium and the fine. These are quite perfectly expressed in the three orders, and accordingly, there is no need for the other two."

Chambray's approach can perhaps be explained by taking the Ionic order as an example. As he considers Classical Antiquity his ideal, he does not take a specifically French angle on the issue. He adduces detailed grounds for rejecting the Ionic order of Philibert de l'Orme (1514–1570), not without wondering in ten lavishly worded lines how something like this could happen to de l'Orme, who, after all, "had a great natural love of architecture." For practical and iconographic reasons, Chambray renounces caryatids and persians – a special theme in French architecture since Jean Goujon (c. 1510–c. 1568). On the one hand, the column which was turned into a female form was uncomfortable for the architect as the circumference of the robes made the passageway too narrow and upset the symmetry; on the other hand, in Vitruvius the women from Carya were prisoners and had to wear these robes a penalty, so the use of these figures was only considered decorous in but a few cases. In spite of Chambray's rejection, Errard's illustrations are very beautiful. A similarly picturesque composition was used to illustrate the legendary invention of the Corinthian capital. Too much decoration of the Corinthian was not to be recommended, even if there is a Classical example, as this "confusion offends the eyes of the knowledgeable." Philibert de l'Orme's proportions are also savaged in this chapter, and Chambray almost apologetically adds that de l'Orme's strengths lay more in directing construction work and in the cutting of stone than in the composition of the orders. Chambray was very clear-sighted in recognizing a fundamental problem for the 16th-century travelling Frenchman: de l'Orme had seen "the most beautiful things in Rome as if with Gothic eyes."

Chambray kept the section on the non-Greek (in other words Latin) Tuscan and Composite orders very brief, not least because not all authors expressed themselves on the subject and the Composite was not dealt with at all by Vitruvius. It is, however, interesting to note an easing in his strict stance on the order of the Temple of Jerusalem, which he categorizes as Corinthian and represents according to Villalpando (1552–1608). The proportions are Corinthian, the acanthus leaves are replaced by palms, and the frieze has Doric triglyphs and metopes, which are not really appropriate to the "delicate" Corinthian order. Chambray lets this pass, as Solomon's Temple falls into the category of the incomparable.

Chambray applied his somewhat rigorous view on art to painting as well, likewise by the translation of the reference work *Traité de la peinture de Léonhard de Vinci*, 1651 (*Critique of Leonardo da Vinci's Painting*), which he followed in 1662 with his own investigation: *Idée de la perfection de la peinture* (*An idea on the perfection of painting*). In 1663, he wrote a discussion on perspective, *Perspective d'Euclide* (*Euclid's Perspective*). Chambray, with his *Parallèle*, was an influential advocate of the correct use of column orders, which were essential in the case of exacting building assignments. At the same time, *Parallèle* is a preparation for the dogmatic correctness represented by the Academy of Architecture after it was founded in 1671, and is also a contribution to the *Querelle des anciens et modernes*, the quarrel which breaks out in France from time to time – between the representatives of an authoritative (Classical), indeed schematic adherence to stringent rules, and those of modern liberty and invention.

JK

Des Termes de Diocletian

1 | Construction of the Ionian, "rectangular column"

The proportions of the Ionian order are pictured here using a "rectangular column" from Diocletian's baths in Rome. The proportions of the Ionian order, in this case in the form of a "rectangular column" from Diocletian's baths in Rome, were taken by Chambray from an older elevation and are shown here in full view.
P. 44. Engraving

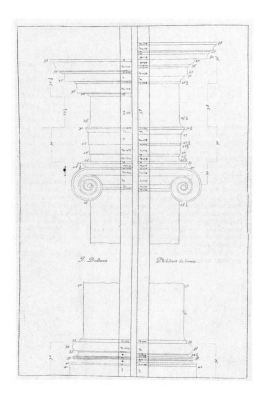

2 | Proportionate comparison of Ionian orders
Chambray prefers Jean Bullant's proposal (left) which follows Vitruvius'
rules for the Ionian order, to that of Philibert de l'Orme (right).
P. 51. Engraving

3 | Illustration of caryatids
Chambray classifies caryatids and Persians between Ionian and
Corinthian. The relief of the triumphal procession is testament
to the character of the caryatids as captives.
P. 53. Engraving

4 | **Illustration of the Persian**
Since neither caryatids nor
Persians are a valid replacement for a column, they are
placed against the wall. The
Persian was sketched from an
ancient figure which used to
be in the Palazzo Farnese.
P. 54. Engraving

5 | Callimachus devises the Corinthian capital
Chambray dryly commented that this engraving is "merely an illustration
of the story of Callimachus … which is used decoratively here."
P. 63. Engraving

6 | Construction of the Corinthian order
Chambray gives the Corinthian order of Diocletian's baths only a limited
recommendation since they are "richly ornamented and embellished."
P. 69. Engraving

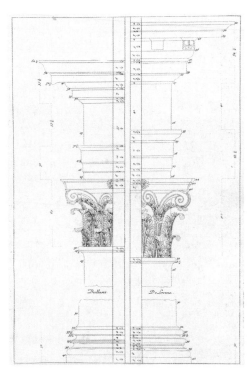

7 | Construction of the Solomonic order
The Solomonic order has been handed down by God and is incomparable,
which is why Chambray accepts the irregularities (Corinthian proportions,
the Doric entablature, palms instead of acanthus).
P. 71. Engraving

8 | Comparison of proportions of the Corinthian order
The comparison of proportions of the Corinthian order by Jean Bulland
and Philibert de l'Orme turns out, as with the Ionian, badly for l'Ormes.
P. 81. Engraving

Claude Perrault (1613–1688)

Les dix livres d'architecture de Vitruve, corrigez et traduits nouvellement en François

PARIS, 1673

The ten books on the architecture of Vitruvius, corrected and in a new French translation

Ordonnance des cinq espèces de colonnes selon la méthode des anciens

PARIS, 1683

A treatise of the five orders of columns in architecture. London, 1708

When the French Academy of Architecture was founded in 1671, its primary aim was to develop a comprehensive architectural doctrine by which the outstanding cultural heyday of French architecture under Louis XIV (reigned 1643–1715) could be presented in an understandable fashion and above all be continued into the future. The basis of the detailed discussions was to gain some clarity with regard to Vitruvius' *Ten Books about Architecture*, the only text about the architectural theory of Classical Antiquity that had been passed down the ages, but one that in many respects was mysterious and prone to misinterpretation. For this very reason, around 1666 Claude Perrault had been commissioned to produce a new translation of the work, including a detailed critical commentary. The ensuing work, however, did not come up to the Academy's expectations at all. There could, he suggested, be no formulating absolute rules for the correct proportioning of architectural elements, society was responsible for deciding what was to be considered "beautiful." This triggered a veritable scandal and prolonged debate, which formed part of the argument between the Ancient and the Modern, between advocates of the Classical and Baroque styles, which also found literary expression in particular in the form of *Querelle des anciens et des modernes* by Claude's brother Charles Perrault.

Claude Perrault came from a respected family of scientists, literati and architects, and initially studied medicine and physics. Early on, in the 1650s, he taught physiology and

anatomy and was elected a member of the Académie des Sciences. He wrote several treatises on physics as well as being one of the most important architects under Louis XIV. With his knowledge of the natural sciences, he was predestined to become the architect of the Paris Observatory (1667–1669). His knowledge of architectural theory led him to be commissioned Chief Architect for the renowned re-design of the east façade of the Louvre and in 1672 to be elected to the Academy of Architecture.

Perrault's translation of Vitruvius, *Les dix livres d'architecture de Vitruve*, which appeared in 1673, and in a later edition in 1684, complete with commentary, began with a rich frontispiece by Sebastien le Clerc which at the same time advertised the author's own architectural works. In the background, the colonnades of the Louvre (still under construction at that time), together with a monumental triumphal arch with an equestrian statue of Louis XIV, designed by Perrault, bear witness to the Sun King's lavish building projects. In the foreground on a sort of stage, an allegory of architecture explains the *Ten Books* – these are held aloft by personifications of sculpture, geometry and painting. They are addressing the enthroned personification of France as ruler of the world, whose attention is being drawn by *abundantia* (abundance) to the architectural works that stand in the background. In the dedication, the aspect of cultural blossoming as intimated here is defined more clearly by detailed reasons for France's magnificence. As in the times of

A

Roman Emperor Augustus Caesar, extensive building in peacetime corresponded, or so the explanation reads, to acts of conquest in war. France alone, Perrault continues, enjoyed a culture that was dominated by civilization, science and good taste, which also had to be expressed in its buildings. But what – such was the tenor of the many commentaries and observations that followed publication of the newly translated Vitruvius text – is perfectly beautiful architecture? To begin with, beauty is but one criterion, for the most part perceived of as a subjective image ("phantasie") by several external circumstances (such as level of education and fashion). However, to attain to the deeper, rationally justifiable rules on beauty, a careful philological analysis of the ancient authority Vitruvius was necessary, Perrault opines. Yet Vitruvius' writings, he goes on, are frequently mysterious and moreover had been translated incorrectly. However, here Perrault does not then offer a precise definition of the correct proportions of various elements of architecture, but rather a significant sub-division of various levels of perceiving beauty in architecture. Absolute proportions, which can be found in the universe and in the human body, cannot be discerned in architecture. What is considered beautiful in the way parts of buildings are proportioned is therefore much more the result of a social consensus on perception, and in no way necessarily the product of logical reasoning or the laws of nature. How else could architectural details that were quite clearly absurd be deemed beautiful, even by experts? And in no way had the highly praised architects of Classical Antiquity used the natural model of the human being when proportioning their columns. Relating base, shaft and capital to the human body could not, Perrault avers, be correct, and furthermore just as with columns there are many variations of the human body, so there is also no way that ideal proportions can be derived from it. As such, the perception of beauty on the level of a correct, proportioning of architectural elements can only occur in accordance with a relative understanding of beauty. In this sense, beautiful means what most educated people of taste enjoy, but it cannot be proved by the laws of nature. However, it is certainly possible to formulate an objective principle. This is based on the functions of a building, i.e. its stability, its hygiene and its comfort. Any aesthetic judgement therefore must take into consideration the connection between the building's purpose and decorations before reaching any verdict. There is no way that giant columns in front of a modest building can be beautiful, even if the architect has otherwise adhered to every rule of proportion. Later, in his work *Ordonnance*, Perrault adds general characteristics such as the richness of the material used, the quality of workmanship, the mirror symmetry of the grounds as well as the "magnificence" of the architecture as additional objective criteria.

The response to the "scandalous" conclusions was not long in coming. The whole of François Blondel's (1675–1683) *Cours d'architecture* is devoted to a rejection of Perrault's expositions. Yet the latter did not give in, and in his treatise on columns published in 1683, *Ordonnance des cinq espèces de colonnes selon la méthode des anciens*, he expanded on his arguments and was not sparing with his sideswipes at the usefulness of a programme of surveying Roman buildings that Antoine Desgodets had undertaken at the time. Despite the precise nature of the study, this had also not resulted in any binding rules on the laws of proportion. So there are, Perrault went on, seemingly no binding rules and Blondel's precise rules on measurement are evidently absurd. Perrault proposed instead a system of simple, complete module values for each individual order of columns. These represent, so to speak, median values of the systems of measurement used until then, and they form a rule of thumb on which contemporary architects could base their work, in the same way as their fellow architects in Classical Antiquity would have done, without having to descend to the level of pedantry in the proportions.   CF

1 | **View of the Hall of the Caryatids in the Louvre**
These sculptures, which were created from 1550/51, are a remarkably
accurate reproduction of the ancient caryatids of the porch of the
Erechtheum at the Acropolis in Athens.
2ⁿᵈ ed., Paris, 1684, pl. 5. Engraving

2 | **Reconstruction of the Temple of Diana in Ephesus**
Perrault utilizes this remarkable illustration of a dipteral temple
with a row of Ionic instead of the usual Doric columns.
2nd ed., Paris, 1684, pl. 13. Engraving

3 | **Illustration of the Corinthian capital**
Note how the anecdote about originating from a funerary urn covered
by acanthus is pictured in all its growth phases.
2nd ed., Paris, 1684, pl. 23. Engraving

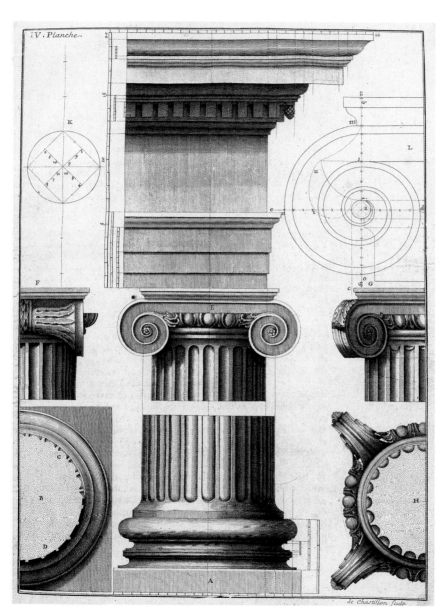

4 | **Base, capital, entablature and details of the Ionic order**
The illustrations 6–8 show Ionic, Corinthian and Composite column orders. The engravings are tables which open out so that they can be viewed and compared next to each other.
Pl. 4. Engraving by Chastillon

5 | Base, capital, entablature and details of the Corinthian order
Pl. 5. Engraving by Chastillon

6 | Base, capital and entablature of the Composite order
Pl. 6. Engraving by Chastillon

François Blondel (1618–1686)

Cours d'architecture

5 PARTS, PARIS, 1675–1683

Course in architecture

In the history of the theory of architecture François Blondel is widely considered the main exponent of a conservative direction in the *Querelle des anciens et des modernes*. In this argument between representatives of Classical and Baroque taste in the late 17th century, he devoted himself entirely to proving that there was a model for an absolute, binding theory of beautiful, harmonious architecture established in Classical Antiquity. Yet this attempt to define an unequivocal canon within the framework of the newly-founded Royal Academy of Architecture should not be understood to simply reinforce those rules that had been passed down through the ages, but was the result of the discovery of history as a discipline, new at the time, and the multiplicity of solutions to architectural questions in individual epochs.

Blondel, who was born in Ribémont in 1618 and died in Paris in 1686, had a long, eventful military career, which is where he would have received his training as an architect. Having started out as a master builder of fortresses, from mid-century onwards he was the guardian of the sons of several ministers of state, including Colbert, and in his capacity as a builder of fortifications journeyed throughout Europe and even as far as the Caribbean. However, in 1671 Colbert appointed him to head of the newly-founded Académie Royale d'Architecture, which had the task of formulating a theory of architecture that, on the one hand, set out valid norms and, on the other, laid the foundations of the supremacy of France in the field of architecture. Moreover, in

1674 Antoine Desgodets was commissioned to carry out a precise survey and documentation of the buildings of Classical Antiquity, which appeared in the form of detailed copperplate engravings in 1667 and 1695. Also, Claude Perrault (1613–1688) had been commissioned to undertake a critical translation and commentary of the standard work on Classical architectural theory, namely Vitruvius' *Ten Books on Architecture*. As a result of his research, however, Perrault came to the conclusion that architectural beauty should be defined as a consensus rather than as an absolute norm. This "scandalously modern" position had been vehemently rejected by Roland Fréart de Chambray in his treatise of 1650, a rejection which François Blondel now took up again in his lecture on architecture, which appeared in 1675–1683 as *Cours d'architecture*, a second edition being published in 1698. Here, Blondel makes an attempt to derive the definitive order of columns from the writings of earlier authors, and to relate them to one another in endless rows of numbers from which he then endeavoured to derive a valid system of measurement. Time and again, he attempted to undermine Perrault's position with somewhat trivial or circular counter-arguments. What was more important was that Blondel tried to identify a developmental line that purportedly had its origins in a primitive model that would have been subject to the laws of nature: the primordial hut described by Vitruvius, which Blondel reconstructed with four tree trunks and a platform and roof of branches on top. The idea that there

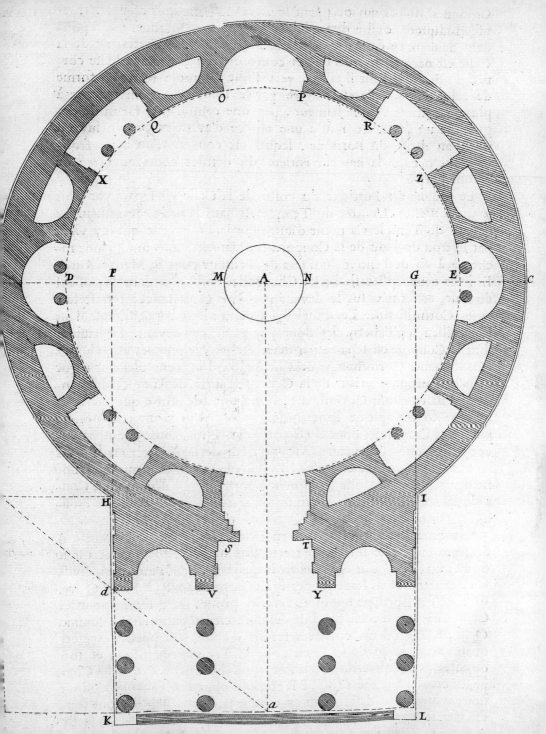

could be any form of advance on this state is the prerequisite for architecture being considered capable of improvement at all. Only in this way could it be clearly and reasonably proved that under Louis XIV (reigned 1643–1715), the arts surpassed Classical Antiquity itself. The principles of imitation and refinement thus become the basis for the development and the evaluation of architecture. As regards the primordial hut, the first human beings imitated and perfected nature, and the Greeks used the same principle for their temples. And yet Blondel did not let himself become an uncritical admirer of all things Classical. Quite the contrary, here too he points out mistakes and deviations. Even in ancient times the good rules were in danger, one reason more for codifying them now. The ensuing detailed depiction of the column orders in all their elements and proportions was integrated by Blondel into a developmental process that had undergone a period of decadence in the Middle Ages. Yet this does not apply universally, as Blondel even makes reference to some Gothic buildings which exhibit successful proportions. However, in the 16th century under Francis I (reigned 1515–1547) the new principles were given a fresh lease of life and then brought to perfection under the Sun King. The argument here was that Classical Antiquity had continually improved on a primordial architecture based on the laws of nature, and that this obliged contemporary architects not just to superficially imitate but to pursue the task of improving and refining. This allowed, indeed demanded for the new period of French glory, a new order of columns based on the last preceding historical order, the Composite. Just as the great empires of Antiquity had developed their columns, the Greeks the Doric, the Ionic and the Corinthian, and the Romans the Composite, now it was up to the architects to enter the competition launched by Colbert in 1671 in such a way that the good rules were applied and continued without extravagance.

For all the debate on architectural beauty, Blondel and his adversaries agreed that building technique and practical functionality are the deciding factors in determining architectural quality. This is tantamount to an admission specifically since the 17th century architecture was having to respond to changing ceremonial needs and higher standards in terms of living and social representation, an aspect that was set to become a fundamental feature of the architectural debate in 18th century France. That said, Blondel's "conservative" position, as promulgated in his aesthetics of architecture, also had far-reaching ramifications. Combining the authority of ancient principles with suitable refinement and bringing them up to date represented both for the young Blondel, and for the Modern Movement in 20th-century France, an ideal method for re-establishing a specifically French tradition. Around 1700, German architectural theory, represented by the likes of Nikolaus Goldmann (1611–1665), Leonhard Christoph Sturm (1669–1719) and Christian Wolff, also adopted Blondel's position in order to propose an absolute, mathematically-based interpretation of architectural aesthetics. CF

Fig. p. 157
1 | **Ground plan of the Roman Pantheon**
Blondel stresses the exemplary character of the building and the way in which it is well-planned, uniform, and conceived with harmoniously geometric proportions.
Part V, p. 750. Etching

2 | **Individual architectural forms, the "primordial hut" and the Doric order**
Architectural expressions are valid for primitive mythical models in architecture as well as for modern column orders.
Part I, pl. 1. Etching

L'Origine des Chapiteaux des Colonnes.

3 | **The origin of capitals**
In an ancient necropolis, the various crowns of the grave
stele are sketched. They are models for classical capitals.
Frontispiece, part II. Etching by Broebel

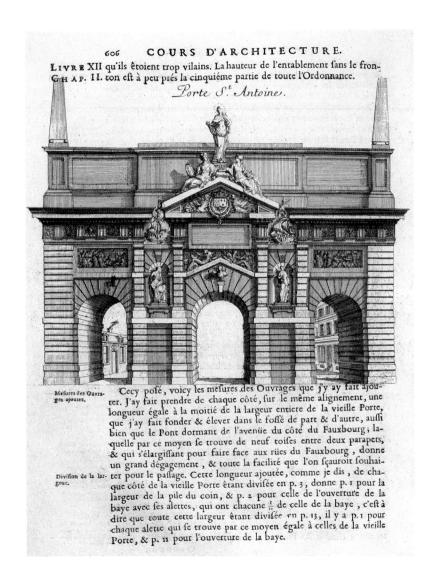

606   COURS D'ARCHITECTURE.

LIVRE XII qu'ils étoient trop vilains. La hauteur de l'entablement sans le fron-
CHAP. II. ton est à peu prés la cinquiéme partie de toute l'Ordonnance.

Porte St Antoine.

Mesures des Ouvra-   Cecy posé, voicy les mesures des Ouvrages que j'y ay fait ajou-
ges ajoutez.   ter. J'ay fait prendre de chaque côté, sur le même alignement, une
longueur égale à la moitié de la largeur entiere de la vieille Porte,
que j'ay fait fonder & élever dans le fossé de part & d'autre, aussi
bien que le Pont dormant de l'avenüe du côté du Fauxbourg; la-
quelle par ce moyen se trouve de neuf toises entre deux parapets,
& qui s'élargissant pour faire face aux rües du Fauxbourg, donne
un grand dégagement, & toute la facilité que l'on sçauroit souhai-
Division de la lar-   ter pour le passage. Cette longueur ajoutée, comme je dis, de cha-
geur.   que côté de la vieille Porte étant divisée en p. 3, donne p. 1 pour la
largeur de la pile du coin, & p. 2 pour celle de l'ouverture de la
baye avec ses alettes, qui ont chacune ¼ de celle de la baye, c'est à
dire que toute cette largeur étant divisée en p. 13, il y a p. 1 pour
chaque alette qui se trouve par ce moyen égale à celles de la vieille
Porte, & p. 11 pour l'ouverture de la baye.

4 | **Plan for the Porte St.-Antoine in Paris**
The continuous use of the Doric order signals valour and strength.
Part. IV, p. 606. Etching

Augustin Charles D'Aviler (1653–1701)

Cours d'architecture qui comprend les ordres de Vignole

2 VOLS, PARIS, 1691

Course on architecture, including Vignole's column orders

D'Aviler, who was born in Paris in 1653, was one of the important proponents of Vignole's canon, though he does add suggestions such as how the rigid system of five column orders can achieve much greater forms of expression by varying the motifs. D'Aviler's expertise as an architect won him a scholarship from the French Academy in Rome, where he spent the years 1676–79. Immediately following his return, he began work on the annotated edition of Vignole's theory of columns, which appeared for the first time in 1691, entitled *Cours d'architecture qui comprend les ordres de Vignole*. Though as a result he was highly respected as an architectural theorist, he enjoyed little professional success in Paris, and in 1689 was forced to move to Montpellier where he lived until his death. In 1693, he was appointed Provincial Architect of Languedoc and as such, in addition to several private residences in Montpellier, he constructed the Archbishop's Palace in Toulouse, his pièce de resistance.

As in the case of François Blondel's *Cours d'architecture* (1675–1683), Claude Perrault's translation of Vitruvius (1673), and Antoine Desgodets' survey of the buildings of Classical Antiquity, the publication of D'Aviler's *Cours d'architecture* should be considered in the context of strivings undertaken by the Académie Royale d'Architecture, founded in Paris in 1671, to formulate an official academic doctrine. It was D'Aviler's explicit goal to find a solution to the problem of the normative ideal, and current needs and expectations. Ultimately, it was a matter of emphasizing the ideal conditions that had prevailed under Louis XIV for developing a perfect form of architecture that would surpass even that of Classical Antiquity. Vignole's treatise on columns was also considered to be one of the definitive modern manuals of rules, albeit one which, because of its sparse text, required detailed commentary on, among other things, the orders and their proportions. D'Aviler expanded on the Italian-style collection of doors and window patterns by adding French samples. He exemplified the application of these basic elements using a large family house, in which above all the importance of *distribution*, i. e. the spatial layout, within the narrow confines of the ground plan is demonstrated. Bearing in mind the density of buildings in Paris, these skills were among the most important things a good architect could bring to bear. D'Aviler added a series of original shapes for columns and balustrades to Michelangelo's building motifs, which had been included in Vignole's early editions. This is evidence of the wish to provide the various building projects with suitable ornamentation. As such, we find columns that are "historical" (with narrative reliefs), "rural" (with shafts resembling tree trunks) or "maritime" (with cliff-like embossing) and, under the heading of "symbolic," he provides a discourse on a French order. The variations in meaning are achieved by amendments to the leaf shapes of the Corinthian capital. Just as Villalpando (1552–1608) had suggested for his reconstruction of the Jerusalem Temple, D'Aviler proposes palm fronds instead of acanthus leaves. The French order

Porte Cochere avec Ordre.

called for a combination of ostrich and cockerel feathers as well as military medals. This method of varying the column orders contrasts with the rigid limitation of orders to the three originally mentioned by Vitruvius, Doric, Ionic and Corinthian, as expounded by the theorist Roland Fréart de Chambray (1606–1676). It was these alone that had developed from the wooden primordial hut and the archetypal laws that this illustrated. Even the two later Classical orders, the Tuscan and the Composite (or Roman) were, in his view, subsequent revisions of the ideal triad. In accordance with this adherence to rules, variations in the order of columns was permissible only in particular areas, for example in the fluting, in the decoration of the bands around the shaft, and in the choice of foliage for the capital. The difference is that D'Aviler tried to interpret the abundance of shapes in architecture as a form of language. Thus, the curvatures of the cornices are read as letters, which are meant to enable "words" to be made from them. As a result, striking motifs in architecture are able to "speak." This is a property attributed by D'Aviler, as by later French architectural theory, particularly to the crowning cornice. With simpler constructions there is no need whatever for a special arrangement that relies on the column motifs, since the specific form of the crowning cornice makes the building's statement. Thus, D'Aviler was one of the early champions of what later became known as the Reduced order, which later on was used in numerous settings.

The second volume of *Cours d'architecture* consists of a detailed specialist encyclopaedia. Here, again, D'Aviler's desire that things be manageable, complete and up to date is manifest. In addition, the work appeared in an easy-to-use quarto format, but one that was in no way detrimental to the quality of the illustrations. They are exceptionally detailed and precise and sometimes cover two sheets. The practical nature of D'Aviler's objectives is also evident in his deliberations on the way architects should be trained. A master builder should not just be familiar with the laws of nature and art, he must have a practical approach, and learn for himself through study trips. Here, needless to say, it was

Classical Rome that remained the undisputed ideal. D'Aviler's treatise was a huge success, and between 1710 and 1760 several extended new editions appeared, in addition to unauthorized copies. These took into account the growing requirements of comfort and the most efficient use of space by including further examples of the ground plans of private residences and above all examples of interior decoration. In Germany, too, D'Aviler's œuvre became a basis for contemporary architectural theory. As early as 1699, Leonhard Christoph Sturm translated it into German and in his own writings attempted to make the ideas, including those on national building decorations, more suitable to German readers.

Overall, the *Cours d'architecture* fits in with the debate on the exemplary nature of Classical Antiquity as initiated by Louis XIV's ideology of kingship and as continued in the *Querelle des anciens et des modernes* on the one hand, and with the acknowledgement that architecture is subject to historical development on the other. Over the years, architecture had taken on various shapes and levels of quality, and having been in decline since Late Antiquity, in France it had been given a new lease of life, ultimately enjoying under Louis XIV an unknown level of *magnificence*. In his treatise, D'Aviler thus clearly takes a conservative stance that places him emphatically in the one camp for the *Querelle*. For him, the qualities of Classical Antiquity were an absolute norm, but the rules that since then had been regarded as valid (for example, those formulated by Vignole) needed to be preserved at all costs from being undermined. So, on the one hand, emphasis is placed on the authority of the Ancients, whilst on the other a wide range of permissible variations is presented, creating *architecture à la française*, an explicitly French form of architecture, which then points forward to *architecture parlante*, the "speaking" architecture of the 18th century. Like François Blondel, D'Aviler offers bad examples that should be avoided at all costs, such as the broken pediments, cartouches and other extravaganzas that the Italian Baroque architects Borromini, Cortona and Rainaldi so preferred.   CF

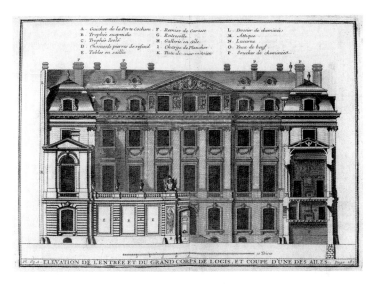

ELEVATION DE L'ENTRÉE ET DU GRAND CORPS DE LOGIS, ET COUPE D'UNE DES AILES.

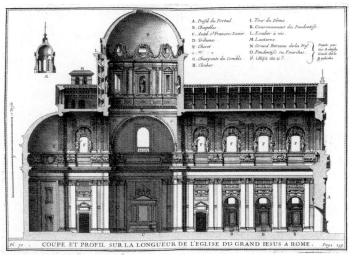

COUPE ET PROFIL SUR LA LONGUEUR DE L'EGLISE DU GRAND IESUS A ROME.

1 | Sketch for a city palace

Using his own rules on architecture, D'Aviler sketched a city palace himself. It follows the plan of a Parisian city palace and serves as a comprehensive model.
Vol. I, pl. 63 A. Engraving

2 | Sectional elevation of Il Gesù in Rome

D'Avila also illustrates Vignola's principle works: in addition to the Palazzo Farnese in Caprarola, we also find a ground plan and sectional elevation of Il Gesù, the mother church of the Jesuits in Rome.
Vol. I, pl. 70. Engraving

Porte-crois

Porte Flamande pour un Iardin .

Porte en Tour
ronde .

Porte Cochere avec Ordre .   Porte Bâtarde .   Porte Cochere ave

Pl. 43 B.

DIVERSES ESPECES

3 Toises.

Porte en Tour creuse.

Porte de Clôture pour un Parc.

Porte Bourgeoise.

Porte Cochere en Niche.

PORTES

page 115.

3 | **Plans for portals**
In addition to the column orders according to Vignola, the treatise contains a number of sketches which quickly turned into a frequently used catalogue of models.
Vol. I, pl. 43 B. Engraving

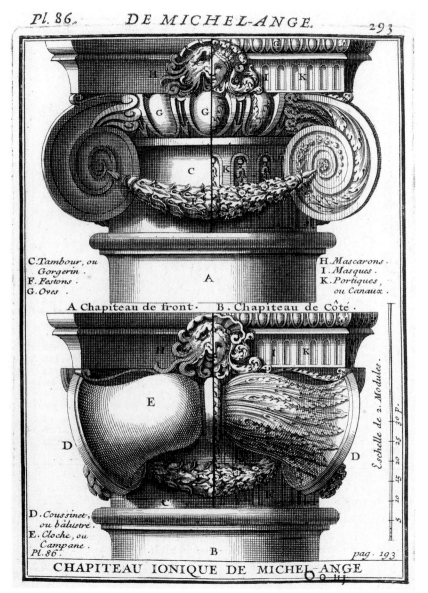

Pl. 86.   DE MICHEL-ANGE.   293

C. Tambour, ou
   Gorgerin.
F. Festons.
G. Oves.

H. Mascarons.
I. Masques.
K. Portiques,
   ou Canaux.

A Chapiteau de front.   B. Chapiteau de Côté.

Eschelle de 2. Modules.

D. Coussinet,
   ou balustre.
E. Cloche, ou
   Campane.
Pl. 86.

B   pag. 193

CHAPITEAU IONIQUE DE MICHEL-ANGE

4 | **Illustration of a capital by Michelangelo** Peculiarly, not only are Vignola's "classical" rules presented, but also the uncanonical forms of Michelangelo, specifically, the bell-like volutes of the Capitol palace. *Vol. II, pl. 86. Engraving*

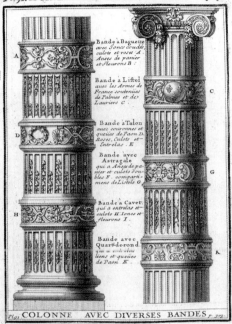

5 | Illustration of a Corinthian capital
D'Aviler argues for a "symbolic" decoration of Corinthian capitals: ostrich feathers and military decorations for the French order and palms leaves and antlers for the capitals of the Temple of Salomon.
Vol. II, pl. 89. Engraving

6 | Decoration of column shafts
The column shafts can also be decorated with attributes which make their classification into a particular type of architecture more precise than by using just Vignola's models.
Vol. II, pl. 91. Engraving

Statüe Heroïque.   Statüe Auguste.

Col. Bellique.

Colonnes Colossales, Solitaires, Creuses et Statüaires.

C.Torse Can.   C.Pastorale.   C.Hydraulique.   C.de Tre

Colonne Cylindrique et massive.

Col. Historiques .par Bandes et en vis. C.Astronomique. C.Milliaire.   C.Marine.   C.Rudentée.   C.Torse e

Pl. 93.   DIVERSES ESPECES DE COLONNES EXTR

Statüe Pedestre . Statüe Equestre .

Colo. en Baluſtre .

Couronnes

Triomphale

Ovante

Cirique

Paliſſaire

Obſidionale

Murale .

Navale .

ullie . C.Canelee Torſe .

Colonne Cylindrique .

ndée . C.Gnomonique .C.Funeraire . Colo.Rostrale . Col .Triomphale .

NAIRES ET SYMBOLIQUES .

page .307 .

7 | Comparison of columns
Columns are more than just useful supports. The shaft also forms part of their expression: in addition to martial columns, there are also provincial, astronomical, funerary and "hydraulic" columns.
Vol. II, pl. 93. Engraving

Jacques-François Blondel (1705/08–1774)

Architecture françoise

4 VOLS, PARIS, 1752–1756

French architecture

Cours d'architecture ou Traité de la Décoration, Distribution & Construction des Bâtiments

6 VOLS OF TEXT, 3 VOLS OF ILLUSTRATIONS, PARIS, 1771–1777

Architectural course or treatise on the decoration, division and construction of buildings

In his own day, as well as once again in 20th-century France, Jacques-François Blondel's architectural theory provided a role model for a rationalist approach to architecture, with its campaign against self-indulgence and illogical decoration in architecture, as had been witnessed in early 18th-century Rococo and in Art Nouveau around 1900. Even the very title of Blondel's main work, *Cours d'architecture ou Traité de la Décoration, Distribution & Construction des Bâtiments contenant les leçons données en 1750, & les années suivantes*, provided evidence that the eminently didactic element of his influence and writing formed part of the tradition of attempting to use academic education to impart knowledge of a system of norms based on reason. Having been begun by François Blondel, this was further developed by Antoine D'Aviler and is continued up to Julien Guadet's *Eléments et théorie de l'architecture* (*Elements and Theory of Architecture*) from 1900 and Gustave Umbdenstock's *Cours d'architecture* from 1930.

Born in 1705 or 1708 in Rouen or Paris, Blondel very early on ventured into the publication of architectural texts, from 1727 for example with Jean Mariette's *Architecture françoise* (*French architecture*), in addition to practising as an architect. In 1737 his first works on architectural theory followed, and in 1739/40 he opened his own school of architecture, the École des Arts, which was soon officially recognized by the state Académie d'Architecture. The large format, four-volume edition of *Architecture françoise ou Recueil des Plans,*

Elévations, Coupes et Profils des Eglises, Maisons royales, Palais, Hôtels et Edifices les plus considérables de Paris from 1752–1756, which above all presents sizable Parisian buildings of the 17th and 18th centuries, was expanded to include Blondel's contributions on architecture for Diderot and D'Alembert's *Encyclopédie* (1751–1772). Having been admitted to the Académie d'Architecture in 1755, Blondel was awarded several large-scale architectural commissions, in particular to redesign the centres of Metz and Strasbourg, projects that were however only completed in part. In 1762, he was appointed Professor at the Academy of Architecture, though he continued teaching at his own school and was responsible for numerous large-scale projects, including some in Moscow and Germany. From 1771 onwards the texts of his lectures appeared in *Cours d'architecture*, the completion of which was taken over by his pupil Pierre Patte in 1777, following Blondel's death in 1774.

Architecture françoise, with its many excellent copperplate engravings, showed a resolute commitment to continuing Jean Mariette's 1727 work, though it was enhanced by a short historical survey of architecture, a history of the city of Paris and an introduction to the basic principles of architecture. The *Cours d'architecture* expanded on these topics, though not without an element of verbosity and repetition. Blondel was well aware of the many solutions to architectural problems in various times and countries. The decision about what was judged to constitute good architecture, he

MAISON ET BUREAU DES
MARCHANDS DRAPIERS.

A

suggested, was subject to good taste, something that was not easy to determine. In general though it was considered desirable to strive for a harmony ("ordonnance") that was appropriate to the building's function, achieved a unity in all its parts, complied with the laws of nature and therefore satisfied common sense as well as being pleasing. Such quality however presupposed a knowledge of the rules of good architecture, and even forbade the pursuit of transitory fashions or capricious fantasy. Even if Blondel naturally considered Classical Antiquity to be an ideal model, there was no way that blind allegiance could be considered. Conditions in France were different from those in Greece and Rome. Rather, what was of critical importance was the challenge of harmonizing the outward appearance of architecture with the structural principles, and above all with convenience of layout and use. Simply designing façades was not hard; what was difficult was to design the façade such that it reflected both the projected use of the building in its social context and the interior layout. The basis of this is the link, known as "convenance," between the intended use of a building ("destination") and the character ("caractère") used to express this. Thus this describes an expression of quality that works in the same way as language and can be immensely diverse. There were for example mysterious and impudent "characters," as well as feminine and superficial ones. All this was the general expression of a new culture of dialogue that likewise aimed to transfer to architecture a new discovery, that of the human soul. This applied equally to the attempt to give beams facial qualities. In the illustrations, various profiles of men's faces in the style of Palladio, Scamozzi and Vignola were projected over the beams. The character's system of language also determined the artistic value of the design, since the arrangement of the architectural elements was to be so harmonious that it became a sort of "silent poetry." It is only then that the highest criterion for quality, a "true style" of architecture, is fulfilled.

The express demand that buildings fitted out with the full range of architectural motifs must obey the rules of structural composition – in keeping with natural laws governed by reason – led to a whole host of problematical and improper solutions: heavy objects clearly placed above light;

columns or pilasters that extended over several stories or whose axes were not properly aligned one above the other; a lack of correspondence between pilasters and columns placed before them; supporting motifs that cross; gables breaking through rafters; overlapping gables; sections of walls that were narrower than the windows in them; windows that were wider than they are high. None of this in any way corresponded to the intended appearance of a sensibly arranged construction, based on the original model of a frame with a protective gabled roof. And yet Blondel was well aware of the fact that these strict rules could not always be adhered to, and as such a good architect needed a few tricks to ensure that he appeared to be listening to the call for sensible constructions. Thus true architecture had to be distinguished from that which appeared to be true, something that in some cases was necessary in order to create a particular effect with a façade, such as balancing out certain visual effects. Here again the principle applied of not blindly following rules. On the contrary, sensible reflection on the part of an architect was evident in the ability to design what seemed to be true architecture without going against its principles. Limitation to what was necessary and appropriate led Blondel to champion the cause of "noble simplicity."

It is clear that Blondel's many-faceted demands for good architecture could scarcely be fulfilled. Yet it is the exacting intention of creating a perfect unity out of the function, use and decoration of a building, a unity that is also immediately recognizable as being based on reason, which explains why Blondel was regarded as the role model for French neo-Classical architectural theory in the 20th century, such as for Auguste Perret (1874–1954), the architect renowned for his use of concrete. Blondel was not just the last theorist who fully believed in the traditional syntax of columns, and who started using this again to replace the "irrational" lawless rocaille architecture of the Rococo. He was also the last author to develop a school of architecture before the fall of the Ancien Régime. This was what "good" French modern architects aimed to follow on from, vaulting over the disastrous 19th century, and combining new techniques with Blondel's classic rules.

CF

Fig. p. 173

1 | **The cloth merchants' building in Paris**
Blondel criticized this façade for its cluttered ornamentation and because the windows were too big. It was probably designed by Libéral Bruant around 1650.
Vol. III, pl. 307. Engraving

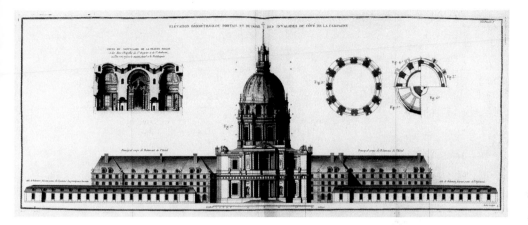

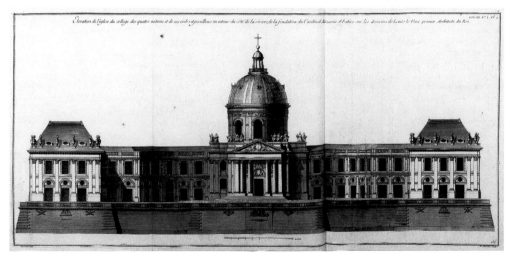

2 | Façade of the Church of the Dome, Les Invalides, Paris
Originally, the domed monument, built from 1680–1690, was to house the grave of Louis XIV as well as the relics of St. Louis (died 1270).
Vol. I, pl. 8. Engraving by Blondel

3 | Court façade of the Collège des Quatre Nations
The Collège was built from 1663–1674 by Louis Le Vau under the auspices of Cardinal Mazarin and was intended to be a lecture hall for foreign students. Today it houses the Institut de France.
Vol. II, pl. 156. Engraving by Blondel

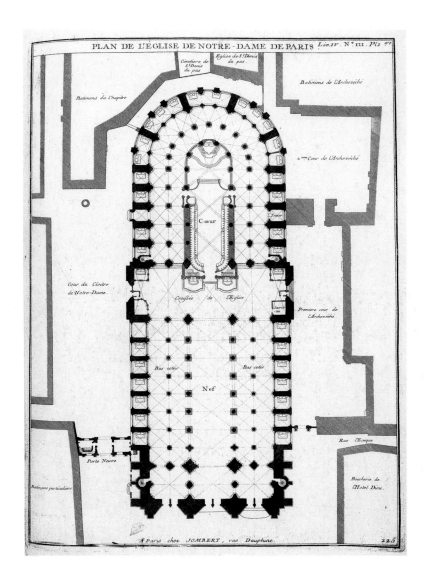

4 | **Ground plan of Notre-Dame Cathedral in Paris**
This illustration of the Gothic cathedral is remarkably
precise in numerous details.
Vol. II, pl. 225. Engraving

Liv.IV. N.° XI Planche I.re

Elevation Géometrale de l'Arc de Triomphe erigé l'an 1670 en l'honneur de Louis le Grand à l'extrémité du Fauxbourg S.t Antoine. Sur les desseins de Claude Perrault.

Babel Sculpsit.

A Paris chez I Sommers rue Dauphine.

N.° 262.

5 | Louis XIV's triumphal arch
The construction of this monumental triumphal arch, designed by Claude Perrault, began in 1670.
Work continued in wood and plaster and in 1716 it was taken down.
Vol. II, pl. 262. Engraving

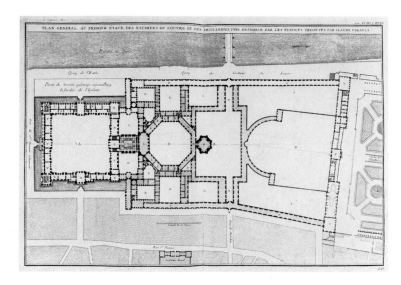

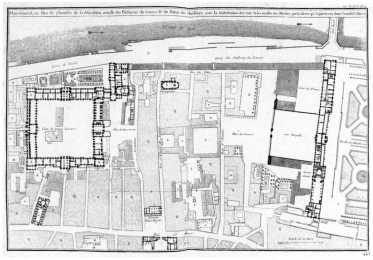

6 | Plans for enlarging the Louvre by Claude Perrault
Blondel's treatise gives a detailed list of the projects which were proposed
to connect the Tuilerie Palace (right) with the Louvre.
Vol. IV, pl. 442. Engraving

**7 | The quarters Louvre and Tuilerie Palace after the middle
of the 18th century**
Note how near the two palaces are to each other.
Vol. IV, pl. 445. Engraving

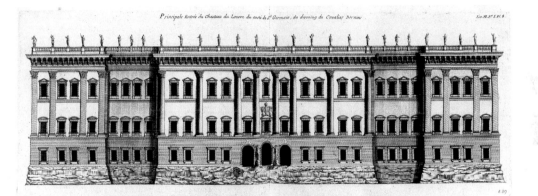

Principale Entrée du Chasteau du Louvre du costé de St Germain, du deessing du Cavalier Bernin

8 | **The eastern façade of the Louvre**
Gianlorenzo Bernini also created a design for the eastern façade of the Louvre
which led to intense discussions about genuine French architecture.
Vol. IV, pl. 449. Engraving

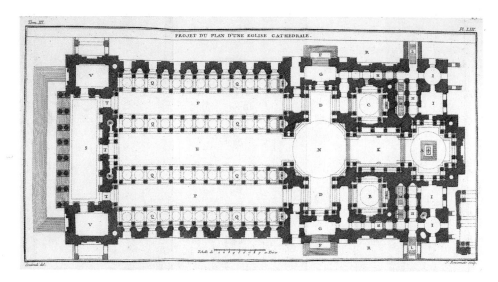

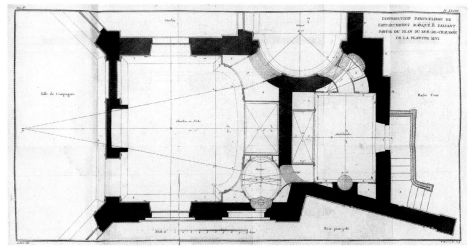

9 | **Plan for an ideal cathedral**
The massive Baroque building has almost completely given way
to a Classicistic structure with free-standing columns.
Illustrated vol. III, pl. LIII. Engraving by N. Ransonnette

10 | **Detail of a ground plan for a room arrangement**
In spite of the irregular ground plan, even the
smallest rooms are symmetric and regular.
Illustrated vol. IV, pl. XLVIII. Engraving by N. Ransonnette

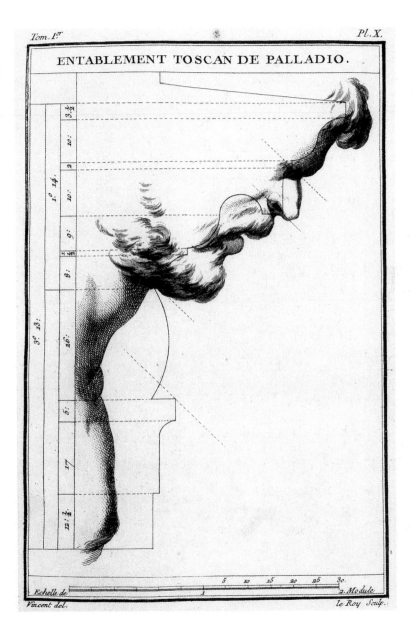

ENTABLEMENT TOSCAN DE PALLADIO.

Echelle de

Vincent del.   le Roy Sculp.

11 | **Hiding the profile of an entablature with the profile of a face**
Architecture begins to take on an individual character. The entablature is now just as exclamatory as a human face. *Illustrated vol. I, pl. X. Engraving by le Roy*

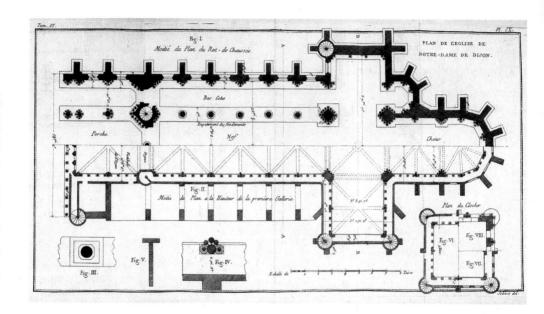

12 | Ground plan of Notre-Dame in Dijon
The Gothic structure has been measured out with an exactness remarkable
for the 18th century. The same applies to its structural details.
Illustrated vol. VI, pl. CXI. Engraving by N. Ransonnette

13 | **Cross-section of**
Notre-Dame in Dijon
Illustrated vol. VI, pl. CX.
Engraving by N. Ransonnette

Marie-Joseph Peyre (1730–1785)

Œuvres d'architecture

PARIS, 1765

Architectural works

Alongside Étienne-Louis Boullée (1728–1799) and Jean-Nicolas-Louis Durand (1760–1835), Marie-Joseph Peyre was another important architect who was influenced by the young Blondel, and further developed the architectural theory of the late Enlightenment, which in his case, against the backdrop of the 19th century École des Beaux-Arts, was to have worldwide implications. His enormous projects, strictly axial and symmetrical in their conception and delicate in their composition, were to influence the teaching at the most prestigious institute of architecture in France until well into the 20th century.

The architect was born in Paris in 1730, began studying under Jacques-François Blondel (1705/08–1774), and in 1751 was awarded the Academy's Rome Prize. During his stay in the Italian metropolis, he busied himself with surveying the thermal baths of Diocletian and Caracalla. These complex, domed structures were just as much an influence on the project he embarked on as a result of the prize, and which he then submitted to the Accademia di San Luca, as was getting to know Giovanni Battista Piranesi (1720–1778) and his fantastic architectural visions. Peyre submitted the plan for an immense archiepiscopal cathedral with four columned porticoes, flanked concentrically by a colonnade based on Bernini's surrounds for St Peter's Square in the Vatican. Two enormous four-wing complexes, to be used as palaces for the canons or the archbishop, were linked to the circular colonnade. Following his return to Paris in 1756, Peyre acted as

head architect for a number of royal premises (Palais du Luxembourg, Choisy-le-Roi). In 1765, he published twelve of his ideal projects in Œuvres d'architecture, of which a further edition appeared in 1795. His main piece of architecture was the Théâtre de l'Odéon (1769–1782), devised together with Charles De Wailly (1729–1798). Peyre died in 1785 in Choisy-le-Roi.

His treatise is basically a presentation in large-format copperplates of his colossal projects, as well as the plans for smaller constructions, especially fountains. Characteristic of all his projects were the shapes (derived from both Roman vaulted buildings and circles), which were to become the most important compositional items in his interiors. In particular, semi-circular niches and apses, exedras and circuses create dominant axes that are crowned by cupolas and further segmented by emphatic use of colonnades and porticoes. Peyre did not consider the orders of columns as important principles of Greek, let alone Roman Antiquity. What was decisive in truly great architecture was the correct order "des pleins et des vides," of "full and empty spaces." Here, he suggests, modern architecture must apply itself in order to achieve the sublime. The overall visual impression made by a building is therefore decisive, if it is to be of outstanding quality, and this can only be conceived by an ingenious architect who is able to create this unique character in such proportions. Too much decoration is not decisive; on the contrary, it is more likely to weary the view. Novelty per se is

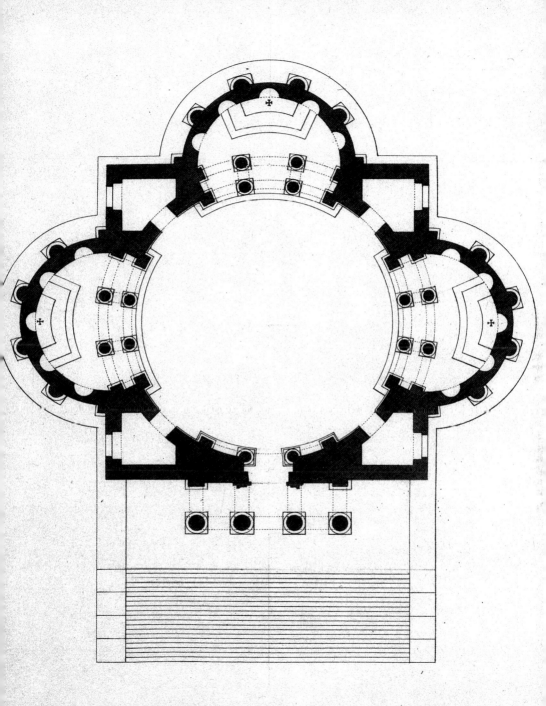

likewise not the aim of architecture. Instead the architect should endeavour to kindle as great an emotional response as possible, such as shock, fear, reverence, sweetness, calm, or passion. Simply copying older things, though, is not enough, they need to be surpassed, just as modern times are outdoing ancient times. Out of temples, he continues, churches for a whole community arose, which in turn had become temples to the Supreme Being, requiring space for a multitude of people. The basis of such architecture is an exact knowledge of Roman Antiquity, whose quality of the distribution of space had hitherto not been considered closely enough. The variety of the many rooms, often round and occasionally enormous and vaulted, all housed on a single floor, is the key characteristic of this architecture. Such an approach covered a multitude of functions, e. g. assembly rooms, museums, baths or rooms for sculpture collections, which Peyre feels should always be furnished with valuable, but in each case different, materials and well lit from above. Besides, if one considers the sheer number of illustrious buildings in Rome – 80 thermal baths alone – only then, Peyre asseverates, does one realize the true greatness of Classical Antiquity and thus the yardstick for the present. As such it is still appropriate today to construct enormous, well-lit suites of rooms, of necessity in one-storey, which requires generously proportioned palaces. The correct distance be-

tween columns in particular imparts an impression of solidity and strength. Gothic architecture should therefore be ignored, Peyre opines, as its delicate nature means that it can only instil fear. The proportioning of details in the order, however, a topic discussed at great length in Peyre's day, is, he contends, essentially of minor significance.

Basing himself on these theories, Peyre develops ideal projects, whereby well-known building tasks are inflated to immense proportions, while integrating and thus preserving elegant models. Thus, the Academy project quadrupled the size of the Collège de Quatres Nations of Louis Le Vau (1612–1670) to a square ground plan curving deeply inwards on four sides. Around this, four wings were added, from which two hippodrome-like courtyards lead off. The chapel is an outsize combination of the Caecilia Metella mausoleum in Rome and the Pantheon. The project is an enormous synthesis of the palaces in Versailles and Würzburg. Astonishingly, Peyre limits written explanation to a few laconic sentences. He wastes precious little space with thoughts about the functionality of his architecture, with its limitless courtyards and rooms. What was decisive was the monumental visual impact – to be integrated into the following century's great projects for magnificent town gardens and squares.

CF

Fig. p. 185
1 | **Ground plan of a chapel rotunda**
Peyre sees this design of a small chapel rotunda in the tradition of Baroque rotundas in Rome, e. g. Vignola's St. Andrea in the Via Flaminia and St. Andrea al Quirinale by Bernini.
Pl. 11. Engraving by Loyer

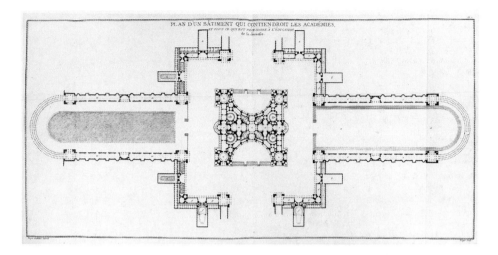

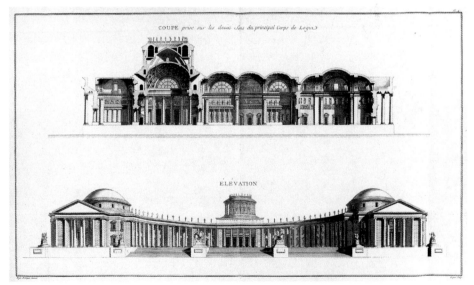

2 | Ground plan of an academic building
The gigantic plan of an academic building combines lecture halls
and libraries as well as an art academy, a dance school, a military
academy, halls of armaments, publics baths and space for ball games.
Pl. 3. Engraving by Loyer

3 | Elevation und sectional elevation of an academic building
The central building is strictly designed along two symmetrical axes.
The interior is divided into a row of domed halls and the exterior
consists of endless colonnades.
Pl. 4. Engraving by Loyer

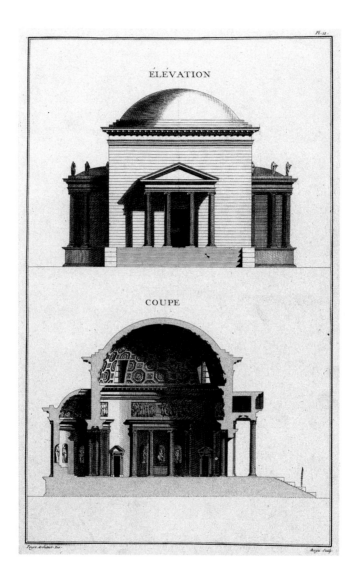

ÉLÉVATION

COUPE

4 | Elevation and sectional elevation of a chapel rotunda
The interior and exterior views of the round chapel make clear the
influence of the Roman on the French: the coffered ceiling is in
accordance with shapes found in the church Val-de Grâce in Paris.
Pl. 12. Engraving by Loyer

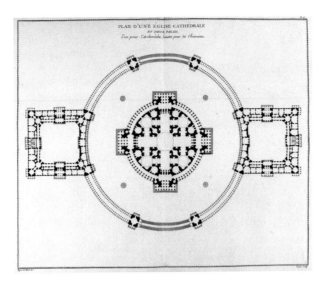

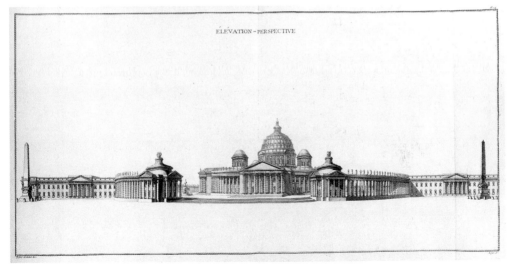

5 | **Ground plan of a cathedral**
The project for a gigantic cathedral attempts to standardize St. Peter's in Rome. The cruciform interior is inserted into an ordered circle surrounded by colonnades.
Pl. 13. Engraving by Loyer

6 | **Elevation of the cathedral**
The design of the exterior of the cathedral makes clear the desire to enlarge Bernini's colonnade around St. Peter's square to colossal dimensions.
Pl. 14. Engraving by Loyer

Claude-Nicolas Ledoux (1736–1806)

L'Architecture considérée sous le rapport de l'art, des mœurs et de la législation

PARIS, 1804

Architecture in its relations to art, customs and legislation

Like many other important architects of the Revolutionary period, such as Étienne-Louis Boullée (1728–1799) or Jean-Baptiste Rondelet (1743–1829), Claude-Nicolas Ledoux had also attended the influential school of Jacques-François Blondel (1705/08–1774). He very quickly assumed the position of an architect much in demand, and from 1771 onwards held the high-ranking position of Inspector of the Royal Salt Mine in Franche-Comté. This line of employment proved to be decisive in the development of his theories since, being so far away from Paris, he was more involved with engineering projects, forestry, canal building and questions of logistics and organization than designing illustrious buildings. As was the case with Boullée, Ledoux cannot be considered an architect of the Revolution, as is sometimes maintained. This would almost have brought him to the scaffold, and anyway the architect had been involved in his theoretical work long before 1789.

With its opulent text and pictures, the treatise *L'Architecture considérée sous le rapport de l'art, des mœurs et de la législation*, (and he had planned to be even more magnificent) was not the first work that attempted to structure the new utopian society along strict architectural lines, or to express itself through architecture. Nevertheless the work is without doubt one of the most demanding examples of a tradition that, in a particular way, was to become so established in the 20th century. In verbose language, dripping in pathos, he presents a world-embracing architectural vision that knows no social barriers in terms of the different estates, but that sets out to structure society according to its activities, in a monumental and highly visual way by means of architecture. On the one hand, there is an element of Rousseau's idea of the social contract, as well as the notions of the Physiocrats that developed in France in the second half of the 18th century. This initial model of a national economy is based on a natural cycle within a closed state system. A never-ending succession of acts of exchange, as in a "natural" sense of order like the circulation of blood, was supposed to constantly maintain the production, processing and circulation of goods. Within this system all social classes, in particular those working in agriculture, were to play a relevant part. For Ledoux this meant that architecture should no longer bear witness to the social standing of the owner or user, but should rather be an expression of the crafts and labour carried out there, and of their social relevance. For this reason, the concept of *architecture parlante*, "speaking" or "eloquent"descriptive architecture, is given a completely new function. In place of *convenance*, or appropriateness in terms of the social hierarchy, comes education. Ledoux exemplifies this especially in his project for the salt-producing town of Chaux in the French Jura. The major part of the project, the salt factories and the workers' houses, was realized between 1774 and 1779. But in the treatise Chaux becomes the example idea of a complex ideal town. The individual occupational groups should live in or use monuments that vi-

sually express the activities in which they are involved. And so the hoop-makers, so vital for the manufacture of barrels, should be accommodated in enormous houses shaped like wheels. The communal house of the "Pacifère," the peacemaker, was shielded by fasces, symbolizing unity. In the case of the house of the river inspector, the river was simply diverted through the house. It was not so easy to find a symbolic form for the school. There was to be a chapel in the middle of the cross-shaped building, enabling the individual subjects taught in the arms of the cross to be directed towards a common, ideal goal. Moreover from here it was possible to keep a careful watch over all the pupils. Of particular curiosity was the plan for an enormous brothel in the shape of a gigantic phallus. Yet here again the educational aspect was decisive, since visitors to the building were not meant to satisfy their carnal desires, but rather attain moral maturity by recognizing the repulsiveness of the activities taking place there.

This system no longer provides for the demonstration of social status by the orders of columns. Ledoux prefers to use for the most part original orders, taken directly from nature as it were, like the Doric, in order to create a sense of the sublime in the city. To this end, the house belonging to the director of salt production has a massive entrance hall in which the column shafts were interrupted by thick square slabs at regular intervals, as a kind of bossage. Otherwise architecture that embraces the structure of society as a whole does not permit any ornamental accessories. Even the elaborate carved foliage of the Corinthian order is useless, indeed damaging to the economy.

Ledoux' adherence to natural cycles also entailed a growing criticism of towns, something immediately apparent in the engravings. Rousseau's ideas of a natural community living away from destructive towns is to be encountered in all the projects, located as they were in balanced, undulating countryside interspersed with abundant vegetation. This paradise is cultivated for mankind and structured with the help of architecture. The workers' houses, set radially around the sorting works and the director's house, are plain and single-storeyed, and thus quite unmistakably subordinate to the central director's house. Yet they all have a small garden where the inhabitants could grow their own produce. Around 1800, Ledoux was unique in his radical formulation of architecture as fulfilling complex social functions that governed life in an almost totalitarian way. Architecture was meant to constantly highlight the goodness and the quality of this utopia. Its true creator, however, is the architect, who let "the poor" have a share in the "grace" of reason. In a famous illustration of the "poor man's shelter," a naked man is shown under a forlorn tree on a beach. The muses in the distant Olympic heaven wish to ease the burden of his homelessness. According to Ledoux, an architect was one of the gods destined to satisfy man's basic needs. Poor original man is no longer granted the natural ability of making his first home, as handed down in the trope of the primordial hut originating from Vitruvius. This idea was to catch on. Even Le Corbusier (1887–1965), for example, was to maintain that architecture alone could stop the proletarian revolution.

CF

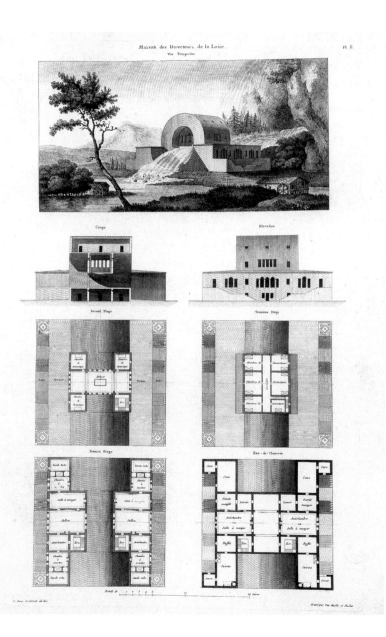

1 | **The river guard's house on the Loue**
The inhabitant defines himself through his metier. Therefore his house is in the shape of the mouth of a pipeline. *Pl. 6. Engraving by van Maëlle and Maillet*

Ledoux Arch.^{te} du Roy.

Vue perspective de la Ville

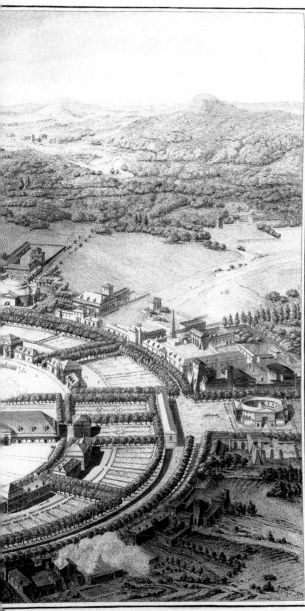

2 | **General view of the saline town of Chaux**
The centre of the complex consists of the graduation works
and the manager's house; the workers' homes surround
the centre.
Pl. 15. Engraving

Coupe de la Porte d'entrée de la Saline de Chaux, sur la Ligne. AB.   Coupe sur la Ligne AB. du Batiment des Berniers.

Le Deux Architecte du Roi

Pl. 36.

3 | **The saline town of Chaux; cross-section of the entry building and the salt refinery**
Exposing the function of the town, the entrance is designed like a stone grotto
from which salt is mined.
Pl. 36. Engraving

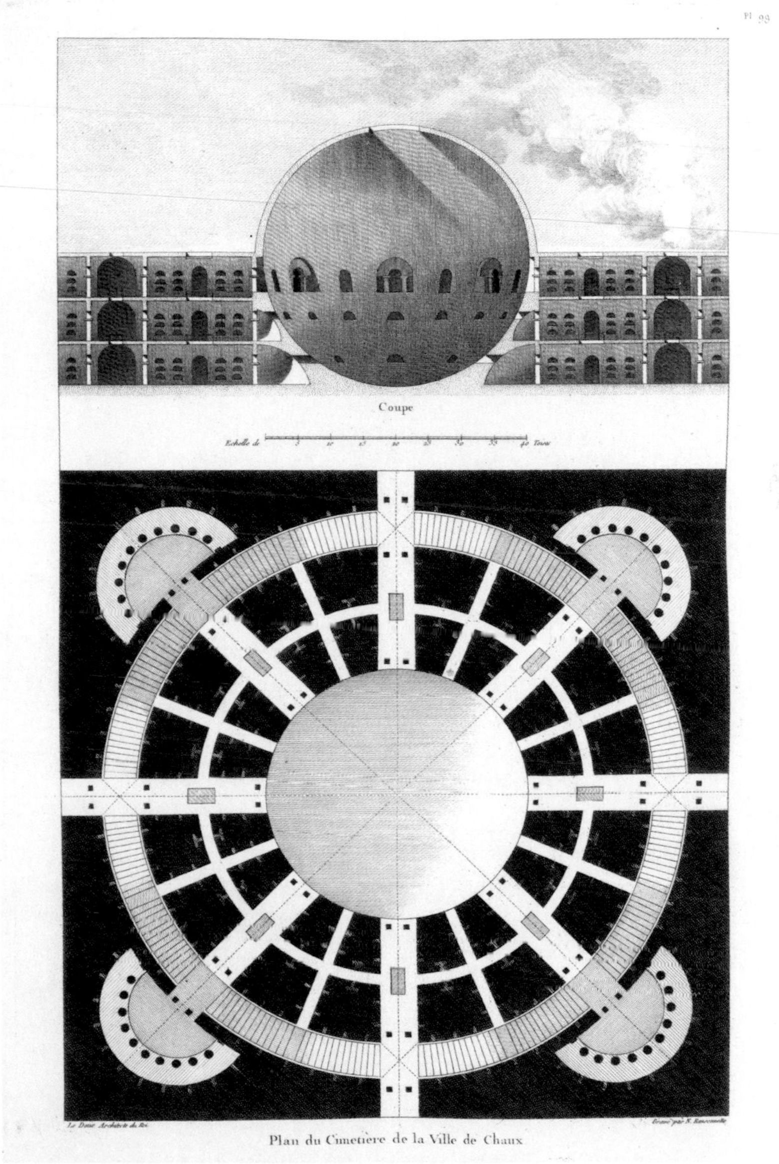

Coupe

Plan du Cimetière de la Ville de Chaux

4 | **The saline town of Chaux; plan of the cemetery**
The immense round shape of the central room of the terrifyingly dark building should bring lofty thoughts to mind.
Pl. 99. Engraving by N. Ransonnette

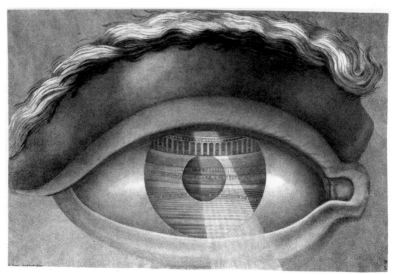

5 | **View of outer space**
The seemingly ironic perspective is to be understood as a reflection of
the eternity of the cosmos into which life and death are integrated.
Pl. 100. Engraving by Bovinet

6 | **The auditorium of the theatre in Besançon is reflected in an eye**
Contact between actors who are watched and the audience who is
watching becomes educational.
Pl. 113. Mezzotint engraving

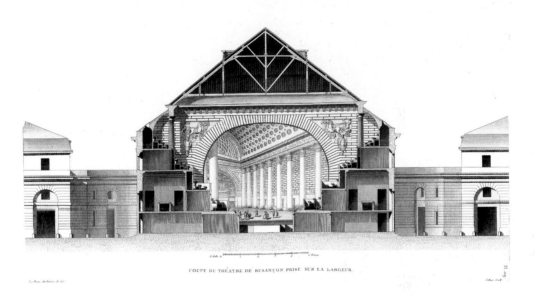

COUPE DU THÉÂTRE DE BESANÇON PRISE SUR LA LARGEUR.

7 | **View of the stage of the theatre in Besançon**
In order to augment the monumentality of the performance,
the stage is framed like a triumphal arch.
Pl. 119. Engraving by Sellier

Jean-Nicolas-Louis Durand (1760–1835)

Recueil et parallèle des édifices de tout genre anciens et modernes

PARIS, 1800

Depiction and comparison of all types
of new and old buildings

Précis des leçons d'architecture

2 VOLS, PARIS, 1802–1805

Précis of the lectures on architecture. Los Angeles, 2000

Jean-Nicolas-Louis Durand's treatise on architecture enti-tled *Précis des leçons d'architecture* offers the reader an aston-ishing standardization and systemization of the concepts of architecture. It distances itself clearly from his work *Recueil et parallèle des édifices de tout genre anciens et modernes*, pub-lished shortly before. It was an extensive attempt to place the world architecture of former days in an historical context, to present it in a sort of imaginary museum but at the same to distance it clearly from the architectural trends of the day.

Born in Paris in 1760, and having enjoyed early success as an architect under the patronage of Étienne-Louis Boullée (1728–1799), from 1796 Durand taught at the recently found-ed École Polytechnique. This was to remain his major em-ployment until 1833, two years before his death. In line with his didactic orientation, *Précis des leçons* is, as it were, the script of a well-illustrated lecture that deals with all aspects of architecture in concentrated form. The difference from the verbose, unmethodical *Cours d'architecture* (1771–1777) of the younger Blondel could scarcely be greater. Durand is consistent in his defence of the main goal of architecture being its use to society. The social appropriateness of any building as well as the profitability of its construction are subjected to this principle. This includes stability, hygiene and comfort, whereby the latter is considered to extend to symmetry, regularity and simplicity. The principle of prof-itability therefore relates to the efficiency of the design, clear technical computation, and the logistical execution of build-ing work. Underneath all this, there is a moral duty placed on the architect, namely to consider an egalitarian society as a whole, one that can be held together only to the mutual benefit of individual members and by the joint use of their produce. The profitability of the architectural product also plays a part in this. Durand tries to guarantee this by a radi-cally systematic principle, one that provides for a square grid as the basis for the walls and supports, which can be joined together to form various buildings, as in a set of building blocks. Needless to say, the size of the basic axis can differ according to the building in question, but the underlying grid always determined the system of construction, which can consist of walls, arcades, buildings and inner courtyards etc. By combining horizontal and vertical building blocks, any building task can be planned and executed with ease. In his lectures, then, Durand always used squared paper (which was occasionally used for architectural drawings in the 18th century, and from which modern graph paper is derived). Standardization means above all that he can devise a univer-sal range of building units, the combination of which enables any type of building to be conceived. Moreover, this process is easy to teach and put into practice, and can in principle be realized with prefabricated elements, the first large-scale ex-ample of which was the giant Crystal Palace in London, dat-ing from 1851. And yet Durand was not bothered with the technical, engineering side of his projects; for him, the eco-nomics and rationality of the design was the deciding factor.

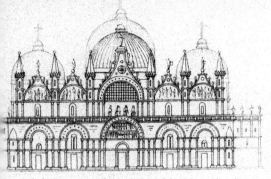

des Invalides

St Marc de Venise bâtie sous Urséolo 1er vers l'an 977.

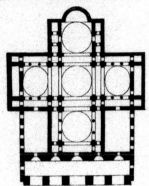

Invalides, bâti par Jules Hardouin Mansard en 1693.

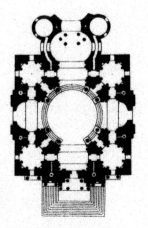

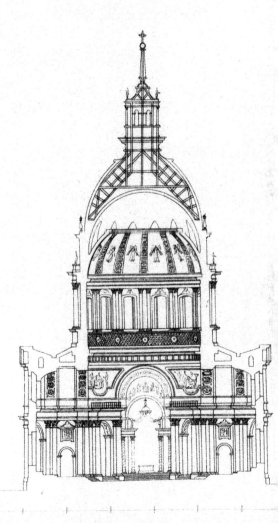

200 Mètres

Architectural traditions, symbolic levels of expression and topography play no further role and thus no longer stand in the way of the goal, a use to society based on the fulfilment of elementary purposes. This can be assured principally through public building projects, and thus Durand's manuals are mostly concerned with enormous public buildings, each strictly symmetrical and organized on an axial basis, frequently arranged around several courtyards. During his study of architecture, however, these are nothing more than long, abstract exercises for designing the basics of architecture, such as entrance halls, arcades, courtyards, and halls, before, at the end of the period of study, they are all combined to form specific types of building with specific functional requirements. These monumental buildings require instrumentation, albeit on an economic basis. Durand's method therefore, founded as it is on standardization, also impacts on the sequence of the traditional five orders of columns. Hitherto, the proportions of these had been defined through a complicated historical process and by means of a constantly rekindled debate. Now they became part of a mathematical formula by which the distance between columns from Tuscan to Composite was reduced in steps, by a column-radius at a time, whereas the height of the columns was increased at each step by the full diameter.

Durand's *Recueil et parallèle des edifices,* published in 1800, is a compendium of historical motifs, a true *Musée imaginaire* of world architecture. This is evident from the front cover, where the margins present illustrations of the major works of world architecture inserted between emblems representing the continents. The giant set of plates does not stand in contrast to *Précis des leçons,* since it is a further part of the new discourse on architecture that was emerging. In it the process of designing buildings and the history of architecture are kept strictly separate, as are teaching and the practice of design in *Précis. Recueil* was used for the teaching and design-practice of historical building until the late 20th century with great success. An index of the building tasks and motifs dealt with allows the reader to quickly skip to the appropriate synopsis. Everything is illustrated in precise copperplate engravings, all to the same scale, and limited to sharp outlines of the ground plan and/ or an elevation: everything is treated, from aqueducts to Turkish buildings, from pump rooms to mosques, from all types of temples imaginable (which are distinguished typologically as either rectangular or circular) to theatres, from the ancient buildings in Palmyra to the innumerable decorations for capitals and ceilings. Durand marks the dawn of a new systematic approach to the history of architecture. On the one hand, buildings are arranged by individual plates according to their typological characteristics, for example "vaulted main buildings" or "monumental portico courtyards," so that the buildings' specific aspects, compared with similar architectural solutions, become readily apparent. On the other hand, there is a brief caption to every building and every reconstruction, stating its location and name, and sometimes the date of construction or the person responsible for the particular reconstruction, such as Villalpando in the case of the reconstruction of the Temple in Jerusalem. If these captions have the effect of picture titles, then the layout of the plates goes a step further in the direction of a museum-like presentation. They appear as tableaux or exhibition walls that are frequently focused by means of prominent large illustrations of buildings on the central axis. To the side, smaller projects are presented symmetrically, forming a harmonious pattern with the regular ground plans and vertical elevations. The historical principle in the section on architectural motifs is of particular significance. The column capitals are not categorized in the traditional manner of Tuscan, Doric or Ionic, but according to the historic succession of existing examples in Egypt, Greece and Rome. In this way, the traditional succession from Doric to Corinthian appears as a side effect, and the main methodological principle is provided by the topographical, historical headings.

CF

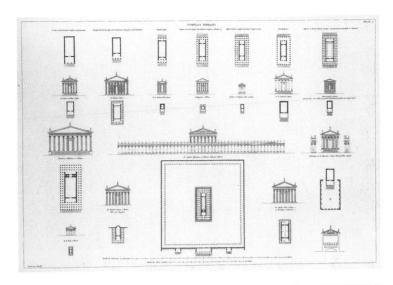

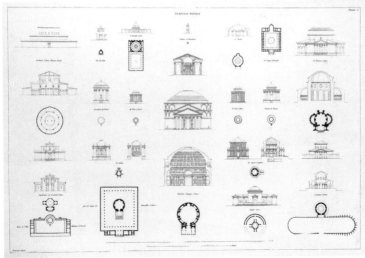

1 | Synopsis of Roman temples
Temple types named by Vitrivius are listed above; underneath
are examples which were actually constructed.
Pl. 2. Engraving by Reville

2 | Synopsis of circular temples
Durand uses two scales: a large one for the cross-sections
and a smaller one for the ground plans.
Pl. 3. Engraving by Coquet

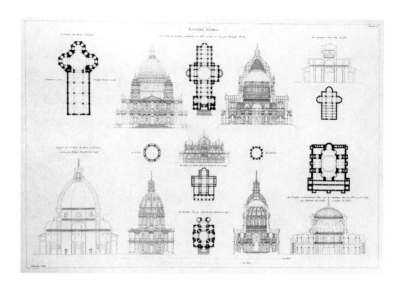

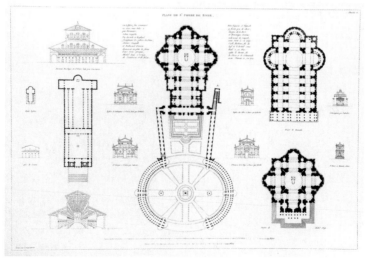

3 | Synopsis of domed structures
Exemplary domed structures in world architecture: the cathedral in Florence, St. Paul's in London, the Church of the Dome in Paris, St. Mark's in Venice, the Hagia Sophia in Istanbul and St. Augustine's in Rome. *Pl. 9. Engraving by Gaille*

4 | Plans for the reconstruction of St. Peter's in Rome
The table shows old St. Peter's and one plan each from Bramante and Michelangelo as well as the executed total plan. *Pl. 11. Engraving by N. Ransonnette*

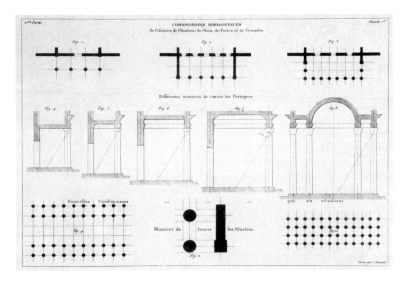

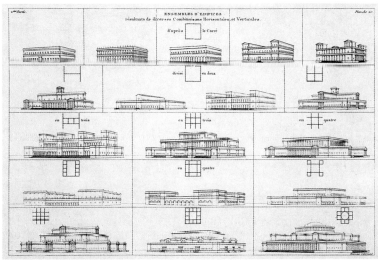

5 | Horizontal connections between columns, pilasters, doors and windows
Easily recognisable here is the rigorous geometrical scheme which allows a variety of vestibules be drawn out on a square grid.
2ⁿᵈ edition, Paris 1817–1819, pl. I. Engraving by C. Normand

6 | Various types of building developed from a square ground plan
The buildings have not been designed purpose in view, but on the basis of formal divisions of a square.
2ⁿᵈ edition, Paris 1817–1819, pl. XX. Engraving by C. Normand.

Jean-Baptiste Rondelet (1743–1829)

Traité théorique et pratique de l'art de bâtir

7 VOLS, PARIS, 1802–1817

Theoretical and practical treatise on building

Guillaume Abel Blouet (1795–1853)

Supplément

PLATES. PARIS, 1847

Supplementary volume

Jean-Baptiste Rondelet belonged to the era of upheaval of the French Revolution, and he played a major role in the shift in architecture from being primarily aesthetic and symbolic to becoming a technically rational discipline.

Born in Lyons in 1743, he attended Jacques-François Blondel's (1705/08–1774) school of architecture and was a pupil of Étienne-Louis Boullée (1728–1799). In particular he was able to gain an extensive technical knowledge when working under Jacques Germain Soufflot (1713–1780) during the building of the Sainte-Geneviève church, which was later to become the Panthéon. Rondelet's remarkable skills in the cutting of vault blocks and in civil engineering were acquired during many years working on the above-mentioned audacious construction, from 1806 onwards as senior architect. They often proved to be of importance when fending off criticism regarding structural safety, especially that of the dome. Between 1783 and 1785, when construction work was halted, he took the opportunity to embark on a protracted study trip to Italy. He was soon considered one of the best structural engineers in France and his expert reports were constantly in demand. During the Revolution, when in 1793 the royal academies were dissolved and in their place new schools of engineering geared to technical expertise were founded, Rondelet was one of the eminent organizers. Ever since 1789, he had called for such an institution to be established, and in 1794 the École Centrale des Travaux Publics was founded in Paris, initially teaching architecture and engineering. Yet one

year later it began to concentrate solely on the study of technical and practical skills and was re-named École Polytechnique. The military needs of the revolutionary armies were a major reason for the school's existence in this form. It was imperative to teach a precise knowledge of building, based on exact calculations and used efficiently, one that could subsequently be further deepened in specialist areas such as artillery, mining, bridge-building, roadbuilding and ship-building. In 1799, Rondelet was appointed Professor at the École d'Architecture, one of the predecessor institutions of the École Impériale et Spéciale des Beaux Arts, which was founded in 1807. Rondelet taught stereotomy and building construction in the Department of Architecture and in 1815 was appointed a member of the Académie des Beaux-Arts. He died in Paris in 1829.

Rondelet penned his thoughts on building problems in numerous expertises and studies. His major work, which appeared in several editions, is the textbook entitled *Traité théorique et pratique de l'art de bâtir*, published for the first time between 1802 and 1817 in five volumes, with an extensive set of plates. In the introduction, he states that the aim of architecture was to make a contribution to progress. Architecture has at least a claim to be not simply the work of an engineer, since in addition to providing stability it must also fulfil the criteria of appropriateness and beauty, so that safe, convenient, splendid buildings could be constructed, giving towns a claim to fame. These were principles that had

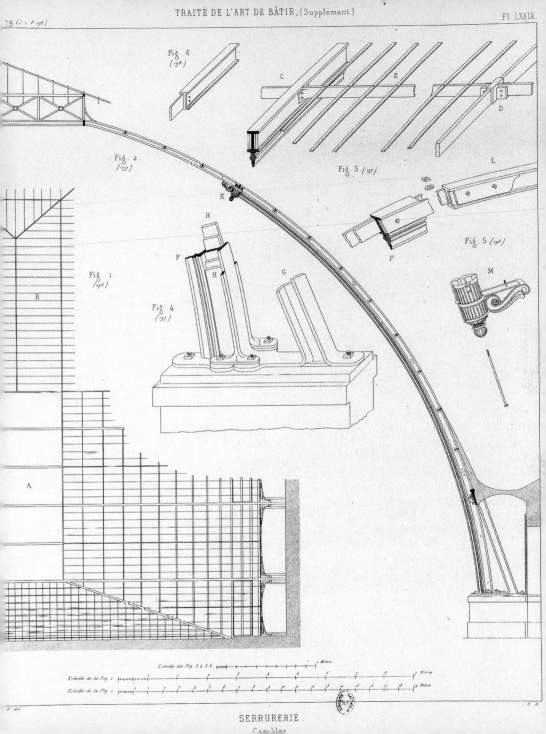

Fig. 6
(198)

Fig. 2
(197)

Fig. 3. (197)

Fig. 1
(196)

Fig. 4
(197)

Fig. 5. (198)

Echelle des Fig. 3. 4. 5. 6.

Echelle de la Fig. 2

Echelle de la Fig. 1

V. del.

E. R.

SERRURERIE.

Combles.

been adhered to in Classical Antiquity; but since the 14th century, when most master builders had trained as painters, a building's decorations had become the centre of attention and technical skills been neglected. For this reason the priority must now, he suggested, be on mastering the skill of building from a practical and theoretical point of view. By this Rondelet means, on the one hand, how workers treated their materials (production, treatment, transport), and, on the other, calculating the structural and load-bearing properties of a building and the costs to be incurred. For this reason the treatise contained no lengthy, traditional formulae, but was rather the sum total of the author's own experience. The new scientific approach to teaching architecture is thus sub-divided into military architecture, shipbuilding and civil architecture, which as far as Rondelet is concerned consists exclusively of public buildings and gardens: temples, palaces, schools, theatres, triumphal arches, fountains, water pipes, bridges, harbours, squares and streets. The extensive main section of the treatise provides detailed information on materials, describing and listing in tabular form the deposits, treatment and behaviour of the most varied sorts of stone, brick, cement and earth, including foreign types. There was a detailed presentation of how to calculate vaults and roof frameworks. The use of iron as a building material is de-scribed exactly for the first time, and illustrated using examples such as the Iron Bridge at Coalbrookdale, the Pont des Arts and the Pont d'Austerlitz. Furthermore Rondelet gives detailed instructions on how to calculate costs based on the metre, the new unit of measurement introduced in 1795. Anthropometric measurements had no further part to play, and thus it is not surprising that Rondelet declines to mention the classical system of proportions.

In terms of structure, Rondelet's work, which has occasionally been described as the engineering counterpart to Durand's teachings on architectural doctrine, was mid-way between older treatise literature and the more recent genre of a manual in several parts. Although Rondelet's work appeared in five volumes, it is strictly structured into seven parts. Each of these is a work in its own right, as each is devoted to a single topic: part 1 to stones, part 2 to bricks and cement, part 3 to the technical aspects of constructing vaults, part 4 to mathematics. Part 5 is devoted to the laying of foundations and earth moving, and part 6 contains a section on carpentry. Only part 7 embraces varied subjects such as roofing, wall panelling, railings and finally the new building material iron, which is obviously still not considered as such and thus does not warrant its own volume.

CF

Fig. p. 207
1 | **Iron skeleton construction as a covering**
The riveted t-section girders and hoop-irons resulted in a skeleton which was amazingly transparent and delicate.
Pl. LXXIX. Steel-engraving by H. Roux the Elder

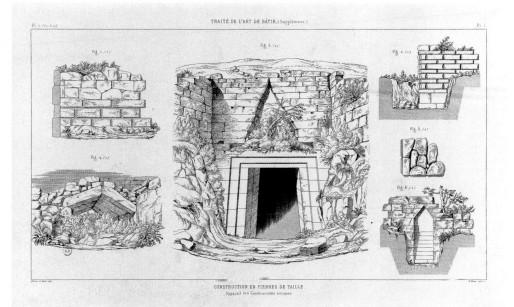

2 | **Ancient masonry techniques**
Also in the ancient cultures, cutting the stone correctly was a necessity
for good and rational construction.
Pl. I. Steel-engraving by H. Roux the Elder

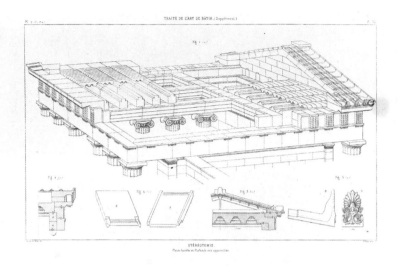

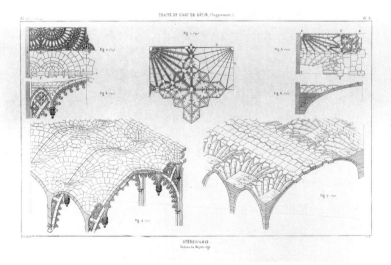

3 | System of construction of the Greek temple
Blouet expressly uses designs from Karl Friedrich Schinkel's
Vorbilder für Fabrikanten.
Pl. VII. Steel-engraving by H. Roux the Elder

4 | Vaulting of the English Flamboyant Gothic
It is once again shown that the correct cut and joining together
of the stone is a prerequisite for the construction of vaulting.
Pl. X. Steel-engraving by H. Roux the Elder

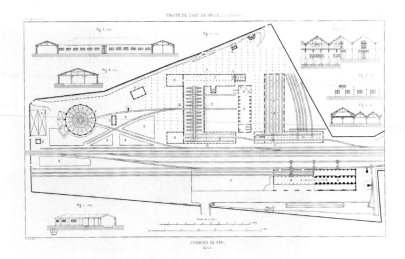

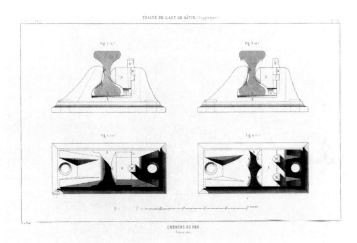

5 | Layout of tracks in a station for freight trains
This is the original plan for the Gare d'Orléans railway station which
was replaced by the Gare d'Orsay (now the Musée d'Orsay) in 1900.
Pl. XVI. Steel-engraving by H. Roux the Elder

6 | Track fasteners
In addition to masonry and carpentry, track building is now
considered part of architecture.
Pl. XX. Steel-engraving by H. Roux the Elder

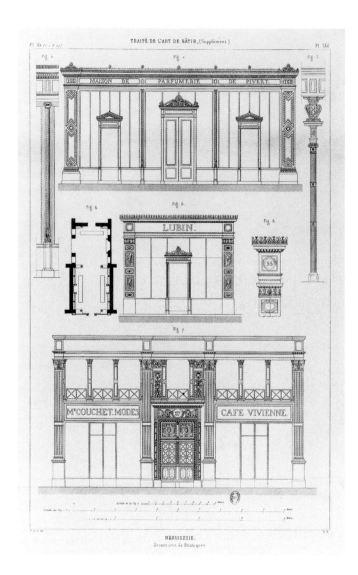

7 | **Shop inserts made of metal**
In the chapter on "construction fittings," various economical
built-ins for shops and shop windows are described.
Pl. LXII. Steel-engraving by H. Roux the Elder

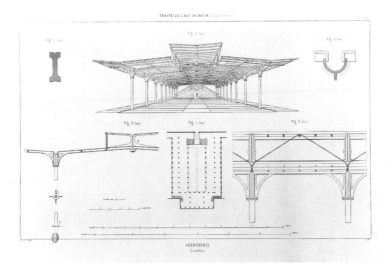

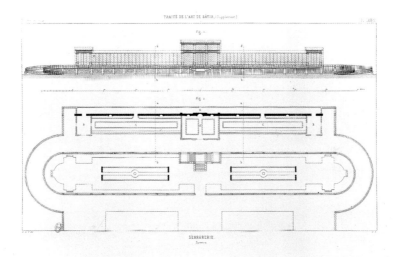

8 | The market halls of Hungerford
The peculiarity of this iron construction was the use of projecting
t-pillars, which made an external support system unnecessary.
Pl. LXXX. Steel-engraving by H. Roux the Elder

9 | Greenhouse in the botanical garden of Rouen
The iron and glass construction with its three pavilions and
majestic ramp is reminiscent of Baroque palaces.
Pl. LXXXVII. Steel-engraving by H. Roux the Elder

Eugène Emmanuel Viollet-le-Duc (1814–1879)

Dictionnaire raisonné de l'architecture française du XIᵉ au XVIᵉ siècle

10 VOLS, PARIS, 1854–1868

Detailed encyclopaedia of French architecture from the 11th to the 16th century

Entretiens sur l'architecture

2 VOLS, PARIS, 1863–1872

Discourses on architecture, USA 1889

Viollet-le-Duc's interpretation of architecture had an almost unparalleled impact on the conceptual tools of modern 20th-century architecture. The structure and function of architecture as its sole determinants, i. e. as the result of historical, sociological and above all technological analyses, would appear to have been culled straight from the extensive writings of this all-round genius. This effect is above all due to the fact that Viollet-le-Duc no longer regards the theory of architecture as a speculative, aesthetic system, but rather as the result of seemingly unassailable empirical scientific research. It is only logical that in addition to Greek Antiquity the emphasis is on the architecture of the Middle Ages since, or so it is alleged, the architecture of modern times is only effective because of its decorative facings and these have nothing to do with construction. From the very beginning, scientific laws of physics could not be derived from this form of architecture.

Eugène-Emmanuel Viollet-le-Duc's theories can be traced back to biographical circumstances; born in 1814 into an educated middle-class family, he trained early on with several architects and, following extensive journeys in France and Italy, had close links to the state's chief building inspection board. His rise to emerge as the greatest restorer of the time began in 1838 when he was appointed press spokesman of this board, which had recently begun surveying and restoring medieval churches and fortresses. Through the Commission des Monuments Historiques, Viollet-le-Duc

was awarded several contracts to restore major items of French medieval architecture, including the cathedrals in Paris, Amiens and Clermont-Ferrand as well as the large abbey churches of Saint-Denis and Vézelay, and the old fortifications in Avignon and Carcassonne. In 1853, he became *Inspecteur général des Edifices Diocésains*, inspector-general of all French ecclesiastical buildings. The expertise he acquired in this role formed the basis of the extensive first edition of the *Dictionnaire raisonné de l'architecture française du XIe au XVIe siècle* that appeared between 1854 and 1868. As opposed to other works of this genre, such as Quatremère de Quincy's *Historical Dictionary of Architecture* from around 1800, this is a painstaking record of real facts about an historical epoch. Here, Viollet-le-Duc's fundamental theories on architecture are dealt with explicitly in several important articles on such matters as construction, restoration and style, but otherwise are implicit in the numerous other entries (for example cathedral, dungeon, pointed arch). In 1863, Viollet-le-Duc was appointed professor at the École des Beaux-Arts, a post that he had to relinquish a year later as a result of his extensive but futile attempts to reform the training of architects. However, his teachings did appear between 1863 and 1872 under the title *Entretiens sur l'architecture*. There he presents his system of architecture, structured by epoch and by basic issues on architecture. But the success of his doctrine was due to several didactic writings that, in addition to several other publications, he authored towards

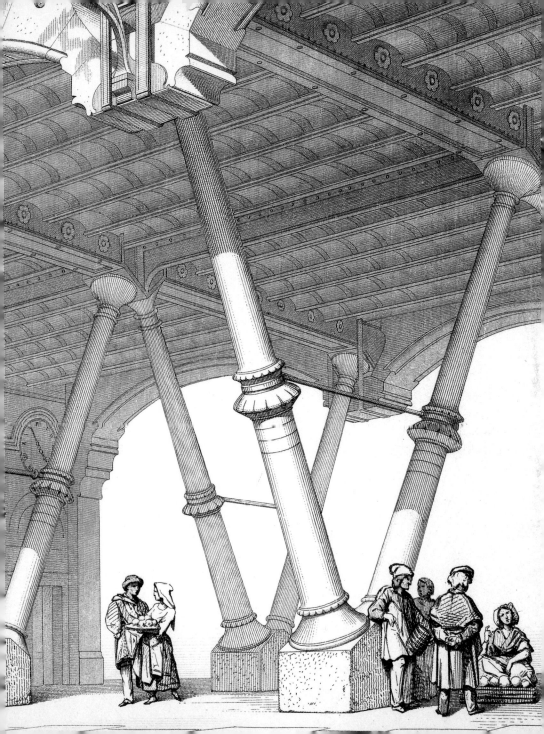

the end of his life: *Histoire d'une maison*, 1873 (*The story of a house*) and *Histoire d'une ville et d'une cathédrale*, 1878 (*History of a town and a cathedral*) describe, in a narrative and easy to understand way, the history and the problems of building.

Viollet-le-Duc's theory of building is based on the precise and extensive knowledge of building and construction techniques in the Middle Ages that he acquired as a restorer. The principles that had emerged in the 13th century of a logical and efficient, i. e. economical way of building, had resulted in a skeleton form of architecture that was elaborated with in a quite unprecedented audacity in the large cathedrals. In this regard, Viollet-le-Duc takes a definite anti-clerical or bourgeois and anti-religious stance. It was only once the rigid laws on building, dating from the monastery culture of the Romanesque period, had been overcome by a secular urban culture, he suggests, were free citizens able to commission large-scale projects on their own behalf, and only then did ingenious constructors enjoy the freedom to work logically and sensibly, according to the laws of nature, when fulfilling these contracts. The consistent application of the principles of reason and logic is thus the driving force of progress, which then forms the focus of good architecture in an emancipated society. This is true, he claims, in particular of the Greek and Gothic styles of building. Thus, he identifies the factors hampering progress as: formal adherence to tradition, conventional academic rules, and authoritarian structures, which above all in his opinion means, clerical and monarchical structures. He combines these factors to offer a universal history not just of architecture but also of the civilizations as reflected in their buildings. The constant force behind progress is, however, dependent on "race," by which he evidently means certain mental characteristics and qualities in peoples, as well as conditions determined by material resources and climate. Moreover,

progress has to contend with historical events and aesthetic premisses. Blindly following purely physical laws of nature is therefore not sufficient for achieving ideal architecture; additional criteria are required, such as how resistant a building is to attacks in war. Ultimately, it is also a case of trying to achieve an ideal system of proportions, and therefore the Gothic skeleton form of architecture constitutes the pinnacle of progress. There, the overcoming of theocratic structures, the quality of material and the genius of the French nation (in which the Aryan and Gallo-Roman races had, he claimed, been happily combined), leads to a way of building that can accommodate structural elements in a dynamic relation of forces. This quality justifies the opinion that Gothic architecture constituted a unique "style." Any object that fulfils this function by adhering so perfectly to the laws of nature possesses this, the greatest of qualities, or so he avers. This is also true, for example, of a vase, a steamer, or a locomotive, produced using a certain material for a particular function. Conversely, this interpretation entails an obligation to find a "rational" technical explanation for every single detail of ideal Gothic architecture, just as in an engine.

There can be no doubt that a theory of architecture that pays attention to every detail and penetrates several other areas of wisdom is a construct that, in addition to many correct assertions, also gives rise to several untenable premisses and conclusions. The relevance to a Modernist approach stems above all from the fact that Viollet-le-Duc developed counter-positions with a radicalism hitherto unknown: Gothic versus Classicism, construction versus ornamentation, truth versus lies, progress versus academicism, engineering versus architecture as art. It was this polar form of argumentation that harboured the potential for later Modernist discussions on the function and nature of architecture. CF

1 | **The ideal cathedral**
Knowledge of the "correct" Gothic architecture leads Viollet-le-Duc to design the ideal church: a synthesis of high Gothic structures.
Vol. II, p. 324. Wood-engraving

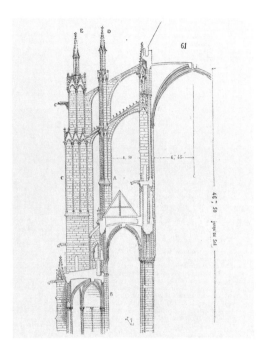

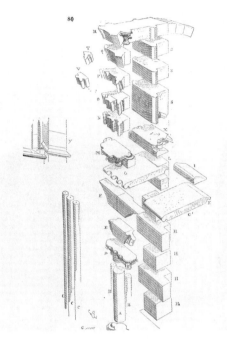

2 | **Cross-section of the choir of the cathedral of Beauvais**
The delicate and daring construction is "not without mistakes."
Viollet-le-Duc claims to know the reason for its collapse in 1284.
Vol. I, p. 70. Wood-engraving

3 | **Drawing for the arched parts of Notre-Dame in Dijon**
The "building block" system is good in the especially complicated
area at the beginning of the arches.
Vol. IV, p. 141 Wood-engraving by G. Jeune

4 | **Cross-section of the eastern transept of St. Nazaire in Carcassone**
Gothic construction cannot do without iron arms at different heights.
Vol. IV, p. 202. Wood-engraving by G. Jeune

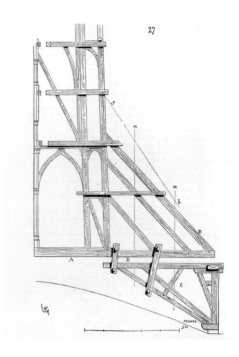

5 | Detail of arch in St. Nazaire in Carcassone
Vol. IV, p. 203. Wood-engraving by G. Jeune

6 | Wooden construction of the turret of the Cathedral of Amiens
The daring of Gothic construction is to be seen not only in the
masonry but also in the carpentry work.
Vol. IV, p. 470. Wood-engraving by G. Jeune

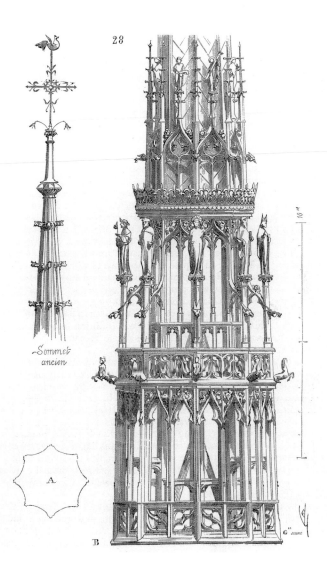

7 | **View of the turret of the Cathedral of Amiens**
Vol. IV, p. 471. Wood-engraving by G. Jeune

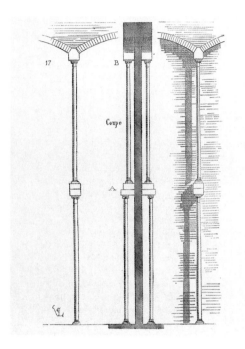

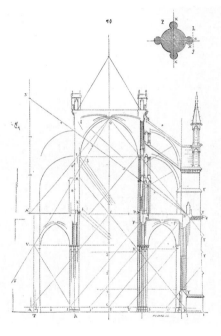

8 | Vertical supporting elements
Wall mass can be reduced by vertical supports made
of stone or iron.
P. 298. Steel-engraving

9 | Proportional analysis of the cross-section of the choir of Amiens
The interior structure of the building is harmonious because it follows
the proportions of the same particular triangle.
P. 406. Steel-engraving by Pégard

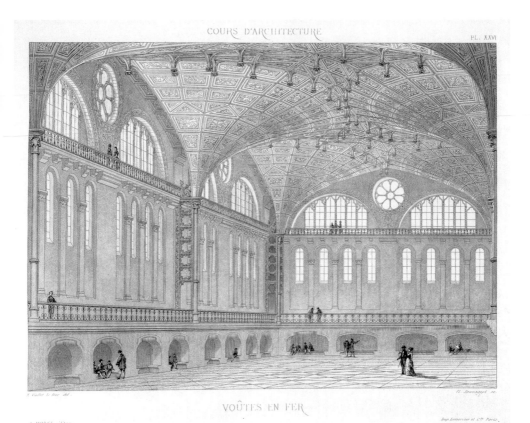

10 | **Design of a large hall with iron skeleton arches**
The new building material, iron, not only allows the breaching
of wider distances than stone arches, it is also more economical.
Atlas, pl. XXVI. Steel-engraving by Sauvageot

E. Viollet-le-Duc del.

A. MOREL. Editeur

MAÇONNERIE

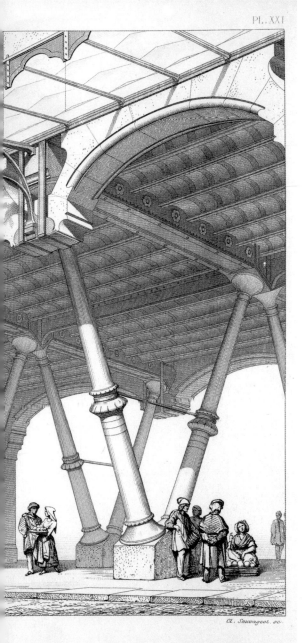

PL. XXI

Cl. Sauvageot. sc.

Imp. Lemercier, Paris.

11 | Market building on iron supports
Derived from the principles of the elastic Gothic
skeleton construction, iron now takes on the
functions of supporting and covering.
Atlas, pl. XXI. Steel-engraving by Sauvageot

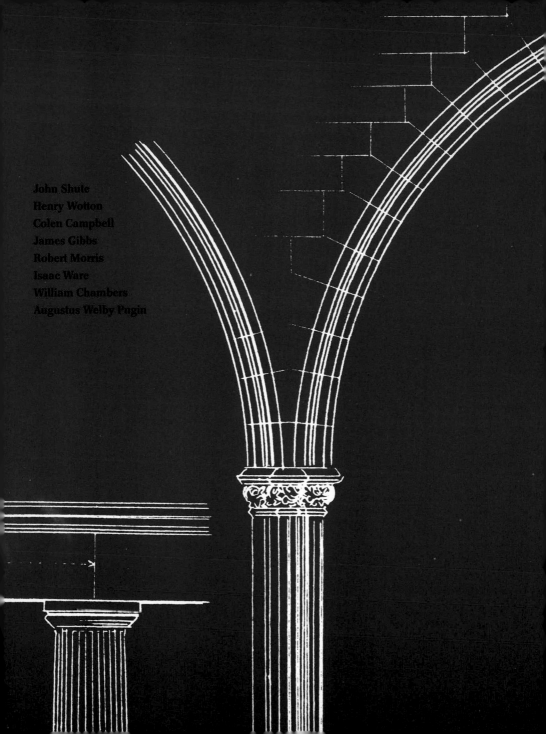

John Shute
Henry Wotton
Colen Campbell
James Gibbs
Robert Morris
Isaac Ware
William Chambers
Augustus Welby Pugin

England

DRVIDICAL

John Shute (d. 1563)

The First and Chief Grounds of Architecture

LONDON, 1563

The publication *The First and Chief Grounds of Architecture* by the miniaturist John Shute must be considered the earliest literary evidence of an exploration of classical architecture in England. In his dedication to the Queen, Shute confidently emphasizes that his work is the result of intensive reading of the most important literature on architectural theory and of his own studies during his stay in Italy in 1550. In fact, Shute's importance lies less in his independent deliberations on architecture and more in the fact that he introduced the discussion on Classical architecture to England through his book on columns, which was published four times, in 1563, 1579, 1584 and 1587. Shute's comments basically paraphrase Vitruvius' architectural theory with which Shute was familiar through the commentary Guillaume Philander produced in 1544. This already becomes apparent in Shute's outline of architectural history, as it not only takes up Vitruvius' concept of architecture as one of man's existential needs, an *initium topos*, but also includes Vitruvius' legend about the origin of the three Greek column orders. But what is unusual is that Shute does not assign the origin of the column orders to the Greeks, but derives them from Noah's Ark. In doing so, he attempts to reconcile the pagan sphere with the Christian sphere in the context of the Counter Reformation. Thus, the Greeks did not derive their architectural principles from nature. Rather, what served as a model was the architecture of the Tower of Babylon, as impressively presented by Peter Brueghel the

Elder (1525/30–1569) in the same year Shute's book was published.

Furthermore, Shute's definition of the general qualifications and duties of an architect is essentially based on Vitruvius' comments. For instance, Shute emphasizes how important a comprehensive knowledge of geometry, optics, arithmetic, music and astronomy is for an architect's complete training. The orders of columns as depicted in woodcuts are extremely sketchy, and scarcely convey the impression that Shute had actually studied the architecture in question *in natura*. Rather, he is guided by Serlio's *Regole generali di architettura sopra le cinque maniere degli edifici* (*General rules on the five orders of buildings*) of 1537, in which the five column orders are systematically elucidated for the first time. True, a complete English translation of Serlio's five books did not appear until 1611, under the direction of artist Robert Peake (1551–1619), but in the mid-16th century a copy of Serlio's fifth book on column orders already existed. It was produced by the Flemish painter Pieter Coecke van Aelst (1502–1550), so it seems likely that Shute was familiar with it given the intensive cultural exchange between Antwerp and London, especially in the field of architectural decoration.

Like Serlio, Shute begins with the Tuscan order and ends with the Composite order. However, he takes the anthropomorphic interpretation of architectural forms since Vitruvius a little too literally when he places a none-too-

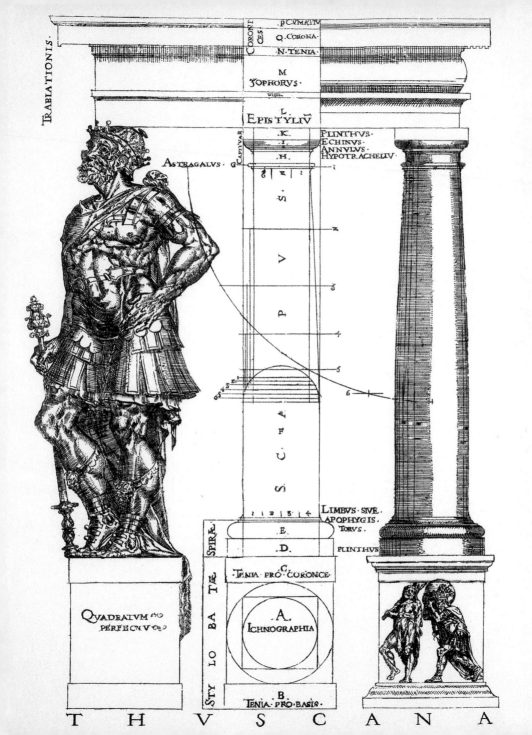

TRABIATIONIS.

P·CVMATIV
Q·CORONA·
N·TENIA·

M
JOPHORVS·

L
EPISTYLIV

·K·
·I·
·H·

PLINTHVS·
ECHINVS·
ANNVLVS·
HYPOTRACHELIV·

ASTRAGALVS· G

CAPITVLVM

S·

V

P

F

C

S

LIMBVS· SIVE·
APOPHYGIS·
TORVS·

E·

D·

PLINTHVS·

SPIRA·

TENIA· PRO· CORONCE

A·
ICHNOGRAPHIA

QVADRATVM
PERFECTVOR:

STYLOBATE·

B·
TENIA· PRO· BASIS·

CORONICES

T   H   U   S   C   A   N   A

well-formed caryatid at the side of each of his columns. Evidently, these sculptures are intended to express the columns' respective characters as determined by Vitruvius. For example, the Doric order stands for the male principle in the form of Hercules, and the Ionic symbolizes the female principle. Vitruvius himself describes it in his fourth book as the expression of "feminine gracefulness."

On the whole, the relatively superficial presentations of columns would seem to suggest that Shute was not really addressing architects with his treatise. Rather, his intention is to provide models of Classical decorations for all the arts. This becomes evident when he generally dedicates his remarks to goldsmiths, engravers, glaziers and other craftsmen. It should be remembered that Shute's publication appeared at a time when the arts were still largely viewed as a craft, as *artes mechanicae* or mechanical arts that managed without any theoretical or scientific foundation. Nowhere is this clearer than in the contemporary understanding of "design" as merely the artisan's study that precedes practical execution, in contrast to the Italian "disegno," the expression of the artistic idea shaped by scientific rules. For example, in his 1598 translation of Giovanni Paolo Lomazzo's *Trattato dell'arte della Pittura, Scultura ed Architettura* (1584) (*Treatise on the Art of Painting, Sculpture and Architecture / A Tracte containing the Artes of Curious Paintinge, Carvinge, and Buildinge*), Richard Haydocke still reduces the meaning of "disegno" to the mere outline sketch ("quantitie delineated"), and it is not until the mid-17th century that this expression is understood as referring to presentation of the "idea," and is thus clearly distinguished from mechanical drawing as an aid to execution. In connection with this general evaluation of artistic activity, for the first time in England the arts were granted the status of a science.

Thus it is no coincidence that it was only in this context that the architectural discourse in England transformed from the medieval understanding of "building" to the classical notion of "architecture." After all, apart from continental influences, it was above all English Late Gothic and its medieval concept of architecture that shaped English architecture up until the 17th century. Accordingly, Shute's reference to "architectura" is by no means a natural one in 16th-century England. In fact, in order to avoid confusing the reader, he initially describes architecture as "a manner of erecting excellent buildings."

Taking this idea as his starting point, the scholar John Dee (1527–1608) referred in his translation of Euclid's geometry (1570) to the architect as the intellectual co-ordinator (or "Chief Master" as he put it) of the various crafts, and architecture as one of the liberal arts ("Artes Mathematicall Derivative"). However, it was not until the architecture of Inigo Jones (1573–1652) at the start of the 17th century that the view of architecture as a science also asserted itself in practice, although Jones' argument with the poet Ben Jonson (1572–1637) on the status of architecture demonstrates that there was a long way to go before Shute's concept of architecture became generally accepted. The Secretary of the Royal Society, John Evelyn (1620–1706), therefore bemoaned in his *Account of Architects and Architecture* (1664) the English elite's lack of familiarity with the Classical architecture discussion, and consequently included an introduction to its basic expressions, which he referred to, following Vitruvius, as "firmness" (*firmitas*), "commodity" (*utilitas*) and "delight" (*venustas*). At the same time, Evelyn took the opportunity to alert his readers once again to the necessary distinction between the untrained mechanic and the highly-qualified architect or *Architectus Ingenio*. Evelyn considered the widespread ignorance about this distinction to be the cause of the poor architecture which he associated above all with the supposed deformed architectures, the "concentration of heavy, dark, melancholy and monastic pillars" of contemporary Baroque. In this context, Evelyn called for the first time in England for the establishment of a school of architecture to help ensure English architects met certain quality standards. However, this early thirst for an institutionalized form of architectural training was not to be satisfied until one hundred years after the foundation of the French Académie Royale d'Architecture (1671): The British Royal Academy opened in 1768. Shute's book on column orders represents a modest beginning in this context since he is the first to make people aware of the high set of qualifications required by an architect in the sense of Vitruvius.

CR

Fig. p. 229
1 | **Illustration of the Tuscan column order with Atlas**
Fol. IIII. Woodcut

2 | Illustration of the
Doric column order
with Herculean Atlas
Fol. VI. Woodcut

3 | Illustration of
Ionian column order
with caryatid
Fol. VIII. Woodcut

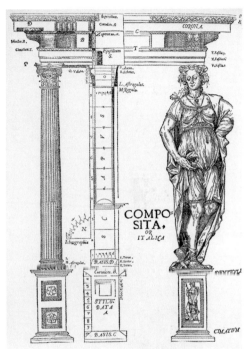

4 | **Illustration of Corinthian column order with caryatid**
Fol. XI. Woodcut

5 | **Illustration of Composite column order with caryatid**
Fol. XIIII. Woodcut

Henry Wotton (1568–1639)
The Elements of Architecture

LONDON, 1624

The work *The Elements of Architecture* by the English diplomat and scholar Henry Wotton, can, in many respects, be
considered the single most important architectural treatise
to be composed in England in the 17th century. It represents
the first intensive investigation of Vitruvius' theory of architecture within the context of English intellectual history. In
the context of European thought it forms part of the body of
new architectural criticism that was not written by architects
themselves but by amateurs interested in architecture. Such
attempts made architecture the topic of intellectual enquiry.
Accordingly, Wotton conceives his short essay not as a professional textbook with explanatory illustrations, and does
without pictures. His sole intention is to convey architectural
categories and quality standards that he considers vital to
enable a scholarly, aristocratic, lay public to form critical
judgements. Wotton's upgrading of the architecture critic
vis-à-vis the architect is in keeping with this objective. As he
explains: "I should thinke it almost harder to be a good Cen-
surer, then a good Architect: Because the working part may
be helped with Deliberation, but the Judging must flow from
an extemporall habite." The basis for such a judgement
stems from the training in the theory of architecture which
Wotton acquired during his frequent stays in Venice as English ambassador between 1604 and 1623. As one of the first
Englishmen or women with an interest in culture to travel to
Italy, Wotton's attention was drawn to the classical theory of
architecture from Vitruvius to Palladio. Essentially, he takes

Daniele Barbaro's translation of Vitruvius (1565) and Palladio's *Quattro libri* (1570) as his points of reference. Naturally,
Wotton is also familiar with the villas and palaces of the
Venetian Renaissance, which he saw on his diplomatic visits
to high-ranking Venetian personalities. As a guide to the
sights of Venice, he ultimately played an important role in
ensuring that English architects and other cultured tourists
noticed Palladio's architecture at all. Thus, Wotton was in-
strumental in paving the way for the English enthusiasm
for Palladio, which emerged following the first Palladian
plans by England's court architect Inigo Jones (1573–1652)
shortly before the publication of the *Elements*.

At an early point in his essay, Wotton emphasizes the
range of his architectural knowledge, never tiring from aver-
ring that Vitruvius had always been his "principal Master."
However, in keeping with the new liberties accorded the
critic, Wotton simultaneously points out some of his master's
errors. Having already made readers aware in the foreword
that Vitruvius had a truly pitiful style of writing, throughout
the rest of his work he repeatedly refers to the latter's non-
sensical prescriptions. For instance, he rejects the circle as
the ideal basic architectural form since it is of no use in the
field of private building; the entasis seems illogical to Wotton
since there is no example of it given by nature, and Vitruvius' instruction to make superposed columns a quarter
shorter than the columns below contradicts all the rules of
optics. Once Wotton has likewise rejected Vitruvius' fluted

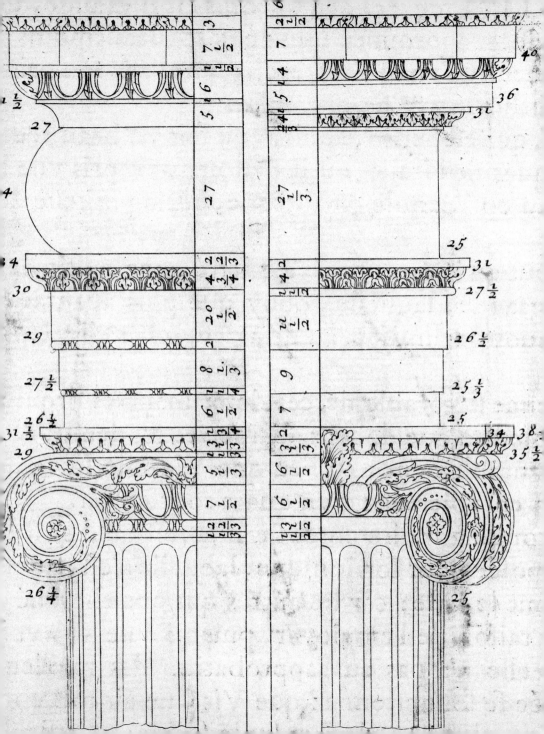

6

3

1½

27

4

34

30

29

27½

26½

31½

29

26¼

7½

6

5

27

2 2/3

4 3/4

20 ½

2

8 ½

2¼

6½

3¼

3 3/3

5½

7½

2 2/3

6

2½

7

5

2¼

40

36

3℄

25

3℄

27½

26½

25⅓

25

34 38

35½

27⅓

2

2¼

2½

9

7

3²

6½

6½

2½

25

columns, he is similarly scathing of the latter's concept of *venustas* (beauty or "delight"). He claims Vitruvius expressed himself very vaguely, and ultimately two of the six construction principles Vitruvius proposed were superfluous. For example, Wotton dismisses *ordinatio* (the principle of proportional order) and *dispositio* (of appropriate combination), and claims ingenuously that *eurythmia* (regularity), *symmetria* (proportion), *decor* (error-free and suitable execution), and *distributio* (economy of construction and propriety) were perfectly sufficient as architectural assessment criteria.

Wotton follows Vitruvius from a critical distance. This is already evident in the overall structure of his text, for unlike Vitruvius he accords greater importance to utilitarian aspects and thereby deviates from the architectural theory based on the three concepts of *firmitas* (robustness or "firmness"), *utilitas* (utility or "commodity") and *venustas* (beauty or "delight"). He sees the origin of all beauty in architecture as deriving from utility, and views the latter as a universal principle: " ... it plainly appeareth, as a Maxime drawn from Divine Light; That the Place of every Part, is to be determined by the Use."

All in all, in his *Elements* Wotton consistently assumes that empirical experience regulates theories of architectural principles, and in so doing he takes up a new scientific model that essentially was founded by Wotton's contemporary and friend Francis Bacon (1561–1626). After all, it was Bacon who in 1620, when laying the foundations for new science in his *Novum Organum*, described it as a virtue to liberate oneself from traditional theories and to observe objects in an unbiased manner. Ultimately, Bacon's own exploration of architecture also meets this dictum, for in his essay *Of Building* (1625) he concentrates solely on the aspect of "utility," and from it derives his critique of architecture. Based on everyday experience, he asserts that houses are not primarily built for their beauty but rather for reasons of commodity. As such, architectural beauty could no longer be derived from the cosmological concept of the universe, but had to seek its legitimacy through the empirically identifiable *utilitas* of the architecture. In this way, Bacon demystifies architecture.

Even though Wotton was strongly influenced by Bacon's empiricism, he nevertheless does not ignore the Vitruvian architectural tradition. Rather, taking the new empiricism as his point of departure he subjects it to critical examination, cloaking it in an easily understandable form for the circles of amateurs he is addressing. It is also in keeping with the particular interest of this group in the building of country properties that Wotton's chief focus is on the correct location for a manor house, and its creative complementation through painting, sculpture and landscaping. Once again, in this field the traditional comments on Italian villa architecture are examined to see how they stand up in the light of practical experience. After Wotton has dealt with hygienic and climatic matters, as well as the aspect of *firmitas*, he ascertains that by his notion of commodity, the enfilades of classical Italian villas are impractical for the colder regions of England, and must therefore be rejected: "The thing I meane, is, that they so cast their partitions as when all Doors are open a man may see through the whole House, which doth necessarily put an intollerable servitude upon all the Chambers save the Inmost... A thing most insufferable, in cold & windie Regions..." His underscoring of man's personal experience is in line with his emphasis on the special quality of human vision ("Royaltie of Sight"). He argues that the garden of a manor house should be arranged to satisfy the latter, by providing a wide variety of aesthetic attractions that contrast with the strict regularity of the architecture itself. And in the same way as the garden's arrangement should underline the effect of the architecture, painting and sculpture are also subordinated to the overall work of art, the country home. In this context, Wotton repeatedly appeals to the aristocrat's critical powers of reasoning, arguing that he should not let his appraisal of art be influenced either by the authority of great artists' names or the unchallenged nature of artistic and architectural conventions. Rather, Wotton demands that logic should serve as a measure of criticism, and thus goes some way anticipating the critical method of Claude Perrault (1613–1688). It becomes clear that Wotton views critical judgement based on logic to be part of a larger pedagogical framework when, at the close of his treatise, he refers to another planned essay dealing precisely with "Morall Architecture."

It is above all due to Wotton's own "moral architecture" in his critical exploration of Vitruvius' architectural doctrine that the *Elements* was accorded much importance well into the 18th century. Just as English enthusiasm for the villa reached its climax, his architectural work was re-published in 1723 together with the English translation (*A Comparison of Classical and Modern Architecture*) of Fréart de Chambray's *Parallele de l'architecture antique et de la moderne* (first published in French in 1650), Alberti's *De Statua* (c. 1434), and John Evelyn's *Account of Architects and Architecture* (1644). The most prominent English authors and architects from John Harris through to Isaac Ware (c. 1707–1766) always referred to Wotton as the first authority on architectural theory in England.

CR

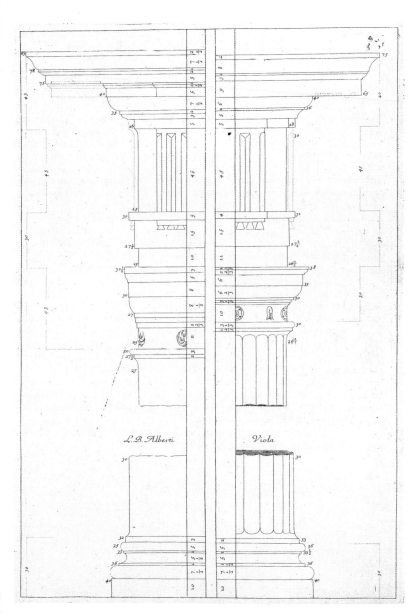

L. B. Alberti

Viola

1 | Illustration of Doric
column order according to
Leon Battista Alberti and
Gioseffe Viola Zanini
*In: Roland Fréart de
Chambray*, Parallèle de
l'architecture antique et de
la moderne, *Paris, 1650.
English ed. from 1723, together
with Wotton's* Elements, *p. 29*

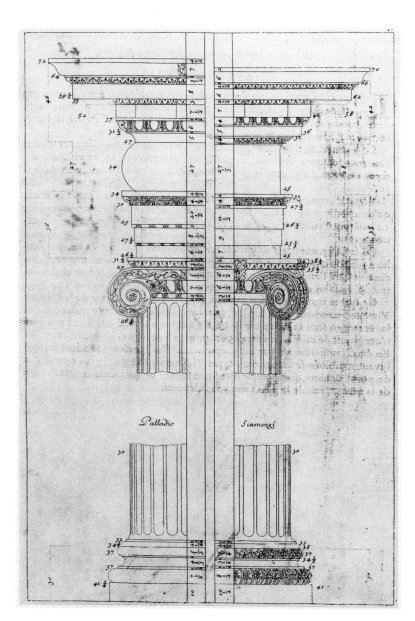

Palladio

Scamozzi

2 | Illustration of Ionian
column order according
to Andrea Palladio and
Vincenzo Scamozzi
In: Roland Fréart de
Chambray, Parallèle de
l'architecture antique et de
la moderne, Paris, 1650.
English ed. from 1723, together
with Wotton's Elements, p. 43

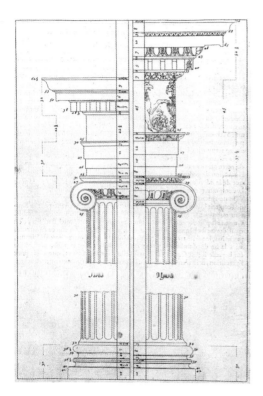

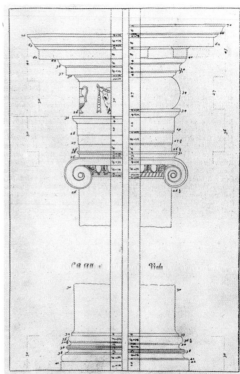

3 | **Illustration of Ionian column order according to**
Sabastiano Serlio and Vignola
In: Roland Fréart de Chambray, Parallèle de l'architecture antique et de la
moderne, *Paris, 1650. English ed. from 1723, together with Wotton's*
Elements, *p. 45*

4 | **Illustration of Ionian column order according to**
Leon Battista Alberti and Gioseffe Viola Zanini
In: Roland Fréart de Chambray, Parallèle de l'architecture antique et de la
moderne, *Paris, 1650. English ed. from 1723, together with Wotton's*
Elements, *p. 49*

Colen Campbell (1676–1729)
Vitruvius Britannicus

3 VOLS, LONDON, 1715–1725

The three-volume publication *Vitruvius Britannicus* by the English architect Colen Campbell is considered to be the manifesto that established English Palladianism. However, the work in question is not a literary reflexion but an extravagant compendium of illustrated plates containing a total of 295 architecture engravings. The text section consists of no more than a brief foreword to the first volume, and explanations of the illustrations. Nonetheless, the publication's objective is expressed unambiguously by the title. For the first time in the history of English architecture, attention was drawn to the genuine achievements of the English architect, the "Vitruvius Britannicus."

Accordingly, in the 100 engravings of his first volume Campbell presents a panoramic view of English architecture since the early 17th century. In this context the works of Andrea Palladio (1508–1580) are mentioned as the greatest model for English architecture. Indeed, their influence is already evident, he says, in plans by the English architect Inigo Jones (1573–1652) for the Banqueting House in Whitehall (1619–1622) and the Queen's House at Greenwich (1616–1635), which even surpassed Palladio's work in beauty. In the first volume Campbell presents these projects by Jones, in the second volume he also shows Jones' proposals for Whitehall as well as the architecture for the piazza at Covent Garden. He also maintains that there was also an abundance of great architects ("learned and ingenious Gentlemen") in his day, such as Christopher Wren (1632–1723),

John Vanbrugh (1664–1726), Nicholas Hawksmoor (1661–1736) and John James (1672–1746), "who have all greatly contributed to adorn our Island with their curious Labours." As such it is surprising at first that Campbell begins the introduction to his first volume by presenting St Peter's in Rome. However, seen in connection with his highly polemic foreword, in which he rejects the Baroque architecture of Gianlorenzo Bernini (1598–1680), Francesco Borromini (1599–1667) and Carlo Fontana (1638–1714) as "licentious," the purpose of this example becomes clear. For Campbell it represents the sum total of all architectural mistakes and therefore functions as a contrasting backdrop against which the special achievements of the English architects are expected to shine forth in an even brighter light. Campbell cleverly formulates his criticism of this building as being the general consensus of all architectural critics. ("The Criticks generally condemn the excessive Height of the Attick ... That the Pediment, supported by a Tetrastyle, is mean for so great a Front, which at least would demand an Hexastyle; that the Breaks are trifling, and the Parts without any Proportion ...")

Indeed, for Campbell St Peter's is by no means merely an especially striking expression of architectural abuses on the Continent: it also stands for Italy's cultural decline. As such he emphasizes in his foreword that in the post-Palladian era Italy had not only become estranged from the true "taste of building," but also from the roots of its culture, the Latin language. From this perspective, Italy could no longer

be the destination of the Grand Tour. Campbell considers such undertakings to be "Mistakes in Education." As the *Vitruvius Britannicus* is intended to demonstrate, it is now the architects and artists of England who are to take Italy's place as the preservers of timeless, classical taste.

Campbell's self-confident support for English culture is to be seen against the background of the general national euphoria following the stabilization of political conditions after the Whig party assumed power in 1714. A prominent Whig, Anthony Ashley Cooper, 3rd Earl of Shaftesbury, had already, in his 1712 *Letter concerning the Art, or Science of Design,* called for an anti-Baroque national architecture founded on a well-informed taste. Not only could the Baroque not meet Shaftesbury's aesthetic objectives, it was also viewed in England as the symbol of an absolutism and Roman Catholicism that was thought to have been overcome. However, Shaftesbury's criticism did not stop short at the architecture of the English Baroque, which he primarily identifies with Christopher Wren's work. In contrast to the latter, Shaftesbury commends the architectural and artistic simplicity of Classicism as an expression of particularly enlightened rationalism.

With his *Vitruvius Britannicus* Campbell takes up this call and fleshes it out by defining Palladian architecture as the due expression of this ideal. Unlike Shaftesbury, however, Campbell is at pains to present the development of English architecture since the early 17th century as a homogeneous national trend, which amazingly – in contrast to Shaftesbury – even includes England's great Baroque architects. In order to foster this new national identity, Campbell reserves his spite for continental Baroque. This explains why after St Peter's, he chooses to present St Paul's Cathedral by Christopher Wren and in particular Wren's design for the Greenwich Hospital (1704). He pays tribute to Wren's pupil John Vanbrugh for Blenheim Palace (1705–1724) and Castle Howard (1699–1712), which he refers to respectively as a "noble fabrick" and a "noble seat." Nonetheless, Campbell cannot wholly deny that influences other than Palladio played an important role in these buildings. Consequently, Campbell presents himself as the architect who actually overcomes the Baroque, by following Wren's St Paul's Cathedral with his own ideal design for a church "most conformable to the Simplicity of the Ancients." In other words, Campbell's motivation is not entirely disinterested; indeed, his book served as an effective means of promoting his own work.

Another person who also vied for the favour of Whig clients was the Venetian architect Giacomo Leoni (1686–1746),

whose translation (1716) of Palladio's *Quattro libri* was deliberately published around the same time to compete with Campbell's publication. Leoni had moved to England in 1715 to capitalize on the English enthusiasm for Palladian architecture. However, his hopes of success were in part unfounded. For while Leoni realized several Palladian projects such as Queensbury House (1721) or Argyll House (1723), he did not land a truly major success. In fact, his Palladio translation quickly came to be viewed as a disparagement of the great model, and was replaced by Isaac Ware's solid rendition (1738).

By contrast, the *Vitruvius Britannicus* was an enormous success for Campbell. All the more so since prior to the work's publication he was hardly known as an architect, and it was only due to its publication that he received a long list of commissions to design country houses for English aristocrats. Alongside the aforementioned church in the first volume of *Vitruvius Britannicus,* an important inclusion is Campbell's influential project for Wanstead House, which he created for Richard Child between 1715 and 1720. Campbell succeeded in producing a synthesis of the traditional English country house and the Palladian villa, and thus developed the prototype for a whole series of country manors that were subsequently built by Palladian architects, such as Wentworth (1733) by Henry Flitcroft, or Prior Park (1735) by John Wood. Campbell devoted the third volume of *Vitruvius Britannicus* (1725) to documenting the successful creative period that followed the first volume's publication. In addition to views of Burlington House (1717), Houghton (1722), Stourhead (1721) and Lord Herbert's house (1723–1724), he also included his copy of a rotunda for Mereworth Castle (1722), as well as the early designs of his patron Lord Burlington (1694–1753).

All in all, there is no underestimating the influence of *Vitruvius Britannicus* on English architecture. Both Campbell's panorama of English architecture as well as the presentation of his own designs make this lavish publication a virtually inexhaustible trove of architectural ideas, which like the later "pattern books" was to exert a considerable influence on architectural practice. Campbell's Palladianism also had an indirect influence on the architectural thinking of his patron Lord Burlington, who following a trip to Italy in 1719 himself became an architect and finally replaced Campbell at the head of the Palladian movement. Owing to his comprehensive archive of Palladian studies of Classical buildings and design sketches, Burlington developed a stringent form of Classicism quite unparalleled in his day.

CR

Extends 400.

a Scale of 200 Feet

The Elevation of S! PETERS CHURCH at ROME Founded by CONSTANTIN the Great Anno 310. The present Fabrick was begun by
POPE IULIUS the II conducted by BRAMANTE Anno 1513 to whom SANGALLO and the Famous MICHEL ANGELO BONAROTI Succeeded.
The Frontispeece and Body of the CHURCH was Erected by P. PAUL the V. under the direction of CARLO MADERNO 1613. and the Balustrade and
other Ornaments were added by CAVALIER BERNINI 1640.

L'Eglise De S! PIERRE a ROME .

Co Campbell Delin:

1 | Façade of Christopher Wren's St. Peter's Basilica
Vol. I, pl. 6. Engraving

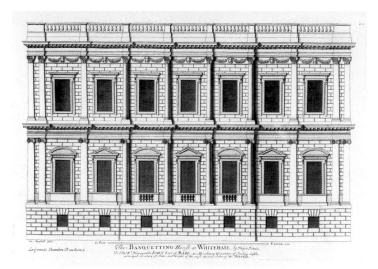

2 | Façade of Inigo Jones' Banqueting House
Vol. I, pl. 13. Engraving

3 | Alternative façade for Colen Campbell's design for Wanstead House
Vol. I, pl. 22. Engraving

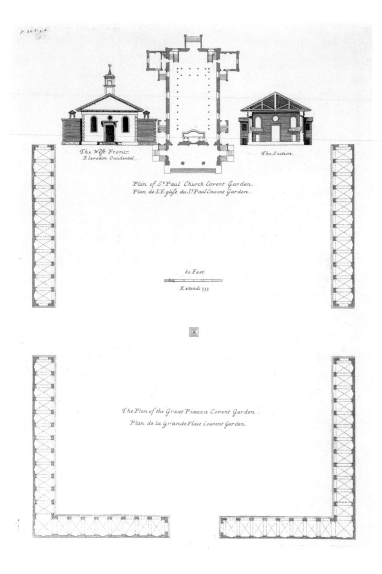

p.20.V.2.4

The West Front.
Elevation Occidental.

Plan of St Paul Church Covent Garden.
Plan de L'Eglise du St Paul Covent Garden.

The Section.

60 Feet.
Extends 333

The Plan of the Great Piazza Covent Garden.
Plan de la Grande Place Covent Garden.

4 | Inigo Jones' design for the square at Covent Garden, ground plan
Vol. II, pl. 20. Engraving

5 | View of Inigo Jones' architecture on the square at Covent Garden
Vol. II, pls. 21 and 22. Engraving

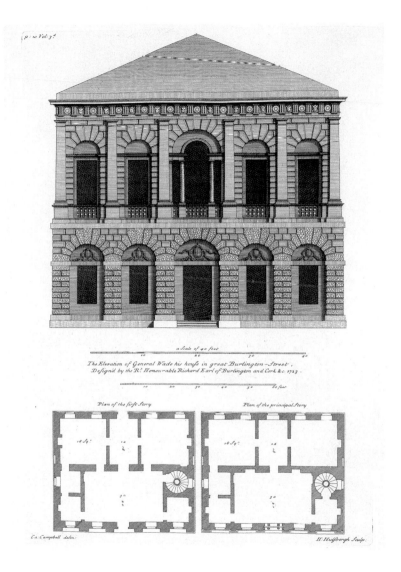

The Elevation of General Wade his house in great Burlington-Street,
Design'd by the R.t Honour-able Richard Earl of Burlington and Cork &c. 1723.

Plan of the first Story

Plan of the principal Story

Ca: Campbell delin:

H: Hulsbergh Sculp:

6 | **Façade and ground plan for Lord Burlington's General Wade House**
Vol. III, pl. 10. Engraving

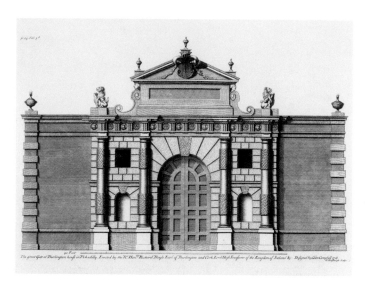

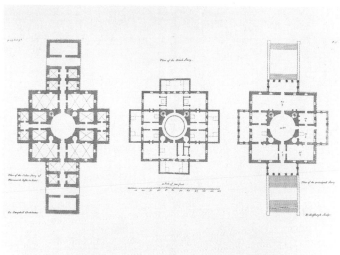

7 | Campbell's design of a gate for Burlington House at Piccadilly
Vol. III, pl. 25. Engraving

8 | Ground plans for Campbell's rotunda variant at Mereworth Castle
Vol. III, pls. 35 and 36. Engraving

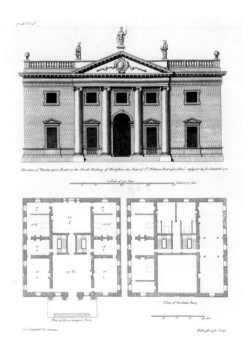

9 | View of Campbell's rotunda variant at Mereworth Castle
Vol. III, pl. 37. Engraving

10 | Façade and ground plan for Campbell's design for Stourhead Castle
Vol. III, pl. 46. Engraving

James Gibbs (1682–1754)

A Book of Architecture, Containing Designs of Buildings and Ornaments

LONDON, 1728

Rules for Drawing the Several Parts of Architecture

LONDON, 1732

The *Book of Architecture* by English architect James Gibbs is the first English architectural publication to only contain plans by the author, and is intended to serve as a pattern book. In contrast to the numerous pattern books by other authors, however, Gibbs' book does not address practising architects but rather "such Gentlemen as might be concerned in Building, especially in the remote parts of the Country, where little or no assistence for Design can be procured." In other words, in the manner of his great model Andrea Palladio, Gibbs intends to improve the inadequate education of provincial architects by providing examples from his own practical (and to his mind, professional) experience in order to avoid "abuses" in architecture. In a sense, Gibbs' *Book of Architecture* provides a store of architectural forms from which the layman is expected to select the suitable subjects for any of a wide variety of construction tasks. Accordingly, it contains a whole series of different projects from church building to villa architecture. This set of folios is rounded off by details for interior decorations such as doors, windows and fireplaces. Gibbs emphasizes in the introduction that he produced the latter "in the best taste," in other words on the basis of his substantial knowledge of Italian architecture.

However, Gibbs' motivation for this unusual project is by no means restricted to conveying correct architectural subjects, but is also to be understood as a response to the architectural doctrine of the Palladians. Indeed, Gibbs' concept of taste coincides perfectly with the Palladian movement when he sees his ideal of architectural beauty realized in a simple, and virtually unadorned façade: "It is not the Bulk of a Fabrick, the Richness and Quantity of Materials, the Multiplicity of Lines, nor the Gaudiness of Finishing, that give Grace or Beauty and Grandeur to the Building; but the Proportion of the Parts to one another and to the Whole, whether entirely plain, or enriched with a few Ornaments properly disposed." Nevertheless, it emerges that Gibbs' designs are not only influenced by Palladian architecture, but above all by the buildings of Christopher Wren (1632–1723), and the Italian Baroque. Moreover, it is evident from the preface to the *Book of Architecture* that Gibbs harbours no liking for Colen Campbell's (1676–1729) architectural doctrine that had been expounded once again in the third volume of the *Vitruvius Britannicus* of 1725. Gibbs likens orthodox Palladianism to a "dictatorship of taste" that does not allow any architectural alternatives, and therefore must be viewed as an unnatural restriction of taste. In this Gibbs anticipates the more liberal concept of taste favoured by the English poet Alexander Pope (1688–1744), who in a letter on the subject dated 1731 places intuitive feeling or "sense" above "taste," and accordingly rejected the mere copying of Palladian architecture as inadmissible.

This discussion on taste must also be viewed against the background of opposing political views. Gibbs did not share Campbell's Whig sympathies. As a convinced Catholic

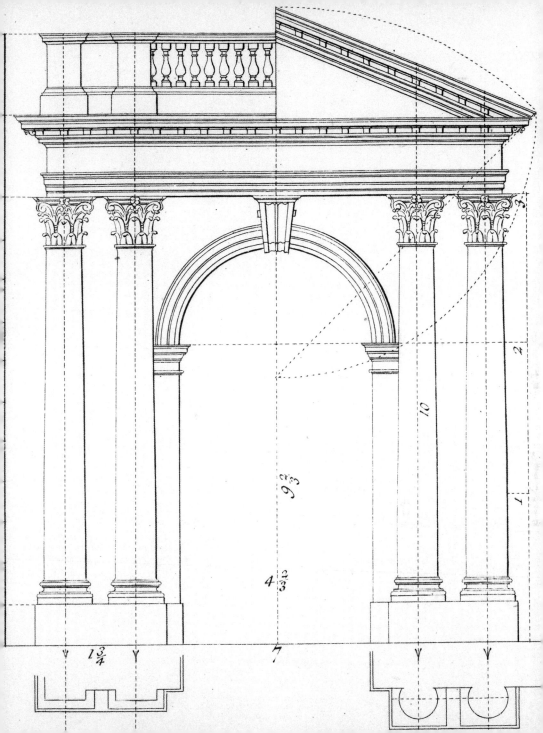

and Tory who supported the expelled Stuarts, he brought together the values and ideas of English absolutism. As a result, his patrons tended to come mainly from the Tory aristocracy, who had lost their power when the Hanoverians ascended the throne. It follows then that his buildings could not be interpreted as an adequate expression of the new situation. Rather, they could only be viewed as symbolic of the old, non-enlightened England. Gibbs did not attempt to disguise the fact that he sympathized with Italy's Baroque architecture so criticized by Campbell. Fully aware that he was the only English architect of his generation to enjoy a training in Italy, he even emphasizes how much he learned from the Italian masters of the Baroque. Specifically, Gibbs worked between 1703 and 1709 in the office of the Roman architect Carlo Fontana (1638–1714), whose "licentious" architecture Campbell mocked.

Against the background of these irreconcilable differences, it makes sense that Lord Burlington decided to replace the Tory architect Gibbs by Campbell for the renovation of his house in Piccadilly, and thus to ensure that his town house would be remodelled along the lines of the new Palladian architectural ideal. In the third volume of his *Vitruvius Britannicus*, Campbell presents his project for Burlington without making any mention of his predecessor, who is otherwise totally ignored in this presentation of English architecture. Despite this open rejection of his person, at the time that Gibbs was writing his *Book of Architecture* he could look back on a successful career, even though his divergent political views precluded his being awarded the really important assignments. For instance, in 1713 he was appointed one of the surveyors for the Fifty New Churches in London, and through his projects for St Mary-Le-Strand (1714–1717), St Martin-in-the-Fields (1722–1726), and country houses such as Ditchley (1720–1722) or Sudbrooke Lodge (c. 1728), he was able to realize several important projects of renown. He must have been all the more annoyed that Campbell's table book on English architecture contained none of his designs, although other representatives of the English Baroque such as John Vanbrugh (1664–1726) and Nicholas Hawksmoor (1661–1736) were included. The fact that Gibbs only presents his own designs in his *Book of Architecture* can be understood as a response to this systematic ignoring of his own work. Moreover, Gibbs' preface sometimes reads like a direct response to Campbell's foreword in the first volume of *Vitruvius Britannicus*. In contrast to the latter he emphasizes the importance of a trip to Italy for an architect's training, and simultaneously criticizes those architects who, like Campbell, never studied the great Italian architectural models, and were therefore at best in possession of superficial architectural knowledge, "... for a cursory View of those August Remains can no more qualify the Spectator, or Admirer, than the Air of the Country can inspire him with the knowledge of Architecture." By underscoring the importance of drawing skills and the study of Classical and Italian models for an architect's training – in keeping with the traditional view – Gibbs is guided by Palladio's maxims unlike the amateur architects Campbell and Burlington. This gives rise to the paradox that the representatives of English Palladianism totally ignore the architectural practice of Palladio, the intensive study of Classical Antiquity, while Gibbs, acting as the intermediary between the Baroque and Palladianism, continues to support it.

Gibbs' second publication, entitled *Rules for Drawing the Several Parts of Architecture* (1732), is also to be seen in this context. Basically, the book follows the tradition of the books presenting column orders since Serlio. It can be interpreted as a concession to the Palladian movement that Gibbs adopts Palladio's column proportions, which like Claude Perrault (1613–1688) before him in *Ordonnance des Cinq espèces de colonnes*, 1683 (*Instructions for the five orders of columns*), he then transfers on to a simplified calculation system. However, unlike Perrault's book on columns, Gibbs' publication does not contain any theoretical reflexion on the status or character of the five column orders. Gibbs did not feel inclined to make such speculations since he was little interested in citing either the architects of the Palladian circle or his own publications in theoretical justification of his architectural œuvre. Gibbs' intention was restricted to a visual aesthetics like the numerous pattern books of William Halfpenny (d. 1755) or Batty Langley (1696–1751), even though in his *Book of Architecture* there is greater evidence than in other pattern books of a classical architectural attitude. Unlike the Palladians, it allowed for various influences, and for this reason attracted a wide public even after the English enthusiasm for Palladio diminished. This is the only explanation for the fact that Gibbs' architecture books exerted considerable influence on architectural activity in Great Britain over a lengthy period of time, not to mention America in the late 18th and early 19th centuries.

CR

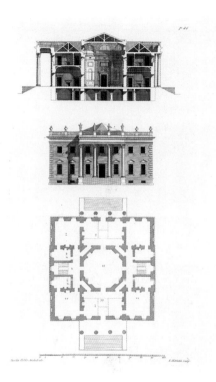

1 | **Western façade of the design for the church of St. Mary-le-Strand**
Pl. 17. Engraving

2 | **Cross-section, view and ground plan for a house with a Corinthian portico and an octagonal hall**
Pl. 44. Engraving

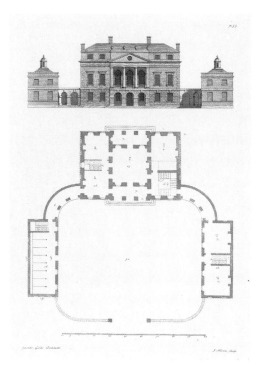

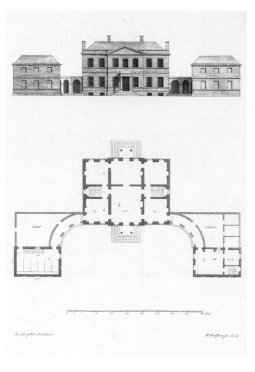

3 | View und ground plan of a house for Matthew Prior in
Down Hall/Essex
Pl. 55. Engraving

4 | Design for a house in Yorkshire
Pl. 63. Engraving

5 | Designs for garden pavilions for Count Cobham in Stowe
Pl. 77. Engraving

6 | Designs for garden pavilions for Count Cobham in Stowe
Pl. 78. Engraving

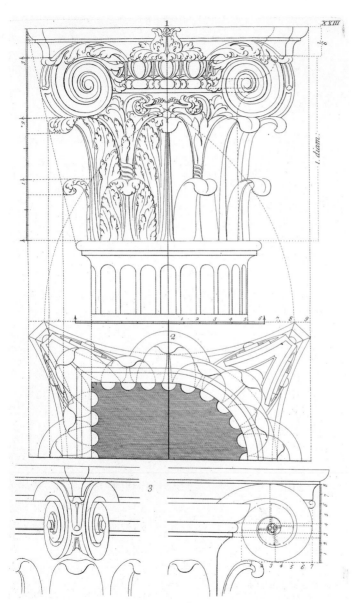

7 | **The Composite capital**
2nd ed. London, 1736, pl. 23. Engraving

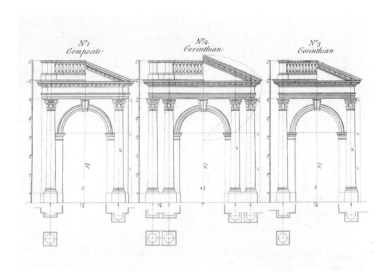

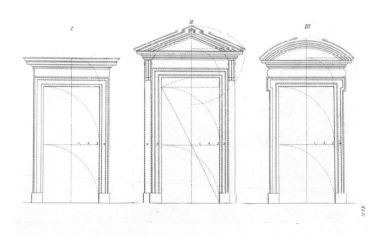

8 | **Composite and Corinthian variants of arcades and gables**
2nd ed. London, 1736, pl. 40. Engraving

9 | **Various door designs**
2nd ed. London, 1736, pl. 42. Engraving

Robert Morris (1701–1754)

An Essay in Defence of Ancient Architecture

LONDON, 1728

Lectures on Architecture

LONDON, 1734–1736

The English amateur architect Robert Morris delivered the ultimate theory on English Palladianism in the course of a whole series of writings such as his *Essay in Defence of Ancient Architecture*, his *Lectures on Architecture,* the *Essay upon Harmony* (1739), and *The Art of Architecture* (1742). This makes it all the more amazing that so little is known about Morris, even though he must doubtless be considered a member of the closer circle of Palladians. Evidence of this would, for example, be the fact that Morris rated particularly highly the architecture of his prominent relation, the Palladian architect Roger Morris (1695–1749), and by way of emphasizing this esteem, dedicated to the latter the second part of his *Lectures* (1736).

However, Morris certainly did not view himself as an architect. Indeed, he repeatedly points out that he has no interest in the constructional theories pertaining to architecture. By contrast, he refers to himself in *The Art of Architecture* as a "poetical architect" who views writing about architecture as a literary art that serves solely to reflect on the beauty of architecture. As such, the contents of his œuvre differ radically from those of the traditional architectural treatise. Nonetheless, Morris' writings are not restricted to some general definition of the beauty in architecture. They constantly serve to justify contemporary Palladianism as a normative taste, and as such already hint at the specific connection made in the 18th century between architectural theory and aesthetics. Accordingly, it is only logical that Morris

scarcely refers to Vitruvius' architectural theory in order to establish his architectural aesthetics. Above all the aesthetic models of the early English Enlightenment, as articulated by the philosophers Anthony Ashley Cooper, 3rd Earl of Shaftesbury (1671–1713) and Francis Hutcheson (1694–1746), as well as the journalist Joseph Addison (1672–1719) and the poet Alexander Pope (1688–1744), provide Morris with his theoretical tools.

However, an essential problem of the new aesthetics was the attempt – given the increasingly subjective focus of philosophical questions since the late 17th century – to arrive at a universally binding definition of taste. He considered the concept of a "man of taste" to deliver a solution to this problem, for such a notion was founded solely on inherent morality, rather than referring to an abstract idea that judges objects of sensual perception to be beautiful or ugly, and applies the words "pleasure" or "dislike" to express this judgement. The concept of a moral sense derived from classical notions of order was intended to guarantee that the aesthetically active subject would only feel attracted by objects that were likewise classically composed. Accordingly, the symmetry, proportion and stereometrics of Classical architecture ultimately reflected the components of a beautiful soul, which Shaftesbury contended was the work of art proper to the enlightened "man of taste." Thus the appraisal of Classical architecture was ordained by nature and did not require any further justification.

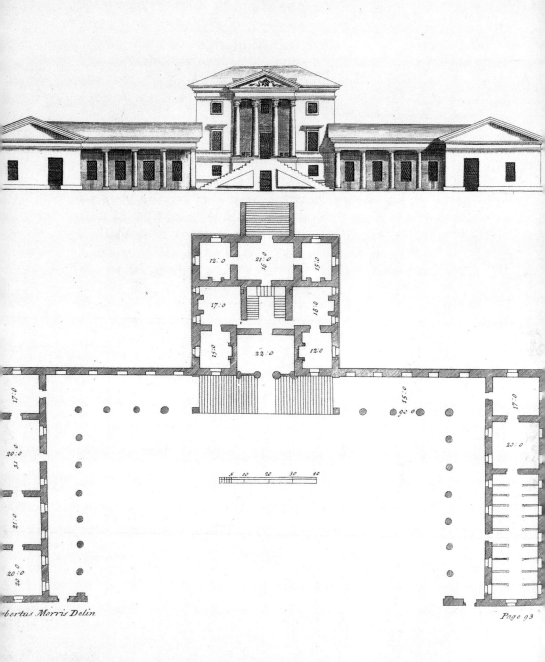

In line with this self-evident conviction, Morris likewise assumes that there is a special correspondence between the structure of the mind and artistic architecture. However, the latter's emotional character meant that there was no means of describing it more precisely, and it thus eluded a concrete definition of architectural beauty in the sense of the Italian Renaissance. Beauty revealed itself in the act of spontaneous, sensory perception, and its effect on the observer. Since aesthetic feeling is now raised to the status of a criterion for appraising beauty, the architectural object is only interesting inasmuch as it must convey the impression of architectural order to the beholder: beauty is only characterized in very general terms as "order in disposition, and variety in matter." At the same time this should not be understood as a plea for permissiveness in building. On the contrary, the aesthetic approach to architectural questions initially led paradoxically to a greater demand for architectural classicism, which should guided by Palladianism. Aesthetically, architecture should have a more austere and rational impact than contemporary Baroque offerings. In this context, the Baroque is rejected since its supposed lack of regularity is also understood as an expression of moral deformity in the guise of continental absolutism.

In his more systematic *Lectures on Architecture*, Morris takes up this conceptual model once again, claiming that "a Plain regular Front, without Dress or Ornament, if justly proportion'd will better satisfy the Taste of the judicious, and more immediately strike the Eye, than all the gay Dress and Decoration of an ill proportion'd Design: There is a kind of sympathizing Pleasure from Nature, when a just Proportion is observ'd in the Performance of a Building." Morris' design of a villa in chapter 12 of his *Lectures* can be understood as an illustration of this architectural ideal. It is based completely on his own schematic proportional system of cubes. The villa has a virtually unadorned, nine-unit façade, and Morris only creates highlights in the form of the Ionic portico, the dome with its graduated tambour and the pyramid roofs of the two wings. However, the simplicity Morris demanded was not to be restricted to the field of architecture. Rather, his *Lectures* define the country house as a complete work of art, combining architecture and garden design. However, while for him architectural simplicity rests on a particular form of classicism, Morris understands simplicity of garden design in the sense of the English landscape garden, as an art with a subtle effect, which, unlike the geometry of Baroque parks, attempts to perfect nature using its own means.

Considered superficially, Morris' comments on the English country house seem at first sight to be a reference to those chapters of classical architectural literature listing the criteria for selecting a suitable building location. Yet it rapidly emerges that Morris' interpretation of "situation" has little in common with the traditional understanding of the Latin term *situs*. On the contrary, he brings his own aesthetic beliefs to bear in developing a theory of the Palladian country house that only takes into account the house's aesthetic impact and not the aspects of "convenience." This is evident when Morris adopts a painter's viewpoint in considering the correct choice of location for a villa. Accordingly, Morris sites his villa designs on hills, from where the observer might enjoy a view of a Classical landscape à la Claude Lorrain with Classical buildings, ("some distant landscape, a beautiful Prospect to a fruitful Vale, or some remarkable Objects"). "Serpentine Walks" provide access to the garden and villa, and he intended that these paths should likewise afford attractive views of the temple and other Classical buildings.

Morris suggests that the architecture of Lord Burlington (1694–1753) represents the prime realization of this exacting task. Burlington's life corresponds exactly with the aesthetic ideal of the "man of taste." An amateur architect trained in the Palladian school, he always realized his designs in co-operation with the architects of his circle, and was willing to forgo seeing his own ideas manifested on paper. Like Morris, Burlington was interested in architecture solely as an art. Only against this background does it become clear why in Chiswick House (1725–1729) Burlington was prepared to forgo all functional purpose of the architecture in favour of the new aesthetic approach. In this instance, architecture is viewed as an autonomous art that has almost completely liberated itself from specifications dictated by architectural theories. The comparison of Morris' aesthetics and Burlington's architectural objectives would seem to suggest that here we have an *avant-la-lettre* formulation of the concept of architecture as an autonomous art, as would be expressed in a much more extreme form in the aesthetic architectural visions of Étienne Boullée (1728–1799), towards the end of the century. The special quality of Morris' writings lies in the fact that they represent the first and only summary of the architectural aesthetic thinking that characterized the early 18th century, both as a return to the design ideal of the Renaissance and also as a precursor of the new architectural aesthetics.

CR

Fig. p. 259

1 | **Elevation and ground plan of a villa**
The design is based on Palladio's Villa Ragona.
P. 93. Engraving

2 | **Design for the façade of a villa**
The design is reminiscent of Roger Morris' villa, Marble Hill.
P. 84. Engraving

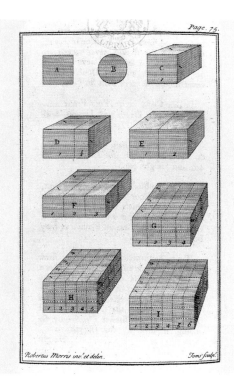

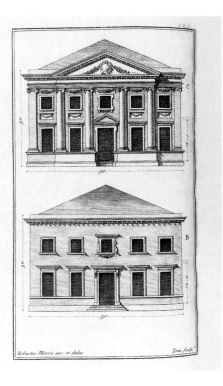

3 | **Morris' system for the proportion of space**
2nd ed., London, 1759, p. 75. Engraving

4 | **Study for an ornament for a façade**
2nd ed., London, 1759, p. 127. Engraving

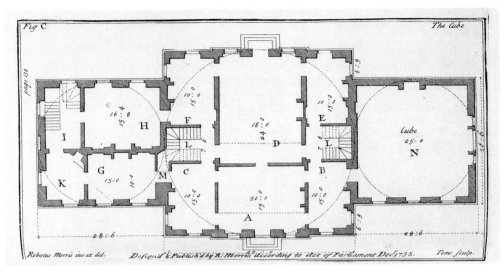

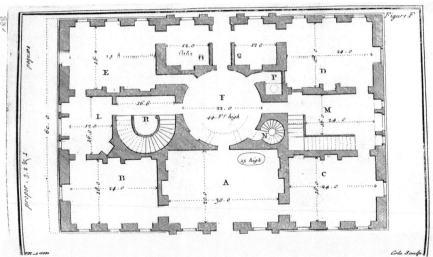

5 | Ground plan of an ideal Palladian villa with an Ionian portico
2ⁿᵈ ed., London, 1759, p. 138. Engraving

6 | Ground plan of an idealized Palladian villa with a dome
2ⁿᵈ ed., London, 1759, p. 188. Engraving

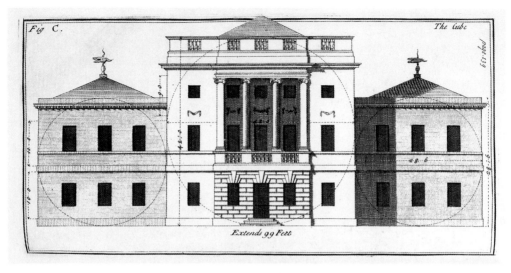

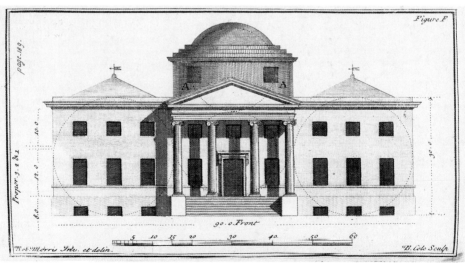

7 | View of an idealized Palladian villa with a dome
2nd ed., London, 1759, p. 139. Engraving

8 | View of an idealized Palladian villa with a dome
2nd ed., London, 1759, p. 189. Engraving

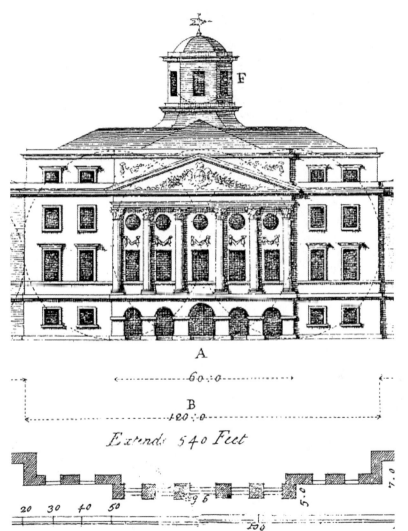

9 | **Design of a large
Palladian country palace**
*2ⁿᵈ ed., London, 1759,
p. 201. Engraving*

Isaac Ware (um 1707–1766)

A Complete Body of Architecture

LONDON, 1756

This work by the Palladian architect Isaac Ware is an architectural treatise of encyclopaedic dimensions. *A Complete Body of Architecture* addresses both property owners and architects, since it was Ware's intention to present a comprehensive treatment of architecture in all its facets. This objective is underscored by the external form of his publication, which through its division into ten books (a "compleat library on this subject") is influenced, in appearance at least, by Vitruvius and Alberti. By contrast, as regards content, Ware refers to questions of more recent and contemporary architectural theory, which he attempts to reconcile with his Palladian architectural ideal.

Ware was one of the most prominent architects in the Palladian circle around Lord Burlington (1694–1753), whose extensive patronage he enjoyed. Ware made a strong name for himself both as regards practical building matters and in literary terms as an authority on Palladian architecture – both through his designs for Palladian manor houses such as Clifton Hill House (1746–1750) and Wrotham Park (1754), and various early works on architecture such as *Designs of Inigo Jones and others* (1731) or *Four Books of Andrea Palladio's Architecture* (1738), with which he provided England with the first sound translation of Andrea Palladio's *Quattro libri*. Accordingly, in his foreword to *Four Books* Ware sets himself off from the earlier Palladio translations by Giacomo Leoni (1716) and Edward Hoppus (1735), which were somewhat careless, incomplete interpretations of the great original.

With his book *A Complete Body of Architecture* he ultimately pursues no less ambitious a goal than to render superfluous those publications that had previously appeared on architecture, and to explain architecture "from its first rudiments to its utmost Perfection." In this context, Ware attaches great importance to the didactic treatment of this complex project. Indeed, after the preface he includes an extensive glossary of architectural terms from "Abacus," "Ancient Manner," "French Order," through to "modern" and "Zoophoros." As an initial basis for instruction, this system of architecture is intended to provide a brief survey of the diverse connections in architecture, and ultimately to act as an introduction to the comments following in the *Complete Body*.

In the latter, Ware refers constantly to *utilitas*, utility/commodity, as the paramount principle of architecture. In doing so he consciously joins the debate on the side that opposes a completely aesthetic approach. Nonetheless, it is evident that Ware was open to the aesthetic architectural concepts of his time, when in his chapter on locations, or as he calls them "situations," he takes up the aesthetic concept of the English landscaped garden as that of a "moving picture." However, Ware considers such aspects to only be of relevance once due consideration has been given to meeting the practical constructional specifications.

Hence it is only logical that Ware, in common with his great model Palladio, begins his publication with an investigation of different building materials, before elaborating the

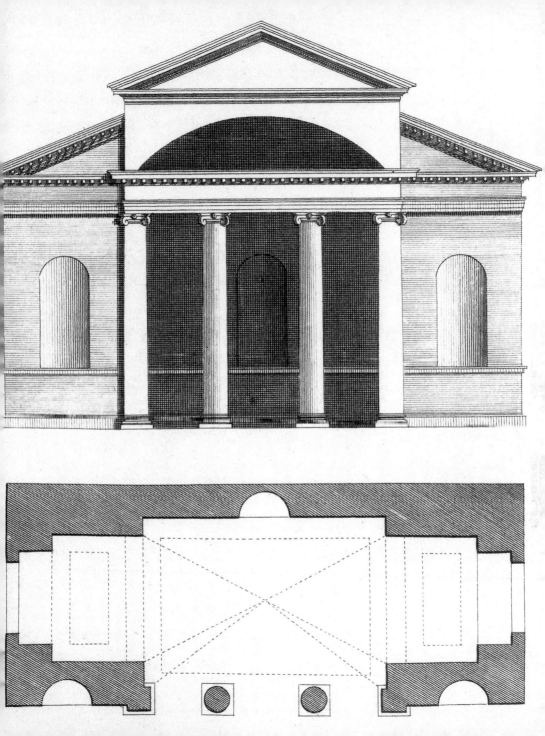

criteria for the correct choice of situation as well as for the construction of the building itself, and finally arrives at a discussion of column orders. For Ware these represent the field of the beautiful in architecture. However, in a departure from the works of his Italian models he no longer considers columns to be "essential parts" of the architecture, but considers them "ornamental parts," according them a mere accessory function. Thus Ware was able to conceive of architecture without columns: "Among the ornamental will fall the orders of architecture, which give the greatest beauty that can be communicated to a building, but they are not essential parts, because very good, nay very elegant, edifices and houses may be erected wholly without them."

In other words, Ware's *Complete Body* can by no means be understood solely in the context of Italian architectural theory. Rather he expands the topic by taking up issues addressed in French architectural theory since Claude Perrault, whose *Ordonnance des cinq espèces de colonnes*, 1683 (*A treatise of the five orders of columns*) had already been translated by the English architect John James (1672–1746) in 1708. In particular, Perrault's criticism of the traditional concept of a certain arrangement of columns as the basis of beauty in architecture probably prompted Ware to conclude that there were no final, objective rules for beauty (as there were for aspects such as *firmitas* and *utilitas*), and that columns could not therefore be considered to belong to the "essential parts." Just as a face can also be described as beautiful even when it changes owing to facial play and mood, there also exist within architecture "certain limits within which the genius may display itself in variations." Ware believes that Ancient Greek architecture testifies to this scope for variation. He argues that the Greeks were influenced directly by nature and derived their ornaments, in other words, the three column orders together with the entablature, from nature. By contrast, imitating existing architecture was a wholly unfamiliar concept to the Greeks. Accordingly, Ware demands that architects should revert to the very beginnings of architecture in nature in order to find the principles from which the Greeks evolved their art of building.

He contends that only this approach could produce an architecture as worthy of imitation as that of the Greeks. However, a glance at the history of architecture reveals that unconsidered imitation has always exerted the greatest influence, and that the art of melding imagination and logic in harmonious balance was lost with the end of Ancient Greece.

Consequently, Ware exposes the proportions handed down since this time as uninspired habit and concurs with Perrault in asseverating that such systems were arbitrary: "The proportions we have shewn varied greatly in their several works: we may now add they were arbitrary." However, this connection was not recognized until the Age of Reason, and in this context Ware draws attention to the particular achievements of his own epoch.

Ware's self-confidence is shared by the French architectural theoretician Marc-Antoine Laugier (1713–1769), whose rational *Essai sur l'Architecture* (1753) was translated into English as *Essay on architecture* as early as 1755. Ware borrows from the latter the theories that are central to his own publication, not only adopting Laugier's concept of the primordial hut but also his appraisal of architectural imitation and his ideas on architecture devoid of columns. Ware also believed that all the essential elements of architecture derived from the primitive hut with its simple columns, entablatures and gables. Fully in keeping with Laugier's views, he therefore also criticizes the use of decorative elements such as fluting, half columns and arcades, and calls for constructional simplicity in architecture. Palladian villa architecture serves him as an example of this architectural ideal. Moreover, Ware attacks the unqualified admiration of Palladio in England, and, with an eye to the student of architecture, comments: "We have shewn him Palladio can do wrong, and that may be an answer to such, as, being bigotted to his opinion, would give it their voice against truth." To Ware's mind, slavish imitation of Palladio goes against reason. Ware understood the Palladian architecture of his time representing enlightened architecture par excellence through its strict emphasis on the unadorned wall, as occurs in the designs of Burlington and Kent, as well as the restriction of arbitrary column decoration to the portico. In this Ware represents a concept of architecture similar to that held by the Palladian theoretician Robert Morris (1701–1754). That said, Ware does not consider Morris' pure aestheticism to represent a practical solution of architectural problems. For him architecture must be viewed both as a science and fine art if it is to meet the demands of his time. It would seem very likely that Ware's synthesis of utilitarian and aesthetic aspects to form a rationalist architectural ideal had a great influence above all on the later work of the English architect William Chambers (1723–1796), *A Treatise on Civil Architecture* (1759).   CR

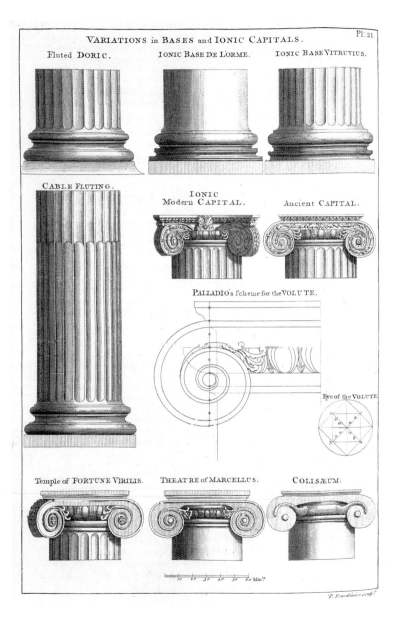

1 | **Variations of bases and Ionian capitals**
Pl. 21. Engraving

2 | **Illustration of variations of the Corinthian capital**
Pl. 23. Engraving

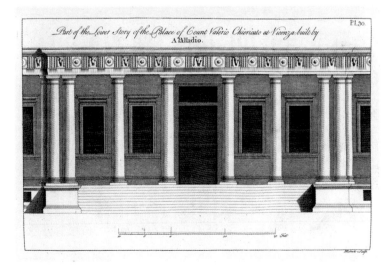

3 | Illustration of the five column orders with base and entablature
Pl. 2. Engraving

4 | Representation of the façade of Palladio's Palazzo Chiericati
Pl. 30. Engraving

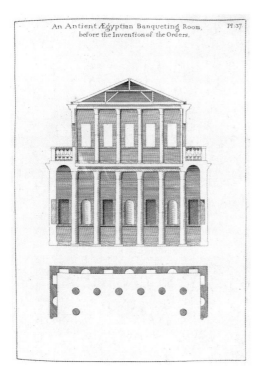

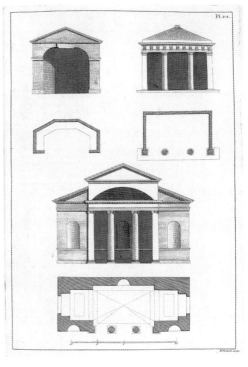

5 | **Ground plan of an ancient Egyptian banqueting hall**
Pl. 37. Engraving

6 | **Designs for various garden pavilions**
Pl. 101. Engraving

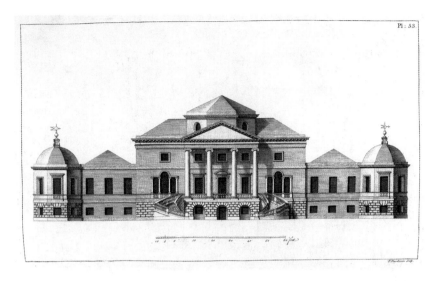

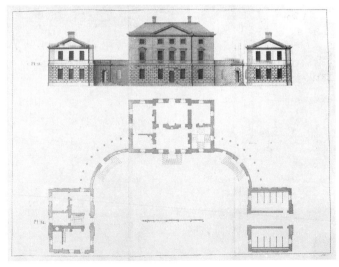

7 | **Design for Wrotham Park villa**
Pl. 53. Engraving

8 | **Design of a villa for Alexander Johnston**
Pls. 54 and 55. Engravings

William Chambers (1723–1796)
A Treatise on Civil Architecture

LONDON, 1759

A Treatise on Civil Architecture by William Chambers, an architect to the English court, represents one of the most influential English publications on the subject. Not only because it was reprinted twice during Chamber's lifetime and four times in the course of the 19th century (1768, 1791, 1825, 1826, 1836, 1862), but also because it offered the most systematic and easy-to-use survey in the English language of the use of column orders. In order to ensure greater accessibility Chambers concentrates exclusively on decorative architectural elements, amongst which – like Ware – he numbers columns, and completely omits issues relating to materials or construction. In keeping with this focus in his third (self-edited) version (1791), Chambers expands the title to read *A Treatise on the Decorative Parts of Architecture*, even including new text passages, which he refers to as the fruit of more than 30 years' experience as an architect. Accordingly, it is above all the third edition of his treatise that offers an especially valuable insight into Chambers' views on architecture – his outlook had been shaped at a very early date by numerous intensive impressions gathered as a student of architecture – first in Paris (1749), and subsequently in Italy. Indeed, it was this comprehensive training that essentially ensured that Chambers emerged in the second half of the 18th century as one of England's most important architects alongside his lifelong rival Robert Adam (1728–1792).

On returning from Italy, Chambers' career developed in a manner that was unprecedented in England, and which was crowned in architectural terms by his being commissioned to design Somerset House (1776–1786), and in terms of professional distinction by his appointment as Surveyor General and Comptroller of the King's Works (1782). In addition, Chambers enjoyed quite a reputation as a lecturer at the Royal Academy, of which he was one of the founding members. As early as 1757, he was appointed tutor to the Prince of Wales (later King George III). Chambers' *Treatise* was a direct result of this tutoring work. He makes constant references to architecture's importance for the state, both as an instrument of representation and in economic terms. Chambers also intended through his treatise to draw attention to his comprehensive training, which was to earn him various public commissions.

However, it was by no means Chambers' first publication. As early as 1757 he published his observations on Chinese architecture under the title *Designs of Chinese Buildings*. It would be wrong to conclude that Chambers viewed himself as a proponent of such exotic architectural ideas. Instead, he emphasizes the negligible importance of Chinese taste for the situation in Europe, claiming that it is of lesser beauty compared with the Classical architectural tradition, and that its employment only makes sense in the area of landscape gardening.

In keeping with this architectural appraisal, in his treatise (which appeared shortly afterward) Chambers focused on the Classical architectural idiom. Unlike Ware, however,

The Primitive Buildings &c.

The First sort of Huts.

The Second sort of Huts.

The Third sort of Huts which gave birth to the Doric ORDER.

The Doric Order in its Improved State.

Origin of the Corinthian Capital.

The Doric Profile of the Temple of Theseus at Athens one of the most Antient Monuments of that Order non Existing.

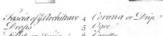

A	Plinth	K	Conge	T	Fascia of ye Architrave	4	Corona or Drip
B	Lower Torus	L	Fillet or upper Cincture	V	Dress	5	Ogee
C	Fillet or Square	M	Astragal	W	Fillet or Tenia	6	Cavetto
D	Scotia	N	Neck or Frise of ye Capital	X	Triglyphs	7	Fillet
E	Fillet	O	Fillets or Annulets	Y	Capital of the Triglyph		
F	Upper Torus	P	Ovolo, or Echinus	Z	Ovolo or Quarter round		
G	Fillet or lower Cincture	Q	Abacus	1	Mutule or Modillion Band		
H	Conge	R	Inverted Cyma or Ogee	2	Mutules		
I	Shaft of the Column	S	Fillet	3	Ogee		

Chambers did not set out to produce a comprehensive encyclopaedia on architecture. On the contrary, the special quality of his writing lies in the reduction of the object of study to the columns and landscape gardening, and also in the emphasis on his own aesthetic experience when passing architectural judgement, and using reason to give them a clearer theoretical edge. Thus, apart from the introduction and a critical survey of the history of architecture, the publication concentrates primarily on a discussion and presentation of the columns based on the writer's own observations and opinions. It is obvious that in this context Chambers likewise relies on Perrault when in the preface he criticizes the unconsidered glorification of Classical architects and a static notion of taste, attempting instead to lend his own comments the suggestion of objectivity.

It is also in the spirit of the Enlightenment that Chambers strives to imbue his explanations with the greatest possible transparency. In the philosophical tradition of essayistic empiricism since Bacon he therefore pursues in his treatise a style characterized by "precision," "perspicuity," "brevity," and "simplicity." In doing so, his intention is not to explain architecture mainly from the viewpoint of abstract principles and rules, but rather all the essential truths should result from a readily understandable experience, and its comprehensible presentation. In the introduction Chambers accordingly opines that this quality (alongside a knowledge of mathematics, geometry and perspective) is one of the most important elements in an architect's training. Travelling is of particular importance for the aforementioned skill, he claims, since the many encounters with different cultures and architectural ideas serve to kindle the "imagination" and "fancy." By contrast, an obedient adherence to models would result in a superficial study of architecture far removed from the attainment of true taste. Thus Chambers underlines the independent character of his explanations while borrowing from Marc-Antoine Laugier (1713–1769).

In the process, Chambers adds to the traditional qualifications of an architect the aesthetic experience of the architectural expert, whose spontaneous appraisal of perceived objects is based solely on a cosmopolitan taste, in other words aesthetic experience. The architect must take this fact into account by considering the aesthetic eye of the observer when devising buildings. It follows that the correct selection of proportions does not depend on a specific relationship between the various architectural elements, but on the architect's dexterity in handling the aesthetic impact of the elements employed. As an art that especially addresses the imagination of the cultivated observer, architecture is no longer assigned to the sciences or reasoning, but primarily to the field of fine arts, in other words the imagination. As a result, Chambers returns to a concept of architecture that began with the discussion on aesthetics in England, starting with Addison's series of essays *Taste and the Pleasures of the Imagination* (1712), and was already incorporated into the early publications on architecture by Robert Morris. Unlike Addison, however, Chambers assigns to architecture the capability to convey, in addition to sensory pleasures ("primary pleasures"), concepts and ideas with no direct relation to perception ("secondary pleasures"), which consequently have no need to simply imitate nature. Accordingly, like the other arts, architecture furnishes a high degree of associations and aesthetic pleasures that can, however, only be appreciated by "persons of enlightened conception."

This special aesthetic quality does not, however, hold for Classical architecture. For while Chambers (above all against the background of the passionate debate on Greece) refers to the particular achievements of Classical Roman architecture, he equally emphasizes the beauty of Gothic in England. In doing so he seconds the views of his colleague Joshua Reynolds (1723–1792), President of the Royal Academy. In keeping with his concept of architecture as a science and an art, Chambers equally praises the structural inventiveness and aesthetic impact of Gothic architecture, which, he thought, at times even surpassed the Classical models. Consequently, to his mind it was a failing that not a single author had explored this architecture – an undertaking all the more pressing since its most attractive examples were rapidly disintegrating: "Would our dilettanti instead of importing the gleanings of Greece; or our antiquaries, instead of publishing loose incoherent prints; encourage persons duly qualified, to undertake a correct publication of our own cathedrals, and other buildings called Gothic, before they totally fall to ruin; it would be of real service to the arts of design." Thus, as early as the 18th century, Chambers also proposes that one urgent task is to preserve and appreciate Gothic architecture, already anticipating the antiquarian interest in this architecture that developed in the 19th century. By contrast, Chambers' own architectural work was influenced by a strict academic Classicism which – like Laugier and Ware – he derived from the archetype of a primordial hut.

CR

To the Lord Viscount Charlemont, is humbly Inscribed by his Lordships

This Design of his Lordships Casine at Marino, most Obedient Servant, William Chambers.

Fig. p. 275

1 | Development of architecture from the primitive hut
to ancient architecture
P. 1. Engraving

2 | Design for a casino for Count Charlemont
P. 35. Engraving

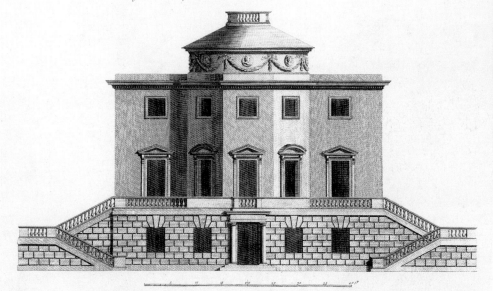

To Lord Bruce, this Design for the Casine at Tanfield Hall in Yorkshire, is humbly Inscribed by his Lordships most Obedient Servant, William Chambers.

3 | **Design of a casino for Lord Bruce**
P. 38. Engraving

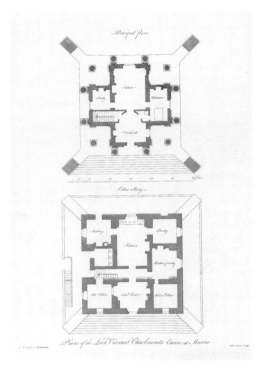

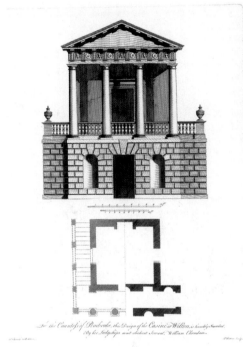

4 | Ground plan for the design of a casino for Count Charlemont
P. 36. Engraving

5 | Design for a casino for the Earl of Pembroke in Wilton
P. 37. Engraving

To the Earl of Tilney, this Design is humbly Inscribed by his Lordships most Obedient Servant, William Chambers.

6 | **Design of a Doric octagon temple for the Earl of Tylney**
P. 41. Engraving

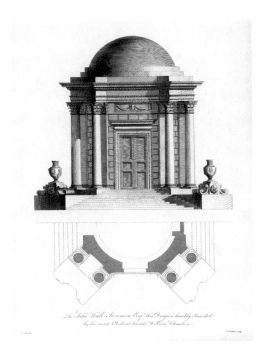

7 | Design for a Corinthian octagon temple

P. 42. Engraving

8 | Design of a Corinthian prostyle temple for Kew Gardens

P. 43. Engraving

Augustus Welby Pugin (1812–1852)

Contrasts: Or, A Parallel between the Noble Edifices of the Middle Ages, And Corresponding Buildings of the Present Day

LONDON, 1836

The True Principles of Pointed or Christian Architecture

LONDON, 1841

The writings of the architect and decorator Augustus Welby Pugin mark the first complete break in England with the Classical architectural idiom as a natural system of reference. Both in his 1836 work *Contrasts: Or, A Parallel between the Noble Edifices of the Middle Ages, And Corresponding Buildings of the Present Day* (2nd edition, 1841), and in *True Principles of Pointed or Christian Architecture* (1841), Pugin presents a totally new evaluation of the history of architecture by not interpreting Classical architecture and its renaissance as an architectural high point but as a sign of decay: Pugin argues that it should be replaced by the Gothic architecture of the Middle Ages whose renaissance Pugin vehemently calls for in the form of a "Gothic revival."

However, Pugin was by no means the first English architect in England to harbour such ambitions. As early as the 18th century Gothic architecture was certainly viewed as an aesthetic alternative to the Classical architectural idiom, even though its employment was initially restricted to English landscaped gardens like those at Stowe or Stourhead. It was only with Horace Walpole's (1717–1797) country house Strawberry Hill (1750–1777) that the Gothic was consciously employed to counter the prevailing Classicism of a Palladian such as Lord Burlington (1694–1753). As evidence of an expanded concept of taste, Walpole's architecture was intended to make people aware of the monotony criticized in Classical architecture. However, Walpole's prime objective was an aesthetic expansion of architecture; he was less concerned about a comprehensive revival of Gothic architectural principles.

Pugin, by contrast, voices a radical rejection of Classical architecture, a rejection that in addition to functional and structural aspects embraces above all non-architectural issues. In this context Pugin's preference for Gothic architecture was decisively influenced by collaboration with his father, Augustus Charles Pugin (1769–1832). On arriving from France, the latter settled in London in 1792 and worked as an architect's draughtsman in the office of the eminent John Nash (1752–1835). Moreover, Pugin's father attained a certain reputation which was largely due to his publications on Gothic architecture, such as *Specimens of Gothic Architecture* (1821–1828), to the second volume of which Augustus Welby Pugin was already a contributor. It seems probable that other authors who began to explore Gothic in the early 19th century – in part from an archaeological perspective – reinforced Pugin's view that Gothic architecture represented an extraordinary achievement, especially as regards structure.

It comes as no surprise that Pugin expounds a functionalist architectural ideal in *Contrasts* by comprehending beauty as "fitness of the design to the purpose for which it was intended." Furthermore, in *True Principles* he calls for structural simplicity ("pure architecture") to which all architectural ornaments should be subordinated. However, the historical model for such architecture is no longer Classicism, as was the case in the 18th century, but Gothic archi-

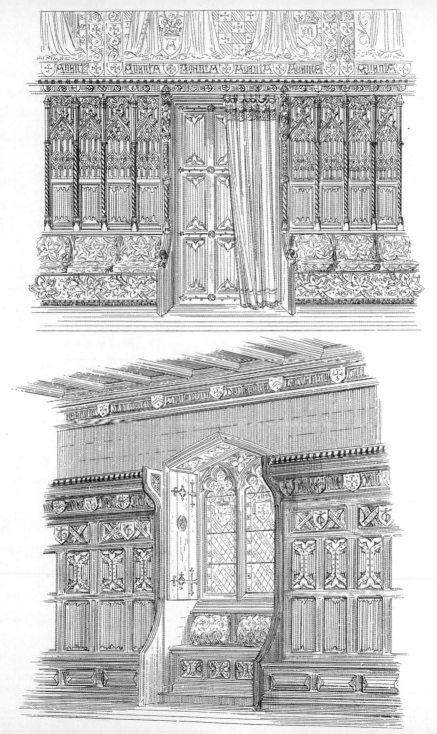

tecture with its flying buttresses, engaged columns and cross-ribbed vaults. Thus for all their ostensible similarities, Pugin's rationalism has little in common with the architectural ideals of Laugier or Ware. Rather, by underlining the structural logic of Gothic architecture he moves towards the position of his French contemporary Eugène Emmanuel Viollet-le-Duc (1814–1879). This becomes evident when Pugin observes that the model of the primordial hut is unsuited to Christian architecture. He finds absolutely absurd the idea that the stone buildings of the Greeks should have originated from a primitive wooden hut. And he continues: since stone offers totally different structural and design opportunities from wood, Greek buildings had not fulfilled their potential. In the final reckoning, therefore, their architecture must be described as primitive. By contrast, the invention of the flying buttress and the airy height of Gothic vaulted structures demonstrated impressively the use to which medieval master builders had put stone. Furthermore, the structural logic of this architecture at the same time determined its façade, as can be proved by the buttress work on Gothic cathedrals. Christopher Wren's Baroque St Paul's Cathedral serves him as a negative contrast since its buttress work is concealed by facing which has no structural or functional purpose.

However, it is not only structural and functional reasons that cause Pugin to reject the adaptation of Classical architecture since Antiquity. In *Contrasts* he explains his attitude above all by citing religious considerations. For instance, Pugin criticizes the use of Classical architectural elements since they originate in Greek temple architecture, and are thus to be seen in a totally different cultural context from the Christian sphere. Ultimately, the great buildings of Antiquity such as the Greek temples evolved from religious motives. The logical conclusion is that adapting such heathen architecture in Christian societies, especially since the Renaissance, would be to worship false idols, testifying to an inability among Christians to create an architectural and cultural expression of their own. To prove his point Pugin refers to European architecture since the 15th century, and its false interpretation of Classical architecture as a treasure trove of forms freely available for anyone to use. Furthermore, Pugin claims to recognize such a superficial attitude in the contemporary architectural ideas of John Nash (1752–1835), John Soane (1753–1837) and Robert Smirke (1781–1867).

On the whole Pugin interprets the aforementioned development as evidence of a gradual drop in standards, whose

origins he sees above all in the weakness of Catholicism as a "triumph of these new and degenerate ideas over the Ancient and Catholic feelings." This situation had only come about, he argued, because English society had proved to have little religious faith at the time of the Reformation. Accordingly, Pugin – who himself converted to Catholicism in 1834 – contended that the reformation of the Catholic church laid the foundations for good architecture, such as evolved in the 13th and 14th centuries, in complete accord with religious and social ideals. Consequently, Pugin does not tire, especially in *Contrasts*, of underlining the perfection of medieval society, and simultaneously creating the association of a social utopia. For in contrast to the society which, around the middle of the 19th century, was characterized by a complex web of problems due above all to the rapid pace of industrialization, the Middle Ages represented for Pugin an epoch of social harmony. This becomes clear when he pronounces the unselfishness of the believer – which spanned the entire hierarchy – to be an essential characteristic of medieval society. Ultimately, it was this all-encompassing religiosity that enabled the building of the great cathedrals, which were effectively nothing other than piety transformed into architecture. It goes without saying for Pugin that the basic elements of this architecture could be derived from Christian symbolism, for example with the cross as a model for a cross-shaped ground plan or a striving for heaven as the reason for the enormous height of the nave. By contrast, those forms of Classical architecture taken from the ancient civilizations bore no correlation to the basic values of Christian society, and were therefore to be viewed as empty adornments that stood for a society devoid of orientation and values. It emerges that Pugin is referring to the contemporary England of the industrial revolution when he compares a "Catholic town" of the year 1444 with the same town in the year 1840. The homogeneous architectural appearance of Gothic towns is contrasted with early industrialized town with its hodgepodge of Classicist architectural styles and purely functional buildings with their attendant factory chimneys. The modern prison in the foreground is intended to allude to the desolate state of secularized societies such as England. Thus Pugin presents a positive image of the Middle Ages such as was to shape the progressive ideas of John Ruskin (1819–1900) and William Morris (1834–1896), though these men certainly did not share Pugin's religious fanaticism.   CR

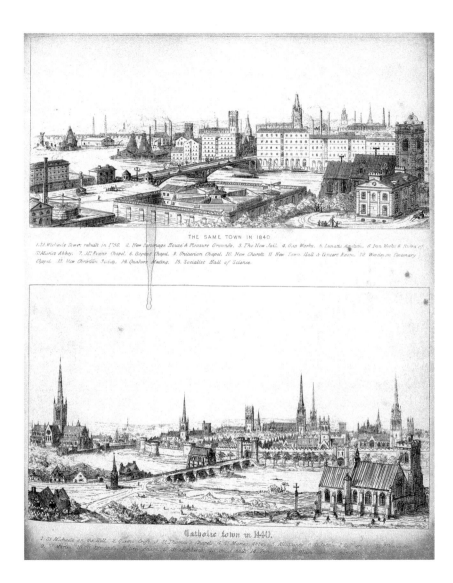

THE SAME TOWN IN 1840

1. St Michaels Tower, rebuilt in 1750. 2. New Parsonage House & Pleasure Grounds. 3. The New Jail. 4. Gas Works. 5. Lunatic Asylum. 6. Iron Works & Ruins of St Maries Abbey. 7. Mr Evans Chapel. 8. Baptist Chapel. 9. Unitarian Chapel. 10. New Church. 11. New Town Hall & Concert Room. 12. Wesleyan Centenary Chapel. 13. New Christian Society. 14. Quakers Meeting. 15. Socialist Hall of Science.

Catholic town in 1440.

1. St Michaels on the Hill. 2. Queens Cross. 3. St Thomas's Chapel. 4. St Maries Abbey. 5. All Saints. 6. St Johns. 7. St Peters ... 8. St Thomas ...
9. St Maries. 10. St Edmunds. 11. Grey Friars. 12. St Cuthberts. 13. Guild Hall. 14. Trinity ...

Fig. p. 283

1 | Wainscoting
Illustration of interior decoration in Gothic style based on Horace
Walpole's Strawberry Hill.
In: True Principles, *pl. VIII. Woodcut*

**2 | A catholic town in the middle ages compared with how it was
imagined to be in the 19th century**
In: Contrasts. *Woodcut*

3 | **Comparison of John Nash's All Souls' Church and the Radcliffe Church in Bristol**
Woodcut

4 | **Comparison of the university portals of King's College with Christ's College in Oxford**
Woodcut

REFERENCES TO THE
NEW HOVSE.

AAA. THE NVRSERY WINDOWS.
B. AN ILL SHAPED MITER.
CCC. THE DRAWING ROOM.
D. THE STREET DOOR.
EE. THE PARLOVR.
F THE WAY DOWN THE AREA.
THIS HOVSE HAS BEEN BVILT WITH DVE
REGARD TO THE MODERN STYLE OF EPISCO-
PAL ESTABLISHMENTS. ALL VSELESS BVILD-
INGS SVCH AS CHAPEL HALL OR LIBRARY
HAVE BEEN OMITTED, AND THE WHOLE
IS ON A SCALE TO COMBINE ECONOMY
WITH ELEGANCE !!!

References to the
Old Palace +

a Sᵗ Etheldreda's chapel +
b Part of the library +
c The east cloister +
d Lodgings for guests +
e The great hall +
THIS VENERABLE PALACE WAS SOLD
TO THAT EMINENT SVRVEYOR C.COLE
WHO VTTERLY DESTROYED IT AND ON
ITS SCITE ERRECTED THE PRESENT
HANDSOME AND VNIFORMᵗ STREET WITH
ITS NEAT AND APPROPRIATE
IRON CATES IN 1776.
+ brayleys londiniana

ELY HOVSE DOVER STREET
1836

CONTRASTED EPISCOPAL RESIDENCES

ELY PALACE HOLBORN 1536.

5 | Comparison of an Episcopal residence from 1536 with an Episcopal residence from 1836
Woodcut

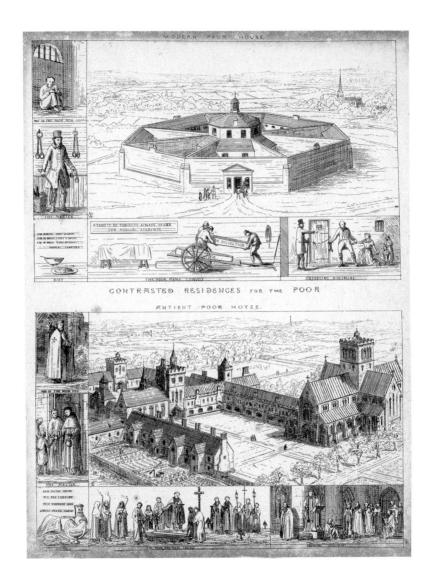

6 | **Comparison of a medieval poorhouse with a poorhouse from the time of Pugin**
In: Contrasts. *Woodcut*

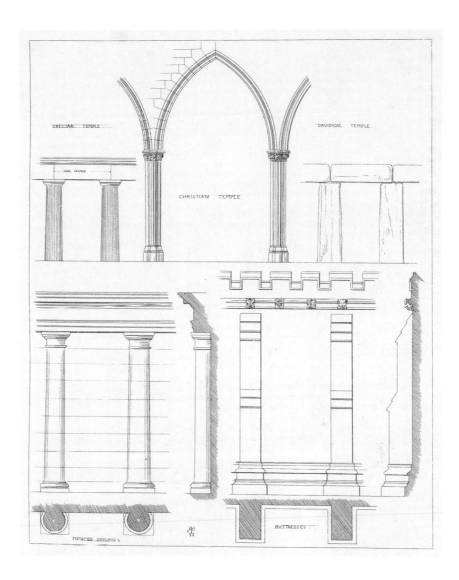

GRECIAN TEMPLE

ONE STONE

DRUIDICAL TEMPLE

CHRISTIAN TEMPLE

ENGAGED COLUMNS

BUTTRESSES

7 | **Comparison of Greek and**
Christian religious architecture
In: True Principles, *pl. 1*

Germany

ning of building with wood, the use of wood was not bound to produce a Doric temple, could equally have produced a northern-style log cabin, only served to elucidate what was meant.

In Italy, the approach to Vitruvius and architecture itself had long since moved on from an interpretation that was limited to a particular era. One year earlier Rivius, well read as he was, had already added another great work on architecture to his work on Vitruvius, one that discussed a wide range of questions to do with geometry and ballistics. In it he reproduced many of Serlio's illustrations, insofar as they had been published by 1546, i. e. for the most part from his books I to III. Others came from Tartaglia (1546), Orontius Fineus' book on geometry (1543) and other sources. In the course of a dialogue included in this compendium of architecture, his interpretation of the architect's rank as an all-round artist who instructs the master builder and craftsman is clearly expressed, which should be considered as a homage to Dürer's *Etliche underricht zu befestigung* (1527). Like the compendium of architecture, the *Vitruvius Teutsch* addresses itself to both the educated architect as well as the craftsman, and to a greater degree also to the client, who often enough had a knowledge of building. With his translation, Rivius intended to formulate a new, broadly based interpretation of both architecture and those professions connected with the building trade, to elevate architecture to a science comparable, say, to mathematics. In the Middle Ages the term *sapiens architectus* had already existed, but this referred mostly to the client, who gave the building a purpose that was determined by God's wisdom. The reference to the architect as the highest craftsman, in the sense meant by Rivius, was also known in the 13th century, such as from St Thomas Aquinas (1224/25–1274). And yet in practice these functions often still lay too far apart. Uniting them, in order to realize the architecture "according to Antiquity," i. e. that of Vitruvius, was particularly important. Rivius was in favour of furthering the

architector doctus, the cultured, educated architect who was in a position to conceive the buildings independently, according to their purpose, and follow their construction in a professional manner, something that required extensive technical and practical skills. Furthermore, those new instruments available in architecture, i. e. the orders of columns, could only be used correctly and purposefully by those who were familiar with both their construction and their purpose. That said, there had always been good and not so good architects, even in the Middle Ages, and it was of no great importance what styles they were using. Rivius' goal lay not in propagating a "new style" of architecture, though he did point out that if the aim was to produce a quality in buildings that had been commonplace in Classical Antiquity, this called for then a wider horizon than that of most craftsmen.

Of the 190 woodcuts in *Vitruvius Teutsch*, 115 are based on 102 illustrations from Cesariano's Vitruvius edition of 1521, and are more or less straight, in some cases simplified, copies. Some of them however were new creations on the topic provided in 1521. 14 woodcuts are taken from Serlio's first four books, and parts of an additional eight are based on the pictures from the *Hypnerotomachia Poliphili* of 1499. Further sources were Hans Brosamer's illustrations of the works of Petrus Apianus, the Paris commentary on Vitruvius by Philandrier and others. Only in the case of 14 of the woodcuts was no model mentioned. On the basis of the monogram P F the woodcuts had earlier been credited to the Nuremberg printmaker Peter Flötner (c. 1495–c. 1546); since Röttinger's investigations in 1914 they have been considered to be by Virgil Solis (1514–1562), with just a small number by other designers or woodcut makers such as Georg Pencz (c. 1500–1550) or Hans Springinklee (1490/95–1540). Further editions, with only minimal alterations, were published in Basle in 1575 and 1614, and there was a reprint of the 1548 edition published in Hildesheim in 1973.

JZ

2 | **Tools of the architect**
"Circles, compasses and all
useful geometric instruments
for artistic education."
*Fol. XI. Woodcut, ascribed
to Virgil Solis*

3 | **The mausoleum of Halikarnassos**
Based on Cesariano's edition of Vitruvius.
Fol. LXXXIIII. Woodcut, ascribed to Virgil Solis

4 | **Eight-sided tower**
Tower of the winds in Athens.
Based on Cesariano's edition of Vitruvius.
Fol. XLVI v. Woodcut, ascribed to Virgil Solis

5 | **Primitive hut**
This first wooden building in Colchis.
Based on Cesariano's edition of Vitruvius.
Fol. LXIII. Woodcut, ascribed to Virgil Solis

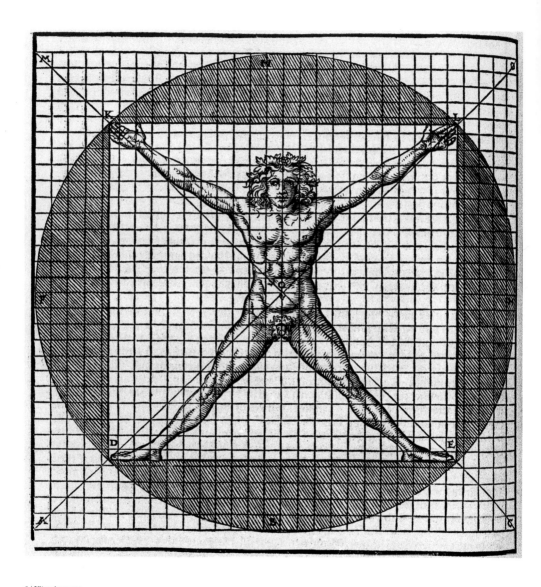

6 | **Vitruvian man**
Based on Cesariano's edition of Vitruvius.
Fol. CI v. Woodcut, ascribed to Virgil Solis

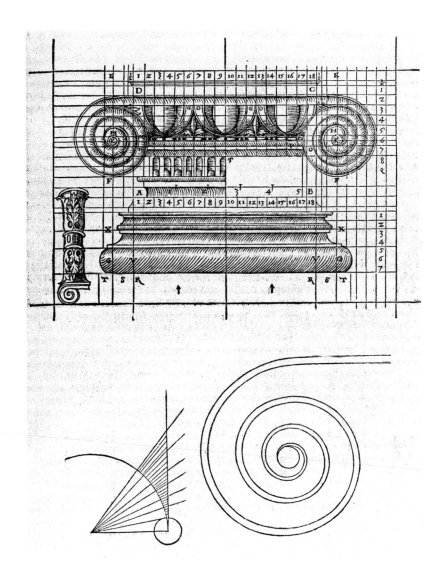

7 | Proportions of an Ionic capital
Based on Cesariano's edition of Vitruvius.
Fol. CXXVI. Woodcut, ascribed to Virgil Solis

8 | **Column orders**
Based on Cesariano's edition of Vitruvius.
Fol. CXXXIIII r and v. Woodcut, ascribed to Virgil Solis

9 | **Six capitals**
Based on Cesariano's edition of Vitruvius.
Fol. CXXXIIII. Woodcut, ascribed to Virgil Solis

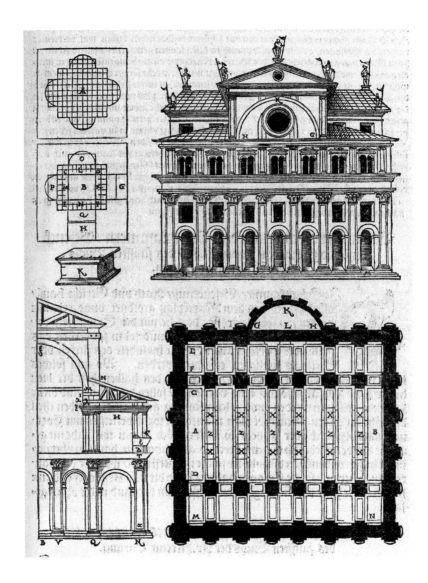

10 | **Ground plan and elevation section of the Julia Basilica**
Palace ("basilica") for Julia, the daughter of Augustus, built
by Vitruvius. Based on Cesariano's edition of Vitruvius.
Fol. CLXIIII. Woodcut, ascribed to Virgil Solis

11 | Roman house
Interior of a Roman house with impluvium in the Corinthian manner.
Based on Cesariano's edition of Vitruvius.
Fol. CC v. Woodcut, ascribed to Virgil Solis

12 | **Apparatus for lifting**
Based on Cesariano's edition of Vitruvius.
Fol. CCXCIIII v. Woodcut, ascribed to Virgil Solis

Hans Blum (born c. 1520/30)
Von den fünff Sülen

ZURICH, 1550

On the five columns

Seldom has so little been known about the life and personality of a successful author as in the case of Hans Blum. Research has shown that there were no less than 39 editions of his book about columns, published before the end of the 17th century in the German-speaking countries, the Netherlands, France and above all in England, where they were in print for longest of all. The fact that he became a successful author at all was due to his development of a practicable method of construction for the orders of columns that was relatively easy to apply. Its wide acceptance accounted for the large number of editions of Blum's work, which could easily be followed not just by master builders but also by joiners and other craftsmen. Even the authors of books about architecture and columns that emerged from the joinery profession, such as Hans Jacob Ebelmann (c. 1570–c. 1609), Rutger Kassmann (c. 1589–after 1645) and Johann Georg Erasmus (1659–1710), used Blum's teachings on columns, and Julien Mauclerc's book on architecture (1600) makes reference to him, as does Abraham Leuthner as late as 1677. The number of copies of Blum's book on columns that actually survived seems, however, to be very small. Nothing is known about the number of copies printed per edition, but one can assume that numerous copies were worn out on building sites and in workshops.

Nothing is even known about what skills Hans Blum learnt, or what his main trade or profession actually was. In the preface to *Kunstreych Buoch* (c. 1560) he simply

mentioned that he had built "numerous ordinary houses" (dwellings), i. e. he was a master builder, and the 1627 Bodmer edition of his works states that "this was written by the famous mathematics scholar M. Hans Blum from Lor on the River Main." Judging by the fact that several woodcuts in his books contain the monogram HB, it can be assumed that he also worked in this trade.

There is no trace of him in the archives of the little town of Lohr on the River Main, where he would have been born between 1520 and 1530; only later in Zurich is he said to have lived from 1542 at the earliest and 1549 at the latest as a "foreigner," although it would appear that he was never accorded full civic rights. On 18 July 1549 or 1550 he married Rägali Kuchymeister in Zurich Cathedral. On 16 May 1550, likewise in the cathedral, a son, Christoffel, was baptized and on 21 January 1551 a second son, Hans. Soon after 1552 Blum, together with his wife and elder son, is said to have left Zurich, leaving his son Hans behind to be brought up by the printer and publisher Christoffel Froschauer. It is not known when and where he died. Blum was presumably a Protestant, and had left Lohr at an early age to embark on an educational journey or the traditional craftsman's "wanderings" to Italy, from where he emigrated to Switzerland.

His book about columns was dedicated to the Zurich municipal building official, Andres Schmid (1504–1565, in charge of building 1544–1552). The edition published by Bodmer in 1627 is addressed to Caspar Schmid, Andres

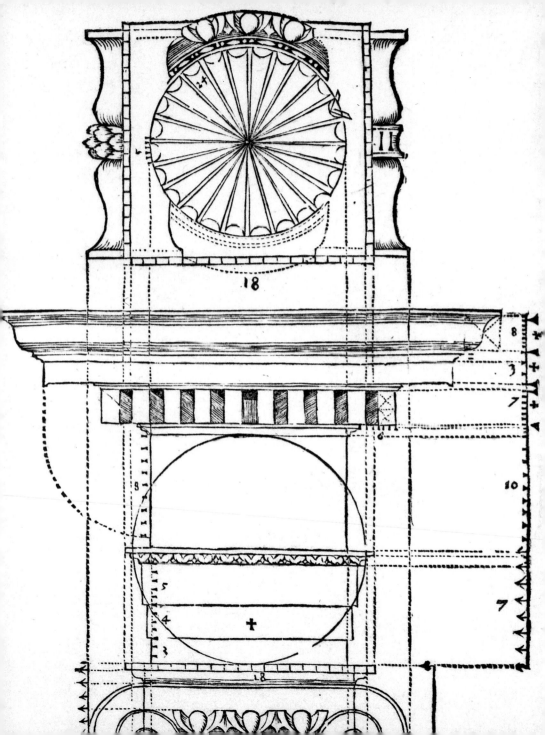

Schmid's grandson. Andres Schmid had most probably supported Blum's work in some form or other. In addition to the book about columns, Blum published *Ein kunstreych Buoch von allerley antiquiteten, so zum verstand der fünff Seulen der Architectur gehörend* (*An elaborate book about all sorts of antiquities, contributing to an understanding of the five columns in architecture*) (undated, probably Zurich c. 1560), which was reprinted in 1596, 1627 and 1662. It quite clearly belongs in the same category as the book about columns; the preface makes reference to the latter and remarks that its recipients had been calling for this supplement. At a later date a further collection was added to these works: *Architectura antiqua, Das ist, Warhaffte vnnd eigentliche Contrafacturen etlich alter schönen Gebeuwen,* (*Ancient architecture, that is true and actual reconstructions of numerous old, beautiful buildings*). This collection of woodcuts of various buildings, for the most part imaginary (no text is given), does not, or at least not exclusively, stem from Blum, but was added by the publisher, who presumably wished to bring out a comprehensive book about architecture. The sequel, which had appeared as early as around 1527, was probably added to Blum's works around 1558, but certainly by 1561 at the latest. Individual woodcuts bear the monograms RW and/or IW, a reference to the draughtsman Rudolf and the carver Jeremias Wyssenbach. At most, the reproduction of Bramante's Tempietto might be attributable to Blum.

The book about columns first appeared in German in 1550, though only one copy of this edition is known. The Latin version of the same year, until now considered to be the first edition, is in fact a translation of the German. Blum's appropriation of Serlio's teachings on columns (Book IV) probably occurred via the Dutch translation by Pieter Coecke van Aelst (1542), which in turn was translated into German by Jacob Reichlinger. While Book IV holds a solitary position of its own in Serlio's œuvre, Blum distinguishes completely between column theory and general architectural theory, and simplifies the method of proportioning in the process. His method presumes a predetermined height that is divided up into individual units. A certain number of these units determine either the height of the column pedestal or, in the case of those columns with no pedestal (of which he presents two examples) the side length of the base. The diameter of the bottom of the shaft is then derived from these measurements. With Tuscan columns this involves dividing the height of the column by six, of which two parts are subtracted for the base and cornice, with the remaining four parts forming the length of a side of a square in which a circle is drawn and in turn a square in the circle. Multiplied by six, the length of the side of the final square corresponds to the height of the column, while the circle inscribed in the final square accords with the circumference of the bottom of the shaft. Using the same method, Blum then developed his own individual procedure for each different column order. The diameter of the bottom of the shaft is considered the module for the height of the shaft, capital and entablature, with the exception of the Corinthian capital, whose height is determined by "symmetric construction." In the case of the superposition of columns, Blum follows Vitruvius' rule and shortens the height of the higher column by a quarter of the height of the lower.

What remains important is the symbolic significance that Blum attaches to the orders of the columns, an aspect that was already evident in Vitruvius. For his symbolism, however, Blum resorts neither to the gods of ancient mythology nor to Serlio's Christian premises, but limits himself to estates and genders. In his way, he compares the Tuscan form with a "coarse farmer," the Doric with a "strong hero," the Ionic with a "brave woman" and the Corinthian with a "beautiful maiden." The Composite was the "compilation or mixture of the other columns." Here, he takes into account the post-Reformation society of northern Europe. This methodology was also the reason for the enormous success of his slim volume. He is considered to be the creator of the northern reference work on columns, since many continued to follow his remarks on columns, which were both practical and adequately reinforced by understandable scholarship. For almost 150 years his methods gave northern Europe access to the forms of Classical Antiquity and the Italian Renaissance. In England, they remained the only practical set of instructions on the construction of columns through till the end of the 17th century.

JZ

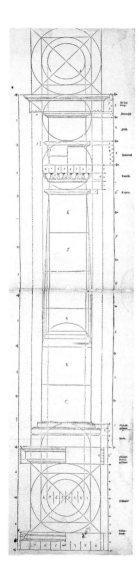

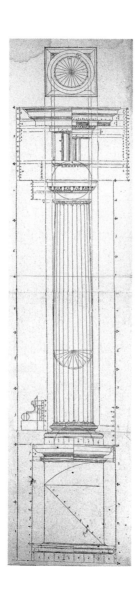

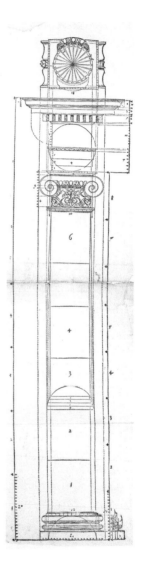

1 | **Construction of the**
Tuscan column order
Ed. from 1627. Woodcut

2 | **Construction of the**
Doric column order
Ed. from 1627. Woodcut

3 | **Construction of the**
Ionian column order, first variation
Ed. from 1627. Woodcut

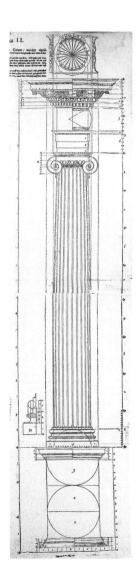

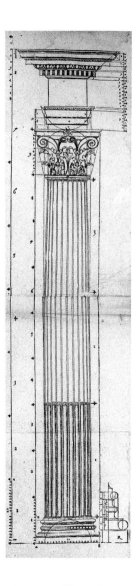

4 | **Construction of the Ionian column order,
second variation**
Ed. from 1627. Woodcut

5 | **Construction of the Corinthian column
order, first variation**
Ed. from 1627. Woodcut

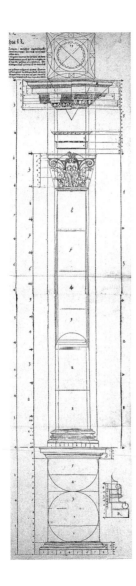

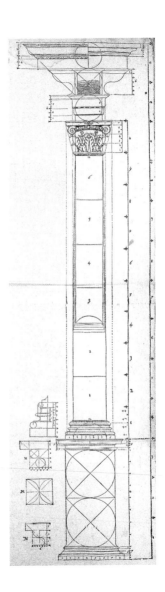

6 | **Construction of the Corinthian
column order, second variation**
Ed. from 1627. Woodcut

7 | **Construction of the
Composite column order**
Ed. from 1627. Woodcut

Wendel Dieterlin (1550/51–1599)

Architectura von Außtheilung, Symmetria und Proportion der Fünff Seulen

NUREMBERG, 1598

Architecture of division symmetry and proportion of the five columns

The painter Wendling (or Wendelin) Grapp, otherwise known as Dieterlin, was born around 1550/51 in Pfullendorf, near Lake Constance, probably as the son of the painter Balthasar Grapp. He served his apprenticeship as a painter with Philipp Memberger in Constance and there is a record of his marriage to Katharina Sprewer in Strasbourg on 12 September 1570. Following the purchase of a house there in 1571 he acquired the rights of a burgher of that city, where he died in 1599, leaving his wife and their children Hilarius, Wendel (the younger), who became famous for his ornamental engravings, and Rosina. His mainly large-scale paintings on façades were in great demand well beyond the borders of Strasbourg, as were those on canvas, which were used as interior decorations for illustrious royal and public buildings. In 1583, he was employed in Haguenau, in 1589 in Strasbourg, where he worked on the New Building, and in Oberkirch in the Black Forest. From 1590 the large commission awarded by the Duke of Württemberg to provide paintings for the Summer House ("Neues Lusthaus") in Stuttgart bound him to the city for best part of the next three years. The "modello" (Staatsgalerie Stuttgart, Prints Collection) for one of the three large ceiling paintings he produced there, depicting the Last Judgement, documents the creative power of his paintings – the finished work unfortunately vanished along with the Summer House. Compared at times with that of Michelangelo, his work scarcely complied with iconographic conventions, or else reinterpreted them. Only one

panel painting signed by him has survived, the Raising of Lazarus of 1587, now on show in the Kunsthalle in Karlsruhe. In 1593 he returned to Strasbourg, where he worked as an artist in the Hôtel de Commerce and other public buildings. In his later years he was involved with the production of draft plans and sketches for architectural projects.

As is immediately evident, it is impossible to slot *Architectura* into any category of architectural theory before or since. Dieterlin was neither a mathematician nor an architect like the other theorists, but instead an artist who showed great independence and creativity in his work and who, as it were, had to get to grips with the space available in the interiors of buildings. Yet there was more to his knowledge of architectural theory. It is most probable that in this area he learned much from a Dutchman, Daniel Soriau (?–1619), one of the founders of the town of Hanau, to whom he dedicated *Architectura*. He was one of the first to perceive Vitruvius' orders of columns as a universal system that could be brought to bear on the arts, including painting and applied art; in his own *Architectura* published in 1577, Hans Vredeman de Vries (1526–1609) had already put forward the method and system of this interpretation. The orders provide the structure for the etchings Dieterlin drew for his *Architectura*. They number more than 200 and show astonishing, almost overflowing imaginativeness. In addition, 171 preliminary drawings or designs have survived (Copperplate engraving collection, Dresden). Presumably, the series was gradually built up

I.
TVSCANA

from 1590 on, and at the latest from 11 May 1592, when Dietterlin submitted his formal application for the Imperial Charter at the Court of Prague. The first book, containing 40 plates, was published as early as 1593, with a Latin edition following later the same year. The second book, with 58 sheets, was completed in 1594, and the Latin version came out the following year. The entire opus was completed in 1598, generally regarded as the year of publication. It was initially published by Jobin in Strasbourg, though the first book was actually printed in Stuttgart. Presumably the complete work, together with a Latin version, was not brought out until after Dietterlin's death, namely by the Nuremberg publishers Hubert and Balthasar Caymocx, who were of Belgian descent. This is the earliest etched work of any size to appear prior to Jacques Callot (1592–1635); the admittedly small print run was subjected to proven amendments and commanded a handsome price in the trade. It nonetheless enjoyed widespread distribution to which various reprints (whether legal or pirate copies) contributed, such as that of 1655 in Nuremberg. From 1609, Daniel Mayer (1576–1630) reprinted sections of the work with altered engravings and published them in Frankfurt am Main in 1612, together with reproductions of Vredeman de Vries; on occasion, sheets copied from Dietterlin were also circulated together with Hans Blum's *Von den fünff Sülen* (1550). From the middle of the 19th century, several reproductions were published, of which the French edition of 1862 (Liège and Paris) is a true historical reproduction. It has been proved that the work was used by artists and craftsmen alike soon after it appeared, yet it was most certainly not meant to be a pattern book. It is much more the individual artistic achievement of a very busy, temperamental and pensive artist, who chose the world of architecture to tame his imagination. We have mainly his marvellously vivid engravings to thank for the fact that although none of his impressive painting has survived, Dietterlin is still considered to be one of the most interesting artists in south-west Germany in the second half of the 16th century – and many of them are duly presented in his *Architectura*. This is generally considered to be the most important printed work of the German Late Renaissance, and has at times been referred to as a "novel of development," to quote

Hans Gerhard Evers. This was doubtless meant to mean a novel that traverses the maze that was the world of Late Renaissance forms by means of the Ariadne's thread of the architectural orders. In doing so, Dietterlin takes into account the associated hierarchies and symbolism, and enriches them both formally and in content. He also enables the dimensions of space and time to be perceived by presenting the seasons and periods of life, the breadth of the social fabric, human activity and passions, the sacred and the profane, nature and art, as are all to be found in those ennobled orders from Roman history. For each order, he played through each of those forms pre-defined by architecture and open to experience by the beholder: columns, pedestals, portals, windows, fireplaces, fountains, coats of arms, graves, and epitaphs. In this way he reaches fantasies of architecture and scenes almost removed from architecture, as on page 18 with the exotic "Tuscan" fireplace elephant. Ornamentation is the component that must be considered the most important by all those who consider the work to be a collection of specimens, as was the case above all in the 19th century. Ornamentation is developed logically from the orders with incredible richness, overflowing imagination, and great confidence in form, rather than being imposed upon them, and even the appearance of Late Gothic tracery within the Composite order should not appear too strange.

Many have referred to the influence of *Architectura* on those 17th-century compendia of architecture and columns that were created as pattern books by joinery architects such as Johann Jakob Ebelmann (c. 1570–c. 1609), Jakob Guckeisen (active at about the end of the 16th century), Rutger Kassmann (c. 1589/95–after 1645), Gabriel Krammer (c. 1550–c. 1611) and others. If the book is not primarily a pattern book, but an independent work of art on a different level from the theoretical works of mathematicians and builders of fortresses, there nevertheless contain "uses" that build on his ideas and the richness of his forms. In this respect reference to the "Gods' Gate" in the Golden Room at Bückeburg Castle by the brothers Ebert and Jonas Wulff (1604/05) as well as other works associated with the Court of Bückeburg must suffice.

JZ

Fig. p. 311
1 | **Tuscan column order**
Pl. 6. Etching

2 | **Portal in Tuscan order**
Pl. 26. Etching

3 | **Doric column order**
Pl. 46. Etching

4 | **Doric column order, architrave and entablature**
Pl. 50. Etching

5 | Ionic column order
Pl. 95. Etching

6 | Fountain in the Ionic order
Pl. 117. Etching

7 | Ionic column order, bases and capitals
Pl. 96. Etching

8 | **Corinthian column order**
Pl. 136. Etching

9 | **Composite column order**
Pl. 176. Etching

10 | **Capitals in the Composite column order**
Pl. 179. Etching

Joseph Furttenbach the Elder (1591–1667)

Architectura civilis, das ist Eigentliche Beschreibung wie man nach bester form und gerechter Regul, Fürs Erste: Palläst ... erbawen soll

ULM, 1628

Architectura civilis, that is an actual description of how, according to the best method and fair regulations to build, to begin with: palaces

The author of *Architectura civilis* was born on 30 December 1591 in Leutkirch or in Constance. He died on 12 or 17 January 1667 in Ulm. Since he apparently came from a well-to-do family he was destined to become a merchant, and educated accordingly. In 1607, i. e. at the age of 16, he embarked on an extended journey through Italy, only returning to Germany in 1620 or 1621. He learnt Italian in Milan and spent seven years in Genoa alone. The influence of the Florentine architect Giulio Parigi (1571–1635) apparently played a crucial role in his decision to become an architect later on. Following his return he designed a system of grottoes for his brother Hieronymus, the mayor of Leutkirch. In 1621, he joined a company of merchant traders in Ulm. Through his marriage to Anna Katharina Strauss, who came from a local patrician family, he was apparently granted the freedom of the city in 1623. *Architectura civilis* was proof of his expertise in the field of architecture, and thus in 1631 he was entrusted with the position of head of the Ulm municipal building department. In 1636, he became a senator and councillor in Ulm, a free Imperial city, and in addition, from 1639 he was head of the municipal timber department. None of his five children survived him. His son Joseph worked for his father as a copperplate engraver. In 1649, he began publication of a projected 15-part series of monographs of different types of buildings, which he however did not continue until some time after the early death of his son in 1655, but which he failed to complete.

Furttenbach was a successful burgher of an imperial city that was still flourishing at the time of the Thirty Years' War. His house contained a famous, much visited chamber of art including a cabinet of models, not to mention a library. Scarcely any of the buildings that he was responsible for whilst in office in Ulm, and had perhaps even planned himself, have survived. His theatre, built in 1641 in the former Dominican friary, became famous, and it is quite certain that his activities were not limited to supervising the construction work. He was also involved with occasional architectural projects such as monumental funeral biers, triumphal arches and theatre decoration.

He first catches the eye as a writer in 1626 with *Newes Itinerarium Italiae*, the fruits of his extended stay in Italy, which has long been used as a guide by visitors to the country. In 1627, there followed a short paper on fireballs – he had learnt the art of fireworks in Genoa. *Architectura civilis* is his earliest work of architectural theory and appeared two years after the Italian *Itinerarium*. It is a short formal compilation of all that would later occupy him on a practical level and in addition, in more precise works of architectural theory. It is essentially a typology of building which, following a hierarchical structure, begins with princely palaces, juxtaposing these with a "heroic court," with a palace each for the rulers and nobility, followed by an alternative, "another princely palace." A dignified staircase was still regarded as a "necessary" inclusion in upper-class residences. The por-

trayal of the "scena comica," the Vitruvian scene from ancient Greek comedy (which at first sight seems somewhat out
of place here) marks the beginning of the somewhat lighter
part of architecture for the ruling classes, with the pleasure
and zoological gardens; Furttenbach devotes seven plates to
the grotto alone, from the façade, via the ground plan to the
cross-section and the grotto itself, with its large coral ornaments and rosettes of shells individually depicted. The typology continues with a "private house," belonging probably to
a burgher or a patrician family, followed by ground plans for
town houses, including an orangery. Church architecture,
which is kept to a minimum, is represented solely by the
front view of a church, the ground plan and a view of the
interior, and in terms of interior design, altar pieces are
shown. There are, however, numerous ground plans of three
variations of a monastery, each two storeys high. They are
all highly symmetrical square layouts laid out around one
or several courtyards; this is also the shape taken for the
grounds of a hospital, a fortified hospital and a graveyard,
which brings the *Architectura civilis* to a close. The plates
were engraved by Raphael and Jacob Custos in Augsburg,
and "Ioseph Furttenbach. Inventor" appears in the bottom
right hand corner of each one. The book was doubtless
aimed at both master builders as well as their clients.

The work is clearly influenced by impressions of Italy.
Furttenbach had set out to adapt the architecture he had
seen in Italy to the climate in Germany, although he did not
develop any system of architectural theory to this end. Like
Paulus Decker (1677–1713) after him, he refers any questions
about the orders of columns and the *Principia architecturae*
to the rules that had appeared previously in Italy, such as
those of Vignola (1507–1573). His later writings at best reveal
a system for the various tasks involved in building: *Architectura civilis, – navalis, – martialis, – privata, – universalis, –
recreationis* (civil, naval, wartime, private, general architecture and landscape gardening.)

The idea of presenting a typology of buildings or
building tasks was obvious: it appeared in the work of Vitruvius and had been continued by his followers in the 15th and
16th centuries. Furttenbach and a short time later Goldmann
advanced the typology. The focal point of Furttenbach's *Architectura civilis* was the building of palaces with gardens and
grottoes as well as the construction of middle-class residential premises. He was the first to tackle this subject in any
detail. With regard to the princely palaces, in addition to
"necessities" he suggested "several little luxuries" to com-
pensate for the prince's "heavy duties" and to dispel any
"seriously melancholy thoughts." He considered work and
leisure to be complementary forms of existence, and followed this premise in the construction of his palaces, houses
and places of leisure. Before Furttenbach little interest was
shown in the residence as a specific building type in its own
right. As was to be expected, his suggestions are based on
Italian models, whereby the influence of Peter Paul Rubens'
engraving *Palazzi di Genova* (*The Palaces of Genoa*, 1622) is
unmistakable. What was new was the fact that individual
rooms were allocated specific functions: chapel, library, theatre, a room for antiques and art, halls, rooms for the chancellery, for consultations, and for banquets. In *Architectura
recreationis* (1640) he expanded on the topic of palaces and
gardens and dealt with it more extensively. Furttenbach was
likewise one of the first to elaborate on public buildings,
dealing first with hospitals, clinics and graveyards. Churches,
town halls, schools and universities were the subject of later
publications. Furttenbach is also the only architectural theorist to present a "purely bourgeois community" in his town
concept.

Furttenbach's œuvre endeavoured to bring country
buildings and gardens closer to the people: it was after all
the time of the Thirty Years' War, and as such *Architectura
civilis* has been referred to as the "architecture of peace."
There is no trace of religious conflict in it, which is what
the Thirty Years' War was superficially all about, yet it is
probable that he favoured the Catholics, if he was not one
himself.

JZ

1 | "Heroischer Hof"
Pl. 4. Engraving by Raphael Custos

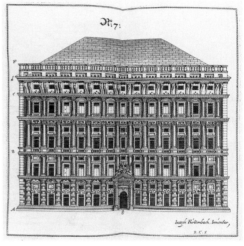

2 | Palace for the gentry
Pl. 5. Engraving by Raphael Custos

3 | Princely palace II
Pl. 7. Engraving by Raphael Custos

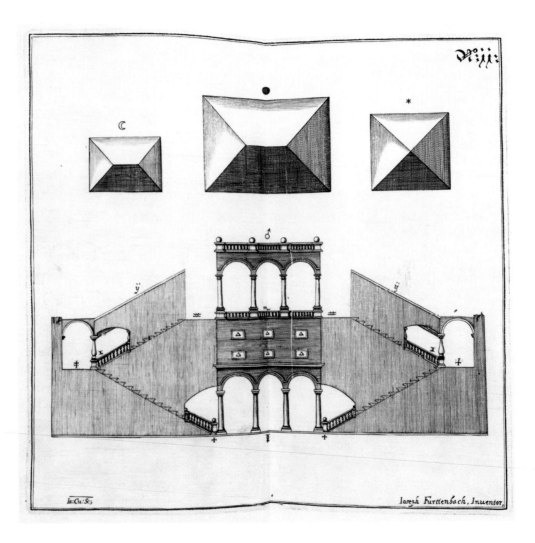

4 | **Stairway**
Pl. 11. Engraving by Jacob Custos

5 | Theatre set: *Scaena comica*
Pl. 12. Engraving by Jacob Custos

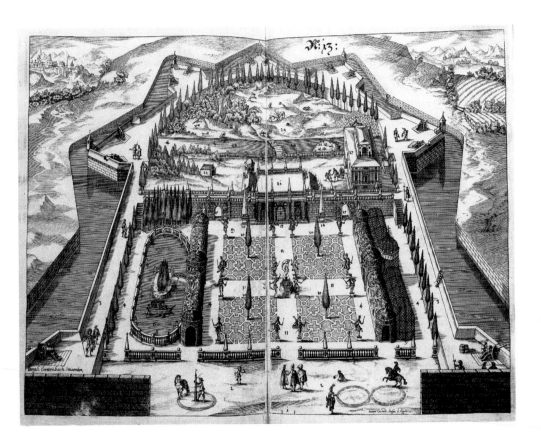

6 | **Pleasure garden**
Pl. 13. Engraving by Jacob Custos

7 | **Façade of a grotto**
Pl. 14. Engraving by
Jacob Custos

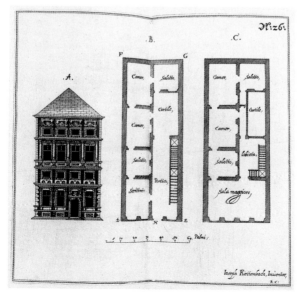

8 | **House in a city,**
with ground plan
Pl. 26. Engraving by
Raphael Custos

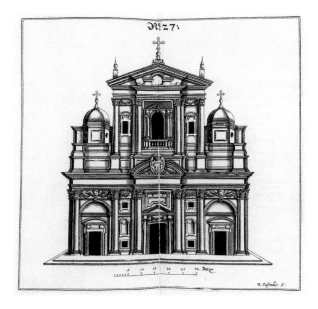

9 | Façade of a church
*Pl. 27. Engraving by
Raphael Custos*

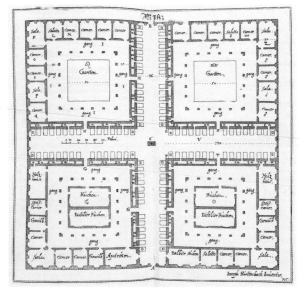

10 | Ground plan of hospital
*Pl. 31. Engraving by
Raphael Custos*

Abraham Leuthner von Grundt (1639/40–1701)

Grundtliche Darstellung Der fünff Seüllen wie solche von dem Weitberühmbten Vitruvio Scamozzio vnd andern Vornehmben Baumeistren Zuesamben getragen

PRAGUE, 1677

Thorough presentation of the five columns like those compiled by the world famous Vitruvius, Scamozzio and other distinguished architects

Abraham Leuthner was born around 1639/40 in Wildstein (now Skalná), to the north of Eger in Bohemia, (now Cheb in the Czech Republic), and died in Prague in 1701. On one of the plates in his treatise he notes that he had also been in Italy during his journeyman years, though recent fundamental research has not busied itself with this question, as presumably no further evidence has been discovered. In 1661, Leuthner was admitted to the guild of masons in the Old Town of Prague, and on 6 November 1665, being a self-employed builder, he became a burgher of the New Town of Prague. On 26 June 1667 he married Maria Glotz or Klotz in the church of Our Lady of the Victory in Prague, and by 1680 had fathered three sons and two daughters. In 1668, together with Johann de Capaoli (d. 1678) and under the supervision of the architect Francesco Caratti (d. 1679) he was involved in the construction of the Černin Palace in the Castle district of Prague, in 1674 in building the pilgrimage church in Stará Boleslav, and between 1674 and 1688 in construction of the Dominican church in Cheb. He is also credited with the construction of a burgher's town house in Cheb in the 1680s. From 1674 until 1688, he was master builder to Duke Julius Franz of Saxe-Lauenburg in Ostrov and between 1674 and 1683 planned and constructed a small summer residence for the latter. In the years following 1682, he started work on his magnum opus: planning the Cistercian monastery in Waldsassen in the Upper Palatinate region of Germany, where the foundation stone was laid in 1689. For this task, he engaged

the five Dientzenhofer brothers. Christoph Dientzenhofer (1655–1722), a foreman, had been his deputy in Ostrov since 1685. Between 1682 and 1687, together with Johann Aischer Leuthner he built the town hall in Loket, which he had designed himself, and in 1687 Leuthner was appointed master fortress builder in Cheb, where six years before he had bought a house at the "Kleist Gate." In 1688, he acquired a house in the Prague New Town for his son Leopold, and bought a house in Prague called "Zum Blauen Hirschen" (The Blue Stag), which was said to have been linked to the "von Grundt" title of nobility. Until then he had simply called himself "Master Mason of Prague Royal New Town." From 1691, his title was "Master Builder of the Eger [Cheb] Fortification Works, Official Trench Master" and "Building and Fortifications Trench Master of the Royal Border Town of Eger [Cheb]." In addition, from 1693 as the successor to Carlo Luragos (1615–1684) he was involved in the construction of a new system of fortifications in Prague and used the title "Imperial (Royal) Master Builder of Overground Constructions and Trenches in the Kingdom of Bohemia." He reached the pinnacle of his career in 1695 when he became "Chief Imperial Master Builder in the Kingdom of Bohemia." He died in his house "Zum Blauen Hirschen" in the Malá Strana district of Prague on 12 January 1701, aged 60.

The summary of Leuthner's life illustrates the work of a highly successful architect and building contractor in the second half of the 17th century who, together with the

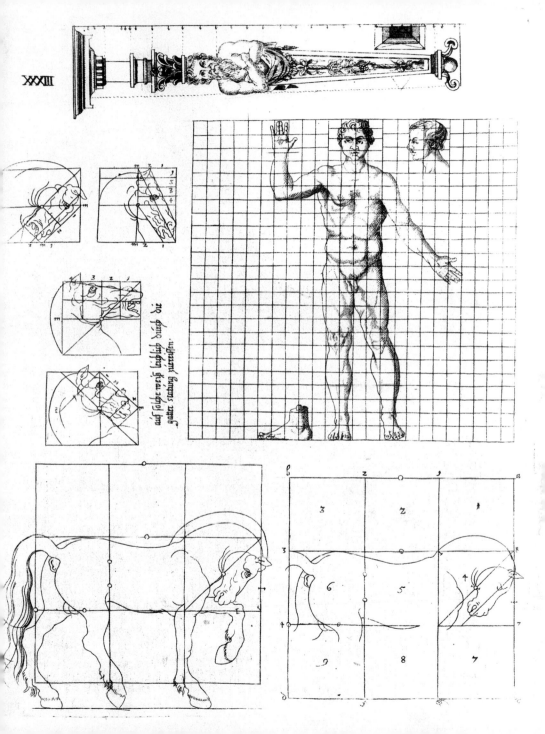

XXXIII

Dientzenhofer brothers, had a not insignificant influence on Late Baroque architecture in Bohemia and southern Germany. By publishing his book on columns he was endeavouring to acquire fame as an educated architect in addition to that he already enjoyed as a result of his expertise in the fields of craftsmanship and planning. Naturally enough this included reference to Vitruvius. Leuthner did this by referring to the origins of architecture, aesthetics and building practice with regard to the primordial hut, the Vitruvian man illustrating human proportions, and hoisting devices. In this he was following the models presented by Giovanni Antonio Rusconi in *Della architettura … secondo i precetti del Vitruvio*, 1590 (*About architecture … according to Vitruvius' Rules*). The basic tenet of the treatise, or rather pattern book, is reminiscent of the early pattern books used by joiners-cum-architects, particularly Hans Jacob Ebelmann's 1609 *Architektur und Kunstbuch* (*Architecture and art book*).

Leuthner's work, which is addressed to "all novices and lovers of architecture," and in no way to "experienced and famous architects," is actually a compilation of well-established books on architecture since 1550. His doctrine on columns is that of Hans Blum (1550), his imaginative cartouches and capitals follow those of Agostino Mitelli (1636), the masks Cornelis Floris and Frans Huys, his connections between architecture and ornaments are based on inventions by Georg Caspar Erasmus (1666); Rutger Kassmann (1630) was the source of his scroll and conch ornamentation, the supporting figures ("Persians") and herm pilasters, by contrast, are influenced by Rusconi (1590), Johann Christoph Feinlin (c. 1670) and Hans Sebald Beham (1528), whereas his examples of architecture from Classical Antiquity are taken from Giovanni Battista Montano (1636) and Sebastiano Serlio (1540). Further models come from Jean Barbet (1633), Pierre Le Muet (1647), Hans Vredeman de Vries (c. 1560), Jacomo Barozzi da Vignola (1562) and above all the various books and editions of Sebastiano Serlio's architectural œuvre, which appeared between 1537 and 1575. Individual points of agreement with Johann Wilhelm's (1649, 1668) *Holzbau-*

kunst (*Architecture in wood*) could well be based on the same source in Vitruvius. In the treatise there is no evidence of the author having himself personally seen any Italian architecture. Nevertheless, there are no grounds for not believing the caption to plate XXVI: "I saw this altar in St Peter's in Rome."

As examples of existing constructions Leuthner's pattern book cites, in addition to Bernini's Baldachin and Serlio's Villa Poggio Reale near Naples, two contemporary Prague buildings: the façades of Černin Palace and of the Clementinum Jesuit theological college in the Old Town. Eight of Leuthner's own draft plans provide a clue to his ideas about architectural form. The ground plan of a church is reminiscent of St. Jacobus Maior in Jičín and the façade, despite different proportions, of that of the church of Our Lady of the Victory in Prague.

On balance, Leuthner's book about columns does not amount to a synthesis of a hundred years of forms in architecture as derived from the spirit of Classical Antiquity, but in exemplary fashion it does select those elements from the repertoire of forms that remained relevant as long as the early 18th century. Leuthner himself etched the plates, and for a master mason and building contractor showed an unusually sure hand and freedom in the pictures he offered. The Prague publisher Caspar Wussin (1664–1747) later used the printing plates for additional editions, which, unlike the first version, are compilations; he added new plates depicting for the most part garden fountains, and portal and window frames, but which no longer had much to do with Leuthner. If today there are only fifteen proven copies in existence it should in no way be assumed that distribution was not widespread; the etchings no doubt shared the same fate as most of the pattern books, which were "worn out" in workshops and building cabins. The book caused a flurry of building activity in Bohemia and southern Germany scarcely witnessed since. Even today there is no reliable facsimile of the 1677 edition.

JZ

Fig. p. 331

1 | **Vitruvian man**
The Vitruvian man according to Rusconi, the Hermes according the Feinlin and the construction grid for horses and horse heads according to Beham.
Pl. XXXIII. Etching

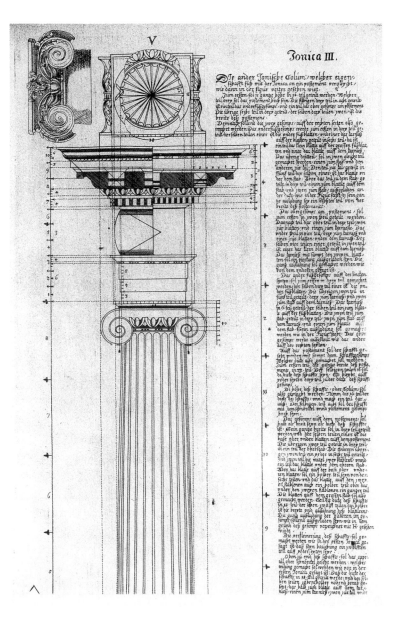

Ionica III.

2 | Ionic column (upper
section) according to Blum;
capital according to Montano
Pl. V. Etching

3 | **Portal**
Pl. XII. Etching

4 | **Bernini's canopy in St. Peter's, Rome**
As well as two capitals according to Montano and
squared stone mouldings according to Serlio.
Pl. XXVI. Etching

5 | **Composita and Corinthia according to Feinlin**
Pl. XXVIII. Etching

6 | Ground plans, elevations
full view and cross-section
of three rotundas according
to Montano
Pl. XXXVIII. Etching

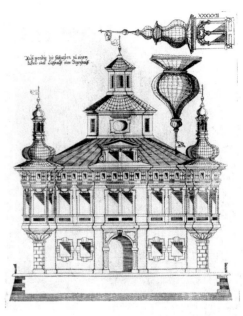

7 | **Part of the façade of the Clementinum in Prague**
And ledge construction according to Blum.
Pl. XXXX. Etching

8 | **Elevation of a country seat, castle or hunting lodge**
Pl. XXXXXIII. Etching

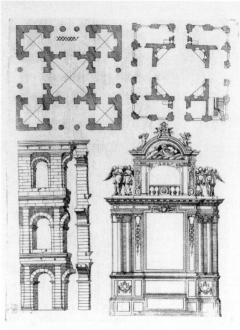

9 | **Elevation of a church façade and mascaron according to Floris**
Pl. XXXXXVII. Etching

10 | **Ground plans according to Serlio and Leuthner**
Partial elevation of the Arena in Verona according to
Serlio and retable according to Barbet.
Pl. XXXXXXV. Etching

11 | **Huts and lifting apparatuses according to Rusconi**
Pl. XXXXXXVIII. Etching

Paulus Decker (1677–1713)

Fürstlicher Baumeister Oder: Architectura Civilis

2 PARTS, AUGSBURG, 1711–1716

Princely architect or: Civil architecture

Though only just 36 when he died, Paulus Decker "the elder," so called to distinguish him from his brother, who was eight years younger and had also been baptized Paul, produced the most elaborately engraved work on the architecture of the German Baroque. The son of a well-established Nuremberg family of metal workers, he was baptized in a Lutheran ceremony on 27 December 1677. From 1695 he was apprenticed to Georg Christoph Eimmart (1638–1705), the first director of the newly-established Nuremberg Academy of Painters, to learn the trade of copperplate engraving. In 1699, having successfully completed his apprenticeship, he moved to Berlin, to be instructed in the field of architecture by Andreas Schlüter (c. 1660–1714). First records of him as an engraver date from 1702, when he was responsible for Johann von Besser's *Preußische Krönungs-Geschichte (Prussian coronation history)*, and in 1703 Schlüter had him engrave his models for the six sheets of *Das berlinische Schloß* (*Berlin Castle*). Around 1705/06, he returned to Nuremberg where, to begin with, he brought out smallish runs of ornaments followed by the *Ausführliche Anleitung zur Civil-Bau-Kunst* (*Detailed introduction to civil architecture*), which evidently soon made his reputation. Thus, in 1708 he was awarded the title of Master Builder of Palatine Sulzbach. In 1710, he was appointed to the court of the Margrave in Bayreuth as inspector of the new princely buildings in Erlangen, and in 1712 Margrave George William appointed him director of building in the Margraviate of Brandenburg-Bayreuth. He

only had one year left in which to carry out his official duties as he died on 3 October 1713 in Bayreuth, unmarried and without issue.

Decker had taken upon himself the task of devising a system of building types that covered all the royal buildings. While carrying out his duties in Bayreuth, the first part of *Fürstlicher Baumeister* appeared, followed by the appendix shortly before his death in 1713. The publisher Jeremias Wolff (1663–1724) compiled the second part in Augsburg and brought it out posthumously in 1716. A third part was meant to cover churches and chapels, and a fourth, town halls, schools, hospitals, stock exchanges and arsenals. Due to his untimely death, the second part only includes those prints that Decker had left behind. Seventeen engravings, for the most part of Augsburg, but also of Nuremberg, assigned Decker's undertaking – and even in fragmentary form it was still overwhelming, with its 130 large-scale plates – a firm place in the Baroque project that the young architect, with noticeable enthusiasm for the absolutist princely display, had devised and offered to those in power. Decker was only able to illustrate a few projects for existing buildings, and these were in a very rich and highly imaginative form, such as the new palace in Erlangen or the nearby summer residence of Mon-Plaisir. However, the book contained no set architectural theory. Even in his *Ausführlichen Anleitung zur Civil-Bau-Kunst* (*A detailed introduction to civil architecture*), which bore no date, Decker was of the opinion that enough

had already been written about these topics. He had therefore simply compiled a few geometric figures and the orders of columns, as well as a collection of models of historical and self-designed examples, not unlike that of Abraham Leuthner (1639/40–1701), but systematically based on well-founded theoretical knowledge. In *Fürstlichen Baumeister* he then endeavours to present a complete set of building types from the point of view of a ruler.

In 1700 the Holy Roman Empire consisted of innumerable sovereign temporal and spiritual electorates, principalities, duchies, dioceses, imperial abbacies, counties and margraviates, all of which were potential clients for Decker and Wolff. These potentates' territories had not only triumphed over the Empire in the political doctrine of the 17th century, gradually they came to claim the status of "majesty," which traditionally, within the Empire, was reserved for the Emperor alone. The social conditions that formed the basis for Decker's monumental undertaking hinged on the view that the office of prince entailed higher power, by which the ruler was accorded complete responsibility for the state, whose supervisory, welfare and planning functions he handled.

The second part of the œuvre, compiled by the Augsburg publisher Wolff, but for the most part prepared by Decker, was a response to the new kingdom of Prussia: it was there, in Schlüter's architectural office, that Decker had acquired his skills or given them greater depth. The introduction to *Fürstliche Baumeister*, the "Princely House," substantiates the close relationship between the work and the architecture of palaces in Berlin around 1700. In addition to French models, examples of work by the Swedish architect Nicodemus Tessin the Younger (1654–1728) for Charlottenburg Palace are also included. The draft plan for a tower refers quite clearly to the 1706 mint tower project for the palace in Berlin. The engraving is considered to be Decker's draft for this building, construction of which was not technically possible as a result of Berlin's sandy soil; it followed the shape of Bellini's project for a bell tower for St Peter's in Rome. In *Prodromus architecturae Goldmannianae*, 1714

(*Introduction to Goldmann's architecture*), which he wrote in disagreement or competition with Decker, Leonhard Christoph Sturm (1669–1719) referred quite clearly to this unfortunate building project and noted that regrettably his sound and generally acknowledged advice had not been followed.

Decker depicted models for all types of illustrious buildings and grounds for residences, and recommended the representatives of the ruling estates to copy these. He brought all these types together in a monumental pattern book *sui generis*: draft plans and recommendations were made for castles, pleasure houses, gardens, orangeries, grottoes, towers and individual rooms in the palaces, even including the ceiling paintings of the main rooms (the dining room, audience chamber and conservatory). Nor were the galleries, with their statues and paintings from Classical Antiquity, omitted; included was the super-elevation of princely rulership by means of iconography, symbolism and iconology (which even went as far as allusions to architecture in the Solomonic style, to which a wise ruler was entitled). For the most part, the models follow the lead of the French court or French architectural theorists such as Claude Perrault (1613–1688), François Blondel (1618–1686) and Marot, whose ideas Decker would have become acquainted with through French emigrants at the Berlin Academy, and so the success of Decker's work is based on these sources. There were many 18th-century architects and decorators who took their cue from Decker, for example Donato Giuseppe Frisoni (1683–1735) in his drafts for Ludwigsburg. Even though he did it elsewhere, the publisher Jeremias Wolff requested the potentates "most respectfully" to forward the plans for their building projects and promised, "no efforts would be spared to complete them as quickly and accurately as possible." Thus the pattern book was at the same time a petition to the princely customers to avail themselves of a sort of agency for princely and later even royal architectural design; the Augsburg publishing house must have operated as such – a rather go-ahead business strategy for the times.   JZ

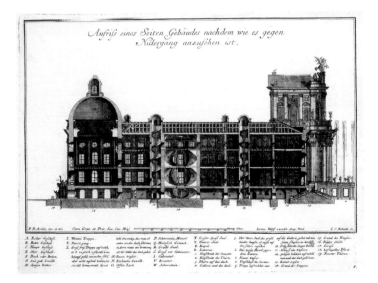

1 | **Façade of the palace**
"Elevation of a building which could be a princely palace as it might look from the front at midday."
Part 1, pl. 6. Engraving by Georg Conrad Bodenehr

2 | **Elevation and cross-section of the northern side wing of the princely palace**
Part 1, pl. 8. Engraving by Georg Conrad Bodenehr

PLAFOND des Vor

Diese Decke wird gantz flach darein die Cupola kan gemahlet werden, unter welchen
stehen kan, der grund dieser decke kan rothlich, und die einfaßungen oder leusten auc
arbeit gemachet ist, welche auch verguldet werden müßen, mus von Spiegel glas gemac
rinnen sich auch alles was in dem Cabinet ist wider representiret. Hier hat der
sen, um zuweißen das diese dinge nicht aus freijen händen oder nach gefallen, son
unter der Cupola kan ein jedweder der sich solcher invention bedienen will selb
nen andern Ornamenten überein kombt u.

Heinrich Jonas Ostertag Sculps.

34.

Ier. Wolff excud . Aug . Vind .

...inets .

...tz oder Stucco gemachte Krantz gantz verguldet-
...seyn . Der ïnere grund aber, worauf die Grodesquen
...ls durch welches man sehr dief hinein siehet, wo=
...rne den Grundriß unter der Cupola stechen las=
...m grund müßen auffgezogen werden, den Krantz
...gnem gefallen doch so machen, damit er mit de=
...schwer aussihet .

3 | **Telescopic representation of dome**
Princely palace, "Ceiling of the entry room"
with painted dome.
Part 1, pl. 34. Engraving by Heinrich Jonas Ostertag

Lange Seiten gegen die Fenster über der Gallerie, in welche man aus dem Cabinet mit Lit: K. bezeichnet, in e entweder von Marmor, oder nur von Gips und hernach Marmorirt oder Metallisirt werden, desgleichen auch die andern Br. Stucco welche an der Maur sehr wohl befestiget werden, auch Verguldet seyn, die 2. Portrait aber seind Mahlereyen, da sollen durch gehends weiß, und mit Marmor Täffelen eingelegt seyn, daran alle Ornamenta, wie auch an denen Wand I Decke durch und durch Verguldet werden mus, da dañ darzwischen allerhand Amourinen als wañ Sie durch die F. köñen allerhand Mahlereyen g

Cum Gratia et Privileg. Sac. Cæs. Maj.

4 | **View of the gallery**
Elevation of the long side of the gallery of a princely palace.
Part 1, pl. 51. Engraving by Johann August Corvinus

A. Rheinl. Schuch.

Iohann August Corvinus Sculpsit.

57

des Haubt Geschoßes, nach dem Spazier Saal komen kan; die Statuen in denen Blinten köñen nach denen Antiquitæeten
denen 4. Bogen Füllungen köñen Zierlich gewürckte Tapeten hangen, die Geñÿ und andere Tugend Bilder follen von
der Thür nächst denen Gevaßen kan man von Kupffer machen und hernach im Feuer Vergulden laßen, die Wände
ſaſst Gesimbse, Holl Kehlen, Capitæle ſambt dem Haubt Gesimbs Verguldet werden. Ingleichem auch die Bogen
die Gallerie flögen, al fresco oder mit oel farben auf tuch köñen gemahlet werden. Uber denen Bilder Blinten
über zu hangen kommen.

Ieremias Wolff excudit Aug. Vind.

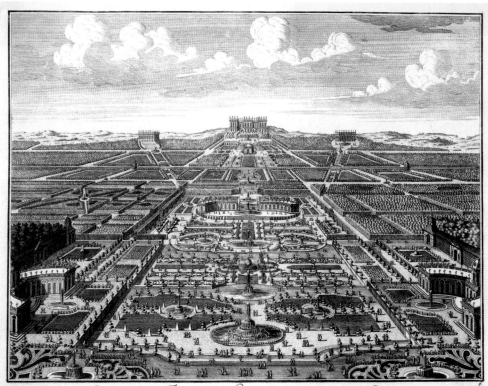

Prospect des Fürstlichen Lustgartens, hinter dem Pallast.

P. Decker Archit. inv. et del.   Cum Privileg. Sac. Cæs. Majest.   Ieremias Wolff excud. Aug. Vind.   Ionas Heinrich Ostertag Sculps.

5 | **Pleasure garden**
"View of the princely pleasure garden behind the palace."
Part 1, appendix, pl. 6. Engraving by Heinrich Jonas Ostertag

6 | **View of the Orangerie**
"Elevation of the Orangerie viewed from a distance."
Part 1, appendix, pl. 8. Engraving by Johannes Böcklin

Lust-Saal, welcher in dem Canal des Fürstl. Lust-Gartens zu Ende des Irr-Gartens ligen kan, das aus der mittlern Platz eine völlige allee dahin gehet.
P. Decker Archit. invent. et del.   Cum. Privil. Sac. C. Maj.   I. Wolff Excud. Aug. Vind.   F. A. Corvinus fecit.

7 | **Garden pavilion**
"Summer pavilion which could be located on the canal
of the princely pleasure garden at the end of the maze ..."
Part 1, appendix, pl. 24. Engraving by Johann August Corvinus

Projoect des Lust Hauses von Sr. Königl. Hoheit Mon-plaisir, wie solches eine halbe Meile von Christian Erlang soll gebauet werden.

Perspectivischer aufzug eines Lustkaußes, wie solches ein Vornehmer Herr auf dem Land erbauen könte.

8 | **Plan for Mon-Plaisir near Erlangen**
"View of the summer palace Mon-Plaisir."
Part 1, appendix, pl. 29. Engraving by Johann August Corvinus

9 | **View of the princely pleasure garden**
"Elevation of a land-house such as a distinguished gentleman could build in the country and viewed from a distance."
Part 1, appendix, pl. 38. Engraving by Carl Remshardt

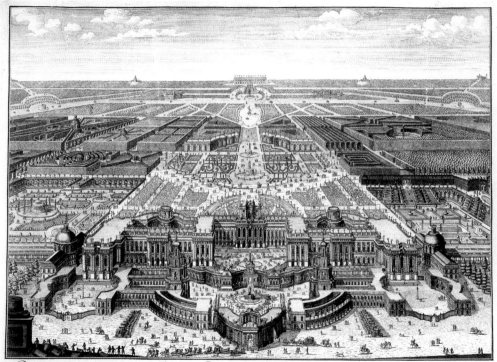

Perspectivischer Auffzug des König. Pallasts mit allen seiten Gebäuden, und einem theil des Gartens.

P. Decker Archit. inv. et del.   Cum Privileg. Sac. Cæs. Majest.   Jeremias Wolff excud. Aug Vind.   Jonas Heinrich Ostertag Sculpsit.

10 | **View of a palace and its grounds**
"Elevation of the royal palace viewed from a distance …"
Part 2, pl. 1. Engraving by Heinrich Jonas Ostertag

11 | **"Orthographic elevation of the tower"**
Part 2, pl. 2. Engraving by Carl Remshardt

Johann Bernhard Fischer von Erlach (1656–1723)

Entwurff Einer Historischen Architectur

VIENNA, 1721

Plan for an historical architecture

Johann Bernhard Fischer von Erlach came from a family of burghers and craftsmen in Graz, Austria, where he was born in July 1656. After training as a sculptor in his father's workshop, the 15-year-old Fischer went to Rome, where he began working in the studio of the Papal Architect and court painter Philipp Schor (1646–end 17th c.). In addition to his activities as a sculptor and wax moulder Fischer familiarized himself closely with the theory of architecture. He made contact with the circle of intellectuals around Queen Christine of Sweden (reigned 1632–1654) and became acquainted with the methods of scientific archaeology, which was in its infancy at the time. Having been in Naples until 1685, from 1687 he was employed as a sculptor by Emperor Leopold I (reigned 1658–1705) in Vienna. That same year he commenced architectural work for Prince Liechtenstein. After the death of Emperor Leopold I in 1705 and the accession of Joseph I (reigned 1705–1711) he was made Chief Inspector of the Court Buildings. In 1712, he handed over the manuscript of his *Entwurff Einer Historischen Architectur* to Emperor Charles VI (reigned 1711–40). Fischer von Erlach died on 5 April 1723.

The set of oblong engravings that make up *Entwurff Einer Historischen Architectur* is one of the most unusual and original works in the history of architectural theory. After commemorative coins, findings from ruins, descriptions of journeys and Classical traditions, Fischer goes on to reconstruct temples, palaces, mausoleums and the squares of ancient Greece and Rome, whilst also introducing the architecture of Egypt and Asia. After lengthy preparatory work, the manuscript itself was actually compiled quickly, presumably in order to be ready for presentation to the new Emperor Charles VI when the latter assumed power in 1712. The contents of the book, which did not appear until 1721, correspond for the most part to the manuscript. It can be gleaned from the first edition's Imperial Charter that Fischer "had spent 16 years on this work on his profession." Thus the project must have been begun around 1705, even if several ideas that Fischer had had during his stay in Rome were incorporated into it.

Fischer quite clearly states his intentions on the title page and in the introduction. He was endeavouring to produce "a history of architecture using illustrations of various famous buildings from Antiquity and foreign countries," to "delight the eye of lovers (of architecture) and to provide inspiration for artists," thus serving to "promote both science and art." Fischer opens the first book, "about a few buildings constructed by ancient Jews, Egyptians, Syrians, Persians, and Greeks" in programmatic fashion with Solomon's Temple. Fischer knew both the interpretation of Ezekiel by the Spanish Jesuit Villalpando (1552–1608), which formed the basis for an architectural reconstruction of Solomon's Temple, and the detailed description of Nikolaus Goldmann (1611–1665), which was based on Villalpando and published by Leonhard Christoph Sturm in 1696. By opening with

Solomon's Temple, Fischer follows a standard publishing tradition, though he uses this architectural model neither to justifies nor to legitimize his own architecture, and instead from this vantage point develops a panorama of world architecture and its individual categories. Solomon's Temple is followed by the Seven Wonders of the world, and the buildings of Persia, Egypt and Classical Greece, whereby the various forms of architecture are not presented on their own but are in each case embedded in the countryside that surrounds them.

The second book, about several "old, unknown Roman buildings," is surprising in its selection. Such icons of Roman architecture as the Pantheon or the Vesta Temple are not included; instead Fischer begins with the ruins of the amphitheatre in Tarragona, Spain. Here, Fischer was not speaking as a scientific archaeologist or learned scholar of buildings, but rather as a courtier, opening the Emperor's eyes to the fact that the architecture of Classical Antiquity once stood on the very ground of the country of which he currently claimed the throne. In this way, continuity between the old and the new Roman Empire is the theme, and historical facts are used to buttress politico-legal claims. This is followed by monuments from Roman Antiquity that were important as architecture, and whose reconstructions were often interpreted very freely, with the imperial character bearing some relationship to Fischer's later constructions. "As far as architecture is concerned, we maintain that the architect must come up with a good idea, and a formula that serves him as both law and insight, as his drafts should be based on order and division, the measurement and harmony of the whole and the parts it is made up of. With regard to the decoration and ornamentation of the column orders, however, the idea must have taken root, and have been confirmed by examples of the Ancients that, through their success based on prolonged studies, determined the type and extent of this art." This was how Giovanni Pietro Bellori had summarized his "ideas about artists" (*L'idea del pittore, dello scultore e dell'architetto*) in a lecture in 1664, demanding that Classical architecture in heroic ruins be reconstructed according to the original ideas and in its original appearance.

During his stay in Rome, Fischer had got to know the General Curator of the city's antiquities, who may well have been responsible for triggering Fischer's interest in Classical Antiquity.

If the manuscript is taken as a basis, the third book, "about buildings constructed by Arabs and Turks, as well as in the modern Persian, Siamese, Chinese and Japanese styles of building" was also meant to include Gothic and Moorish constructions. Fischer used familiar examples from publications of engravings for his reconstructions of the large-scale buildings in the Middle and Far East, which were often set in rural environs.

The fourth book contains only "a few buildings invented and drawn by the author," illustrating the types of buildings relevant at the time: churches, town residences, garden palaces, summer houses, country castles, tombs and festive architecture. Fischer presents a mixture of building projects, some planned, some already completed. Often, rather than presenting the completed building, he shows the plans that were submitted, which gives a far greater insight into the architect's original intentions than the finished product, subject as it was to all kinds of restrictions. The fact that he included his own work in a book about the history of world architecture is evidence of a self-confidence among architects typical of the Renaissance. Here, Palladio (1508–1580), who dealt with his own work in *Quattro libri*, was very much a role model.

Fischer's *Entwurff Einer Historischen Architectur* did not set out to be an objective presentation of the history of architecture, it serves the purpose of legitimizing the Habsburg empire and its interest in ensuring its continuity. His comparative history of world architecture is compiled from literary and pictorial sources that he names individually. At the same time he proves himself to be an ingenious architect and draughtsman, well capable of illustrating the three-dimensional quality of architecture. Fischer overcomes the academic tradition of Vitruvius, which until then had dominated architectural theory, and as architect and artist presents architecture in a historical and contemporary context with his impressive depictions.   BE

1 | Hall of columns
The ancient motif of a hall of columns with Exedra is formulated
by Fischer von Erlach in the language of French Classicism.
The connection with ancient architecture is a conscious one.
Fascicle 1, sheet 4. Etching by Johann Ulrich Kraus

2 | Reconstruction of Salomon's Temple
Like many theoreticians of architecture, Fischer von Erlach places
the "perfect" structure, Salomon's Temple, at the beginning
of his treatise, showing above all the huge substructure.
Fascicle 1, pl. II. Etching

3 | Reconstruction of the Temple of Zeus in Olympia

The reconstruction is based on Pausanias' description, whereby the Corinthian order and the coffered barreled vaulting are borrowed from Diocletian's palace in Spalato.

Fascicle 1, pl. V. Etching

Das Wunder=Bild des Olympischen Iupiter
und Helffenbein; sitzend 60 Schuh hoch; Woran Phidias sein M...
wiesen. Anben der Durchschnitt des Olympischen von den 4 Iah...
berühmten Tempels zu Elis. Nach der genauen beschreibung Pauf.

Ioan Bernard Fischer v C. delineav.

La Statue Colossale du Jupiter Olympien, composée d'or et d'ivoir,
qui étant assise a eü la hauteur de 60 pieds. Le chef d'œuvre de Phidias. On y a ajouté
la coupe du Temple Olympien dans l'Elide, fameuse par les jeux, qu'on y celebroit tous
les quatre ans. Le dessein est aprés la description exacte de Pausanias.

Bold
er=
en

Cum Pri: Sac: Cæsa: Majest:

4 | Reconstruction of the Colossus of Rhodes
Fischer von Erlach continues the theme of
reconstructing the Colossus of Rhodes which
has been a matter of discussion since the
Renaissance. However, the bronze statue did
not stand as a lighthouse at the entrance to
the port but rather at the port itself.
Fascicle 1, pl. VIII. Etching

Le merveilleux Colosse de Rhodes dedié
au Soleil, qui fût jetté en bronze par Care Lyndien,
Soûs le gouvernement de Theagone Prince de Carie,
environ l'an du monde 3600 Il avoit 70. aünes de haut.
Plin: L. 2 cap. 62 et L. 34 c. 7. Strab L. 12.

atua,
n
em
ichtet.

Cum Priv. Sac. Cæs. May.

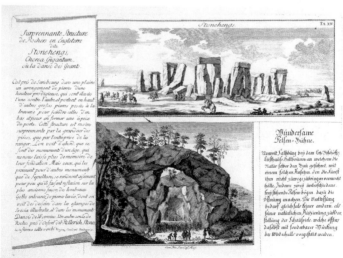

5 | **Trajan's Forum in Rome**
With his design of a central column, a fountain and statues
of two men on horseback, Fischer von Erlach has created
a variation of the classic French *Palace royal.*
Fascicle 2, pl. VII. Etching

6 | **Stonehenge in England and the stone theatre at
Hellbrunn Palace near Salzburg**
Fascicle 2, pl. XIV. Etching

TA. V.

Die grosse Cisterne zu Constantinopel
an dem Marckt Atmeidan sonst Hippodromus genant.

Dessen steinerne Säulen grösten Theils mit Wasser ange=
füllet unter der Erden nicht weiter von einander
stehen als daß man mit Kahnen zwischen durchfahren
kan. Ihrer werden in allen 224. gezehlet. Gegen=
wertige eigentliche Abzeichnung ist samt dem Grund=
riß und anderen Türckischen Gebäuden aus Orient
verschrieben worden, um solche der sonderbahren
Beschaffenheit halber denen Liebhabern mit zu=
theilen.

La grande Cisterne de Constantinople
à la place dite Atmeidan autrefois l' Hippodrome

Les 224. Colonnes de pierre de taille dont elle est
Soutenüe Sous terre sont presque couvertes d'eau
à une distance qui ne souffre que le passage de
petits bateaux. On en a fait venir de l'Orient
cette Elevation avec le plan et avec quelques
autres bâtimens Turcs pour les communiquer aux
curieux a cause de leur singularité.

7 | Reconstruction of the Cistern of Constantinople
Like Diocletian's thermal baths, the aqueduct of Carthage and several bridges,
Fischer von Erlach includes the "The Great Cistern of Constantinople"
among the technical structures in his *Historical Architecture*.
Fascicle 3, pl. V. Etching

Friedrich Weinbrenner (1766–1826)

Architektonisches Lehrbuch

3 PARTS, TÜBINGEN, 1810–1819

Architectural textbook

The life and works of Friedrich Weinbrenner can be divided up into three main stages: his childhood and training as a carpenter in Karlsruhe (1766–1788), his apprenticeship and journeyman years in Switzerland, Vienna, Dresden, Berlin and Italy (1788–1797), and his professional years as a building official for the State of Baden in Karlsruhe (1797–1826). The six-year stay in Italy was a major influence on Weinbrenner; it was here that he found direct on his doorstep examples of Classical architecture, as well as accompanying literature that had been handed down through the ages. During this period he laid the foundation stone for his architectural œuvre, which predominantly features the sober elements of the Greek and Roman style of construction. From August 1800 until his death in 1826 Weinbrenner worked in Karlsruhe, where in his role as chief building officer he was responsible for extensive building activity, and made substantial contributions to the supervision of building work. Primarily his efforts were channelled into extending this Baroque fan-shaped city, paying great attention to the appearance of individual streets and squares. He showed great fervour in his descriptions of the training of architects, which he carried out in his private institution. His pupils' exercise sheets provide an insight into the curricula: simple drawing, geometry, the shapes of buildings and the theory of construction. *Architektonisches Lehrbuch* is at one and the same time a practical instruction manual for his pupils, and an explanation of his architectural theory.

The first sections of Weinbrenner's *Architektonisches Lehrbuch* appeared in 1810. The whole spectrum of architecture was to be explained in four parts (from the theory of drawing and the theory of construction to the history and theory of architecture). While three volumes were completed before Weinbrenner's death, the fourth, *Die praktische Baukunst* (*Practical Architecture*), remained in manuscript form and was not published. Though incomplete, the *Lehrbuch*, being the first practical and theoretical compendium of all the different aspects of the field, quickly became popular, especially in Germany. The plates, with their brief explanations, established a form of German theory of architecture, pushing back the predominant influence of the French and Italian. The publication of the manual actually served a more practical purpose: "Trained for the world, not for scholarly schools, I give with my best will that which the older artist can and indeed should give the younger, by means of drawing and short explanations, without scholarship, for his teaching and education, which is indispensable. I want to elaborate not in a speculative, philosophical or scholarly vein, which is repellent to pupils and practising artists. Scholarship is of little use to us, and the idea of reason in architecture is thus of little value to us if experience is not added to it. At the same time, I was driven by a vivid sense of a lack of formal education in architecture, both written and oral, which during my six-year stay in Rome I often had the chance of observing in myself and others."

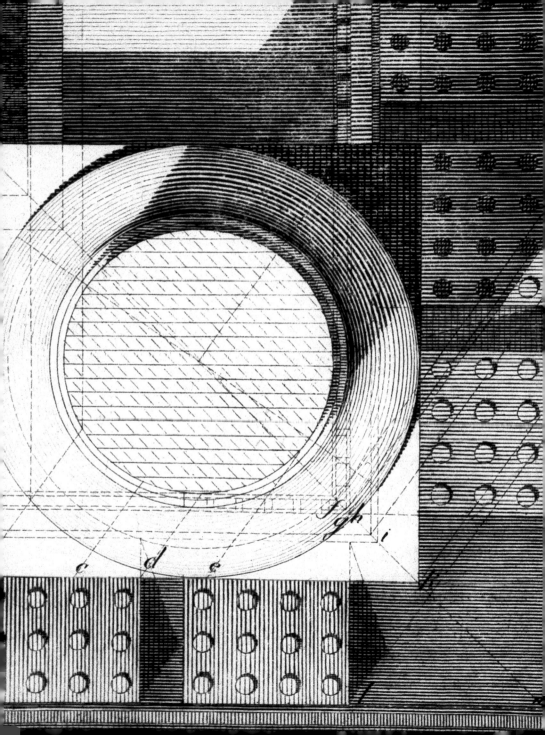

The first two booklets are devoted to the art of drawing perspectives, indispensable practice for future architects in that they are confronted with the fundamental questions of depicting architecture and construction. Not until the third part *Über die Höhere Baukunst* (*On advanced architecture*) does Weinbrenner's actual view of architecture clearly emerge. It talks about the shape and beauty of advanced architecture, about the practice of decoration in architecture and the use of the orders of columns, the division, arrangement and execution of buildings, even if palpably from a highly practical point of view. "In this sense, a figure is beautiful if contours promise a useful completion. The usefulness itself is determined by the concept of the figure." Weinbrenner perceives beauty in the forms, not in the materials used. He describes in the following way how the form of a building must come about: "If commodity is the guiding principle in creating buildings of certain characteristics, so that these conform with our needs and not we with theirs, then a building for a shoemaker, a merchant, a manufacturer as well as that of a rich man can be built with a few, and that of a prince with many aspects of commodity, manifold and as a characteristic whole." Even architectural ornamentation "must have an intrinsic importance that corresponds to the importance of the object it adorns and to the purpose of the building." For Weinbrenner, the key method to illustrate hierarchical structures of importance in architecture remains the orders of columns, as there the various degrees of expression not only accentuate the character of the building but should also contribute to the refinement of the building. Weinbrenner bases his concept of an aesthetics of reception in architecture on the architectural theory that prevailed around 1800, which called for a functional, utilitarian style of building.

In order to study the theory of form in architecture, Weinbrenner provides three plates showing variant systems for ground plans and elevations, derived from basic geometrical shapes. In this way, Weinbrenner arrives at a system of planning for single and multi-use rooms within a building. Complying strictly with the symmetrical alignment, depending on the size and purpose of a building, any number of combinations is possible, based on a grid system. Weinbrenner considers those schemes presented in the manual as visual examples for viewing and teaching, which need some modification during the actual building process in order to do justice to the "multi-purpose" nature of architectural drafts. Here, Weinbrenner was attempting to mediate between Kant's aesthetics and Durand's functionalism.

The fourth, unpublished part is dedicated to practical architecture, and deals with the theory and technical production of staircases, and the practical and technical theory of wooden and stone structures. The work is not organized chronologically. There are various versions of the manuscript entitled *Über die technische Anordnung der Schreiner, Glaser, Blechner und Schlosserarbeiten bey Gebäuden* (*On technical matters concerning joiners, glaziers, plumbers and fitters in buildings*) for the sixth segment of the third part. The detailed explanation of the production and use of gates, doors, shutters, wall and ceiling facings, window frames and iron as used in construction work bears witness to the immense range of Weinbrenner's craft knowledge, which he acquired during his training.

Unlike the typical treatise on architecture, which used as its method the theory of decorum, Weinbrenner developed a manual that provided lessons and exercises with an increasing degree of difficulty. Both in terms of methodology and the demand that the purpose of the building should be the basis of the architectural design, there are parallels with the work of the Frenchman Jean-Nicolas-Louis Durand (1760–1835), whose abstract gridding system introduced modern rationalism to architecture. Since Weinbrenner adhered to the Classical vocabulary of forms, his architecture became subject to criticism soon after his death.   BE

1 | **Detail study**
The task is to determine the illumination and shadowing for a Doric capital which is illustrated from above and in elevation.
Part 1, pl. XIII. Etching

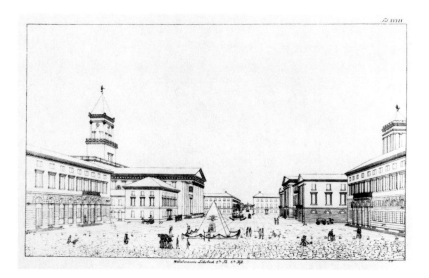

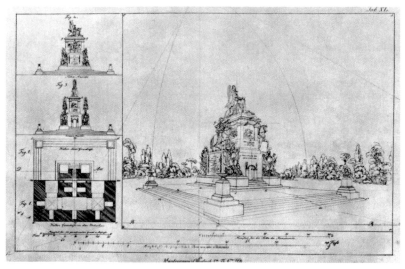

2 | Market square in Karlsruhe
The design of the market square in Karlsruhe is based on a succession
of four different squares which lead to the palace in a type of
Via Triumphalis.
Part 2, pl. XXXIX. Lithograph

3 | Design for a monument
In 1815, Weinbrenner designed a monument based on
the Battle of Belle-Alliance which he intended as a
"Monument for all Europe."
Part 2, pl. XL. Lithograph

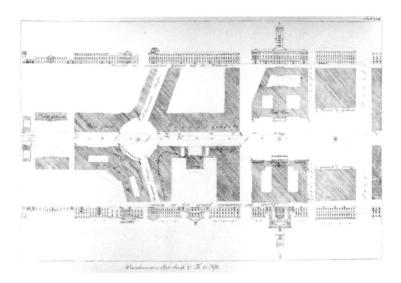

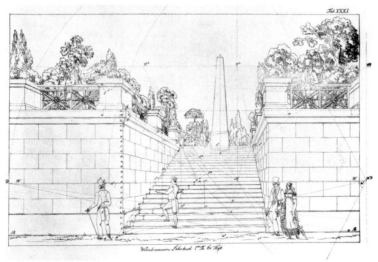

4 | **Design for the former Schlossstraße in Karlsruhe**
The entrance square is followed by the round plot with the
obelisk; then a rectangular square and finally the quadrangular
square with the pyramid.
Part 2, pl. XLII. Lithograph

5 | **Stairway**
Using an illustration of a stairs leading to a terrace,
the textbook assigns the task of drawing the stairs with the
proper perspective and of determining the shapes of the shadows.
Part 3, pl. XXXI. Lithograph

6 | **Decorations**
Part 3, pl. XVII. Lithograph

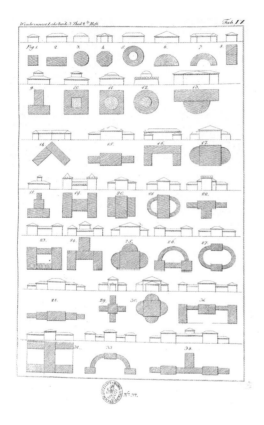

7 | **Ground plans and elevations for buildings
based on geometric forms**
Part 3, pl. IX. Lithograph

8 | **Fluting**
Variations in fluting of column shafts, figures of Hermes, caryatids, Ionian
and Corinthian capitals.
Part 3, pl. XXL. Lithograph

Karl Friedrich Schinkel (1781–1841)

Sammlung architectonischer Entwürfe von Schinkel enthaltend theils Werke welche ausgeführt sind, theils Gegenstände deren Ausführung beabsichtigt wurde

28 FASCICLES, BERLIN, 1819–1840

Collection of architectural designs. New York, 1989

When the 16-year-old grammar-school student Karl Friedrich Schinkel saw Friedrich Gilly's draft for a monument to Frederick the Great at an exhibition at the Berlin Academy in 1797, he decided on the spot to become an architect. Schinkel was born in Neuruppin in 1781, the son of Johann Cuno Schinkel, a superintendent pastor in the Protestant church, and his wife Dorothea (née Schinkel). He was one of the first graduates of the Berlin Academy of Building and his life-long devotion to his teacher Friedrich Gilly (1772–1800) who died at the early age of 28, becomes evident in the autobiography Schinkel published in 1825: "A decisive leaning towards art had manifested itself in him (Schinkel) at an early age and he therefore seized the opportunity offered to him of studying under … Gilly, whose services to the study of architecture were well known through his highly regarded writings. But it was the work of Professor Gilly, the son of the above, that was a particular stimulus for Schinkel's young spirit, which first experienced a closer encounter with this art in the form of these brilliant architectural contrasts, which were dealt with in a highly individual manner."

During his first journey to Italy from 1803 until 1805, Schinkel received a lasting impression both of buildings of Classical Antiquity as well as medieval brick architecture. Following his return to Berlin in 1805, he first of all had to make do with decoration work, but succeeded in gaining public attention by exhibiting large-format dioramas. On the recommendation of Wilhelm von Humboldt, he was appoint-ed a probationary building official (Geheimer Oberbauassessor) in the Prussian government service, a position made permanent with his promotion to Geheimer Oberbaurat in 1815, when he was co-opted to the state's technical building commission. His employment in the public service resulted in supervisory duties throughout the kingdom of Prussia, as well as commissions from ministries and other public institutions. It was not until 1816 that he was given any real assignments, such as the Neue Wache and the re-design of the cathedral at the Lustgarten, followed in 1817 by the royal command to rebuild the theatre on the Gendarmenmarkt, which had been destroyed by fire. Even though his employment in the Prussian civil service precluded any more extended educational travels, later trips on official business took him to France and England (1826), Italy (1824 and 1830), and above all repeatedly to the Prussian provinces, which stretched from the Rhineland to the Russian border. In addition to the numerous architectural designs and projects that were never realized, important buildings Schinkel completed in Berlin include the Neue Wache (1816–1818), the Königsschauspielhaus (Theatre Royal, 1818–1821), the Friedrich-Werdersche Church (1821–1830), the Altes Museum (Old Museum, 1822–1830) and the Bauakademie (Academy of Building, 1832–1836), where he had an apartment, and where he died in October 1841.

"Historical does not just mean retaining or repeating what is old, for this would destroy history. To act in a histori-

cal manner means to introduce something new that at the same time continues history," was how Schinkel accurately described the basic tenet behind his architectural intentions, which indeed became the basis of his building work both in theory and in practice. Schinkel stood out from his contemporaries by his permanent intellectual reflexion, the ongoing deliberation on how to revise his practical approach to building.

In 1819, Schinkel, who was 38 at the time, presented the first part of the series *Sammlung architectonischer Entwürfe*. It contained his own works, inasmuch as they were completed or at least had already been drawn up for actual construction projects. The large-format edition could well have been inspired by *Recueil de Décorations Intérieurs* (*Collection of interior decorations*, 1801) by the French architects Charles Percier (1764–1838) and Pierre François Fontaine (1762–1853), and possibly also by *New Vitruvius Britannicus* (1802–1809) by George Richardson (1736–1817). It is still surprising that Schinkel presented an overview of his architectural work at such an early stage in his career, given that the complete published edition was not finished until a year before his death in 1840.

The volume of plates is a reference work, a monumental catalogue of his œuvre, a sort of biography in pictorial form. Schinkel includes buildings and other completed projects, as well as alternative designs, ground plans and elevations, cross sections, interior and street views, architectural details and gardens, designs for monuments, bridges, furniture, ornaments and handicraft objects, which in many cases were never completed, not even in altered or reduced form. As such, the volume is at one and the same time a pattern book and a textbook for exemplary building and design that was to be of considerable influence for future generations of architects.

Schinkel accompanies each plate with a short text. Even though the theoretical aspect takes back seat to the impressive visuals, the aesthetic arguments are presented in concise, explanatory form. In addition to the question of acquiring land, the conversion of existing buildings, and the diversion of water courses, he goes into the questions of managing client requests, of co-operating with other architects and garden landscapers, and of what to do when plans have to be changed for financial reasons.

In the introductory text, Schinkel defends the Schauspielhaus (Theatre Royal), generally considered his *magnum opus*, against the criticism levelled at it, much of it by people who did not understand it. "There are many who have an obscure one-sided feeling that they are able to change individual things about the finished work, since ignorance and a lack of ability to create unity out of a highly non-uniform starting position blind them to the destruction that these changes would make to the overall construction. The simpler the solution for the immediate outer appearance of a complicated building, the less its artistic value is recognized by the masses." This amounted to a succinct call for an overall architectural concept, whilst neglecting individual aspects of a building. For all the clear description of these individual aspects, the emphasis of the plates is on giving an impression of overall cohesion.

The actual basis of Schinkel's architecture is contained in *Architektonisches Lehrbuch*, which remained a fragmentary work. The theory behind it is not aimed at practical planning and building, but focuses on ensuring that the building is imbued with due artistry. It is proof of Schinkel's ongoing development, a man who brought together all those changes in ideas, aesthetics and technology that occurred between 1800 and 1850. As a result of the possibilities offered by the modern materials of the early 19th century, Schinkel was able to apply new interpretations and uses to Vitruvius' trinity *utilitas*, *firmitas* und *venustas* (utility, strength and beauty). Later editions, which appeared in rapid succession, bear witness to the widespread high esteem in which Schinkel's architecture was held. With *Architektonische Entwürfe* Schinkel established a new form of publication, that of the self-compiled catalogue of an œuvre, a form that would be of significance right through to the publications of Frank Lloyd Wright (1867–1959) and Le Corbusier (1887–1965).

BE

PERSPECTIVISCHE ANSICHT DES NEUEN SCHAUSPIELHAUSES ZU BERLIN.

1 | **Full view of the New Theatre in Berlin**
Fascicle 2, p. 7. Engraving

NEUE SCHLOSSBRÜCKE IN BERLIN.

PERSPECTIVISCHE ANSICHT DES NEUEN MUSEUMS IN BERLIN, VOM STANDPUNKT ZWISCHEN DEM TEICHBAU UND DER NEUEN SCHLOSSBRÜCKE.

2 | **Palace bridge in Berlin**
In 1819, Schinkel designed the new Palace Bridge as a replacement for a wooden bridge. It led over the left arm of the Spree and formed the end of the street, Unter den Linden, in front of the city palace.
Fascicle 3, p. 24. Engraving

3 | **The Neues Museum in Berlin**
The New Museum in Berlin was in the planning from 1824. The main floor was to exhibit sculpture, the upper floor, painting, and the basement was for "economic requirements."
Fascicle 6, p. 37. Engraving

4 | **Design for Krzescowice Palace**
Krzescowice Palace was planned by Count Potócki as a residence
for his family. In 1822, Schinkel was entrusted with the design
but the plans were never executed.
Fascicle 7, p. 43. Engraving

5 | **Church at the Werderscher Markt in Berlin**
Full view of the exterior of the church.
Fascicle 13, p. 79. Engraving

PERSPECTIVISCHE ANSICHT VON DER GALERIE DER HAUPT-TREPPE DES MUSEUMS
DURCH DEN PORTICUS AUF DEN LUSTGARTEN UND SEINE UMGEBUNGEN.

6 | Entry hall to the Neues Museum in Berlin
On the famous page, one can see through the hall of columns to the pleasure garden,
part of the royal palace, as well as to the towers of the Werdersche Church.
Fascicle 17, p. 103. Engraving

SITUATIONS PLAN VON CHARLOTTENHOF MIT DEN GRUNDRISSEN DER GEBÆUDE.

7 | Ground plan for Charlottenhof
Plan for the layout of Charlottenhof as well as ground plan of the
buildings. From the terrace, which can be covered by a canvas roof,
there is a view to the Neues Palais by Potsdam.
Fascicle 18, p. 109. Engraving

Leo von Klenze (1784–1864)

Anweisung zur Architectur des christlichen Cultus

MUNICH, 1822

Instructions on the architecture of the Christian faith

Along with Karl Friedrich Schinkel (1781–1841), Leo von Klenze, who for many years was Director of Court Buildings and the most senior building official under King Ludwig I of Bavaria, is considered the most important German architect of the first half of the 19th century. Even today, buildings such as the Glyptothek, the Alte Pinakothek, the Residence, the Odeonsplatz and Ludwigstrasse dominate the Munich cityscape. Monuments such as the Befreiungshalle (Hall of Liberation) near Kehlheim and above all the Walhalla near Donaustauf still enjoy national popularity. Even during his lifetime, the trend-setting new Hermitage Museum in St Petersburg was internationally famous.

In 1800, the 16-year-old began his studies at the Berlin Academy of Building under David Gilly (1748–1808). His aim was to be admitted to the higher echelons of the buildings section of the Prussian civil service. During a course of studies in Paris lasting several months he was greatly inspired by the architectural theories of Jean-Nicolas-Louis Durand (1760–1835). In 1808, he was summoned to the court of Jérôme Bonaparte (installed as "King of Westphalia" by his brother Napoleon) in Kassel, and in 1816 appointed Royal Court Architect in the Bavarian capital, Munich. On his numerous journeys to England, France, Greece, Italy and Russia, Klenze obtained a broad overview of art-history and in addition conducted archaeological research in Greece and Sicily. He took part in the debates on contemporary architectural research and theory well into a ripe old age. Though

Klenze left behind a vast array of literature on such subjects as archaeology, history and religion, he did not produce any one textbook as such containing a definitive theory of architecture.

The *Anweisung zur Architectur des christlichen Cultus* can be regarded as a pattern book of modern basilica-based church architecture, which Klenze aimed to elevate to a new and higher level of development. Taking sacred buildings as an example, he formulated his neo-Classical approach to architecture in an excursus covering the philosophy of religion, history, aesthetics and the history of art and culture. In the introduction to the work, of which several hundred copies were forwarded free of charge to various religious and secular authorities, he explained its official, governmental character. Klenze justified a state-run, centralized art and architecture policy, citing historical models from Pericles to the art-loving Popes of the Renaissance, in order to propagate a "general fixed interpretation of architectural rules and forms." The instructions are sub-divided into a preface, six chapters and 38 plates. The first four chapters serve to provide theoretical justification for the adoption of a neo-Classical style of building, the fifth summarizes in catalogue form the "requirements of Christian liturgical building," with the sixth and closing chapter containing explanations of the sample plans. The plates present eleven patterns for small village churches, and three for larger ones, two for urban parish churches, two for the main church in large towns and

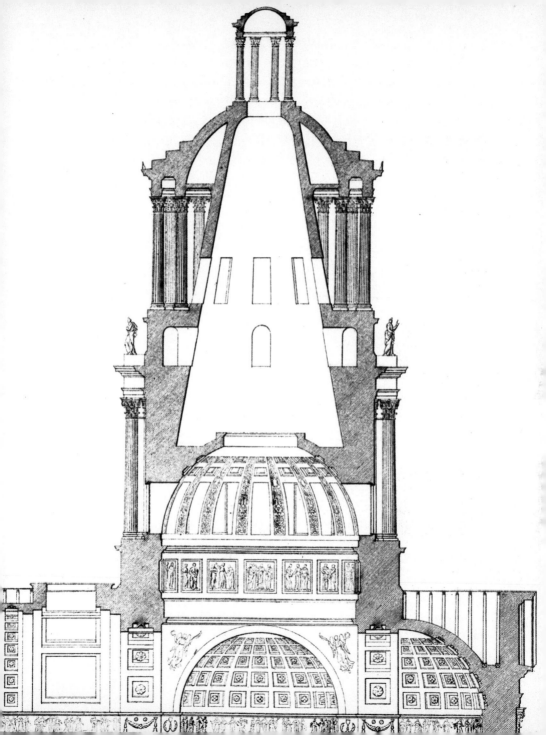

another for a cathedral. What is remarkable is that none of the plans presented displays the cross-section with raised nave and clerestory so characteristic of old Christian church architecture. The chapters on theory illustrate how Klenze handled the central question of whether early Christian basilicas should be interpreted in a neo-Classical or Romantic light. Most of all he was at pains to refute the objections raised by the Romantics around Peter Cornelius (c. 1783–1867) to a neo-Classical approach to modern church building.

In the first chapter, "Earlier religions and their relationship to Christianity," Klenze attempts to prove the inner affinities between ancient pagan religions and Christianity, with the goal of showing that in principle, "liturgical requirements could be satisfied architecturally in one and the same way." The second chapter provides "solid historical justification" for the adaptation of the architecture of Classical Antiquity in early Christian times, arguing that the architecture of this "heroic epoch of Christianity" was, in its turn, highly relevant for the present time, unlike that of a medieval period of decay. In the third chapter, which was devoted to the aesthetics of architecture, Klenze seeks to prove that the basic aesthetic principle of Greek architecture was not diametrically opposed to, but completely at one with the innermost truth of Christian faith. Following Aloys Hirt (1759–1837), he asserts that in terms of the laws of statics, construction and economy, architecture in Greece had reached the highest point of perfection in a harmonious balance between spirit and matter. Greek architecture, because of its perfection and truth, he continues, should be recognized as the "architecture of true, intrinsic and positive Christianity, as truly Christian architecture." This, however, in no way means that Greek buildings should be copied directly. Rather, he calls for a "clear differentiation between individual forms and their composition, analogy and syntax, since although the individual forms that the Greeks and Ro-

mans passed down to us are to be regarded in themselves as perfect, although in no way as final, our requirements, particularly liturgical requirements, are so different from theirs that these forms need to be put together in quite a different way in order to fulfil their function." The violation of the unity of form and structure expressed here, which was derived from French neo-Classicism, aroused contemporary criticism especially. And yet it could be argued that Klenze's "clear differentiation between individual forms and the way they are put together" was just an abstract way of illustrating the superiority of Greek architecture. It was not just the "most perfect, best and most beautiful" architecture, but the "only true and fundamental one … by which measure all that came before could be summarized as the beginnings and an imperfect attempt, and all that came later can be subsumed under the heading of regional and digressive."

The fourth chapter is devoted to a "fleeting glance at the liturgical buildings of Christianity … which time and circumstances inspired, either at one with or in opposition to those principles we have determined." There is much criticism of Gothic, as a "Christian hierarchical style that reflects the baleful hair-splitting of dogmatism and scholasticism." Klenze categorically rejects the Romantic notion that Gothic was German in origin and sees it more as a product of the despicable political system which "used spiritual and ecclesiastical means … to strive for worldly power and possessions, and cause people to cast their eyes upwards towards heaven so as to be able to act and rule on earth unobserved." Despotism, mendacity and a "lack of static harmony" were the characteristics of Gothic edifices with their hidden buttresses, which were "artificial, not artistic." According to Klenze, Gothic was not suitable for reincarnation, but at best for preservation as part of the cultural heritage. It was not until after this theoretical beginning that Klenze embarked on a somewhat unspecific discussion of the architectural design of churches.   BE

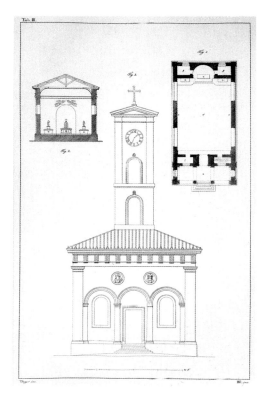

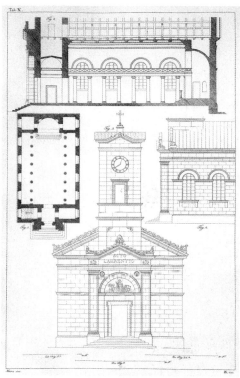

1 | **Plan for a village church**
The prototype for a simple village church is based on "Italian precedents"; in particular the open tower is a repetition of many small Italian bell towers.
Pl. III. Engraving

2 | **Plan of a church**
The galleried church is characteristic of protestant churches in Germany, although Klenze also envisages this style for Catholic sacral structures.
Pl. XI. Engraving

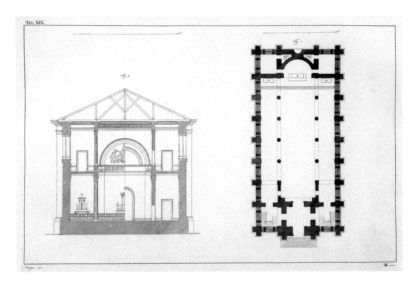

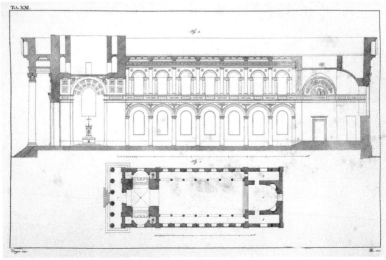

3 | **Cross-section and ground plan for a large church in the city**
Klenze describes this design as a model which can be adapted
to local needs.
Pl. XIX. Engraving

4 | **Sectional elevation and ground plan for a large church in the city**
With this design, Klenze plans a tower, a front chapel
and a raised presbytery.
Pl. XXI. Engraving

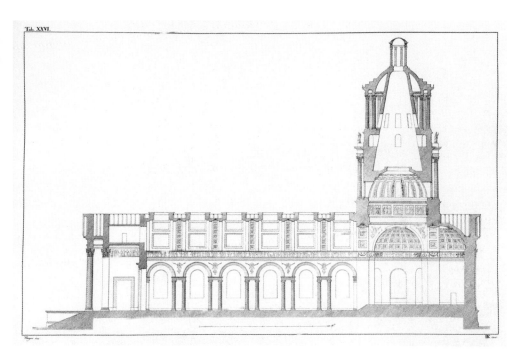

5 | **Sectional elevation of a columned basilica**
The columned basilica is illuminated by high windows in the vaulting and
contains a raised presbytery which is covered by a central dome.
Pl. XXVI. Engraving

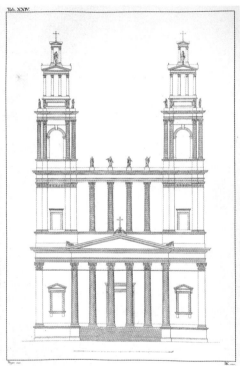

6 | Church tower

The church tower is reminiscent of a septizonium and rises above an entry hall with six columns. The tower is divided into four sections, whereby open and closed stories alternate.

Pl. XXII. Engraving

7 | Façade with two towers

Klenze's design is a conscious reference to medieval architecture.

Pl. XXIV. Engraving

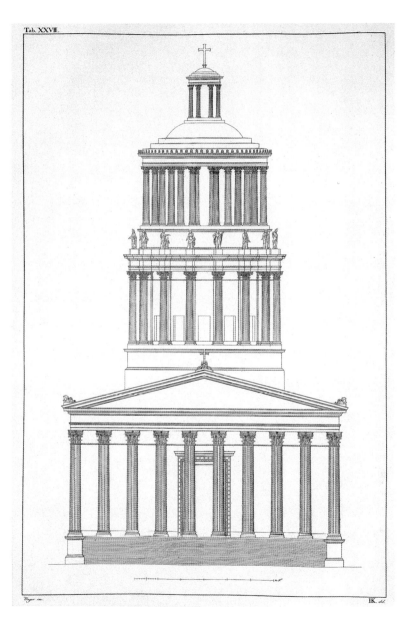

Tab. XXVII.

8 | Façade and central tower of a basilica
The entrance consists of a portico and Corinthian columns; the two-storey central tower is crowned by a cross.
Pl. XXVII. Engraving

Christian Carl Josias Bunsen (1791–1860)
Die Basiliken des christlichen Roms
2 VOLS, MUNICH, 1842–1844

The basilicas of Christian Rome

Johann Gottfried Gutensohn (1792–1851)
Johann Michael Knapp (1791–1861)
Denkmale der christlichen Religion
VOLUME OF ILLUSTRATED PLATES, STUTTGART, TÜBINGEN,

ROME, 1822–1827

Monuments of the Christian religion

Christian Carl Josias Bunsen, a diplomat and theologian, was born on 25 August 1791 in Korbach and studied theology, classics and history from 1808 in Marburg, and from 1809 in Göttingen. Extended journeys to learn foreign languages took him to Copenhagen in 1813, where he learnt Icelandic, and to Paris in 1816, where he learnt Persian and Arabic under Antoine Isaac de Sacy. Barthold Georg Niebuhr appointed him in 1818 to the Prussian Mission to the Vatican where, between 1818 and 1838, he served as secretary, administrator and finally as ambassador. The Archaeological Institute and the protestant hospital were founded as a result of his initiative. In 1828, a visit to Rome by the Prussian crown prince resulted in a life-long friendship with the future King Friedrich Wilhelm IV (reigned 1840–1861). During his stay, Bunsen wrote a five-volume topographical history of the city (*Beschreibung der Stadt Rom*, 1830–1842) (*Description of the City of Rome*) and a series of articles on Roman basilicas that were to have far-reaching consequences for Protestant church architecture. His *Die Basiliken des christlichen Roms* was not illustrated, but rather made reference to the plates by Gutensohn and Knapp. As a result of the so-called Cologne Confusion, the ecclesiastico-political troubles of 1837, he was suspended in 1838 and spent a year in England, before becoming Ambassador to Berne between 1839 and

1841. Following skilful negotiations, the English-Prussian diocese was set up in Jerusalem in 1841. His political and diplomatic goals centred on an alliance between the Protestant states of Great Britain and Prussia. In 1854, he retired from office and moved to Bonn, where he died on 18 November 1860. His extremely varied activities extended as far as supporting expeditions to Egypt (led by Lepsius) and to Africa (led by Vogel). In the United States, his clear stance against slavery was disseminated in the form of a treatise. He saw the future well-being of nations in a lawful, constitutional religious freedom made possible by the Christian faith.

At the beginning of the 19th century, discussions about church architecture centred on the Classical or Early Christian basilica, already praised by Alberti as the archetypal place of Christian worship. It was Goethe who as early as 1787 first expressed his admiration for Early Christian basilicas, specifically for San Paolo fuori le mura in Rome. The Berlin expert on Classical Antiquity, Aloys Hirt, devoted himself to reconstructing the basilica of Classical Antiquity on the basis of Vitruvius' description. Particularly after the Napoleonic wars, the restoration of the Church, not to mention architectural developments, lent some urgency to a standardization in church building practice, and the Early Christian basilica was the predominant model.

That same year the publisher Baron von Cotta commissioned the young Bavarian architects Johann Gottfried Gutensohn and Johann Michael Knapp to make views and building plans of Early Christian basilicas in Rome. The engravings appeared in four volumes between 1822 and 1827. In September 1822, Gutensohn and Knapp announced that they intended to spread their "ground plans, sections and views" over seven volumes each with seven copperplate engravings. The seven plates of volume one, which was printed at de Romanis' press, were devoted to the basilicas of San Clemente and San Paolo fuori le mura. The project continued in fits and starts and it was not until 1824 that the second volume appeared, published by J. G. Cotta in Stuttgart and Tübingen as well as under licence by Scudelari in Rome. The third volume followed the same year and in 1827 the first edition of the joint fourth and fifth volumes was completed. The final edition, published by Cotta in 1843, included a total of 50 plates, and these illustrations covered virgin territory as far as architectural history was concerned, since until then there had been no historical work on Early Roman Christian basilicas. The drawings of ground plans, elevations, sections and views were based on measurements the two architects had themselves made of the buildings, later additions and alterations to the original buildings being indicated by cross-hatching. Bunsen's *Basiliken des christlichen Roms* appeared at a later date as an accompanying text to Gutensohn and Knapp's volume of plates.

What Klenze intended for Catholic church building with *Anweisung zur Architectur des christlichen Cultus* (1822) was what Bunsen endeavoured to achieve for Protestant church building in his work about Roman basilicas, which he dedicated to "his most gracious Majesty Friedrich Wilhelm the Fourth." For Bunsen the question of whether and if so how Early Christian basilicas could be a suitable model for contemporary church building formed the main element of his essay. Bunsen wrote in the preface: "Yes, it is recognized that this knowledge of ancient basilicas is ultimately of major importance for a lively understanding of the Germanic architecture of the Middle Ages and for the ensuing possibil-

ity of its revival." In view of this, it becomes clear that his interest lay not solely in archaeology and the history of building but also in the lively issue of Gothic style, which was equated with Germanic architecture.

In the introduction, Bunsen gives a summary of previous points of view and judgements of Christian basilicas, before describing the basilica in Athens and those in Ancient Rome and then, in the second section, turning his attention to Christian basilicas. The third section is devoted to the Christian basilicas of Rome before submitting them to systematic investigation in the fourth section. The closing section is devoted to contemporary Protestant church building, the structural, liturgical and historical conditions for which he derives from Christian basilicas. "At long last the question of an internal and external connection between basilica building and the magnificent sights of the Late Middle Ages, the Teutonic style of church building, could no longer be ignored. And if all this is to be of any use at this time then one cannot fail to cast a glance at the ideas behind church building and the practical requirements of our time." Bunsen believes the basilica's single hall satisfies the need for Protestant churches to be at one and the same time a church for sermons and a church with an altar. As far as style is concerned he prefers Germanic vaults, and his ideal solution culminates in the sentence: "We have before us the Early Christian basilica, as a model for the Germanic style, for the purpose of a Protestant church service. These three elements result in unending freedom as far as the construction and variety of old and new are concerned."

Bunsen's ideas about the construction of Protestant churches and his pronounced preference for a Gothic style were of far-reaching importance. In *Über den Bau evangelischer Kirchen* (*On the building of Protestant churches*), dating from 1845, Semper specifically quotes Bunsen. The number of churches built in and around Berlin is an indication of the influence of Bunsen's thought, and without this work on basilicas the various planning stages for the reconstruction of Berlin Cathedral would have been inconceivable.

BE

1 | Interior view of S. Paolo fuori le mura seen from the raised area
Pl. VI. Engraving

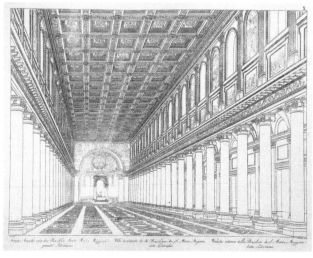

2 | **Interior view of S. Paolo fuori le mura**
Pl. V. Engraving

3 | **Interior view of S. Maria Maggiore**
Pl. X. Engraving

4 | Interior view of S. Lorenzo

Pl. XIII. Engraving

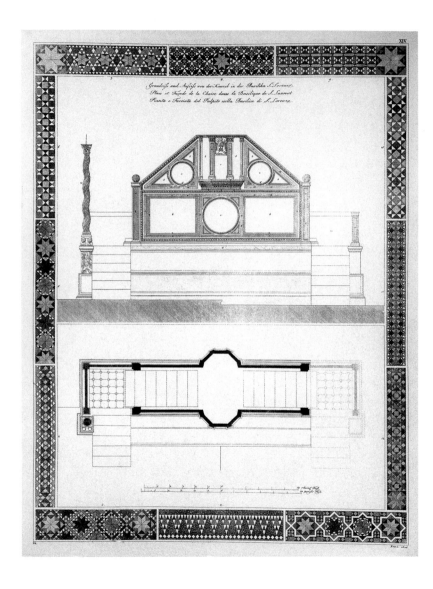

5 | Ground plan and elevation of the pulpit of S. Lorenzo
Pl. XIV. Engraving

6 | Interior view of S. Agnese
Pl. XVIII. Engraving

7 | Interior view of S. Stefano Rotondo
Pl. XXI. Engraving

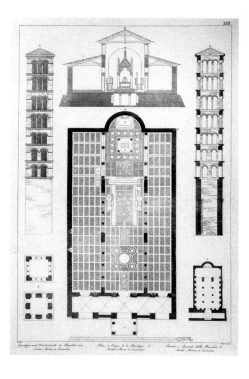

8 | **Ground plan and cross-section of S. Maria in Cosmedin**
Pl. XXII. Engraving

9 | **Interior view of S. Clemente**
Pl. XXXIII. Engraving

XXV.

Auffsüße und Durchschnitte von der Kirche S. Vincenzo alla tre Fontane. | Façades et Coupes de l'Église de S.t Vincent aux trois Fontaines. | Facciate e Spaccati della Chiesa di S. Vincenzo alle tre Fontane.

10 | **Elevation and cross-section of S. Vincenzo alle Tre Fontane**
Pl. XXV. Engraving

Heinrich Hübsch (1795–1863)
In welchem Style sollen wir bauen?

KARLSRUHE. 1828

Which style should we use for building?

Gottlieb Heinrich Christian Hübsch, who was born in Weinheim-an-der-Bergstraße on 9 February 1795, began studying philosophy and mathematics in Heidelberg in 1813, before moving to Karlsruhe in 1815 to study under Friedrich Weinbrenner (1766–1826). This came about as a result of his contact with Georg Moller (1784–1852). Following years spent travelling in Italy and Greece (1817–1820 and 1822–1824), he began working as a teacher of architecture at the Städel Academy in Frankfurt. In 1827, a year after Weinbrenner's death, he was appointed to office in Karlsruhe, initially as palace architect and member of the building commission, before holding a succession of posts in the building department of the government of Baden, culminating in Director of Building in 1842. Since 1832, Hübsch was likewise head of the School of Building at the newly-created Polytechnic, the precursor of today's university. As part of his studies, in particular of Early Christian church building, he travelled frequently, in 1838, 1847, 1849/50 and 1853/54, on several occasions to Italy as well as to France, northern Germany and especially throughout southern Germany. In 1858, the first section of *Altchristliche Kirchen*, (Early Christian churches) appeared, in which he defines architecture as an historical form of art "but not an archaeological form, which is what many want to make it." Hübsch died on 3 April 1863 aged 68.

Publication of the treatise *In welchem Style sollen wir bauen?* in 1828 marked both the middle of Hübsch's life and

a turning point in it. The work triggered a debate on the theory of architecture. The dedication in his essay reveals the widespread influence he intended his work to have: "To those artists who will be gathered in Nuremberg on 6 April, 1828 for the tercentenary [of the death] of Albrecht Dürer." For the first time he was able to make his call for architecture to be freed "from the trammels of Antiquity" independently and without constraint, since his teacher Friedrich Weinbrenner had died two years earlier and for one year he had held a tenured post in the civil service of the Grand Duchy of Baden. The fundamental polemic against the prevailing neo-Classicism of the day was meant to provide theoretically sound basis for a new orientation.

Hübsch opened his work with a very provocative hypothesis: "In modern times both painting and sculpture have long since ceased to be a lifeless imitation of Antiquity. Only architecture has failed to grow up and still continues to imitate the style of Antiquity." Hübsch sees the immaturity of architecture in this lifeless imitation of Classical Antiquity. This amounted to a continuation of his criticism of contemporary neo-Classicism, since as early as 1822 in *Über griechische Architektur* (*On Greek architecture*) he had earned the disapproval of the scholarly Classicist establishment, in particular of its spokesman Aloys Hirt (1759–1837). Hübsch derived his anti-Classicist stance from an investigation into historical architecture. His studies of Classical monuments in Greece and Italy resulted in his differentiating between

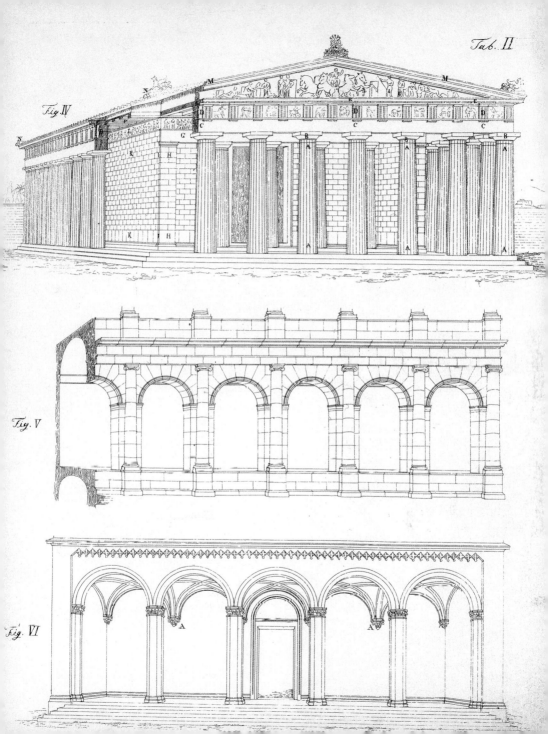

Tab. II

Fig. IV

Fig. V

Fig. VI

Greek and Roman architecture as well in strong criticism of Vitruvius. "If we wish to develop a style that is meant to have the same qualities as those we rate so highly in the types of building of other peoples and recognise as beautiful, then it must emanate not from an earlier but from the current state of things, i. e. firstly, our usual building materials; secondly the current state of knowledge of structural engineering; thirdly, from the type of protection that comes into question for buildings subject to our climate, with regard to durability; and fourthly, the general nature of our requirements, which are founded in our climate, and perhaps in part in our culture, too."

Thus Hübsch defined a set of conditions that had nothing to do with aesthetics, in which building material, knowledge of technology and structures, the climate and its effects on durability, and the general nature of our needs (which are in turn founded in our climate and culture) all play a significant role. In addition to this there is the term "truth," which is the guiding principle of the whole treatise, and which Hübsch regards as the highest principle in art. The criterion of truth is met when both the design and the use of all elements in the building accord with the building's intended function. In his theory, the structure itself is also assigned an elemental function. At the same time, this structural element is assigned an important stylistic function since "with any style the forms of supports and their coverings, being the most prominent and most important for construction, give the style its dominant character." The fact that Hübsch categorized a central facet of his interpretation of style, the appropriateness of the structure, as "truth," seems to point to the moral aspect of a middle-class view of life. He disparages the traditional way of building as a "mendacious style" and criticizes a trend in which structurally necessary architectural elements "are gradually being treated more and more as ornamentation, or rather as a means by which to make more of a building than its function allows it to be."

Hübsch attributes elements of design to the natural circumstances under which architecture arises. He see the basis for this in the building material available, in the level of "technostatic" knowledge prevailing at a given moment, in the attention paid to durability in view of prevailing climatic conditions, and finally in social and cultural requirements. Using these criteria, he then criticizes neo-Classical architecture and counters it with a theory-based "round-arch style." He considers this to be a reincarnation of a Roman style that has been purified of all memories of Antiquity, "just as it would have become if it had been able to develop freely and without constraint, without any reference to the Classical style." For Hübsch a "round-arch style" means the load-bearing, structural frame. Any expansion with regard to ornamentation, indeed any form of decoration, was left to each individual artist. "In any case those buildings that are embellished with the most unfortunate of decorations, but as far as the elements are concerned are consistent in their design, are far more valuable as works of art than even the most faithful reproductions of Antiquity." This consistency is the characteristic of a style which, by taking the basics of architecture into consideration, succeeds "in solving the most varied of assignments with utmost flexibility and in the most direct way." Its works "will assume a truly natural character, where a layman will feel the same sensation as a trained artist."

As a pupil of Weinbrenner, Hübsch was completely under the spell of the architecture of the French Revolution. He shared its overattention to the stereometric proportions while totally neglecting the details. The latter were not an integral part of architecture but is and remains subject to any random use. The match of the load-bearing frame to its function, and this alone, independent of the form of details, is what defines a work of art. Hübsch's architectural theory developed thoughts that were decisive in the development of Revivalism in architecture, architecture that was far more creative than simply imitating a style. Hübsch's contribution was that he developed an approach to architectural aesthetics whose influence stretched far beyond his own time.

BE

Fig. p. 399
1 | "Simplicity of Greek architecture"
Using various examples, including the Colosseum in Rome, Hübsch explains the simplicity of Greek architecture by which no element is used "pleonastically."
Pl. II. Engraving

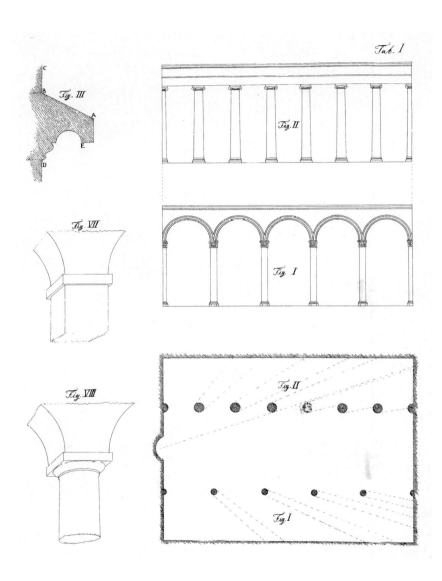

2 | **Comparison of column arrangements**
In a church with three naves the columns should not be placed according to
Greek proportions (Fig. II), but with the distancing shown in Fig. I.
Pl. I. Engraving

Gottfried Semper (1803–1879)

Vorläufige Bemerkungen über bemalte Architektur und Plastik bei den Alten

ALTONA, 1834

Preliminary remarks on painted architecture and sculpture in Antiquity

Die vier Elemente der Baukunst. Ein Beitrag zur vergleichenden Baukunde

BRAUNSCHWEIG, 1851

The four elements of architecture. Cambridge, 1988

Der Stil in den technischen und tektonischen Künsten

2 VOLS, MUNICH, 1860–1863

Style in technical and tectonic art

Gottfried Semper was born on 30 November 1803 in Altona, Holstein, which then adjoined (and is now part of) the Free City of Hamburg. In October 1823, he commenced studies at the University of Göttingen, intending to become either an officer in the artillery or a fortifications engineer. In 1825, he moved to Munich to study architecture under Friedrich von Gärtner (1792–1847) and in 1826 to Regensburg, in order to help with surveying work for the cathedral. Because of a duel, he was forced to flee Germany and found employment in Paris under Franz Christian Gau (1790–1853), an architect who hailed from Cologne. In 1830, he journeyed to the Mediterranean, visiting Provence, Italy and Sicily before staying for some time in Greece, where he researched poly-chromatics in Classical architecture. In 1834, on the recom-mendation of Franz Christian Gau, he was appointed to the position of Director of the Dresden Academy of Building. During the years spent in Dresden he devoted himself to major building projects, such as the Hoftheater (Court The-atre) and the museum, as well as to a fundamental reorgani-zation of teaching methods at the academy. In doing so he sought to unite structural, technical aspects with artistic ele-ments, to discover an interplay between technology and art.

As a result of his involvement in the uprising against the government of Saxony in May 1848, Semper was forced to flee abroad. His participation in the Great Exhibition in London in 1851 and as a teacher of architecture, structural engineering and sculptural decoration at the newly founded School of Drawing and Architecture in Marlborough House opened his eyes to the conditions that prevailed in the crafts. Between 1855 and 1871 he was Professor of Architecture at the Federal Polytechnic in Zurich. Semper died in Rome on 15 May 1879.

The small work *Vorläufige Bemerkungen über bemalte Architektur und Plastik bei den Alten* appeared the year he took office in Dresden and takes up the debate that had been going on among Classical scholars since around 1800. Even though Semper also wished to help settle the debate on the use of colour, his main concern was to improve contempo-rary architecture, which he criticizes as being too rigid and mere imitation. In the preface, he states quite categorically that he has no intention of delivering "a purely antiquarian, scholarly dissertation," but aims to give practical tips and "be of direct use." Contemporary architecture pays, he con-tinues, no heed to the requirements of modern times, where-

as architecture in Classical Antiquity did indeed address the requirements of the day. Semper suggests that cities in Classical Antiquity were governed by the spirit and fate of the community. In an unbridled polemical manner, he lashed out at the "semi-bankrupt architecture" of his day, criticizing the schematic nature of Durand' designs and the pirating of historical styles. This early work of 1834 contained a political as well as a cultural programme, as it already dealt with the connection between architecture and conditions in society.

Die vier Elemente der Baukunst, which he published in exile in 1851, once again takes up the discussion about polychromatics in architecture and is essentially a dispute with the Berlin art historian Franz Kugler (1808–1858). In the fifth chapter, "The four elements," Semper develops his perception of aesthetics in architecture, which he derives from the "primordial state of human society." He describes four basic elements – the hearth, the roof, the enclosure and the embankment, from which he claimed architecture had arisen. He ascribes man's various technical skills to these basic elements: "Ceramic and, later, metallurgical works and art to the hearth, water technology and masonry to embankments, woodworking to the roof and its accessories." Walls originate from a textile, craft background, to the skills of mat weavers and carpet makers. As far as Semper was concerned, art and architecture originated from handicrafts, architecture just adopted the same ideas second-hand, so to speak.

The prelude to *Der Stil in den technischen und tektonischen Künsten* began in 1840 with Semper's Dresden lectures on buildings. The two volumes of his main work appeared between 1860 and 1863 (volume 1, *Die textile Kunst*, [*Textile art*] in 1860, volume 2, *Keramik, Tektonik. Stereometrie, Metallotechnik für sich betrachtet*, [*Ceramics, tectonics, stereometry, metallurgy viewed in themselves*] in 1863). They cover the phenomenon of embellishing and its importance for the development of civilizations. For Semper, embellishing is a basic principle of man's artistic expression, and thus he considers "embellishing" and "covering" always necessary for artistic and cultural expression in those cases "where form is meant to stand out as a significant symbol, as an independent human creation." According to Semper, the symbolic form is achieved in two ways. Firstly it is focused on the building itself and its structural qualities, and furthermore Semper sees the architectural design of a building as the

product of a superordinate idea that characterizes the particular epoch. The symbolic form is borne by the façade, as it were the skin of the building, and not the internal layout. The internal layout is a matter of the client's individual requirements. Through this veiling of the interior by the façade, the building achieves its outwardly visible symbolic content. The surface quality of the stone used was of particular importance for the building's overall effect. Semper made reference to the great Early Renaissance masters in this context. Making the masonry visible, he says, offers a way of giving the various finishes a similar symbolism, instead of the traditional orders of columns, thus giving the building its own characteristic look. Yet for Semper the style of building is not just expressed through technological aesthetics, it is equally important as the expression of a society moulded by religion, social conditions and political circumstances. Semper refers to the basic idea behind Renaissance architecture as the synthesis of two cultural elements: the principle of integrating an individual into a larger community and the opportunity for each individual "to see himself represented in a strong and glorious manner." Semper considered Renaissance architecture a model for contemporary architecture, since by means of "objectivity and freedom in the use of symbols" the Renaissance freed itself from its bonds with regard to the treatment of the three Classical orders of columns and discovered its own individual, characteristic form of expression. According to Semper's theory, the principle of substituting something characteristic for something typical (which had arisen in the Roman Empire and had reached its zenith in the Renaissance) should, he claims, be continued and perfected in contemporary architecture.

As far as Semper was concerned it was no longer Classical Antiquity, but the Renaissance as its legitimate, exemplary successor, that should set the standard for the present day. His extensive writings, which provide information about his artistic intentions, are not pure architectural theory, but rather statements about art in a social, historical context. The importance of Semper in the theory of art and in building practice lies in the political role that he believes architecture plays in society, and in his examination of historical styles of building, by which he hopes to find new forms of expression for contemporary architecture.

BE

1 | **Illustration for the jacket**

2 | **Illustration for the jacket**
"Grey, dear friend, is all theory
And green is the golden tree of life". Goethe, *Faust*

3 | **A section of ceiling in the Temple of Theseus in Athens**
Pl. V. Tinted flat print

4 | **Ceiling painting from the Chapel of St. Catherine in Assisi**
Pl. VII. Tinted flat print

5 | **Detail of architrave**
Crowning sections of the architrave in the opistodom of the Temple of Theseus in Athens.
Pl. IX. Tinted flat print

6 | **Tuscan temple according to Vitruvius**
Pl. XIII. Tinted flat print

Friedrich Hoffstadt (1802–1846)

Gotisches A-B-C Buch, das ist: Grundregeln des gothischen Styls für Künstler und Werkleute

FRANKFURT/MAIN, 1840–1845

Gothic A-B-C, i. e. basic rules of the Gothic style for artists and craftsmen

As the Berlin architect Gustav Stier (1807–1880) observed at the Bamberg Congress of Architects, current European architecture appears "in a coat of the brightest colours: and yet in no country other than Germany are so many thoughts lost on the spirit and purpose of architecture in general, and in particular on the spirit and purpose of architecture in our time … Nowhere else are the various points of view divided up into so many smaller and larger groups."

Friedrich Hoffstadt, by profession a lawyer but in addition not just a collector of art but also an amateur painter, graphic artist and a sculptor, was born in 1802 in Amorbach in Franconia. Having studied law in Erlangen, Munich and Landshut, he initially worked as an attorney in Ansbach, but as a sideline was involved with medieval art, drew book illustrations, and designed stained glass windows from patterns by Peter Cornelius (c. 1783–1867) as well as a carved altar for the Catholic church in Nördlingen. On his transfer to Munich, where he had been appointed junior legal officer to the municipal district court, he began to assemble an extensive collection of medieval works of art. In 1833, he founded the Society for German Classical Studies of the Three Shields, which was intended to be a kind of Old German stonemasons' lodge. His *Gotisches A-B-C Buch,* with illustrations by himself and Karl Ballenberger (1801–1860), was published during his time in Frankfurt, where he was an official at the municipal court. He subsequently worked in Munich and Aschaffenburg. Hoffstadt died in 1846, leaving his wish to construct a Gothic cathedral unfulfilled.

Thus it was not an architect but rather a lawyer who published the most extensive, chronologically ordered work on Gothic style. The preliminary pages entitled *Gotisches A-B-C Buch, das ist: Grundregeln des gothischen Styls für Künstler und Werkleute* appeared in Frankfurt in serialized sections between 1840 and 1845; taken together, they amount to a practical manual on geometry for building work by craftsmen. The compendium – which was 270 pages long, had 40 plates, and remained incomplete – was an explanation of the Gothic style and a description of the history of Christian architecture, and although the national element is downplayed slightly, the Gothic style as a universal German style remains quite clearly in the forefront.

Hoffstadt bemoans the fact that the Gothic style had not been included in the curricula of academies and schools of architecture. By depicting the rules of Gothic for artists and craftsmen in the manual he was attempting to redress this deficit. A contemporary critic praised Hoffstadt as a "Vitruvius of the German style," who revealed considerable knowledge of Gothic ground plans and books on stone masonry. Hoffstadt gives precise instructions for forming individual figures using the laws of geometry, choosing the basic square as his starting point. He was convinced that no genuine work of art could be created as long as just Gothic details rather than the fundamental principles are adopted.

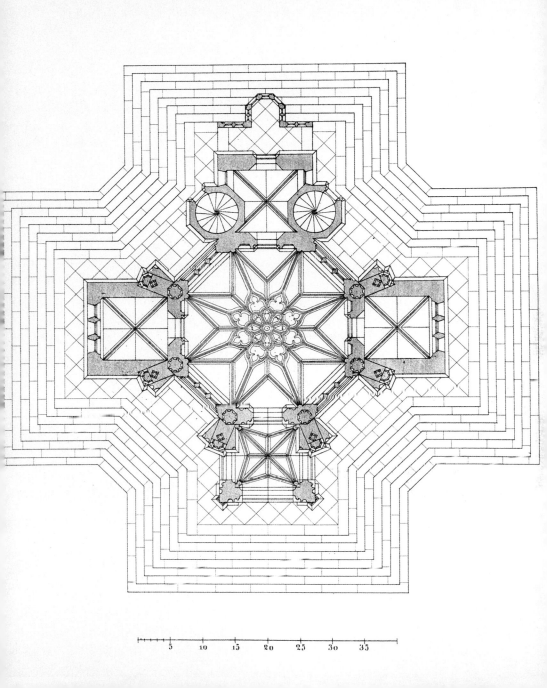

The plates present his own plans, which he had culled from old books on stone masonry, from medieval building plans and reference books. Hoffstadt declares pure embellishment to be of secondary importance and instead begins with the basic geometric forms of individual Gothic elements. He attempts to elaborate the Gothic style by starting with its inner core, by looking for its principles. His investigations centre on Christian cathedrals, Christian churches, as the focal point of all types of art, which by appropriating and reinstating Gothic forms in religious architecture, unite to become a total work of art. With the unity of cathedral, forest and poetry, Hoffstadt repeats the typical metaphor fielded by the adherents of neo-Gothic, who were convinced by this elementary symbolism.

According to Hoffstadt, the "eternal and unalterable laws of geometry" are the root of all forms, whereby the equilateral triangle and the square represent the "key" to the Gothic style. Even in his own day, his insistence on deriving basic shapes from geometrical figures that are then implemented by moving from ground plan to elevation was

criticized for being overly rigid and clinging to rules, and he was accused of having a mania for numbers. Citing crystals as an example, he likewise attributed the forms encountered in nature to geometry: "Since natural formations are subject to the geometrical laws of formation and these same geometrical laws are present in the creations of Gothic style, this explains the relationship in the results." For Hoffstadt, the Gothic style represents the zenith and goal of all architecture.

Hoffstadt's didactic approach with an explanatory pattern dominated by geometry is an important connecting link between the writings of the 1830s and Georg Ungewitter's (1820–1864) subsequent textbook, which attempts to establish a general set of rules for form and construction principles in the Middle Ages. Furthermore, Hoffstadt's manual is an attempt to unite two issues. On the one hand, it aims to provide archaeological, art-theoretical foundations from which to explore the theory of medieval architecture, and, on the other, to provide comprehensible teaching material for theoretical instruction.   BE

Fig. p. 411
1 | **Ground plan of a Gothic monument**
Italian ed. from 1885, pl. XLIII. Etching

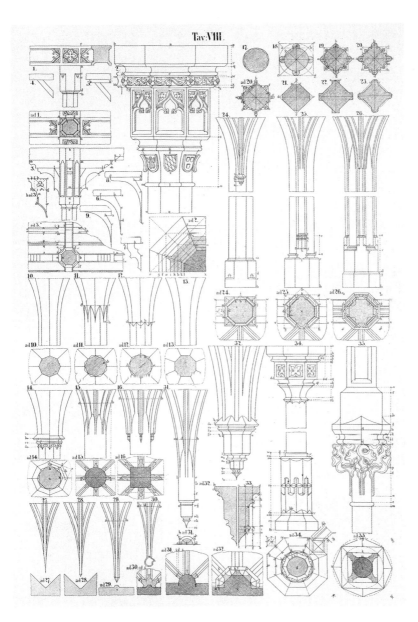

**2 | Constructions of
pilasters and pillars**
*Italian ed. from 1885,
pl. VIII. Etching*

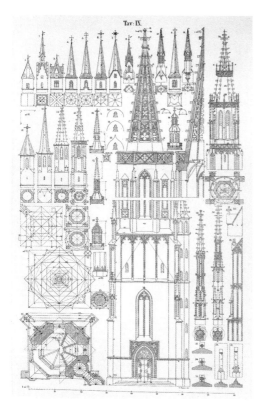

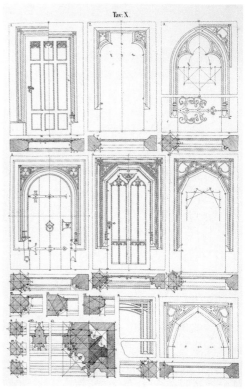

3 | **Constructions of towers**
Based on the use of triangulation and quadrature.
Italian ed. from 1885, pl. IX. Etching

4 | **Different doors and constructions in profile**
Based on the use of triangulation and quadrature.
Italian ed. from 1885, pl. X. Etching

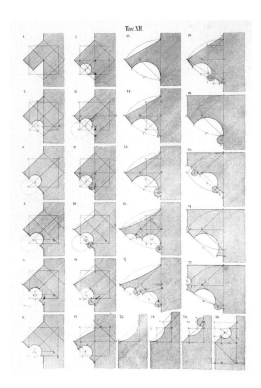

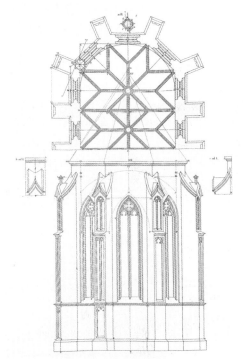

5 | **Plans of the moldings in profile**
Italian ed. from 1885, pl. XII. Etching

6 | **Plan of the choir**
Based on the use of triangulation, quadrature and wall elevation.
Italian ed. from 1885, pl. XIII. Etching

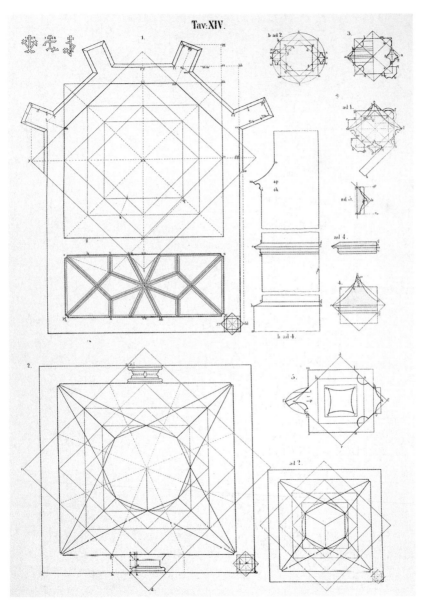

7 | Ground plan of the choir,
based on the use of
triangulation and quadrature,
*Italian ed. from 1885,
pl. XIV. Etching*

Tav: XLIV.

8 | **Elevation of a Gothic monument**
Italian ed. from 1885, pl. XLIV. Etching

Carl Alexander Heideloff (1789–1865)

Der kleine Altdeutsche (Gothe) oder Grundzüge des altdeutschen Baustyles. Zum Handgebrauch für Architekten und Steinmetzen, besonders für technische Lehranstalten

NUREMBERG, 1849–1852

The little Old German (Goth) or the foundations of the old German style of building.
For use by architects and stonemasons, in particular for technical teaching establishments

In 1823, Friedrich Campe from Nuremberg described Carl Alexander Heideloff as "a creative genius, a rare and versatile artist, the like of whom has not set foot in Nuremberg since the days of Albrecht Dürer." And yet on his death, the fame of the artist, who had been so celebrated when alive, quickly waned. Carl Alexander Heideloff was born in Stuttgart on 2 February 1789 into an artistic family with many branches. He trained at the Academy of Art attached to the former Hohe Carls-Schule, and was strongly influenced by the architects Johann Jacob Atzel (2nd half of the 18th century) and Friedrich Thouret (1767–1845). Journeying through south-west Germany, he noted the examples of medieval art that he later used in his compendium *Ornamentik des Mittelalters* (*Medieval ornamental art*), which appeared in sections from 1843. While based in Wiesbaden he was able to deepen his knowledge of medieval architecture in the middle Rhine region, before being appointed to a position in Coburg in 1816. In 1820, he was made head of building in Nuremberg. Here, in addition to his tasks supervising restoration work, his activities as an architect and sculptor grew in importance. In 1823, he became the first director of the City Polytechnic, where, following its conversion to a state institute in 1833, he was given a chair which he held to a ripe old age. He was awarded the title of Royal Conservator in 1837 for his extensive restoration work in Bamberg Cathedral (1831–1834), so that he can rightly be considered one of the founders of the heritage preservation movement. Numerous written works,

in particular manuals for various lines of trade, as well as about the Greek orders of columns, the Romanesque style and stonemason's lodges in medieval times, bear witness to his prolific output. Heideloff died in 1865 in Hassfurt, where he was last employed.

Der kleine Altdeutsche (Gothe) is an excerpt from a work that was planned, but remained incomplete, entitled "Lehre der gesamten altdeutschen Baukunst und ihrer Verzierungen" (Theory of all old German architecture and its ornamentation). From around 1808, Heideloff had been collecting examples of medieval building, such as the "manuscripts" of the construction site for the cathedrals in Strasbourg and Basle. He studied the rich collections of drawings in Vienna and *Von altdeutscher Baukunst* (1820) (*On old German architecture*) penned by Christian Ludwig Stieglitz (1756–1836), which included an excerpt from a booklet on stonemasonry. Heideloff attempted to get to the bottom of the laws of Gothic architecture in order to collate them into a system that could be taught.

Heideloff provided a brief table of contents for his textbook on Gothic building, which was divided up into three "courses." The first course deals with the basic principles of old German architecture, the second the construction of cross vaults, pillars, columns, vault ribs, profiles, windows, and portals as well as the accompanying details and the positioning of pinnacles. "The third course shows the compilation and further application of octagons [triangulation and

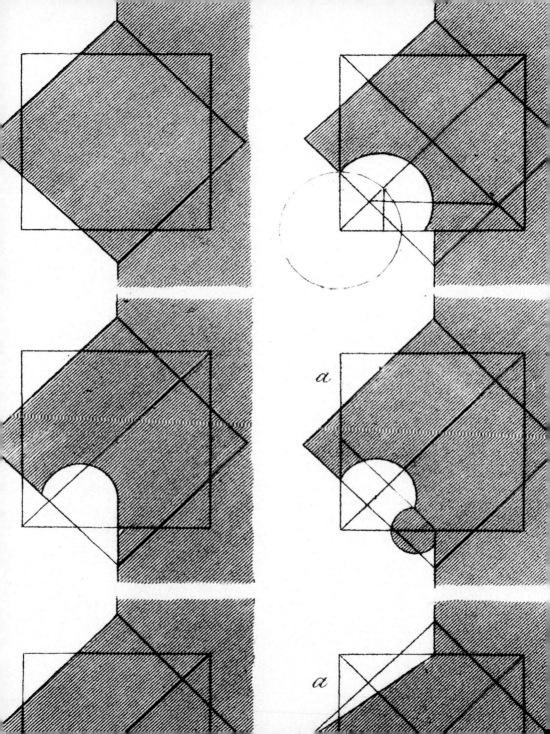

a

a

quadrature] in the ground-plan of cathedrals, collegiate churches, parish churches and chapels, and duly expounds on the four degrees."

The first course contains the theory of triangulation and quadrature, the geometry of the tracery, the construction of the pinnacles and the openwork gablet and, in the style of Matthäus Roritzer, the architect of Regensburg Cathedral in the 15th century, the design of finials, crockets, socles and cornices. The second course explains the construction of the vaults, the ground plan and elevation of the choir and tower from the octagon. There are examples of ribbing, and the treatment of many details, and the design of buttresses. In the third course Heideloff undertakes a classification of the ground plans of Gothic churches, and he determines the elevations with the help of the theory of triangulation and quadrature that was of such decisive influence in the neo-Gothic style. He derived this method from the cross-section of the Milan Cathedral, which Cesare Cesariano (1476/78–1543) used as the basis for his 1521 commentary on Vitruvius. Cesariano is known to have followed the suggestions of Stornalocco, a mathematician from Piacenza, dating from 1392, for the elevation of the cathedral, a prime example of triangulation. It can be taken as certain that Walther Rivius' (c. 1500–1548) works on architecture were the source of this knowledge, works that Heideloff is known to have had in his possession. Heideloff further intended to inform his readers about the life and (alleged) building activity of Albertus Magnus, the "great past master " of the Gothic style. His research led to the opinion that "the German building style had only the German disposition and its creative powers" to thank for its origins.

In his writings Heideloff advocated the resurrection of and a return to Gothic architecture. His theoretical writings were intended to educate both artists and craftsmen alike,

since without knowledge of the laws this renewal would have been unthinkable. The fragmentary condition of his œuvre, the missing solutions to many problems led to resignation and Heideloff's realization that: "I wanted to create a work that would be second to none in its thoroughness and technical accuracy in the basic principles of old stone masons. But there is at present only a small proportion of the population that has any time for Beauty and thus I shall not live to see my great work on old German architecture published in the detail that I would have wished."

Heideloff spurned the architectural theory of Heinrich Hübsch (1795–1863), contrasting the round-arch style with "old German" Gothic architecture, which he considered to be architecture in its consummate state. For Heideloff, unlike Hübsch, ornamentation is an essential architectural element, since it results in a balanced relationship between individual elements and the overall product. The medieval laws of proportion are, he suggests, a theoretical and practical application of these principles. Furthermore, for Heideloff the Gothic style is both a deeply religious and patriotic style, which offers tremendous opportunities for development as long as the laws in question are adopted. Heideloff adheres to the theory of a purity of style, which is reflected in his definition of the "pseudogothicum," whose "style has things in common with no less than true German style, but which, because of some arbitrarily added ornamentation, can be considered a work of German art." In Heideloff's opinion pseudo-Gothic, unlike the authentic neo-Gothic, fails to exhibit any adherence to the basic principles of construction as regards both the overall form and individual forms. *Der kleine Altdeutsche (Gothe)* represents a milestone in the development of teaching concepts for instruction in the Gothic style in polytechnic education.

BE

1 | **Illustration for the jacket**
Portrait of Albertus Magnus.
Engraving by P. Kadeder

2 | **Illustration for the jacket**
Portrait of Erwin von Steinbach.
Engraving

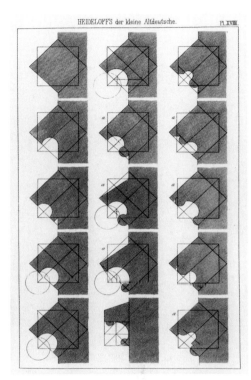

3 | **Christian symbols**
Illustration of the basic idea of the octofoil, the symbol of God's trinity in unity and the gospel; from the old builders' lodge in Zurich and according to a booklet by a Swiss stonemason.
Pl. II. Engraving

4 | **Profiles of protective moldings**
Recorded from existing monuments and old drawings.
Pl. XVIII. Engraving

Georg Gottlob Ungewitter (1820–1864)
Lehrbuch der gothischen Konstruktionen

LEIPZIG, 1859–1864

Textbook on Gothic buildings

Georg Gottlob Ungewitter was born on 15 September 1820 in Wanfried. At the age of 14 he attended a vocational training establishment and the Academy in Kassel before moving to Munich in 1837, where for two years he studied at the Academy of Fine Arts under Friedrich von Gärtner (1792–1847). Following his time in Munich, in 1840 Ungewitter sat a building examination in Kassel, where he distinguished himself in design and draughtsmanship. He was accepted by the state department of building as a trainee, but in 1842 requested he be released in order to continue his studies in Berlin. Ungewitter spent the next six years in Hamburg, where in his own words he completed 24 larger and smaller buildings. During the two years he spent in Lübeck between 1848 and 1849, he turned his attention to the Gothic style under the direct influence of the town's medieval architecture and that of August Reichensperger's *Die christlich-germanische Baukunst und ihr Verhältnis zur Gegenwart* (1845) (*Christian Germanic architecture and its relationship to the present time*). Between 1849 and 1851 he set up shop as a private architect in Leipzig, where he scarcely received any commissions, but for his own study purposes made copies of older historical buildings. Having submitted an application in which he unconditionally supported the reintroduction of Gothic architecture in places of education, technical colleges and academies, he was provisionally employed in the vocational college in Kassel, a position that was made permanent in 1856. There he lectured in structural and materials theory,

architectural drawing, perspective, the history of architecture, the beginnings of Christian architecture, Germanic (or Gothic) architecture in Germany, and the revival of a Christian-Germanic style of building, as reflected in the completion of Cologne Cathedral. He remained unsuccessful in his numerous attempts to move on professionally, for example to the Polytechnic colleges in Karlsruhe or Hanover. Ungewitter died of tuberculosis in October 1864.

Ungewitter developed his theory of architecture in his extensive *Lehrbuch der gothischen Konstruktionen*, limiting himself however to the Gothic style and the precursors of Gothic vaulting he found in Roman and Byzantine architecture. He presented the stylistic developments in all the essential elements of building and decoration in architecture from early to late Gothic, relying on actual medieval buildings, which served as the basis of his encyclopaedic compilation. In doing so he was at pains to remain strictly objective and systematic. Using the Gothic style he took the same amount of effort in attempting to explain building geometry, the production of designs and the shapes of details. The manual is divided up into nine chapters. Having presented individual aspects of building such as profiling, tracery, vault constructions, the design of pillars, columns and cantilevers, Ungewitter devotes a main chapter to the design of ground plans in medieval architecture. There are some shorter sections reserved for towers and portals, interior colours and the positioning of rood screens. Though the treatise is set

out as a practical manual on building, consisting of instructions on how to execute ground plans, elevations and sections, there are also many examples of description, analysis, and interpretation. Ungewitter develops his architectural system by reference to Gothic cathedrals: "The cathedral includes within itself the totality of development in every other architectural work, just as the spirit that resides in its vaults imbues all the rooms … A palace or a town hall is indeed different from a church but we pray in them all, the purposes sanctioned by religion are served by all of them, and their external shape would then contradict the very core of their being if their appearance did not reflect their origin in church design." With this statement Ungewitter directly unites the Gothic style and religion, and in the same way as Hoffstadt, raises it to the status of a principle that can be used for the most varied of building assignments. With regard to the controversy on the correct style that dominated the 19th century, Ungewitter came out clearly in favour of the Gothic style. He justifies this preference on both an aesthetic as well as a functional level, whereby he is able to fall back on his intensive studies of Gothic architecture.

When Ungewitter writes that "the open depiction of all structural relationships forms the vital principle of Gothic architecture," structural composition is no longer a technical expression but an aesthetic category. An appropriate structural scheme is one of the central neo-Gothic arguments in favour of the universal application of the Gothic style. The understanding of truth also plays a decisive role in Ungewitter's theory, by which he attempts to introduce an ethical aspect into architecture. "The characteristic features of Gothic buildings are the strictest interpretation of the conditions that have to be fulfilled, of the prevailing circumstances, and the characteristics of the material, always endeavouring to achieve the greatest goals with the smallest means, but above all the most conscious aversion to any untruth in the development of form and the ensuing avoidance of all surro-

gates." The term truth has many aspects, ranging from the effect of the materials to the design of forms, and is applied to architecture by analogy with the Christian understanding of the term. Ungewitter's explanations appear to be logical and carefully construed in rational terms. This applies to the linkage of form, function, material and construction. In that they are all logically derived from each other – they are mutually defining – a coherent system emerges. The aesthetic level is touched on through "effect," "expression," and "character." Structural composition is considered to be the connecting element between the technical and aesthetic sides.

The proportional figures propagated by the theorists of a German neo-Gothic style are concerned first and foremost with quadrature and triangulation. Ungewitter's numerous publications deal with various aspects of the theory of architecture, whereby his early work clearly demonstrates a Romantically-tinted view of the Gothic style, obviously influenced by Reichensperger, as the unity of religion, fatherland and art. And yet Ungewitter does not persist in his yearning for a unified world, but tries to mould his own age by means of plans, buildings and writings. His written works are shaped by an explicit critique of Classicism, accusing Joachim Winckelmann (1717–1768) of having distanced himself from the local way of building and denouncing Friedrich Weinbrenner (1766–1826) as a purist. His writings create a new type of pattern book in which he combines design practice with systematic theory. An unaltered second edition of *Lehrbuch der gothischen Konstruktionen*, which originally appeared between 1859 and 1864, came out in 1875. It was not until Karl Mohrmann's third edition that there were any changes in the order of the chapters, with additional drawings to explain structural relationships unknown during Ungewitter's lifetime. A fourth edition between 1901 and 1903 was proof of the continued influence of this standard work on Gothic style.

BE

Fig. p. 425
1 | **Study of capitals**
2ⁿᵈ ed., 1875, pl. 15. Lithograph

2 | Table of tracery

Illustration of large rose windows and tracery in galleries.

2nd ed., 1875, pl. 6. Lithograph

3 | Characteristics of net vaulting

2nd ed., 1875, pl. 11. Lithograph

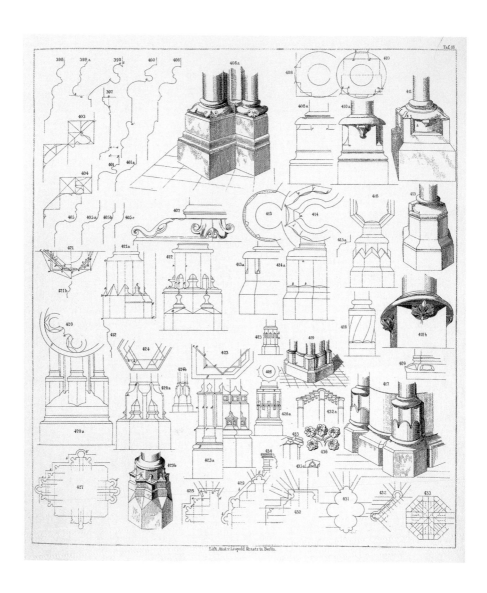

4 | **Socles of pillars and bases in profile**
2nd ed., 1875, pl. 16. Lithograph

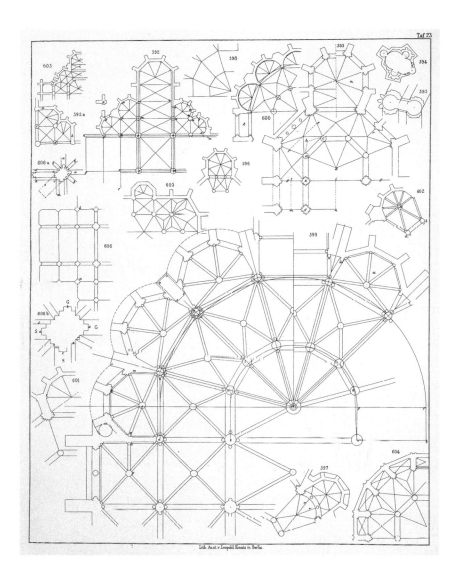

5 | **Choir with ambulatory and chapel cornice**
2nd ed., 1875, pl. 23. Lithograph

675 d

675 e

675 f

675 b

675 g

678

678

g

6 | Gothic gable construction
2ⁿᵈ ed., 1875, pl. 30. Lithograph

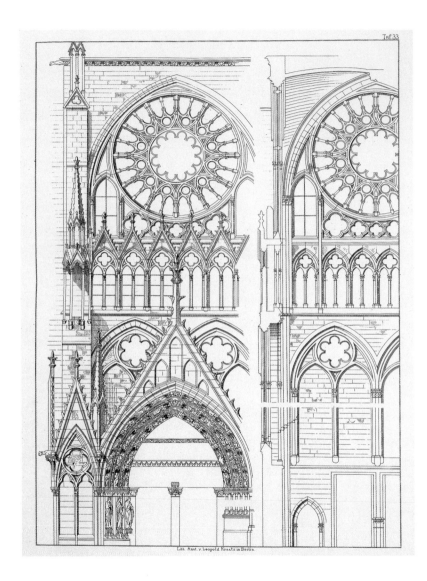

7 | **Elevation of the façade**
Illustration of different parts of buttresses and the development of the triforia.
2nd ed., 1875, pl. 33. Lithograph

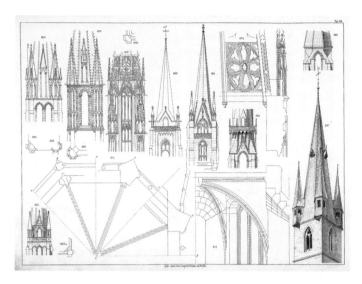

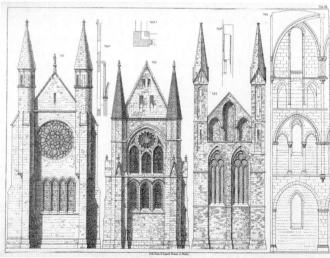

8 | **Gables above the sides of the towers**
2nd ed., 1875, pl. 44. Lithograph

9 | **Elevation of the façade**
Draft of the rose windows in the gabled
walls and draft of the raised areas.
2nd ed., 1875, pl. 38. Lithograph

20th century

Ebenezer Howard (1850–1928)

To-morrow: a Peaceful Path to Real Reform

LONDON, 1898

A slightly modified new edition entitled Garden Cities of To-morrow.
London, 1902

Ebenezer Howard's short book is one of the most important and influential modern programmatic texts on the subject of urban development. It is the earliest attempt to combat the deplorable conditions in growing industrial cities with a re-formed urban structure, thereby abolishing the usual contrast between town and country.

Howard held an office job and worked as a stenographer in London. He was in America from 1872–1876 where, as a young man, he was impressed by some of the many newly founded communities. But he also recognized the dangers of land speculation. Howard was greatly influenced by the social reformer Edward Gibbon Wakefield and his ideas for the settlement of Australia and New Zealand (*View of the Art of Colonization*, 1849), the communistic ideas of the Russian Prince Peter Kropotkin, who lived in London. and the American economist Henry George, whose *Progress and Poverty* demanded the abolition of private property. The utopian novel *Looking Backward*, 1888, by the American Edward Bellamy, which sketched a just and classless industrial society, also helped shape his ideas. Howard wrote his book in the 1880s.

Using a magnet as a metaphor, Howard compared the advantages and disadvantages of living conditions in towns and in the country. His third magnet, "town-country", combines the advantages of both into a future-oriented programme. The realization of this concept is his model of a "garden city." The garden city's most important principles are limited size (not more than 32 000 inhabitants on about 2,400 hectares of land) and the planned regulation and separation of functions. To this end, Howard designed a scheme of radial structures with concentrically organised areas. In the centre there is a round garden area, surrounded by official buildings and cultural institutions. This central section is surrounded by a broad central park which is bordered by a circular glass palace in which the shopping area is to be found. This is followed by concentric strips which make up the residential area, consisting of small detached single-family dwellings with gardens. The plots are narrow and range from 6 x 30–40 metres in size. The residential area is divided by a broad boulevard, the "Grand Avenue," which is enclosed by terrace houses. Factories, warehouses and markets are to be found on the outermost ring of the garden city. These are serviced by a circular railway system with tangential access to the network. A green belt stretches around the garden city. This is free of structures and is reserved mostly for agricultural purposes. It guarantees the self-sufficient production of food for the city. Howard imagined his model garden city as a part of a larger urban system. Several garden cities could surround a "central city" which would not have more than 58 000 inhabitants. All together, the population of such an urban agglomeration would be limited to 250 000.

The structure of Howard's garden city was influenced by ideas of ideal towns during the Renaissance as well as by the tradition of country estates in England. But the garden

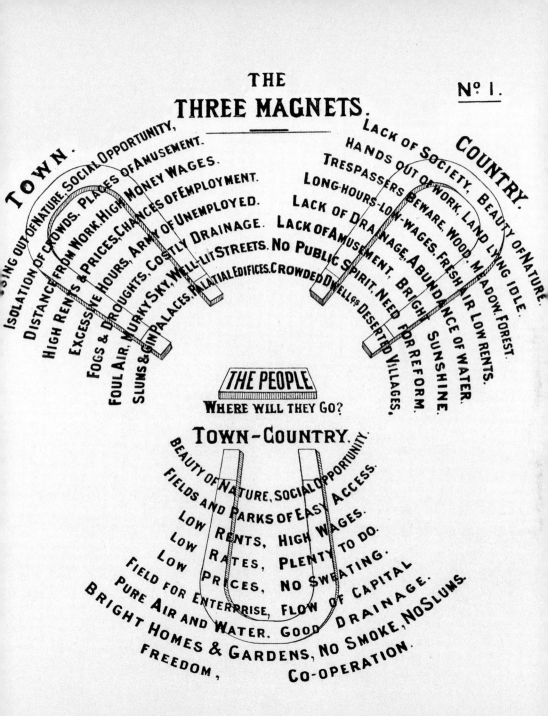

city was to consist of a relatively compact concentration of buildings and population, in other words anything but a rural idyll. Howard's main aim was social, demographic and functional reform. His ideas in this respect stem from utopian socialists like Robert Owen (1771–1858) and Charles Fourier (1772–1837). The prerequisite for his model was the common ownership of land. He insisted on co-operative and collective forms of management for industry, agriculture and retail trade. Private initiative was not to be eliminated but all types of speculation had to be prevented.

Through a more balanced distribution of economic and cultural impulses, Howard wanted to counteract increases of population and poverty in the big cities as well as the intellectual impoverishment outside of them. In many lectures, Howard was able to spread his ideas and even convince business people of the economic feasibility and social desirability of his concepts. The Garden City Association was founded in 1899 and this was quickly followed by similar organisations in most European countries.

In England, two garden cities were soon built in the greater London region. Letchworth was planned and executed beginning in 1903 by Barry Parker and Raymond Unwin, and in 1919 Welwyn was built according to the plans of Louis de Soissons. Both projects were loosely based on Howard's work, though they neither structurally, architecturally nor socially adhere strictly to Howard's programme. They were, in fact, middle-class residential towns whose inhabitants were somewhat reform-minded. In 1909, Hellerau, near Dresden, was the first garden city built in Germany.

Even though Howard's concept of the garden city never really took off, it was nevertheless a great influence on the politics of urban planning in the 20th century. Howard's most important achievement was to be the first person to recognize that the architectural development of urban and non-urban areas are interrelated problems. The big cities continued to grow and the decentralization of industry, which was central to Howard's theses, developed on its own. Nevertheless, many urban planners used Howard's concepts. These included Frank Lloyd Wright (1867–1959) in his model of "Broad Acre City" and Ernst May in Germany. Howard's ideas about garden cities inspired the typical modern suburb and also resulted in today's industrial estates as well as the construction of publicly financed housing estates, especially in Holland and Germany. These, however, are lacking in the urban flair that Howard had imagined.

Howard settled first in Letchworth and later in Welwyn, where he died in 1928. One year before his death he was knighted. A new edition of his work, updated with annotations, was published in 1946 by his former colleague, Frederic J. Osborn. Having inspired the plans for Greater London and Manchester in 1944, Howard's ideas were an important influence for the "new towns" in conurbations in Great Britain, the planning of which started in 1946, and for the so-called "satellite towns" of post-war Germany.   JP

Fig. p. 437
1 | **Diagram of the three magnets**
Advantages and disadvantages of living in the city or the country and better living conditions by combining both as a reform model for the garden city.
No. 1

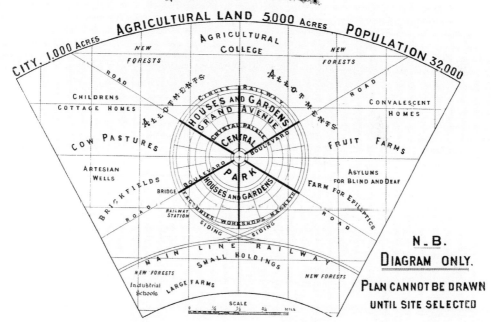

2 | **Schematic diagram**
Illustration of functional and structural divisions of a garden city and its surroundings
with garden allotments, agricultural land, social facilities, and a railway.
No. 2

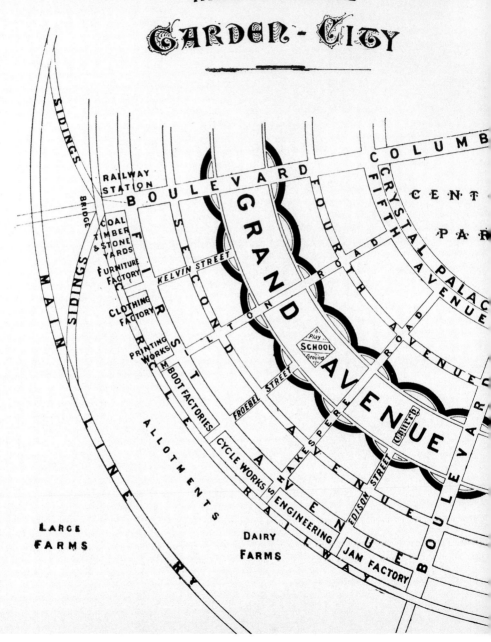

N⁰ 3.

HOSPITAL

LIBRARY

GARDEN
(5 Acres)

THEATRE

**CONCERT
HALL**

N ‒ B.
A DIAGRAM ONLY.
PLAN MUST DEPEND UPON
SITE SELECTED.

SCALE

110   220   440 YDS. = ¼ MILE.

3 | **Functional and structural division of a garden city**
Central garden square with public facilities, crystal palace with
shops, residential areas, factories, craftsmen, and ring railway.
No. 3

Tony Garnier (1869–1948)

Une Cité industrielle: Étude pour la construction des villes

PARIS, 1917

An industrial city. A study in urban planning

Tony Garnier's *Cité industrielle* is the ideal plan for a re-formed industrial city. Every detail has been considered. It stands in clear opposition to the anarchy of industrial city sprawl.

Garnier studied from 1886–1889 at the École des Beaux Arts, where he was strongly influenced by the functionalist/rationalist teaching of Julien Guadet. While studying with a grant from the Académie des Beaux-Arts between 1899–1904, he prepared a plan for an industrial city in Rome. He submitted the two pages of his proposal with the ground plan and the general view to the Academy in 1901, where it was unequivocally rejected. Unperturbed, he continued to work on his proposal and submitted it again in 1904, under the title "Une Cité industrielle." This time, the Academy regarded the work as "successful, but uninteresting." Garnier returned to his hometown of Lyons, where he opened an office of his own in 1905. From 1909–1939 he worked as a professor at the École Régionale d'Architecture, where he enlarged the project to cover a total of 164 designs, which he published in Paris in 1917 with only a short explanatory text.

Garnier wanted to develop the ultimate model for an industrial city in the 20th century. His proposal was for a fictitious city, although the differences in altitude as well as the location on a river and the presence of the mouth of a tributary leave little doubt that the model is Lyons. A fictitious historical town is also included in the plan. In contrast to Lyons, Garnier's model is anti-metropolitan. His *Cité indus-*

trielle is planned for only 35 000 inhabitants – about the same number as Ebenezer Howard's "garden city" model. The most important principle is the functional division of the city in terms of work, social life and living area.

The industrial zone is on low-lying ground. The largest installations are a steel factory and blast furnaces with additionally a port and a dam. The city stretches across a higher plateau and overlooks the valley. It is connected to the industrial area by train. All the administrative buildings (town hall, registry office, court of arbitration) are positioned at the centre of town, along with other public buildings. These include a large assembly hall with a number of different-sized rooms intended for various events, lectures and meetings. There is one large auditorium for 3,000 people, which is equipped with loudspeakers for council meetings or musical performances. There are also theatres, museums, archives, libraries and sports facilities. In addition, there is a job exchange to help people find work. Service facilities are to be found in front of the railway station. These include hotels, department stores and open-air markets. The railway platforms are set along the side of the railway station and the tracks are designed to run dead straight in order to allow access for high-speed trains.

All the buildings are low, with a maximum of three or four storeys. Only the central administrative building is crowned by a clock tower. The residential zones are set on an orthogonal grid with streets and blocks of regular size. Social

institutions like schools are scattered in between. Traffic and pedestrians are separated from each other. The residential buildings are detached, located on gardenlike residential islands which are 30 by 150 metres in size, but without fences. These are subdivided into plots of 15 by 15 metres. The buildings are only permitted to occupy at most half of the plots; the rest is public space reserved for pedestrians. The "Cité industrielle" is an open green city, without enclosed spaces. The number of single-family dwellings is higher than the number of apartment buildings. They are pavilion-like and have one, two or a maximum of three storeys.

In the first proposal made in 1901, the roofs were pitched, whereas in the published version, all the houses have flat terrace roofs. Hygienic standards were important to Garnier. Each bedroom has at least one window which faces south and each room, no matter how small, has a window facing outwards. Interior walls and floors are made of smooth materials and all corners are rounded. The distance between buildings must be at least equivalent to their height. The architecture features uniform design: cuboid shapes, flat wall surfaces and a sparse rationality which was new and provocative in France at the time. Nevertheless, some elements such as cornices, pilaster-like pillars, and tall windows give the structures a neo-Classical look, such as was typical of the œuvre of Auguste Perret (1874–1954). Everything in the *Cité industrielle* was to be built of reinforced concrete – a technology which at that time was still in its infancy.

Garnier's *Cité* was intended to be not only a technological but also a social model. It is in the tradition of model architectural societies of utopian socialists like Charles Fourier (1772–1837) and Robert Owen (1771–1858). It was directly inspired, however, by the socialist ideals of Jean Jaurès and Emile Zola's "ideal city" in his utopian/socialist novel *Travail* (1900). Quotations from the latter book are featured as inscriptions on the blueprint for the assembly hall. Garnier did not envisage either police or military for his model city. There is no prison and no church. The town-planning concept clearly owes much to Ebenezer Howard's garden city.

The draft of "Cité industrielle" met with a degree of recognition when it was presented in 1904, but the actual publication in 1917 went unnoticed. Then, in 1920, Le Corbusier published parts of it in the magazine *L'Esprit nouveau*. He also referred to Garnier in his programmatic essay *Vers une architecture* in 1923. In 1924, the exhibition of designs for the "Cité industrielle" was repeated and this time it received more attention. Tony Garnier's *Cité industrielle* was an important inspiration to many who favoured the *Charter of Athens* for modern city planning drawn up at the CIAM (Congrès International d'Architecture Moderne) in 1933.

As of 1906, Tony Garnier handled a number of public building projects in Lyons on behalf of the socialist mayor Édouard Herriot, who later became Prime Minister and then Foreign Minister. Among other projects between 1920–1924 and 1929–1935, he built the Quartier des États Unis, in which he was only able to apply his principles to a limited extent.

JP

1 | **Meeting halls**
Covered foyer in the form of a spacious portico;
built of reinforced concrete.
P. 17. Drawing

2 | **Administrative and assembly buildings**
Illustration of the town hall and court of arbitration with
quotations from Émile Zola's novel *Travail*.
P. 19. Pen and ink drawing

3 | **Theatre**
Theater and rehearsal building. The dome above the auditorium
is clearly inspired by Charles Garnier's opera house in Paris.
P. 28. Pen and ink drawing

4 | **Complex of various medical facilities**
The medical facilities are located on a hill in the north of the town and
are protected from the cold wind by the hills. They consist of a hospital,
an institute for heliotherapy and an institute for the disabled.
P. 52. Pen and ink drawing

5 | **Residential area**
Detached houses of one and two stories are shown in the foreground
and central area. The space between the houses is for public use.
P. 72. Pen and ink drawing

6 | **Homes with two stories**
The strict cubic form and the radical lack of decoration
anticipate the architecture of the twenties.
P. 75. Pen and ink drawing

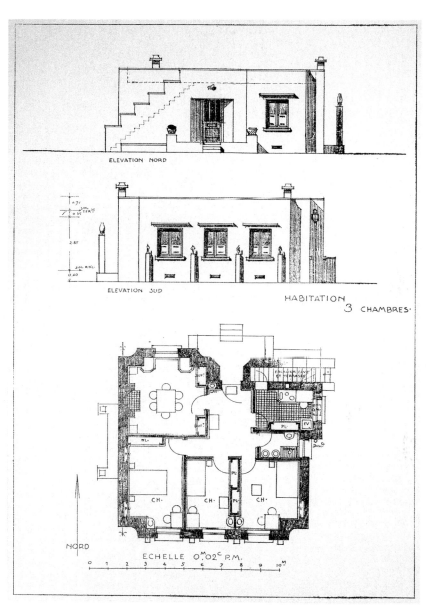

ELEVATION NORD

ELEVATION SUD

HABITATION
3 CHAMBRES·

NORD

ECHELLE 0.ᴹ02ᶜ P.M.

0 1 2 3 4 5 6 7 8 9 10ᴹ

7 | Views and ground plan of a house with one storey
The design of the approximately 80 m² of living space; the entry and the steles of the rear façade add a sense of Classical nobility to the simple form.
P. 103. Drawing

CITÉ INDUSTRIELLE
TONY GARNIER ARCHITECTE

P. 163
VUE DES USINES

8 | **General view of factories, steel mills, industrial port and wharves**
P. 163. Coloured pen and ink drawing

9 | **View of the blast furnaces and the dam with power plant**
P. 164. Coloured pen and ink drawing

CITÉ INDUSTRIELLE
TONY GARNIER ARCHITECTE

LES HAUTS-FOURNEAUX

Bruno Taut (1880–1938)
Die Stadtkrone
JENA, 1919

The City Crown

Alpine Architektur
HAGEN, 1919

Alpine Architecture

"Das bunte Glas zerstört den HASS" (Coloured glass destroys HATE). This is one of a number of somewhat cryptic aphorisms which appeared on a glass pavilion at the Werkbund Exhibition in Cologne in 1914. Bruno Taut designed this polygonal drum of concrete supports and covered it with glass tiles. It was crowned by a prism-shaped glass dome and served as the exhibition hall for the glass industry. The young architect's creation attracted a great deal of attention and quickly came to represent a new Expressionist trend in German architecture. The above-mentioned aphorisms stem from the writer Paul Scheerbart (1863–1915), who wrote fantasy novels and poems and whom Taut considered to be the "only poet of architecture." Scheerbart's article, *Glasarchitektur* (*Glass Architecture*) was published in Berlin by the Expressionist publishing house "Der Sturm" that same year, 1914. Without this stimulus, it would be difficult to imagine Taut's literary creations. Scheerbart presented a series of hypotheses containing ideas that he had been developing over a long period; namely, that brick architecture would be replaced by glass and that this would result in a major change in the earth's surface and elevate human culture to a higher level.

To return to Bruno Taut: he was born in Königsberg (now Kaliningrad in Russia) in 1880, and received his education at the Building College in his home city. After practical training in several towns, Taut collaborated from 1904–1908 with Theodor Fischer in Stuttgart, and in 1908 he settled in

Berlin. There, he worked with his younger brother, Max, without ever entering into a formal partnership. In 1912, Taut became a committed member of the garden city movement and designed the garden city suburbs of Falkenberg in Berlin's Grünau district and the "Reform" garden city in Magdeburg. The garden city philosophy (with all its implications for social reform) was to become an important source of inspiration for Taut's vision.

Taut's practical activity ended with the First World War. He began to write and sketch – not to escape from the brutalities of reality, but rather to oppose it by presenting a positive utopia. On no account can the compositions and sketches which Taut executed between 1916 and 1920 be regarded as a form of therapy for an out-of-work architect. They must instead be seen as a dense and impressive artistic accomplishment situated between utopian social thought and town planning, between the esoteric and the aesthetic, between artistic synthesis and critique of civilization, between the metaphorical properties of glass and abstract art.

The *Stadtkrone* was written in 1916/17 and published in 1919, and reveals a certain relationship to work by utopian socialists such as Charles Fourier (1772–1837), who drew a connection between architectural concepts and secular chiliasm. According to Taut, "socialism in an apolitical and trans-political sense, far from being a form of domination, represents the most basic relationships between human be-

DOMSTERN

26

ings. It bridges the gap between feuding classes and nations and connects people with people." Taut designed an immense circular garden city with a radius of about 7 kilometres for three million inhabitants. The "City Crown" was to be in the very centre. "Mighty and inaccessible," it would have been the culmination of a community and cultural centre, a skyscraper-like, purpose-free "crystal building." "The building contains nothing but one beautiful room which can be reached by either of two staircases to the right and to the left of the theatre and the little community centre. How can I even begin to describe what it is only possible to construct!" Taut based his work on historical models and references, which were appended with illustrations. Above all he referred to the medieval city: "Cathedrals with their purposeless naves and their even more purposeless towers were the true city crowns." This was in accordance with the spirit of the times and the studies of Taut's contemporary, the art historian Wilhelm Worringer. For Taut, the Indian temple was an even better example of the sovereignty of ideas and intellect over profane utility, as well as an example of a combination of the profane and the religious.

In comparison with the relatively realistic *City Crown*, Taut soon took a further, large step in the direction of utopia. One result of this was his essay, *Auflösung der Städte oder: Die Erde eine gute Wohnung oder auch: Der Weg zur Alpinen Architektur (The Disbanding of the Cities or: The Earth is a Good Place to Live or: The Way to Alpine Architecture)*, which was written in 1918 and published in 1920. On the title page,

Taut called the work "a mere utopia and a little entertainment." In 30 artistic illustrations – fantastically visionary fairytales often verging on the biomorphic – he once again developed a residential and social model which is a far cry from metropolitan dimensions. The human communities were to be as small and differentiated as possible, even providing space for eccentrics. Ludditism and the rejection of functional aspects are mixed together with futuristic technological fantasies. In this way, Taut designed a "sanctuary where solar energy is absorbed by glass plates, lenses and mirrors and stowed in towers of light." Of course, this is not all to be taken literally. It is a symbol, not of a new society, but rather of a new humanity which has overcome its earthly fetters. The model of the city crown puts in an appearance here, yet now it is even more ethereal and liberated from any kind of profane functionalism. This "Giant Star Temple" which is – it goes without saying – made of glass, is intended to fuse man with architecture to create a cosmic total work of art set on a theatrical/religious stage. "Art for art's sake has been overtaken; it permeates all humankind."

As a theoretical foundation and protective accompaniment to these artistically high-quality texts, illustrations and plates, Taut included an appendix made up of in some cases arbitrarily isolated passages from works by a variety of authors. These include Friedrich Hölderlin, Friedrich Engels and Friedrich Nietzsche, whose critical tendencies toward the state and capitalism interested Taut. Taut accorded pride of place to the Russian anarchist and communist, Peter Kro-

---

Fig. p. 455
1 | Cathedral star
The cathedral star, a fantastic conglomeration of mirrored arched forms, is the embodiment of Taut's romantic synthesis of art and nature.
In: Alpine Architektur, *fig. 26. Pen and watercolour*

potkin, who fought for a society free of statehood and sovereign authority and without private property. Taut's ideas were similar to those of Kropotkin and his German follower Gustav Landauer. Nevertheless it would not have been possible to describe Taut as an anarchist or communist in the sense of politics and parties.

In 1919, a year before the appearance of *Auflösung der Städte*, *Alpine Architektur* was published. It was an imaginative collection of annotated illustrations about climbing the Alps and reaching ever more transcendental and utopian regions. Even though it was rooted in concrete architectural structures and genuine topographical situations, *Alpine Architektur* amounts to the ultimate Taut fantasy. It is about nothing less than the partial covering of the Alps and its foothills as far as the Mediterranean with crystalline glass structures. "Yes, impractical and useless!", said Taut about his ideas; but then he contradicted himself by defiantly stating that "all that is left for us is restless, courageous work in the service of beauty and in subordination to the higher power."

In the two years following the end of the First World War, just as this and similar compositions like *Der Weltbaumeister (The Architect of the World)* and *Haus des Himmels (The House of Heaven)* were being published, Taut became feverishly active in organizing revolutionary artists and architects. Like many of his colleagues, he was convinced that specifically architects and artists must play a central role in the development of a new society. At the end of 1918, Taut became one of the founders and activists of the *Arbeitsrat für Kunst* ("Working Council for Art") and the "November Group," both short-lived associations of utopian and revolutionary Expressionist minds. His comrades-in-arms included Walter Gropius, Erich Mendelsohn, Paul Klee and Lyonel Feininger. These hopelessly idealistic groups were quickly doomed on the practical political level. At the end of 1919,

Taut developed a new, more private concept of organization. He founded an almost clandestine group; a loose alliance of architects and artists who exchanged projects and utopian ideas by exchanging letters. This union of correspondents included the Luckhardt brothers, Hans Scharoun and Hermann Finsterlin and called itself *Die Gläserne Kette* ("The Glass Chain"). Taut published ideas and designs which resulted from these exchanges of letters in his magazine *Frühlicht*. The end of this alliance came at the end of 1920. Expressionist exuberance, the Dadaistic lack of seriousness and the uninhibited fantasies could not assert themselves against either the new rationalism or, especially, the temptation of specific building commissions.

Bruno Taut was then appointed the local building inspector (1921–1923) of Magdeburg, where he tried to give the city a more attractive look by painting the exteriors of buildings in more expressive colours. In 1924 he returned to Berlin, where he worked as a consulting architect for public-service house-building companies. Using modern technology, he was able to realize a number of housing estates (e.g., the horseshoe-shaped Berlin-Britz), which are considered to be among the most important architectural accomplishments of the Weimar Republic. One should not think of these projects as a betrayal of his earlier idealism or as an expression of the adoption of bourgeois values. Rather, they were an attempt to change these ideals to fit changing circumstances.

In 1933, Bruno Taut had no choice but to emigrate. First he went to Japan, where he made an intensive study of Japanese art and architecture, and then, in 1936, he became a Professor at the Academy of Art in Istanbul. During this period, he constructed a number of school and university buildings in addition to his own residence in Istanbul's Ortaköy district. Before his house could be completed, Bruno Taut died on 24 December 1938.

GL

Kristallhaus in den Bergen

ganz aus Glaskristall
errichtet — farbigem
in der Schnee und Gletscherregion
Andacht
Unaussprechliches
Schweigen

(Tempel)
des
Schweigens

Weg vom
Tal her
Kristallmaste
sind Wegbe-
gleiter.
Sie funkeln
in der Sonne
und besonders
die grössten,
die sich im
Lichte drehen —
Kristall-
Standarten
Plateaus für
Luftlandungen

Dieses
im All be-
Taut dur-
setzen A

bare Gegensätze. Architektur lässt sich nicht „anwenden". Auch nicht auf Ideale. Jeder Menschengeist
soll verstummen, wo die höchste Baulust, wo die Kunst spricht – fern von Hütten und Kasernen

haus soll keine „Krone" sein. Wer kann
en! — — Und keine „Stadtkrone" Bruno
as Höchste, das Leere über eine Stadt
und Stadtdunst bleiben unüberbrück-
LÄCHEN KANTEN WÖLBUNGEN RAUM .

2 | Crystal building
Taut did not ascribe a centralized and community oriented
function to the crystal building in the mountains as he had
done with the crystal building of the City Crown.
Fig. 3. Pen and watercolour

3 | Crystal building
The crystal building in the Swiss mountains was to be a
"Temple of Silence"; its effect was to be the result of
"lofty architecture and tremendous quiet."
Fig. 4. Pen and watercolour

4 | Building plan
Taut's visions of supranational Alpine architecture were partly based on
concrete locations like the alpine foothills of the Upper Italian lakes.
The terraced buildings are remarkable for their lack of expression.
Fig. 14. Pen and watercolour

SCHNEE
GLETSCHER
GLAS

Firnen
im ewigen Eise
und Schnee —
überbaut und ge-
schmückt mit
Umbauungen, Flä-
chen und Bögen
von farbigem Glase
B.Q. Glütus

Die Ausführung ist gewiss ungeheuer schwer und opfervoll, aber nicht unmöglich. „Man verlangt so sollen
von den Menschen das Unmögliche." (Goethe)

5 | **Snow, glaciers, glass**
For Taut, building over the Alps was a triad of snow, glaciers and glass. Its realization
would have been "extremely difficult and full of sacrifices but not impossible."
Fig. 10. Pen and watercolour

ALPENAUSLÄUFER AN DER RIVIERA ·

Glas-
dorn am
Pontofino~
Offene Hallen
mit wechselndem
Durchblick aufs
freie Meer

Ganz
aus massivem
Glas erbaut ~
Glaspfeiler und
- streben ~
Mattglasgewölbe
Nachts farbiges
Licht Darunter ~

Gegend von
Porto Venere
Steiles Seestade mit funkelnden
massiven edelsteinartigen Glas-
kristallen besetzt

Halbinsel davor
mit Bauten von
mattem Glase,
die ins Meer hinunter-
gehen.

15

6 | Fairytale palace
Taut devised a fairytale palace architecture for the Mediterranean coast southeast
of Genoa which he generously considered to be part of the Alpine foothills.
Fig. 15. Pen and watercolour

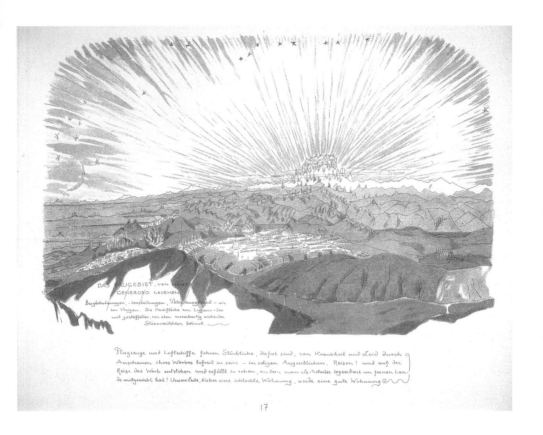

DAS ~~AUGEBIET~~. VON MONT
GENEROSO GESEHEN

Bergbebröpfungen, - benpfleitungen, überpbausorbeit - wie
im Vorigen. Die Hochfläche am Lugano-See
mit gestaffelter, von oben mosaikartig wirkender
Glasarchitektur bebaut.

Flugzeuge und Luftschiffe fahren Glückliche, die froh sind, von Krankheit und Leid durch g
Anschauen ihres Werkes befreit zu sein – in seligen Augenblicken. Reisen! und auf der
Reise das Werk entstehen und erfüllt zu sehen, an dem man als Arbeiter irgendwo im fernen Lan-
de mitgewirkt hat! Unsere Erde, bisher eine schlechte Wohnung, werde eine gute Wohnung

17

7 | View of the city
That Taut was influenced by medieval towns which were characterized
by a towering cathedral can be seen by this sketch.
Fig. 17. Pen and watercolour

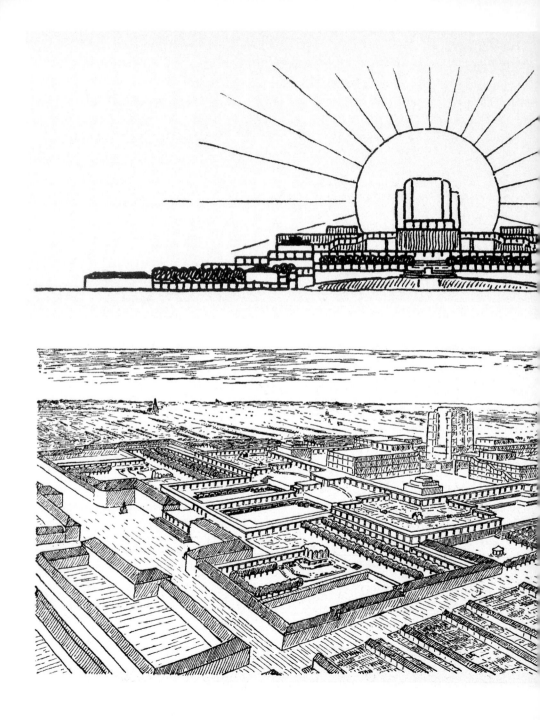

8 | **The city crown**
In the middle of Taut's ideal city is the city crown, from which
a sacral structure free of purpose arises: the crystal building.
Fig. 42. Pen and ink drawing

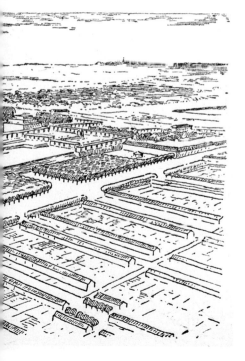

9 | **View of the city**
From this perspective one can recognize the hierarchical
gradation from the low residential buildings to the
community structures and finally to the crystal building.
Fig. 49. Pen and ink drawing

Le Corbusier (1887–1965)

Vers une Architecture

PARIS, 1923

Toward a New Architecture. New York, 1927

Urbanisme

PARIS, 1925

The City of Tomorrow. New York, 1927

La Charte d'Athènes

PARIS, 1943

The Athens Charter. New York, 1973

Le Corbusier's influence on the theory and practice of architecture and town planning in the 20th century cannot be overestimated. Through the publication of his building projects and plans as well as through his extensive theoretical work, virtually no other architect has had such a provocative and standard-setting impact on the discourse of Modernist architecture. He wanted to open "eyes which do not see" ("des yeux qui ne voient pas") – one of his famous statements – to the beauty of Modernist engineering technology. He understood his theoretical explanations as an "appeal to architects" which should serve as an aid to recognizing the road to a style of architecture for modern times, which would be as rational as it would be poetic: a "conscious, exact and splendid game of the buildings assembled under the sun."

The architect and theorist Charles-Édouard Jeanneret was born in 1887 in La Chaux-de-Fonds in western Switzerland, the Suisse Romande. From 1923 he called himself, "Le Corbusier" which is derived from a name on his mother's side of the family, Lecorbésier. In 1917, he went to Paris and from 1920 he published the magazine *Esprit Nouveau* with the painter Amédé Ozenfant. By 1925 they had brought out a total of 28 issues and developed their own platform which was intended to substantiate and publicize an aesthetic for the machine age.

Numerous hypotheses, first published in *Esprit Nouveau*, appeared in 1923 in Le Corbusier's first bound work on architectural theory, *Vers une architecture*, translated as

Toward a New Architecture (although the word "new" is not in the French title). Here he brought together his theoretical principles in a collection of texts which is both appellative and exciting. The book turned its author into an immediate international celebrity and is still today an excellent reference book for the gesture and content of modern architectural propaganda. Although the typographical appearance of this book is somewhat conventional, the reader is captivated by manifesto-like slogans, numerous repetitions and especially by the unusual montage of text and pictures. Polemic intermingles with apodictic proclamations while subjective architectural aesthetics are interpreted as the sum of anthropological constants.

The book is arranged in various chapters, each prefaced by so-called guiding principles. Their impact is due to a series of simple, sometimes short and suggestive sentences as well as to the use of poetic metaphor. The well-integrated illustrations are a surprise. They often do not refer to the actual projects in question, but stem from the stocks of classical architectural history as well as from engineering technology. The confrontation of the Parthenon in Athens with a sports car is a typical example, deliberately chosen for its shock effect. Le Corbusier's arguments often use examples from the Ancient world as models which set a standard of rational logic that has yet to find its due equivalent in the modern industrial age. That is why it is the engineer who, unencumbered by an academic tradition, is able to develop

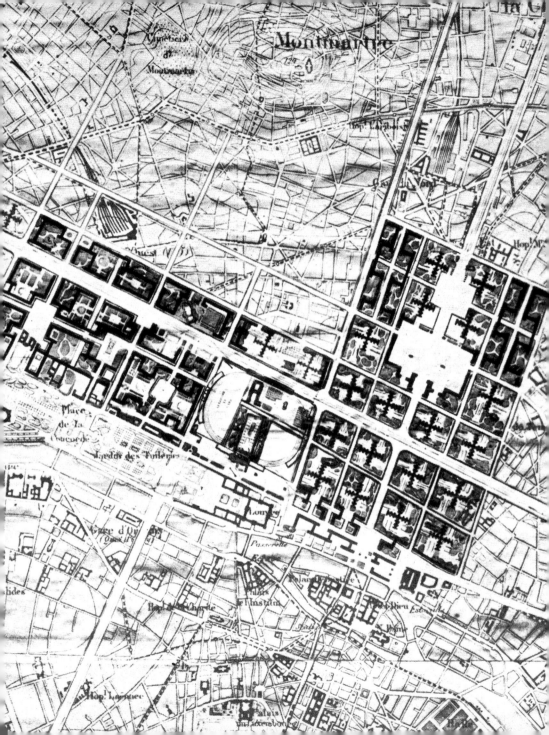

the precise solution to mechanical problems. According to Le Corbusier, what else is a house other than a "machine for living in" ("machine à habiter")!

The new aesthetic was the result of a clear analysis of functions and therefore moved forward the debate on reforming architectural aesthetics, which had been underway since the second half of the 19th century. Form follows function and industrial design is the yardstick for all design. The upper decks of an ocean liner with their railings and spiral staircases, their rows of windows and functional white paint are the illustrative material for an architectural beauty which attests not just to appropriately stringent, but also to hygienic and almost moral qualities. This is what Le Corbusier wrote about an ocean liner: "a pure, clean, bright, correct and healthy architecture." "Styles," however, are "a lie." At the same time, Le Corbusier rehabilitates architecture as an art form, assigning to the architect the duty to rise above simple utilitarian expedience and to work creatively. It is the orderly hand of the artist which first creates the satisfactory aesthetic effect he ascribes to modern architecture. Unusual layouts and creative compositions of "the buildings assembled under the sun" as well as artistic elaboration of freely formed façades become the yardstick for a functionally justifiable yet simultaneously aesthetic understanding of architecture. It is noteworthy that Le Corbusier in no way links his treatise with a revolutionary social utopia. On the contrary, the final chapter, which is called "Architecture or Revolution," makes it clear that the author is not particularly concerned to adapt his aesthetic to a social utopian context. For him, there is a real deficit in the creation of adequate working, leisure and above all living conditions for a progressive industrial society.

The themes of Le Corbusier's ensuing publications are therefore house-building and especially problems related to town planning. *Urbanisme,* translated as *The City of Tomorrow,* which came in 1925, is the fundamental introduction. Analogous to his provocative theorems on Modernist architecture, he defines town planning primarily in functional terms and the city as a tool. Order and straight lines, functional analyses and rigid shapes are the ineluctable consequence of such an approach. Yet in spite of the sobriety of his argumentation, he retains an unmistakable aesthetic approach to questions of the face to be given the city. It is the "eternal forms of pure geometry," which are not only the logical result of this function, but which also appear "full of poetry." The project "Ville contemporaine pour trois millions d'habitants" (a contemporary city of three million inhabitants), which was conceived as early as 1922, illustrates the consequences of these fundamental city-planning consider-

ations. A regular row of 24 skyscrapers is arranged around a central traffic hub, forming a kind of city crown within a large green area, which is divided by a system of hierarchically arranged streets to form a cityscape. The various urban functions like traffic, work, residences, and recreation are clearly defined and relegated to different spaces. With the "Plan Voisin," which was developed in 1922 and refined through to 1929, Le Corbusier applied the concepts devised for the "Ville contemporaine" to Paris. With deliberate polemicism, the old inner-city districts are confronted with the vision of a new city. With the exception of a few historical monuments, the existing urban structure was to be replaced by a radical new solution.

In 1943, *Charte d'Athènes* appeared, becoming Le Corbusier's most successful book on modern city planning. The text is based on statements made during the 4th Congrès International d'Architecture Moderne, which took place in 1933 during a cruise from Marseilles to Athens, and was very much under Le Corbusier's way. The Congress proposals were revised by Le Corbusier in 1941 and published two years later, using in some cases plans first published 1935 in *La Ville Radieuse.* The centre-piece is the precise differentiation of urban functions and how their methodical separation forms the basis of rational city planning. The imperative tone of the Charter makes it come across as a precise analysis and instrument which can and must be used to solve problems in urban planning at any time. It seems altogether *dirigiste* when the author insists that the Charter must first establish its legitimacy with the administrative organs. It thus shows architecture's duty "to create or improve a city, and it also has the responsibility to choose among and distribute different elements, whose correct proportions will provide the basis for a harmonious and durable work. The architect holds the key to all this in his hands."

Today, Le Corbusier still polarizes the critics. His apodictic positions, his absolutist thrust, and not least the enormous circle which has been influenced by his theories, predestine him to be the target of critics of the modern city and the banal and imitative way in which it has been developed in line with his hypotheses. For his critics, the decisive aspects of a failed urban philosophy are his break with tradition, the separation of functions, and the dictate of functional logic. At the same time, there is no question that it was Le Corbusier who was the leading voice calling for an architecture of the modern industrial age. Apart from the historical aspects of his platform, it is artistic quality by which the realization of his vision of urban planning must be measured.

PS

Notre-Dame in Paris.

1 | **Notre-Dame with "elevation governors"**
German ed., 1926, p. 59. Photo

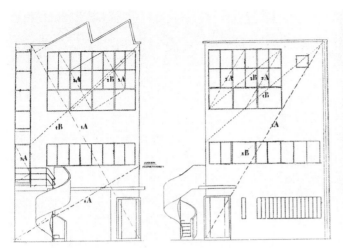

2 | Maison Ozenfant
View and sketch of the façade with elevation governors.
German ed., 1926, p. 63. Photo and drawing

3 | Classic Greek architecture confronted with automobiles
German ed., 1926, p. 108/09. Photo

4 | **The deck of the** *Aquitania*
German ed., 1926, p. 79. Photo

5 | **The Plan Voisin for Paris (1925)**
Model with the hand of the architect. The photo is from the documentary
"Architecture d'aujourd'hui" by Pierre Chenal, 1931.
Additional illustration not included in the treatise.

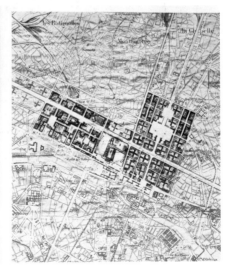

6 | The Plan Voisin for Paris
Model
Additional illustration from: Œuvre Complète, 1929–1934, p. 93

7 | The Plan Voisin for Paris (1922–1929)
In the picture on the left the project is contrasted with the existing city
structure; on the right is the project in the context of the inner city.
Additional illustrations from: Œuvre Complète, 1929–1934, p. 91

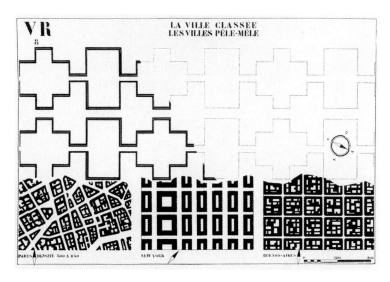

8 | **La Ville Radieuse (1935)**
Study of a plan compared to typical urban plans of Paris,
New York and Buenos Aires.
Additional illustration from: Œuvre Complète, *1934–1938, p. 30.*
Line drawing

9 | **La Ville Radieuse (1935)**
Detailed view of the structure of a typical residential neighborhood.
Additional illustration from: Œuvre Complète, *1934–1938, p. 31*

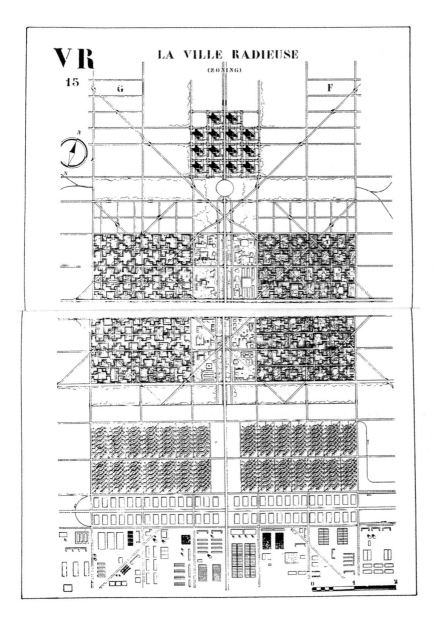

**10 | La Ville Radieuse
(1935)**
Complete plan.
In: Charta von Athen,
*2nd German ed. 1988,
p. 230/31. Drawing*

Henry-Russell Hitchcock (1903–1987)
Philip Johnson (b. 1906)

The International Style:
Architecture Since 1922

NEW YORK, 1932

This book, which was no doubt the most important American manifesto on architecture until Robert Venturi's *Complexity and Contradiction in Architecture* was published in 1966, appeared in connection with an exhibition which was organized by the Museum of Modern Art in 1932, the first exhibition on architecture by the museum, which at that time was a mere two years old. Philip Johnson, the first curator of the MoMA's Department of Architecture until 1934, art historian Henry-Russell Hitchcock, and the MoMA's then Director, Alfred H. Barr, first came up with the idea in the autumn of 1930. For the most part, the exhibition was prepared by Johnson. Years earlier, during a trip to Europe, his interest in modern architecture had been roused by Hitchcock while visiting the German Architecture Exhibition in Berlin (1931). At that time, he also personally made the acquaintance of such architects as Ludwig Mies van der Rohe, Walter Gropius, Erich Mendelsohn, Jacobus Johannes Pieter Oud and Le Corbusier. The exposition was called "Modern Architecture: International Exhibition" and opened on 10 February 1932. It included works by such architects as Mies van der Rohe, Walter Gropius, Hans Scharoun and Otto Haesler from Germany, Le Corbusier from France, Alvar Aalto from Finland as well as other architects from Austria, Belgium, Britain, France, Germany, Holland, Italy, Japan, the Soviet Union, Spain, Sweden, and Switzerland; but also Americans such as Raymond Hood, Frank Lloyd Wright, Howe & Lescaze and Richard Neutra. Only structures which actually had been built were exhibited. There were no visionary projects, not even those of the Russian Constructivists. The centrepiece consisted of four works: the Villa Savoye by Le Corbusier (1930), the Tugendhat House by Mies van der Rohe (1930), which Johnson considered to be the most important Modernist building, Frank Lloyd Wright's "House on the Mesa" in Denver (1931), and the house that the Dutchman J.J. P. Oud had just built for Johnson's mother in Pinehurst. In addition, there was a section on residential building which had been entrusted to the renowned urban critic Lewis Mumford. The exhibition was reconstructed in 1992 by Terence Riley of Columbia University.

The book, *The International Style: Architecture since 1922*, appeared while the exhibition was in preparation. It contains 138 illustrations, exterior and interior photographs, and ground plans in alphabetical order of the architects' names in order to avoid any categorization by country. The relatively short text was written by Hitchcock and contains an introduction by Alfred Barr; Johnson merely edited it. The text is not concerned with the individual buildings. It is an attempt to inductively define stylistic categories based on the common characteristics of modern architecture and according to the principles of the analysis of form used in art history. The basic thesis is that the new edifices presented in the exhibition represent the valid architectural style of the day and that this style is just as "unified and inclusive" as the styles of earlier epochs in art history, such as Gothic and

Baroque. Hitchcock compares the new style not only to the out-of-date Revivalism of the 19th century, but also to the new architecture of the period before the First World War, for example to work by Peter Behrens, Otto Wagner, Auguste Perret and Frank Lloyd Wright, whom he describes as "half-Modern." For him, the pioneers and leaders of the new style were primarily Walter Gropius, J.J. P. Oud, Le Corbusier and Mies van der Rohe and, in the second rank, Gerrit Rietveld and Erich Mendelsohn.

Hitchcock vehemently rejects the functionalist thesis of many architects that the aesthetic element of architecture is meaningless in the technological era because form must be derived automatically from the logic of function and technology. Instead, he points to the essential difference between architecture and construction, emphasizing the artistic nature of modern architecture. Hitchcock defines three basic principles as the constituent characteristics for the aesthetic value of the new style: first, architecture is no longer conceived of as mass, but rather as volume. Instead of solid walls, space now consists of surfaces and panes; in the geometric clarity of smooth surfaces, volume seems immaterial and weightless. The second principle is regularity, which now appears in place of axial symmetry. It is not a monotonous absolute regularity, but rather, the rhythmic composition of regular forms. The third principle is the renunciation of decoration. Its place is now taken by the elegance of material, the technical perfection of detail and correct proportion as an aesthetic quality. All three principles define an aesthetic of abstract mathematical form which corresponds to nonfigurative painting. Hitchcock explains the use of these principles by using examples from the illustrations, and he also devised a series of formulas for architects to help them avoid mistakes.

In the preface to a new edition published in 1965, Hitchcock suggests that his book was less remarkable for what it said, than for the time at which it said it. When it was published in 1932, it was the first positive appraisal of Modernist architecture to use the methods of formal analysis and the scholarly concepts deployed by art historians. It was his intention to show US architects that there was a generally received contemporary international style which had simply not yet been recognized in America. Hitchcock and Johnson were undoubtedly exposed to the expression "international style" through Walter Gropius' essay "Internationale Architektur" (*Bauhaus Bücher 1*, 1925) as well as through the concept of the "international style c. 1400". The book was criticized for the primarily and almost exclusively aesthetic angle it took. The social aspect of the new architecture, which Lewis Mumford emphasized in the exhibition's catalogue, is only mentioned in the final chapter, which has as its the title the German word "The Siedlung" (the "housing estate").

In 1951, Henry-Russell Hitchcock wrote an article entitled "The International Style Twenty Years After" for the *Architectural Record*, in which he relativized many aspects of his 1932 book. He now realized that the International Style was at an end, and found that the claim to absolute validity which he had earlier ascribed to the rationalistic tendency in architectural thought had been a historical mistake. Indeed, the other trends of the 1920s possessed the same historical validity. He stressed this especially in relation to Frank Lloyd Wright, who had strongly protested against the exhibition in 1932, describing it as propaganda and threatening to withdraw from it. Hitchcock had not even mentioned Wright once in his book.

Both the book and the 1932 exhibition, which the Museum of Modern Art also presented in 13 other American cities, met with a lively response. They paved the way for Gropius to be appointed professor at Harvard University (1937), followed in 1938 by Mies van der Rohe in Chicago, and for the total change of direction in American architecture which was to occur after World War II.   JP

1 | Johannes Andreas Brinkman and Leendert Cornelis van der Vlugt,
Van Nelle Tobacco, Tea & Coffee Factory, Rotterdam (1928–1930)
"An industrial building admirably composed of three sections, each devoted
to a separate function but with the same structural regularity throughout."
P. 109

2 | **Le Corbusier and Pierre Jeanneret, Savoye House, Poissy-sur-Seine (1930)**
"The white second storey appears weightless on its round posts. Its severe symmetry sets off the brilliant study in abstract form … the blue and rose wind-shelter above."
P. 119

3 | **Walter Gropius, Bauhaus School, Dessau (1926)**
"The workshops have entirely transparent walls. A good illustration of glass panes as a surfacing material. The projection of the roof cap is unfortunate, especially over the entrance at the left."
P. 141

4 | **Erich Mendelsohn, Schocken Department Store, Chemnitz (1928–1930)**
"Startling ribbon windows made possible by cantilever construction."
P. 177

5 | **Mies van der Rohe, German Pavilion at the
Barcelona Exposition, Spain (1929)**
"The walls are independent planes under a continuous slab roof,
which is supported on light metal posts."
P. 183

6 | **Lilly Reich, Bedroom in the Berlin Building Exposition (1931)**
"A Luxurious and feminine character achieved by a combination
of white materials of various textures."
P. 204

7 | **J.J.P. Oud, Workers' Houses, Hook van Holland (1924–1927)**
"The continuous balcony carried around the curved shops underlines
the simple rhythm of the windows."
P. 195

Walter Gropius (1883–1969)
Internationale Architektur

MUNICH, 1925

International Architecture

Walter Gropius was one of the most influential architects of the 20th century. In 1910, along with his partner Adolf Meyer (1881–1929), Gropius went independent. Gropius, speaking about himself, said that he was unable to "put even the simplest idea on paper" and therefore he needed Meyer so that his ideas could take more formal shape. With their very first big project, Gropius and Meyer made architectural history: with the Fagus factory in Alfeld an der Leine, Peter Behrens' model is easily recognizable, yet in terms of structural and aesthetic radicalism it goes much further.

In 1919, Gropius was appointed the head of the new Staatliches Bauhaus in Weimar. The Bauhaus was experimenting with a holistic approach to art and craftsmanship; the "joining together of all artistic creation; the reunification of all artistic disciplines to a new architecture." Conservative forces drove the institute out of Weimar, and so the Bauhaus master craftsmen chose the industrial town of Dessau as their new headquarters. The Bauhaus building, the Masters' Houses, the Employment Office and the Törten housing estate were the outstanding buildings to emerge. In 1928, Gropius left the Bauhaus and opened an office in Berlin. Obviously, there was no future for the former Bauhaus director in Germany after 1933, so he emigrated to the United States via England. As professor of architecture at Harvard, he embarked on a second career. Gropius had always known the value of teamwork and because of his own inability to draw, he had always employed qualified colleagues. Together with

some Harvard graduates, he founded The Architects Collaborative (TAC) in 1945. It soon became one of the most important architectural offices in the USA. Everyone, including Gropius, subjugated their own ideas to the work of the team. Gropius died in Boston in 1969.

The extent and importance of his published work is little in comparison to that which he produced as an architect and as a university professor. Nevertheless, there are some books and articles which were of great influence. In 1923, Gropius published *Idee und Aufbau des Staatlichen Bauhauses (The Conception and Structure of the Staatliches Bauhaus)*. This essay contained the basic agenda, instructions and a statement of accountability.

The expulsion of the Bauhaus from Weimar seemed at first to be a heavy blow, but relocation kindled new energy. In its orientation, the Bauhaus became more pragmatic and more rationalist. In order to avoid public relations mistakes, Gropius initiated activities which could be described as a multimedia advertising strategy. They included the publication of the *Bauhausbücher (Bauhaus Books)*. The Bauhaus master – teachers were initially called "masters" to stress their craft credentials – László Moholy-Nagy (1895–1946) was responsible for their design. No. 1 in the series was Gropius' *Internationale Architektur.*

"This work is a picture book of modern architecture. It is a brief review of the work of leading modern architects of the developed world and aims to familiarize the reader with

trends in today's architectural design." Thus begins the introduction. It is followed by about 100 pages of photos, isometric sections and illustrations of models. About 90 examples from about a half dozen countries are considered. Of those, about half were buildings that had already been erected, the rest projects and studies. The book thus has the character of a workshop report. The majority of examples are from the period after the First World War, mostly beginning in 1922. Just 14 date from before 1914.

It begins, like a homage, with three factories built by Peter Behrens for AEG between 1910 and 1912. These are buildings which, for all their modernity, portray Behrens' Classicism, an approach Gropius did not share. These are followed by Henry van de Velde's Theatre, built for the Werkbund Exposition in Cologne in 1914, and Petrus Belage's Amsterdam Stock Exchange. After that, Gropius presents his own early work, the Werkbund model factory and the Fagus factory. These are followed by photos of giant grain silos which seem a bit strange – they had been shown by Gropius in 1911 during a lecture on "monumental art and industrial construction". In an article entitled *Grundlagen für Neues Bauen* (*The Basics of Modern Building*) (in *Bau- und Werkkunst*, 1925/26) he describes the ambivalent fascination of these inaccessible edifices and how their "repulsive form [makes one feel] something of the brutal power of capital-

ism." The powerful monumentality of these cubes, which managed to transform themselves into something aesthetic, fascinated other architects as well, who saw in them the archetypal representation of the industrial age. At the end of the picture book, there is an aerial view of Manhattan. Unusually, Gropius offered a short commentary here in which he on the one hand criticizes the lack of planning and dense concentration of "inappropriate building styles," and on the other praises the "gigantic shape of the skyscrapers." If the reader turned back one page, he could see the proposed totalitarian ideal: Le Corbusier's 1922 vision of a high-rise city.

Between Behrens' industrial buildings and the highrise dreams we find utilitarian buildings, residential buildings and housing estates. The main focus is on examples related to the Bauhaus, ten designed by Gropius himself, and others by his colleagues Karl Fieger, Marcel Breuer, Ludwig Hilberseimer, Georg Muche and Richard Paulick (e. g. the experimental steel building in Dessau) as well as by Hannes Meyer, who later became director. A photo shows models of system-built houses which were presented in 1923 in a Bauhaus exhibition in Weimar and represent the "combination of the greatest amount of uniformity of type with the greatest amount of variability."

There is no system to this review of pictures; objects and pictures appear arbitrarily and no explanations are of-

Fig. p. 485
1 | Peter Behrens, small motor factory near Berlin
The beginning of *Internationale Architektur* is marked by a few buildings from the period before the First World War including Behrens' small motor factory. Gropius had worked in Behrens' studio from 1908–1910.
P. 11. Ed. from 1981

fered. Missing are interior views and ground-plans; they were held back for a later publication which never appeared. Nor was there any systematic appraisal of trends to date. Moreover, this work was intended to appeal to a "broad spectrum including lay people," who could obtain an idea of the clarity and objectivity of Neues Bauen or "modern building" as well as of the preference for glass surfaces or combinations of cuboid shapes. Gropius counted on the visual effect of the pictures to influence readers.

The introduction reads like a manifesto on Neues Bauen. Like Adolf Loos (1870–1933), Gropius initially rejected Revivalism with its "use of motifs, ornaments and profiles mostly from previous cultures," which degraded a building to the status of a bearer of "dead decorations." With his "new natural sense of structure," which did not recognize any national boundaries, he offered an alternative to an "academic aestheticism" which closed its eyes to technological progress. Characteristic of the new order is that the form of a building is derived from its "essence" and function. Nevertheless, Gropius was not the proponent of any kind of simple functionalism. Instead, he favoured the integration of "proportion" as a "concern of the spiritual world." It remains dependent on function and construction, but also raises a building to a level higher than simple utility. Artists were necessary if this synthesis of function and form was to be accomplished, and Gropius did not shy away from the term.

Characteristic of the new architecture are its "precisely defined forms, simplicity in multiplicity, repartition according to function and restriction to typical basic forms. It should also be sequential and repetitive." Then Gropius, not for the first time, made use of a poetic formulation, that betrayed the enthusiasm of the times. He insisted that buildings be "shaped by internal laws without lies and games; all that is unnecessary, that veils the absolute design, must be

shed." Gropius finished with a statement in favour of progress and dreamt of "lightly overcoming the sluggish effects and appearance of the earth." This closing statement corresponds to the last pictures. In the preface to the second edition, Gropius took stock of the achievement made: the "new spirit of building," based on technological successes, was, he suggested, about to conquer the "civilized world." The reader almost expects to read a term which Gropius meticulously avoids, namely "International Style." For him there was something bigger, more absolute than style, namely, "building as the way to shape life's processes."

Internationale Architektur established a new kind of architectural literature: the treatise in the form of a book of photographs. This was, however, not without precedent. In 1923, Adolf Behne, an art historian associated with Neues Bauen, completed a manuscript with the title *Der moderne Zweckbau* (*The Modern Functional Building*). In it, he analyzed and provided evidence of trends in architecture. Behne could not find a publisher and therefore his book did not appear until 1926, one year after *Internationale Architektur*. It received little attention, although the argumentation ran deeper. The authors were acquainted and were aware of each other's projects. Behne complained bitterly to Gropius because the latter had taken advantage of him. However, Gropius' book was imitated in its turn. Thus, Ludwig Hilberseimer published *Internationale neue Baukunst* (*International New Architecture*) in 1927 under commission to the Werkbund. The most important publication to take its cue from Gropius and Behne appeared in 1932 in the United States: *The International Style: Architecture since 1922* by Henry-Russell Hitchcock and Philip Johnson. What Gropius had not wanted to discuss was tackled there by the American historians of architecture: they declared that modern architecture was a style. GL

2 | **View of Manhattan (1926/27)**
A view of Manhattan comes at the end: "In spite of complexes without plan
and a conglomeration of subjective building styles, one can see a modern
city characterized by the suggestively immense form of the skyscraper."
Ed. from 1981, p. 106

3 | Fagus factory, near Alsfeld (1910–1914)
Gropius wrote architectural history with this factory. The iron-framed construction
of the façade, which no longer had any useful function, was spectacular and innovative.
Ed. from 1981, p. 17

4 | **Model of serial houses (1923)**
"Variability of the same basic type through connecting and disconnecting repetitive space cells. Basic idea: combining the greatest possible standardization with the greatest possible variability."
Ed. from 1981, p. 103. Model

5 | **The Bauhaus Building in Dessau (1925/26)**
After moving to Dessau, Bauhaus got its own building complex which was designed in Walter Gropius' private office.
It became the incunabulum of modern architecture.
Ed. from 1981, p. 22

6 | Dessau, south side of the Director's House (1925/26)
On the edge of Dessau three duplexes for the Bauhaus masters and a residence
for the director were built. The photo by Lucia Moholy shows the south side.
Additional illustration not included in the treatise.

Frank Lloyd Wright (1867–1959)

Ausgeführte Bauten und Entwürfe von Frank Lloyd Wright

BERLIN, 1910

Wasmuth Portfolio

AUSGEFÜHRTE BAUTEN
UND ENTWÜRFE VON
FRANK LLOYD WRIGHT.

The so-called Wasmuth Portfolio is one of the most beautiful and influential publications of modern architecture.

In 1909, during a crisis in his private and professional life, Frank Lloyd Wright came to Europe. Ernst Wasmuth, a publisher in Berlin, had offered to produce an opulent publication of his architectural plans. Wasmuth had learned about the American architect from one of his European admirers, the English architect of the Arts and Crafts Movement Charles Robert Ashbee (1863–1942), as well as from the German literary historian Kuno Francke (1855–1930), who was a professor at Harvard University and founder of the Busch-Reisiger Museum (he wanted to persuade Wright to move to Germany). Upon concluding the contract in Berlin, Wright retired for one year to Fiesole, near Florence where he put together source illustrations in collaboration with his son Lloyd Wright and the draughtsman Taylor Wooley on the basis of drawings he brought with him. Only a few of the drawings had been done by Wright himself; the majority, including several perspectives done from photographs of existing buildings, were done by his colleagues Marion Mahony, Birch Burdette Long and William E. Drummond.

The book consists of two bound portfolios with 78 tables and 28 plans in landscape format measuring 65 cm x 41 cm. They are exquisitely printed in white, grey, brown and golden ink on grey and white paper, the plans being on translucent silk paper. There are various prints on different kinds of paper and in different colours of ink. For distribution to Wright's closest friends, a luxury edition was prepared which was printed on Japanese paper.

The Wasmuth Portfolio contains nearly all of Wright's projects up to that time, whether executed or not: the prairie houses which include the Robie House in Chicago (1909) and the Coonley House in Riverside, Illinois (1908); commercial projects like the buildings for the Larkin Company in Buffalo (1904) and the bank building for the City National Bank in Mason City, Iowa (1909), as well as the Unity Temple in Oak Park, Illinois (1907/08). Wright wrote an introduction for the portfolio that was translated into German. The original English version was printed in Chicago and was distributed with the copies of the portfolio that came to America.

In his introduction, Wright explained his agenda for an organic architecture for a democratic society. He begins with a hymn to traditional Italian architecture and its simple, natural beauty. He criticizes architecture since the Renaissance, however, as corrupt and inorganic. These buildings only reflected the way in which civilization had distanced itself from nature, the curious is confused with the beautiful and the history of style since the Renaissance is not a development but a disease. Wright's key word is "Gothic." In the tradition of the Gothic interpretations by the early English Romantics, he equates "Gothic" with "organic" and "natural." He calls to the art and the architecture of modern times for a return to the "Gothic spirit." In addition, he adds, it was the responsi-

bility of America, more than any other nation, to create architecture in the spirit of democracy. This must be architecture of individuality ("Individuality is a national ideal."). At the same time, it must be architecture of industrial ideals. In America, everyone has the inalienable right to live the way he wants in his own home. Nevertheless, he treats the usual American practice of choosing whatever style one wants with sarcasm and postulates a new style which should be developed from the American spirit. The willingness to find the true American spirit, though, cannot be found in New York, but rather in the West and Mid-West. The correct, organic style of the Gothic spirit is as natural as a flower; it must develop from the needs of the inhabitants, out of natural materials and out of the natural features of the landscape. If all these components exist, the style will develop itself. Naturally, one necessary requirement is a good working relationship between the client and the architect. The architect must have the same familiarity with his building matter as the musician with his instrument. Wright recognizes an especially traditional sensitivity for the natural beauty of materials in Japan; he also sees this in the new architecture of Germany and Austria.

Wright explains his principles for building homes and prairie houses in this way: the house, its furnishings and its surroundings must form an integrated whole. Everything must stem from the same concept. No decoration and no pictures on the walls; the ceilings must be relatively low and the windows in compact rows. Living space, kitchen and bedrooms must be part of an integrated group. The horizontal is the line of domesticity. It is also the line of the prairie in the Mid-West. Unnecessary height is to be avoided. The horizontal form unites the house with the ground. In its entirety, the house must be as though it were cast and not pieced together: only then is it a true work of art.

In conclusion, Wright explains that the drawings he has presented are meant to show nothing more than the composition and the basic shape of the buildings as well as to give an idea for the feeling that is transmitted by the surroundings. He also stresses his artistic indebtedness to the art of the Japanese woodcut.

One year later, in 1911, after Wright had already returned to the US, Wasmuth published a smaller and less expensive volume of photos that he called *Ausgeführte Bauten* (literally "Constructed Buildings" but known as *The Little Wasmuth*). At the request of Wright it was Ashbee who wrote the introduction. It was this edition that caused Wright to have such an enormous influence not only on young architects in Germany like Peter Behrens, Erich Mendelsohn and Walter Gropius, but also on the likes of Le Corbusier and on the architects of the De Stijl Movement in Holland. Wright, however, was to be disappointed with the response to Wasmuth publication in the USA. The copies which Wright had brought with him to America were destroyed when his home, Taliesin, burned down in 1912. Some of the original drawings were also later lost when Wright was in Japan. The Wasmuth publishing house brought out a second edition in 1924 and several reprints have appeared in the United States since the 1960s.   JP

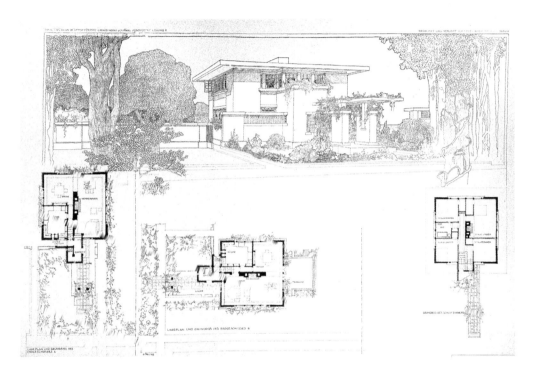

1 | **Concrete house**
This house was publicized by Wright in 1907 in *Ladies' Home Journal* as "A Fireproof House for $5000"; a small version of his praire house, it was condensed into a cube.
Pl. XIVa. Drawing by Marion Mahony

2 | Bradley House (1900)
The Bradley House is one of the earliest praire houses.
The low ceiling, geometric motives in series and the simplicity
of the furniture contradicted the Victorian taste at the time.
Pl. XXII. Indian ink and coloured pencil

3 | Residence for the Curtis Publishing Company
"Typical, cheap house ..." This was the second design
published in 1901 in the magazine *Ladies' Home Journal*:
"A Small House with 'Lots of Room in It'".
Pl. XXIII. Drawing by Birch B. Long

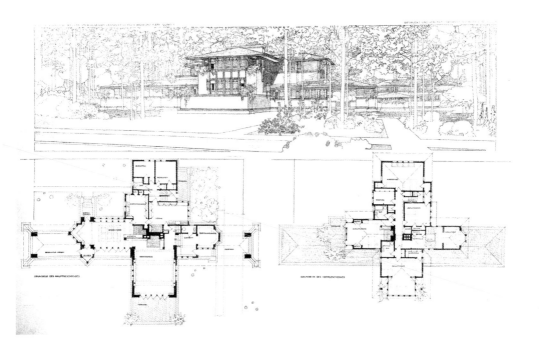

4 | **Willits House (1902/03)**
The series of praire houses begins with the Willits House; typical with its horizontal composition,
the cruciform ground plan radiating from the fireplace, and the interconnecting rooms.
Pl. XXV. Pencil, gouache and Indian ink

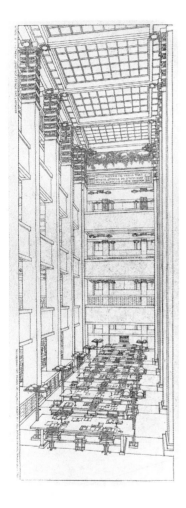

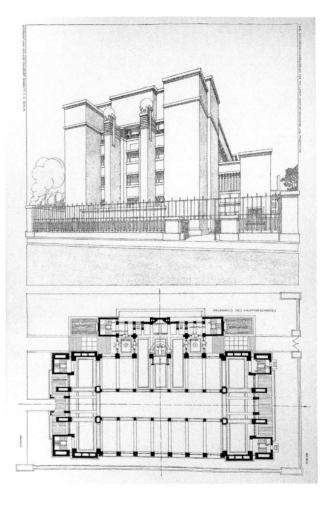

**5 | Administrative building for the Larkin Company
in Buffalo (1902–1926, torn down in 1950)**
The office functions were directed toward the
interior of a high room which was covered by a glass
roof and surrounded by four-storied galleries.
Pl. XXXIII a. Pen and ink drawing

6 | Administrative building for the Larkin Company in Buffalo
Ground plan and elevation of the administrative building of the
Larkin Company. From the outside, the building appears to be
a self-contained monumental cube.
Pl. XXXIII b. Pen and ink drawing

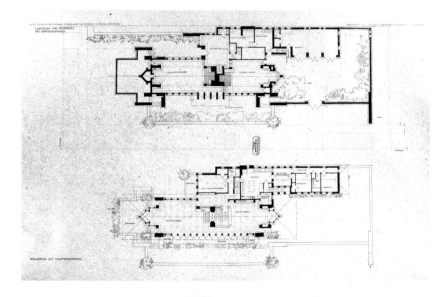

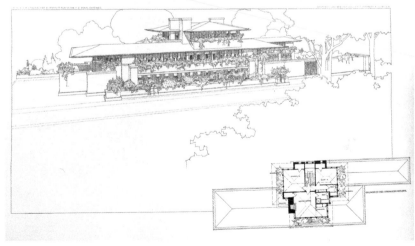

7 | Robie House (1909)
The Robie House is the climax and final example in Wright's series of prairie houses. Because of the narrow building site, the interconnected rooms are in a row.
Pl. XXXVII a. Pen and ink drawing

8 | Robie House
In the Robie House, Wright cultivates the aesthetic of the long drawn out horizontal line as in no other structure. Here is a view and the ground plan of the upper floor.
Pl. XXXVII b. Pen and ink drawing

Paul Schmitthenner (1884–1972)

Das deutsche Wohnhaus

STUTTGART, 1932

The German House

There is hardly another treatise on architecture which has found itself in the middle of more aesthetic and political controversy than *Das deutsche Wohnhaus* by Paul Schmitthenner. The first edition appeared in 1932 and the second in 1940. The controversy is due partly to the content of the book and partly to the personality of the author and the role that he played on the eve of the Third Reich.

Schmitthenner was born in 1884 in the Alsatian town of Lauterburg. In 1909, after studying architecture in Karlsruhe and Munich, he began working for Richard Riemerschmid. In 1918, Schmitthenner was offered a teaching position at the Technical University in Stuttgart. In the 1920s, this became known under the "brand name" of "Stuttgart School" and developed into one of the leading institutes of education for architects. Alongside Paul Bonatz (1877–1956), Schmitthenner became head of the school, which was based on the traditions and local patriotism of Theodor Fischer (1862–1938).

As the Werkbund exhibition "Die Wohnung" ("The Dwelling") was being prepared in Stuttgart in 1927, the local architects and representatives of Ludwig Mies van der Rohe's (1886–1969) Neues Bauen were ignored. This led to a polarization of the architectural camps. Schmitthenner always took the conservative view although he was, in fact, a rationalist and favoured standardization (he advocated a standard type for the middle-class house). In the 1920s, Schmitthenner built tastefully designed good-quality houses for Stutt-

gart's wealthy. It was as a result of these houses that the familiar expression "Schmitthenner house" was coined. At the beginning of the 1930s, he revealed himself not only as a traditionalist in matters of architecture, agitating against Neues Bauen (for example in a dispute about roofs), but he also appeared as a political agitator at events of the "Kampfbund für Deutsche Kultur" ("Fighters for Germanic Culture") which had a close relationship to the Nazi party. In 1932, he signed the appeal for a "Deutsche Geisteswelt für den Nationalsozialismus" ("Germanic intellectual world for National Socialism"). However, Schmitthenner's hopes of using National Socialism for his own purposes were not to be realized. His traditional/romantic sense of architecture and his middle-class postures were out of place. The technocratic planning elite which surrounded Albert Speer had nothing in common with an individualist and advocate of quality craftsmanship.

Schmitthenner's book was to be the first in a series (the others never materialized) entitled "Baugestaltung " ("Building Design "). He used this word instead of "Baukonstruktion" ("Building Construction") to demonstrate that good construction alone was insufficient to meet his requirements regarding design. According to him, and in the tradition of the Werkbund, the architect must "have a thorough knowledge of craftsmanship" and especially of building materials. But his most important duty is to "create order." The book was aimed primarily at his students and therefore it has a personal and instructive character. The photographs,

designs and pictures document examples of Schmitthenner's own buildings from the 1920s in Stuttgart, Berlin, Baden and Alsace. This exposition of his work is enhanced by examples of what Schmitthenner considered to be a typical German house: "Whether a German house stands in Schleswig-Holstein, Westphalia, Swabia, Alsace, Silesia or the Ostmark [i. e. annexed Austria], it always wears a German face. That face is not determined by building materials but rather by something spiritual which creates a relationship of kind."

Using historical examples, Schmitthenner develops an ideal which he then approaches analytically. The ground plan must be clear, simple and readable without explanations. The body of the building must be a closed cube structured with sparingly inserted windows with small panes. Much space was devoted to the roof; Schmitthenner made this the acid test for principled construction. He stressed that the roof was not an aesthetic matter but rather a practical one. He always insisted on the simplest shape for a roof which for him, in Germany, was the pitched roof. The ideal house was unpretentious yet self-assured. Although these ideas originated with the "Homeland Protection Movement" at the turn of the century, they contain modern elements: "The landscape was there first and its rights are older."

Actually Schmitthenner's true interest was not the exterior of a house but rather the arrangement and design of the interior. A house, whether big or small, should be spacious or at least seem so. "Every house, even the very smallest, must have a large living room, something like a 'hall'." Although Schmitthenner's ground plans indicate the exact function of each room, he did attempt to throw Neues Bauen and the Werkbund Exposition of 1927 off balance in this respect: "It is preferable to defer the problem of dining-car kitchens to bloodless problematicians and as for the calculation of how many kilometres a normal cook walks in a decade – well, there are enough ossified statisticians around to work that out." He never intended to design houses for people who desired a totally rationalized household. This is made clear time and again, for example when he describes the complicated access to a house on a hill in Stuttgart: "Nobody will overlook the door to the house. But the handyman, the door-to-door salesman, the baker and the butcher will never reach it because they will have already seen to their business at the window of the pantry or the kitchen where they have long since been sighted by the watchful cook." Like his clients, Schmitthenner represented a rather antiquated upper-middle-class life style. His own house appears at the end of the book. It is the incarnation of his romantic ideals of the past. He had his fellow-Alsatian René Schickele sing the praises of this "Ark above Stuttgart."

The first edition of *Das deutsche Wohnhaus* received a lot of attention and criticism – more for political than architectural reasons. It was, within limits, the first well-founded traditionalist set of opinions that was expressed after the "shock" of the Weissenhof housing estate. However, it was not particularly innovative. The introduction took to task Neues Bauen with its "bloodless mechanical purity," which for Schmitthenner was the epitome of "gross overestimation of technology and economics." In particular he lashed out at "machines for living"; not only as aesthetic and functional problems, but also as the expression of a spiritual and moral crisis. In a pictorial comparison he juxtaposed Hans Scharoun's expressive villa on the Weissenhof with an older iconic prototype and model: Johann Wolfgang von Goethe's garden house in the park on the River Ilm in Weimar, which goes back to 1776. The idealization of this structure was not Schmitthenner's idea. It originated with the reform movement around 1900. Paul Mebes had long before included it in his 1908 work *Um 1800 (Around 1800)* and it had served as Heinrich Tessenow's inspiration for his famous detached house in Hellerau.

In 1934, the introduction to *Das deutsche Wohnhaus* served as the basis for Schmitthenner's publication *Baukunst im neuen Reich (Architecture in the New Reich)*. This was replaced for the second edition in 1940 by a relatively independent text entitled *Vom Unscheinbaren in der Baukunst (On the Unassuming in Architecture)*. In this work he praised the unassuming, the small and modest, and he used the cathedral in Strasbourg as an example. It arises "from the harmony of the unassuming world at its feet, which is what gives its grandeur and charisma." There were literary models for praising the unassuming from the middle of the 19th century: Adalbert Stifter's novella *Bunte Steine (Colourful Stones)* and his Biedermeier novel *Nachsommer (Indian Summer)* in which the "rose house" appears. This may well have been the basis for Schmitthenner's designs. In 1940, this was understood as a subtle criticism of the architectural spirit of the times; especially since Schmitthenner had also commented that it was still the case that "little that is good and plenty and is inadequate" is being built. He also stressed that "the imposing structures of our day" are only impressive against an unassuming background. His quiet reproach did not fall on deaf ears. Friedrich Tamms, a colleague of Albert Speer, published a rebuttal with a closing chapter entitled "Das harte Gesetz in der Kunst" ("The Severe Law of Art").

The preface of the unchanged third edition of 1950 drew a bitter conclusion. Schmitthenner conceded that in the light of the current housing crisis, which was "of terrible proportions", the dimensions of his houses were not "in tune with the times". However, he defended the constants in his work: the importance of building materials as well as their careful adaptation and usage.

GL

Fig. p. 501
1 | **Goethe's garden house in the park on the Ilm River, in Weimar**
Goethe's garden house was built in the 18th century and
was the ideal house for Schmitthenner.
4ᵗʰ ed. from 1984, p. 10

2 | **Paul Schultze-Naumburg,** *Burg Plaue,* **ca. 1900.**
The painter, architect and author, Paul Schultze-Naumburg was
a co-founder of the Werkbund, a representative of the Heimat-
schutzbewegung, and a model for Schmitthenner.
Oil on canvas, 43 x 60 cm. Private collection, Hanover.
Additional illustration not included in the book.

3 | **Strasbourg Cathedral**
"Strasbourg cathedral …
rises from the rhythm and
harmony of the inconspic-
uous world at its feet which
make it radiate in size"
(Schmitthenner 1941)
4th ed. from 1984, p. 11

4 | **The garden city of Staaken**
Schmitthenner's garden city, Staaken, is reminiscent of northern German and Dutch towns.
It was built in Spandau near Berlin from 1914–1917 for employees of the armaments industry.
Additional illustration not included in the book.

5 | **Villa for the family of the manufacturer Roser (1925/26)**
Schmitthenner imagined this villa in Stuttgart as a "large house in an open and elevated location"; it is a typical patrician "Schmmitthenner house." View from the southeast.
4th ed. from 1984, p. 68

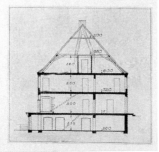

6 | **Villa for the family of the manufacturer Roser, ground plan**
The ground plan has a closed form, typical of Schmitthenner.
4th ed. from 1984, p. 71. Drawing

7 | **Schmitthenner House, stairs (c. 1930)**
A look at the stairs of Schmitthenner's own house in Stuttgart
(destroyed 1944) make it possible to recognize his traditionalist
point of view about living space and family life.
4ᵗʰ ed. from 1984, p. 185

8 | **Kochenhof housing estate near Stuttgart**
This housing estate was built in 1933 as an attempt at mass residential
building; when the Nazis came to power, Schmitthenner cultivated
a kind of Biedermeier idyll.
Additional illustration not included in the book.

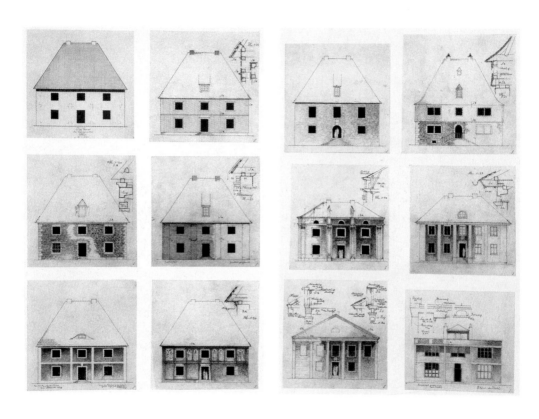

9–10 | **Façade design**
In *Variationen über ein Thema: Gebaute Form*, written from 1943–1949
and published posthumously, Schmitthenner played with the idea of
façade variations with different materials.
Additional illustration not included in the book. Drawing

11 | Königin-Olga-Bau on Schlossplatz in Stuttgart (1950–1954)
The Olgabau on Schlossplatz in Stuttgart is a curious, hybrid and
anachronistic late work of Schmitthenner.
Additional illustration not included in the book.

Council of Ministers of the GDR

Grundsätze des Städtebaus

BERLIN, 1950

Council of Ministers of the GDR: The Principles of Town Planning

The *Grundsätze des Städtebaus*, published in 1950, not only formed the legal basis for the socialist town-planning policies of the GDR in the first half of the 1950s, but they were also the result of a tense and fiercely fought argument on what form an adequate socialist architecture should take. They came about after an intense argument between advocates of the continued development of Modernism, on the one side, and those of an orientation toward traditional prototypes, on the other. This architecture was to be "democratic in content" and "national in form" and its results are still considered today to be not only controversial but also among the most ambitious building projects of the 1950s. At the same time, the conditions for a transformation in architecture and town planning in the GDR exemplify the close connection between politics and town planning in the former communist bloc.

After the principles were approved by the Council of Ministers on 27 July 1950, they were published on 16 September 1950 in the official gazette of the German Democratic Republic. The preamble already contains a definition of the task of the architecture, which was to be not only an expression of the new order of communist society, but also make clear the global claim of the state in these matters. In paragraph 6, the manifesto clearly stresses the necessity of a centre which would not only be the administrative and cultural, but also the political hub. The structure of the city would be strongly defined by axial roads, squares and dominating ar-

chitectural symbols; its architectural expression, according to paragraph 14, should be "democratic in content and national in form." It should implement "the experiences of the people as embodied in the progressive traditions of their past." There are, however, no specific definitions of "democratic content," "national form" or "progressive traditions" in this text. The reference to the necessary adaptation of historical models as well as the rejection in paragraph 12 of a cityscape permeated with green are an obvious rejection of major aspects of the *Charter of Athens*. The communist city was to be a clearly recognizable alternative to the western formalist variant of international Modernism. The publication of the 16 principles went hand-in-hand with the new GDR Reconstruction Law, which was promulgated on 14 September 1950. The cities of Berlin, Dresden, Leipzig, Magdeburg, Chemnitz, Dessau, Rostock, Wismar and Nordhausen were listed as having priority, and were to be rebuilt in an exemplary fashion. At the same time, a new Land Law was introduced. In effect, this provided for expropriation in certain areas, thereby creating the basis for the realization of comprehensive plans.

The 16 principles were developed on the occasion of the famous "trip to Moscow" in 1950. This was a politically motivated study tour which took place from 12 April to 25 May, led by the Minister of Reconstruction, Lothar Bolz. In addition to the Director of the Institute for Urban Planning in the Ministry of Construction, Kurt Liebknecht, other partici-

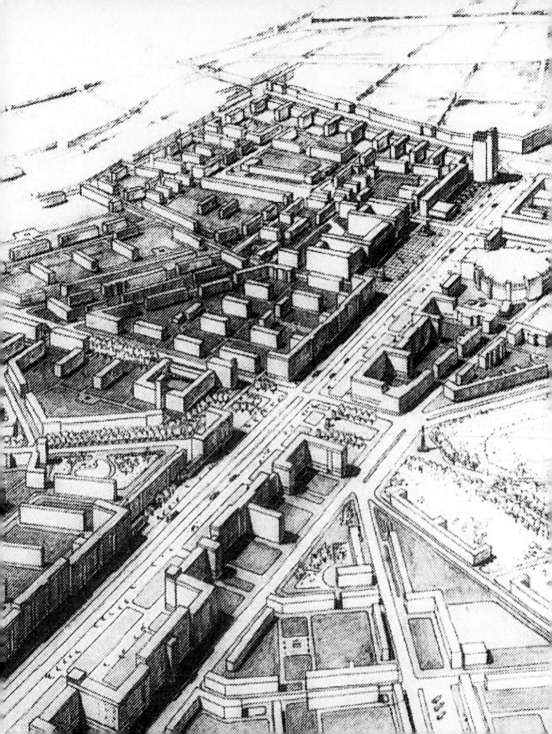

pants were Walter Pisternik of the Ministry of Reconstruction, the head of the Berlin Building Authority, Edmund Collein, the head of the City Planning Office in Dresden, Kurt Leucht, as well as Waldemar Adler who represented the Ministry of Industry. The principles were preceded by a long critique by prominent GDR politicians regarding the decidedly Modernist reconstruction plans for the capital that had been developed since 1946 as part of the so-called collective plan under the leadership of Hans Scharoun. The repeated accusation of "cosmopolitanism" was clearly an issue in the context of the basic cultural and political debates in the nascent GDR. Western "formalism" – another catchword in this long debate – was to be countered by "socialist realism." Instead of universal formal modernity, the new cities should convey a historically familiar, compact, hierarchically organized, regionally based and monumental image. It is clear that these discussions in the GDR reflected the desire to take advantage of and further develop already existing prototypes in the Soviet Union, where such debates had been going on since the 1930s.

Following Soviet stipulations, the delegates sketched the basic agenda for town planning in the GDR during the trip. At the same time, the General Secretary of the Socialist Unity Party, Walter Ulbricht, also involved himself. On the occasion of the 3rd Party Congress in July 1950, Ulbricht recommended "principles of a realistic architecture based on Soviet architecture" in order to set buildings off from "American boxes." Nevertheless, the first plans for the showpiece of the GDR reconstruction, the Stalinallee in Berlin, still showed many Modernistic features in 1951. Even Hermann Henselmann, who would later become the leading planner for the Stalinallee, distinguished himself at first with plans in the Modernist tradition. However, with his project for a high-rise apartment block on the Weberwiese in Berlin in 1951/52, Henselmann completed a paradigm shift which was to have major consequences, for he now combined elements of Schinkel's Classicism with the modern individual skyscraper. A prototype was now achieved which had regional roots, historical grandeur, a high degree of monumentality, and at the same time high-grade fittings and facilities. Kurt Liebknecht praised the project as an expression of "progress in national architecture." In this way, it became possible for Henselmann to become one of the most important planners for the construction of the boulevard. Apart from the dominant high-rises that loom over the squares at the entrances, the boulevard is lined with slender and functional rows of buildings, to which neo-Classical decorative elements have

been added, along with historical references, such as an adaptation of the pair of domes from the Gendarmenmarkt which are deployed at Frankfurter Tor to provide the required regional anchorage.

One of the reasons why only some of the extensive plans for new construction were completed was no doubt another radical transformation in the paradigm of city planning and architecture after 1954. Following Stalin's death in 1953, Khrushchev introduced a change in the nature of construction in the Soviet Union, largely as a result of economic considerations. After a short time-lag, this policy also reached most of the other communist countries. On the occasion of the Union Building Conference in Moscow in 1954, Khrushchev sharply criticized architectural practices up to that time, saying that their decorative expense was not economically justifiable. Consequently, emphasis was now placed on a modern construction industry as well as on the development of new construction types. The standardization of building inevitably led to architectural tendencies which were far more functionalist, although this style had been unequivocally condemned as formalistic just a few years earlier. This paved the way in the communist countries for the urban townscapes which we see to this day. In the GDR, this new paradigm shift handed down by Moscow led, at the latest by the end of the 1950s, to the severing of links with "architecture in the national tradition". Projects in progress like the second phase of the construction of Stalinallee where abandoned or demonstratively corrected. When the name was changed to Karl-Marx-Allee, the distancing from Stalinist policies became coupled with an increasing rejection of their architectural manifestations. It was not until the problems involved in a purely rational and economic view of town planning, namely the monotonous design of its mono-functional neighbourhoods, came under scrutiny in East and West alike, that 1950s GDR architecture started to be re-appraised. The previous verdict on Stalinist architecture as a "wedding-cake style" was countered by post-modern arguments relating to its semantic quality, the functional mix, the existence of a proper centre, and the quality of craftsmanship. Today, this legacy is not judged only as a historical example of the essential fusion of architecture and politics, but also in the context of the fundamental debate on the relationship between tradition and innovation in 20th-century architecture.

Grundsätze des Städtebaus appeared without illustrations. The following selection of pictures serves to visualize urban planning in the GDR.   PS

1 | **Documentary photo**
Walter Ulbricht together with the chief architect of Moscow, Alexander Vlassov, as well as Edmund Collein (2nd from left) and Kurt Liebknecht (right) in front of the model of the high-rise on the Weberwiese, Berlin, December, 1951.

BERLIN STALIN-ALLEE

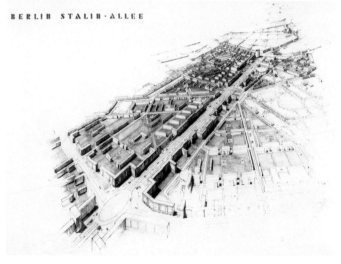

2 | Hanns Hopp, model of the "central high-rise"
in the centre of Berlin (1951)
Model

3 | Egon Hartmann, Plan for the construction
of Stalinallee in Berlin (1951)
Drawing

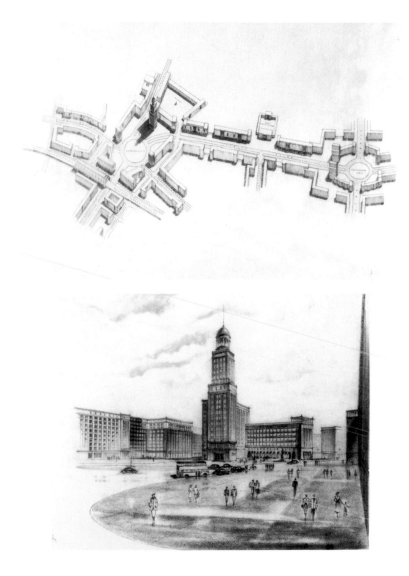

4 | Hermann Henselmann, Plan for the second phase of construction of
Stalinallee between Strausbergerplatz and Alexanderplatz in Berlin (1953)
Drawing

5 | Hermann Henselmann, Plan for the construction
of Alexanderplatz (1953)
Drawing

Archigram (founded 1960)
Archigram

LONDON, SINCE 1961

Hi-tech and Pop culture were the major influences on the international debates in architectural theory in the 1960s. Groups of architects took the stage with sensational manifestos, spectacular utopian urban projects and subversive/ironic observations of late capitalist society. Mobility, cosmopolitanism, and almost limitless optimism in respect of the potential for developing more and better technology symbolize the spirit of an age captivated by space travel as well as by the Beatles' Yellow Submarine. The imaginative architectural comics of the English Archigram group presented serious models for cities as well as others that were amusing, carefree and utopian. These were conceived for a global and highly technological civilization. The aesthetics of Cape Canaveral joined up with happenings and popular everyday culture.

Archigram was formed in 1960 as an association of young and highly experimental British architects who, until 1974, regularly co-operated with each other as a team of independent artistic personalities. Warren Chalk, Peter Cook, Dennis Crompton, David Greene, Ron Herron and Michael Webb created in "Archigram" a group name intended to suggest exaggeratedly succinct messages in matters architectural. Their most important medium was a kind of underground magazine which was also called "Archigram" and, beginning in 1961, appeared at irregular intervals. It contained the most important themes and projects of the individual members of the group as well as other architects with whom they were friends. In the beginning, the magazine circulated only in insider circles but it soon became an institution. It obtained broad international recognition in 1963, when the group held its first joint exhibition, "Living City," at the London Institute of Contemporary Art. Accompanied by numerous articles by the architectural critic and theorist Reyner Banham, Archigram took the stage as the protagonist in a new urban philosophy which aimed to synthesize contemporary Pop Art with the aesthetics of science fiction. With such suggestive utopias as the nomadic "Walking City" by Ron Herron (1964);

"Plug in City" by Peter Cook, Warren Chalk and Dennis Crompton (1964–1966), which could be newly installed at any time; and the "Inflatable Suit House" by David Greene (1968), they became a fixture in the annals of the architectural history of the 1960s. Their projects continued late modern tendencies while including aspects from everyday life and Pop culture. Collage, comic strips and poetic essays were mixed with manifesto-like contributions, clarifying the references of the utopias involved. For example, in *Archigram 4* Warren Chalk satirizes the genre of sci-fi comic strips. He integrates fundamental manifesto sequences into the normal sequence and these lead the reader to the basic position of the authors: "Only those imbued with respect and enthusiasm for today's wish-dreams can adequately implement them in the built environment. The recurrent theme in Space Comic universe is the mobile computer "brain" and flexing tentacles." Their visions of free floating, flexible, adaptable and increasingly ephemeral spatial structure based on advanced technological infrastructures blend the late-1920s "Dymaxion" living machine of Buckminster Fuller or the 1960s expansive lightweight roofs of Frei Otto with the world of images from James Bond films, contemporary flower power covers and multi-media performances. One of the few projects that they were able to realize was the Archigram Capsule conceived for Expo '70 in Osaka. It was hung from Kenzo Tange's roof in the central Theme Pavilion for the duration of the exhibition. With this project in particular, one can sense the closeness of Archigram to the methods of the Japanese Metabolists. It is also similar to contemporary projects by Yona Friedman from France and Hans Hollein from Austria. Their decidedly subversive publication with its specific admixture of popular "trivial" genres and architectural theory set a standard for the contemporary reader, which continued to have an influence even on the literary genre-crossover publications by Rem Koolhaas and his Office for Metropolitan Architecture in the mid-1990s.

PS

Fig. p. 517
1 | **Warren Chalk, "Spaceprobe" Cartoon**
In: Archigram 4, *1964*

2 | **Ron Herron, Walking City**
The city comes to New York …
In: Archigram 4, *1964*

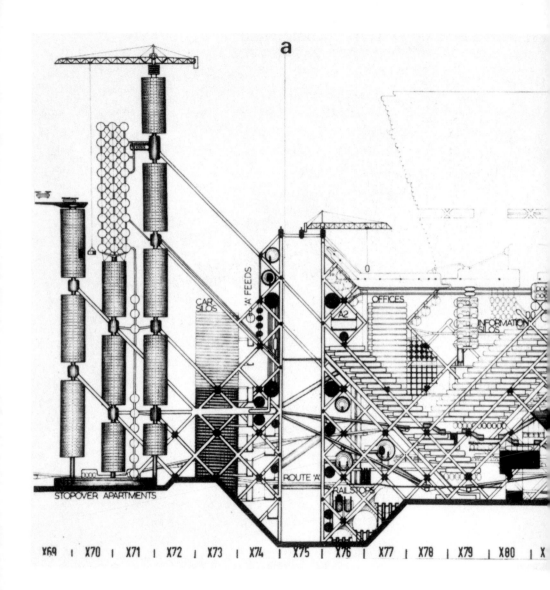

3 | **Peter Cook, Plug-In-City**
In: Archigram 4, *1964*

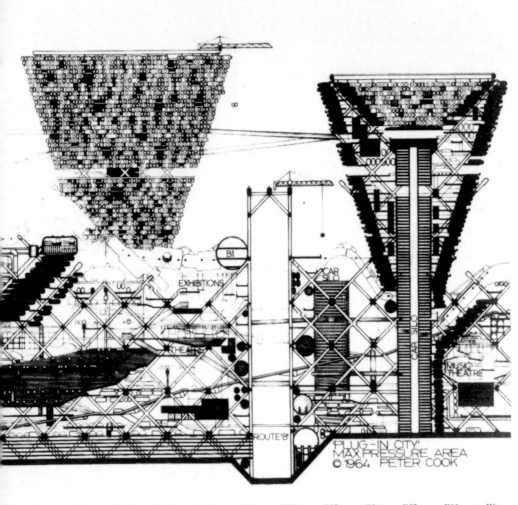

'PLUG-IN CITY'
MAX PRESSURE AREA
© 1964 PETER COOK

Kisho Kurokawa (b. 1934)
Metabolism in Architecture

LONDON, 1977

The architecturally philosophical concept of Metabolism dates back to 1960, when on the occasion of the Tokyo World Design Conference a group of Japanese architects grabbed the eye with manifesto-like texts and sensational projects. The leading figures at the start of the Metabolic movement were Kenzo Tange and Kisho Kurokawa as well as Kiyonori Kikutake and architecture critic Noboru Kawazoe. Their architectural approach linked the late modern, technologized New Brutalism with the concept of architecture as analogous to biology. Like the DNA double helix, their often utopian urban planning projects explain the connection between primary mega-structures and periodically replaceable individual components. Especially the idea of a capsule as an adaptable and minimal microstructure characterized many metabolic projects. In this way, Kikutake's Marine City (1960), Kurokawa's Helix Structure (1961) and Kenzo Tange's Tokyo Bay Plan (1960) with its infinitely enlargeable and exchangeable cell structure, correspond to the picture of a synthesis of fictional outer-space architecture and biological organisms. Mounted in Tokyo from 1970–1972, Kurokawa's Nakagin Capsule Tower is one of the few Metabolic projects to actually be realized. Others include the ephemeral constructions at Expo '70 in Osaka such as Tange's mega-structure in the Theme Pavilion and Kurokawa's Takara Beautilion Pavilion.

These projects were accompanied by numerous publications, Kisho Kurokawa's texts in particular focusing on the philosophy of Metabolism. On the occasion of the Design Conference in Tokyo in 1960, Kurokawa, together with Kikutake, Fumihiko Maki, Masato Otaka, and Kizoshi Awazu published a manuscript entitled *Metabolism 1960 – A Proposal for a New Urbanism*, which expressed the basic outlook of the group members: "We regard human society as a living process ... We do not believe that Metabolism only indicates acceptance of natural, historical processes; rather we are trying to encourage the active metabolic development of our society through our proposals."

In his book *Metabolism in Architecture*, which appeared in 1977, Kurokawa explains *ex post* the concept of a specifically Japanese as well as internationally relevant architectural theory. Assuming an ever increasing technologization of global civilization, the point is to produce "a system whereby man would maintain control over technology." If new technologies were mixed with a system of regeneration and metabolism analogous to that of nature, the result would be not only logical solutions for problems of civilization as well as for the urban environment, but also models for the control of an automated technology and a culture of accelerated transformation. This globally applicable approach is equally brought to bear on a typical Japanese cultural tradition which understands architecture more as a renewable variation of a prototype than as a lasting monument. Kurokawa refers to the tradition of Shinto shrines with their figures, which are fundamental prototypes and have been handed

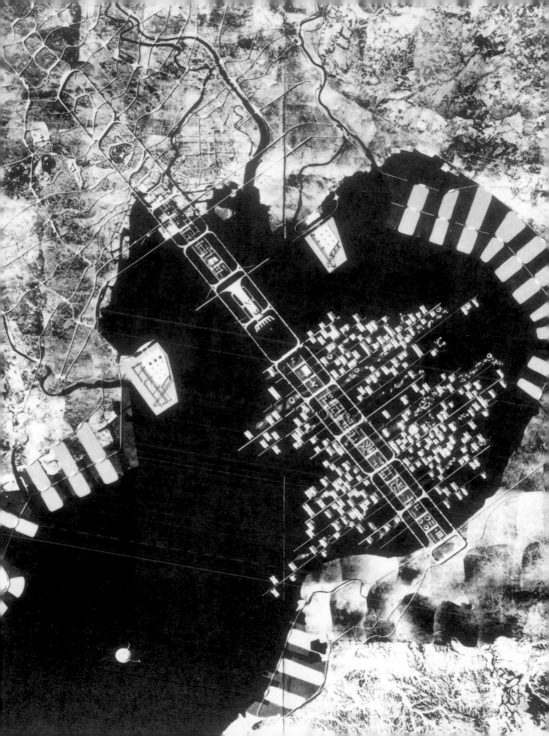

down for centuries, but whose "originality" and authenticity is totally dependent on their material existence. In the light of a background of dramatically swift disintegration of inherited organic city structures, a flexible and adaptive capability in structural systems seems to be an adequate way to enact this form of tradition, which is based on cultural philosophy. With this in mind, Kurokawa justifies the necessity for fundamentally new planning strategies in *Metabolism in Architecture:* "Growth and transformation are taking place at an ever faster pace in modern cities. From the industrial revolution until the middle of the 20th century, the growth of a city meant the expansion of its boundaries until it became a giant; but cities are now about to undergo a metamorphosis entirely different from this pattern. Regardless of whether the city limits its expansion or not, the mobility of people, goods and information is increasing at a drastic pace."

The Japanese Metabolists developed a demanding and coherent theory with many international parallels. In addition to the statements found in Archigram, which alternate between theory and Pop, reference can also be made to the utopian mega-structures of Yona Friedman in France, to the Habitat Project in Montreal, which brought the Israeli Moshe Safdie to fame, and to the projects of Austria's Hans Hollein.

Logically, corresponding contributions to the exhibition were also integrated into the Theme Pavilion at Expo '70. However, on the occasion of the World Fair, many protagonists of Metabolism distanced themselves from the actual trends of their own architectural movement. Metabolic structures with the character of hi-tech toys were gradually no longer primarily the prototypes of new planning approaches. Instead they functioned more and more as fashionable images of a technological society. Their elaborate architectural images had now taken on a life of their own without proving their actual capabilities. Yet despite the crisis in this specifically late-modern architecture in the early 1970s, it retained its fascination. It is not only in light of the sentimental revival of the spirit of the swinging sixties that so many of the Metabolists' ideas and analyses now seem extraordinarily up-to-date. Hi-tech, the ecologically relevant conception of intelligent architecture, from the perpetual relevance of Renzo Piano and Richard Rogers' megastructure, the Centre Pompidou in Paris, to Rem Koolhaas' Masterplan for Euralille and not least the architectural synthesis of "high" and "low," and of theory and Pop culture, are the reasons for Metabolism's enduring importance.

PS

Fig. p. 523
1 | **Kenzo Tange, Tokyo Bay Plan (1960)**
Additional illustration not contained in the book.

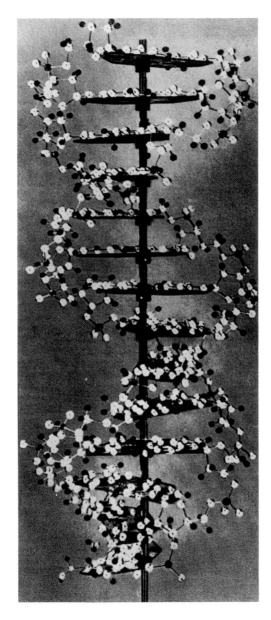

2 | **Double helix of a DNA molecule**
*Additional illustration not contained
in the book.*

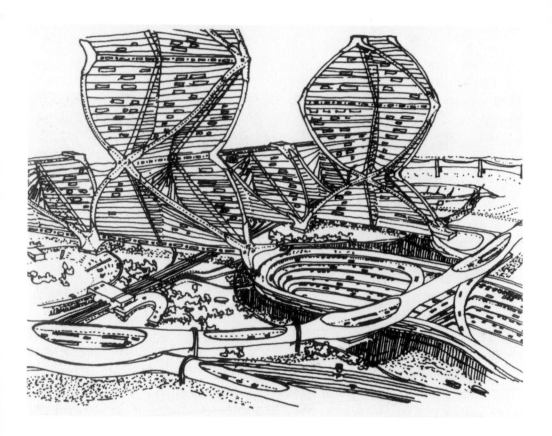

3 | Helix Structure (1961)
P. 56

4 | Kiyonori Kikutake, Marine City (1960)
P. 42. Model

5 | Aruta Isozaki, City in the Air (1960–1963)
Model. Additional illustration not contained in the book.

Aldo Rossi (1931–1997)
L'Architettura della Città

PADUA, 1966

The Architecture of the City, 1984

Essentially his education was "literary," or so wrote the Milan-based architect Aldo Rossi, born in 1931. When he wrote his key architectural œuvre *L'Architettura della Città* in the mid-1960s, architecture was, in his opinion, in "such a disastrous state" that he felt the need to systematically sift through the historical evidence and work it up for scholarly use and to distance himself from the undemanding architecture, bereft of any theoretical underpinnings, being put out by naïve functionalism. He therefore opted to research and write more than to plan and build.

Rossi created a great sensation with his first large structure, which was a subtle violation of functionalist dogmas. The arcaded house, Gallaratese 2 (1969–1973), in a suburb of Milan, is a long, minimalist "bar on stilts." It is austere, emotive, and focuses on the typical. The search for a specific type, simple forms, the inclination towards monumentality and the establishment of historical references characterize his works during the following years: school, cemetery, shopping centre or floating theatre for the Biennale in Venice (1979/80). In the 1980s, Rossi became the most successful Italian architect internationally. He worked in Paris, Berlin (where he designed houses for the International Building Exhibition), Orlando in Florida (an office complex for Walt Disney) and Japan. Rossi's buildings became constantly more colourful, lively and less abstract in their historical roots. Occasionally, this led to the misunderstanding that he was one of the most important representa-

tives of Post-modern architecture. However, Rossi remained faithful to the rationalism he had formulated and his work was a far cry from any ironical games with historical citation. The search for a fundamental prototype, his scholarly and earnest interest in the history of the site and the task in question, as well as the synthesizing of a variety of aspects into one architectural form, remained his goals right up to his final project. Aldo Rossi died in 1997.

Rossi had a broad education and he published frequently. The first edition of his most important book, *L'Architettura della Città*, appeared in Padua in 1966, the same year as Robert Venturi's *Complexity and Contradiction in Architecture*. These two books are the most important and most influential architectural treatises of the 1960s. Their approaches, motivations and objectives are similar. We need only mention in passing that Venturi's treatise is more brilliant, easier to read and contains a more convincing combination of text and pictures. Both men wanted to eliminate the vulgar and commercial form of functionalism (this should not be equated with modern architecture in general) common in the 1960s by returning to wide-ranging historical arguments.

In his book, Rossi analyzes the city, as he says in the introduction, as architecture; however, he understood the city not as a collection of buildings, but rather as the result of a long-term, open-ended process of becoming and passing away. This seemingly simple premise was a radical break

with many conceptions of town planning in the 20th century: for example, Le Corbusier (1887/1965) and Ludwig Hilberseimer (1885–1967) assumed that the ideal city could be planned.

Rossi's treatise can be read in two ways, but both lead to the same result. On the one hand, it is a fair but unmistakable attack on the belief common at the time that appropriate architecture and urban form would automatically develop when a plan was defined. Rossi called this a criticism of the naïve functionalism (including the organic utopia of someone like Hugo Haering) which deprived form and type of the complexity they had achieved over time without filling the ensuing gaps. This central hypothesis was embedded in Rossi's rigorous scholarly argumentation. The second way of reading *L'Architettura della Città* is, therefore, to see it as an often a dry and aloof endeavour, which rests on a critical discussion of secondary literature. Rossi reviewed various approaches to researching the history, the development, the design, and the social and architectural aspects of the town or city. His work spans various methodologies and disciplines, considers Maurice Halbwachs' theory of collective memory as well as Camillo Sitte's theory on town planning, Jean Tricart's research on social structure, Hans Bernoulli's critique of the private ownership of land, Pierre Lavedan's history of the development of Paris, Fritz Schumacher's analyses from the point of view of a practising town planner, and many more besides. Rossi's scholarly accomplishment was that he was able to bring together and examine many different "urban objects" – from the Classical cities of Athens and Rome, to late medieval Vienna, blocks of flats in Berlin and his own home city of Milan – and make a critical evaluation of them. Nowadays, this may seem self-evident, but Rossi was a pioneer of interdisciplinary urban research.

On the basis of his literary analyses, it is possible to imagine what Rossi's own architectural ideas were like. He assumed that the make-up of all urban structures was of a manifold nature, could not be explained by citing single causes nor easily solved. The complex system "city" requires complex answers and interventions. Rossi used the category of permanence, as it relates to individual monuments and streets, to describe function and alterability through the centuries, and is exemplified by the Palazzo della Ragione in Padua. This complex of 13th and 14th-century buildings consists of a town hall, a court building and a market hall. It is proof that different uses can adapt to an architectural shell, but not the other way around. The Palazzo della Ragione is a "monument" but its exterior does not betray its function. Monuments of this type are indispensable as the culmination of every city. Their striking nature, the way they determine the look of a city and their sense of identity do not result, at least not primarily, from their function but rather from

their form. By advocating traditional monuments in this way, which he reinforces with a picture of Cologne Cathedral standing in the middle of the bombed-out old town in 1945, the tradition-conscious European Rossi differentiates himself from the American, Robert Venturi, who without prejudice devotes his attention to everyday symbols and forms. The monuments which Venturi called for are of another type and are found, for example, on the Strip in Las Vegas.

Rossi wanted to return to buildings what was stolen from them by functionalism – meaningful form, weighty expression, a claim to being art and the power to create fictions. However, a city is made up of much more than just individual buildings and structures. The history of a city was, for Rossi, also the history of its architecture; but this simile does not work in reverse.

A central instrument in Rossi's scholarly analyses and in his planning was the search for an architectural "type," for the non-reducible fundamental form. In this respect, he explicitly turned against functionalist points of view that wanted to develop a "type" based on function. Rossi's "type" has, rather, absorbed the traces of life and traditions of generations: what has developed through centuries is both durable and flexible. The "type" is self-evident and it is exactly this which interested Rossi; just as it interested him to know why one eats soup with a spoon. Aldo Rossi was not a passionate and dogmatic opponent of Modernist architecture like many of his Post-modern contemporaries; but he did fight against the idealist notion that form follows from function; he fought against the well-meaning moralizing of architecture; he combated the idea of a quasi paradisac final state. Cities are always dynamic; there are always conflicts between individuals and collective interests in both the private and public spheres.

"The town of Split which developed inside the (late Classical) Palace of Diocletian and therefore had to find new uses and new meanings for unalterable forms, has, because of this very aspect of architecture and its relationship to the city, achieved emblematic importance. The outward concentration of its form is in direct proportion to its great ability to adapt to a variety of functions." Rossi wrote these words as an epilogue to the first German edition of his book in 1973. With his discovery of the historical city and its durable values and its potential for development, Rossi decisively stimulated the debate on town planning and heritage conservation. With his rigorous, disciplined, narrative and emotive structures, he also made his mark.

More so than in the case of other literary architects, Aldo Rossi used his own projects and buildings as the pictorial commentary to his treatise. In keeping with this, the illustrations here will chiefly be of his work.

GL

Fig. p. 529

1 | **Il Palazzo Hotel in Fukuoka**
The Il Palazzo Hotel (1987–1998) combines western and oriental elements and tries to transform the chaos of urban development into a monument.

2 | **Arcaded residential block, Gallaratese 2 in Milan (1969–1973)**
This was Rossi's first big commission. The formal influence of the classical modern cannot be overseen; however, Rossi went even further.

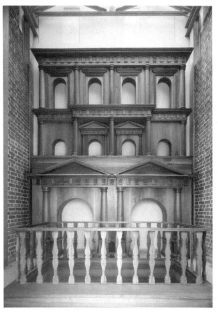

3 | **Expansion of the San Cataldo Cemetery in Modena (1971–1984)**
Rossi tried to bring the monumental forms of the Cemetery
into a relationship with the industrial monuments of the city
(in the background).
Drawing

4 | **Funerary chapel**
Interior of the funerary chapel for the furniture manufacturing family
Molteni in Giussano (1988). The wooden backdrop – in Palladian style –
contrasts with the shell, which is reminiscent of industrial construction.
Model

5 | The Middle School of Broni, Province of Pavia
Aldo Rossi built the school with Gianni Braghieri from 1979–1982.
It is a self-contained ensemble which is designed like a small city.

6 | Residential block in Berlin, southern Friedrichstadt
The block was built from 1981–1988 within the framework of the International Building Exposition (IBA) in Berlin. The characteristic motif of the monumental corner pillar appears here for the first time.

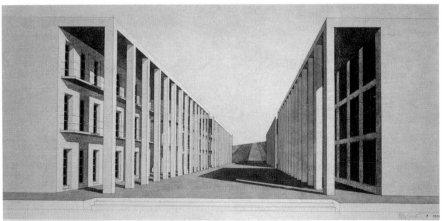

7 | **Model for the Historical Museum in Berlin**
In 1988, Rossi won the competition for the German Historical Museum
in Berlin. The unexpected developments in German history made this
project obsolete.
Model

8 | **Giorgio Grassi, design for student village in Chieti (1979)**
Because of its severity and reduced design, it is easy to recognize
Heinrich Tessenow as the model for this plan.
Drawing

9 | Design for a university village in Chieti (1979)
Rossi was looking for archetypical basic forms and designed the
village with small individual buildings and a community centre.
Drawing

Robert Venturi (b. 1925)

Complexity and Contradiction in Architecture

NEW YORK, 1966

Robert Venturi, Denise Scott Brown, Steven Izenour

Learning from Las Vegas

CAMBRIDGE, 1972

Robert Venturi's study *Complexity and Contradiction in Architecture* was published by the Museum of Modern Art in New York in 1966. It introduced an epoch-making change and influenced the development of architecture more than any other treatise in the last third of the 20th century. The second book that he wrote together with Denise Scott Brown and Steven Izenour, *Learning from Las Vegas*, is of similar importance. It was published by the Massachusetts Institute of Technology.

Robert Venturi was born in 1925 in Philadelphia. He embarked on his career in the intellectual climate of the East Coast. In 1958, Venturi went freelance in Philadelphia. In 1964, he formed a partnership with John Rauch and in 1967 with Denise Scott Brown (born 1931) whom he married in the same year. Venturi taught at the University of Pennsylvania and at Yale, and at other institutions.

Venturi's œuvre is varied. It includes development projects like villas, museums and supermarkets, but also beach houses and research institutes. Guild House in Philadelphia (1960 1963), a retirement home, was built at the beginning of his career and he used it often to illustrate his ideas about what is ugly, banal and symbolic in architecture. About the same time, he built a small house for his mother in Chestnut Hill, which reflected his ideas on variety and contradiction and broke with all conventions of functionalism. Indeed, he did not hesitate to include irritations such as a stairway that leads to a wall. Venturi borrowed from Pop Art for such pro-

jects as the shops for the supermarket chains BEST and BASCO, which were built in the mid-1970s and are nothing more than "decorated sheds." Since the 1980s, Venturi's buildings have been characterized by the playful use of elements of Classical architecture. We can agree with Robert Stern in characterizing his style as "ironic Classicism." The extension of the National Gallery in London (1985–1991) is an example of a both emotive and playful building that masterfully juggles with the idiom and rhetoric of the Baroque.

In the introduction of *Complexity and Contradiction*, Venturi acknowledges that he wishes to offer a critique of architecture and justify his own work. His premise is not objectivity, but rather artistic licence; he examines those aspects of architecture which interest him, namely, complexity and contradiction. In a reversal of the classic dictum of Ludwig Mies van der Rohe that "less is more," Venturi postulates that "more is not less." Such a surfeit of explicit messages of symbolism and decoration was not to be found in the works of classical Modernist architects like Mies van der Rohe or Adolf Loos. According to Venturi, they achieved and cultivated their purity and hermetic style by ignoring many factors and by working against the needs of society. For Venturi, the demonstrative "less," i.e. the renunciation of ambiguity in Modernist architecture, is quite simply boring.

In his historical explorations (which are not intended to meet the demands of rigorous scholarship) Venturi finds enough ambiguity, contradiction and contrast-especially

where the architecture of Mannerism, Baroque and Rococo is concerned. Even in the work of Le Corbusier (1887–1965), one of the only modern architects alongside Alvar Aalto (1898–1976) whom Venturi liked, Venturi identifies the roots of contradiction; for example, the Villa Savoie has a simple exterior but a complicated interior. Le Corbusier was, Venturi claimed, a master of subtle but effective rule-breaking.

Venturi repeatedly refers to literature and art, where variety and contradiction are indispensable. He cites Pop Art as a good example. It works with paradoxes, changes contexts and dimensions and aims to exhaust all potential of perception. It would be short-sighted and inappropriate to call Venturi a Pop Art architect, although there are clear affinities. Like Pop Artists from Robert Rauschenberg (born 1925) to Andy Warhol (1928–1987), Venturi tries to cross the borders between vulgar and high art and (again like them) he extracts familiar objects out of their usual frame of reference and thereby exposes them to new meanings.

Much of Venturi's work, like his emphasis on the complexity of the historical city or his renunciation of the functionalist credo, is similar to that of Aldo Rossi (1931–1997). However, unlike his Italian colleague, Venturi is not primarily interested in questions of typology. His attention is fixed on narrative and symbolic categories which have been frowned on in Modernist architecture since the 1920s.

It was a central concern of Venturi's, as theorist and architect, to rediscover architecture as a bearer of symbols. He found models not only in history, but specifically in his own surroundings – in the trivial buildings of North America. Pop Art pointed the way by opening his eyes to everyday banality as a source of vitality, multiplicity and colour. With typical American pragmatism and optimism, Venturi declared that its pure existence was justification enough for the commonplace and the banal, and it was in this light that he coined the phrase "Main Street is almost alright." Yet as an intellectual, which he most certainly is, Venturi does not leave things at that, but develops strategies for artistic appropriation and transformation.

Venturi's second book, *Learning from Las Vegas*, was written with Denise Scott Brown and Steven Izenour. It is dedicated to the analysis of "Main Street" and was inspired in 1968 by a seminar sponsored by Yale University: it was an examination of the main street of the gambling city of Las Vegas, the so-called "Strip." The central theme had to do less with individual architectural forms and more with architecture as a means of communication. The first part of the book discusses the results of the seminar. Using photos, maps and diagrams, he demonstrates how seductive the characteristic

architecture of Las Vegas is; how parking lots, advertisements, street lights and entrances to casinos are designed. Many references and relationships emerge – such as the historical reference in the costumes of Caesar's Palace casino. According to one result of the study, it is symbols and not architecture which dominate the space with their sculptural form, their silhouettes and their lighting effects. In spite of the chaos and ugliness, which the authors do not dispute, they find clues for the design of an animated, multi-faceted and contradictory city which exists in mockery of modern ideals.

Two significant figures at the centre of the second, more theoretical part of *Learning from Las Vegas* are the duck and the decorated shed. Venturi took the photo of the duck from Peter Blake's critical balance-sheet, *God's Own Junkyard. The Planned Deterioration of America's Landscape*, 1964. It shows a fast-food restaurant specializing in poultry on a country road: the restaurant is in the shape of giant duck. The building is a sculpture in its own right; the symbolic form has taken over the architecture. He contrasts the duck with the decorated shed, which is no more than a functional box. Its decorations and the sign – an ad on the roof, on the grounds, or simply as a fake second front wall – which indicates its function are totally independent of its architecture. Venturi fundamentally accepts the duck and the shed, pointing out that both have their justification in architectural history. Quite respectlessly, he asserts that the Cathedral of Amiens is a giant advertisement with a shed behind, which, because of its symbolic form, is in turn a duck.

However, in modern architecture, he says, the duck plays too great a role. This hypothesis is meant to provoke and does not withstand scrutiny. Nevertheless, Venturi goes on to demonstrate what he means: he contrasts the Guild House, an early work, with an apartment house, Crawford Manor, which is also in Philadelphia and was built by the then well-known Paul Rudolph. Guild House is, to put it pointedly, a function-oriented shed with some ornaments and symbols (it is topped by an ironically placed golden television antenna). Crawford Manor, on the other hand, is a duck; not exactly like the fast-food restaurant, but still a duck because of its sense of feigned expressiveness and because of a design which tries to be heroic and artistic through form for the sake of form.

Post modernism has been popular since the 1960s because it exhibits variety and contradiction through irony, playfulness and an innocent and optimistic relationship to history and everyday culture. It would be almost unimaginable without the theories and sketches of Robert Venturi.

GL

1 | **Robert Venturi's residential block, Guild House, Philadelphia (1960–1963)**
The block became a paradigm for post-modern architecture. *Learning from Las Vegas* offers a precise analysis of its stylistic means and forms. *German ed., 1978, p. 185*

2 | **Vanna Venturi House in Chestnut Hill (1962–1964)**
Venturi built this house for his mother. The front corresponds to a traditional house, but it is not without contradictions. *German ed., 1979, p. 188*

3 | **Benjamin Franklin Memorial in Philadelphia (1972–1976)**
Venturi placed the exhibition rooms of this memorial underground and he marked the location of
Franklin's house with a steel skeleton above them.
Additional illustration not included in the book.

4 | **Country home in Northern Delaware (1978–1983)**
The blind façade made of plywood for this country home ensures an ironic and
estranged relationship between regional designs and classic representation.
Additional illustration not included in the book.

5 | City Edges Planning Study
In 1973, Denise Scott Brown and Venturi produced a study of advertisements for points of interest on the road leading to Philadelphia. They employed the methodology and aesthetics of commercial advertising.
German ed., 1979. Photo montage

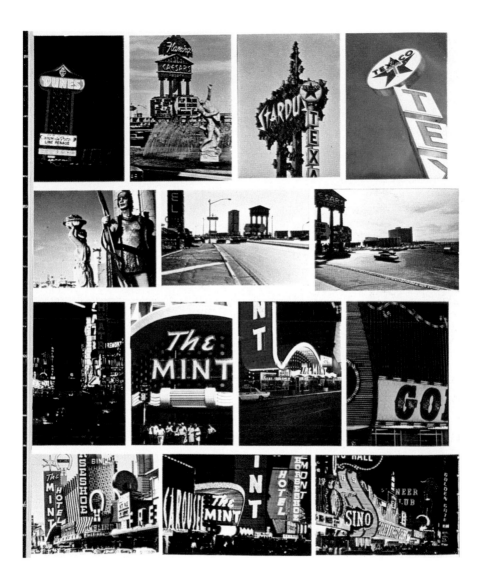

6 | **Study of advertisements**
The analysis of the advertising that dominates public space in the city
of gambling is at the centre of the book, *Learning from Las Vegas.*
German ed., 1979, p. 76/77

7 | Designs for eclectic façades
These eclectic façades drawn by Venturi in 1977 are celebrating
a party of styles in a brief survey of the history of architecture
to be used as a symbolic inventory.
In: A garden party of styles, *1977. Drawing*

8 | **Study of comparisons**
Using examples like Thomas Jefferson's University of Virginia (bottom left),
this page from *Complexity and Contradiction* shows how repetition and
layering can achieve stimulation.
In: Complexity and Contradiction, *English ed., chapter VIII, figs. 94–102*

0 | " I am a monument"
Venturi's proposal for designing a monument in *Learning from Las Vegas*:
no symbolic form; just a box with a sign pointing itself out.
German ed., 1979, p. 184. Sketch

Großes Zeichen — Kleines Gebäude

oder

Das Gebäude ist das Zeichen

10 | **"The Long Island Duckling"**
"The Long Island Duckling," a duck-shaped fast food restaurant, is the subject of Venturi's
illustration for his thesis about a building being dominated by its symbolic form, which
he contrasts with the "decorated shed."
German ed., 1979, p. 29. Photo and sketch

Charles A. Jencks (b. 1939)

The Language of
Post-Modern Architecture

NEW YORK, 1977

This book is one of the most successful works on architectural theory from the post-1945 era. By 1991, it had gone through six editions. It has been translated into ten languages. Charles Jencks, who was born in Baltimore in 1939, first studied English literature and then architecture at Harvard University. In 1970 he took a doctorate in the history of architecture at London University. Jencks is a practising architect and garden designer. His book *Movements in Architecture* appeared in 1972 and in it he used an essay-like English literary style which was based on the provocative tone of Pop Art as well as an armchair style of introspection, with the result that his observations and conclusions are as shrewd as they are inconsistent.

Jencks was one of the first to transfer the term "Post-modern" from literary expression, where it was first used in 1975, to architecture. The descriptions and empirical reflective diagnoses of *The Language of Post-Modern Architecture* have more the character of sharp irony than of a systematic programme, let alone a manifesto; and from the point of view of scholarly architectural history there is much that is disputable, amateurish and factually inaccurate. Nevertheless, the book was very successful as a theoretical foundation for Post-modern architecture.

Part I, entitled "The Death of Modern Architecture", begins with the sentence: "Happily we can date the death of Modern Architecture ... It expired finally and completely in 1972" – namely with the demolition of several high-rises which were built between 1952 and 1955 by Minoru Yamasaki (later to be the architect of the World Trade Center in New York). These were part of the modern residential complexes

of Pruitt-Igoe in St. Louis, Missouri, and they were destroyed because of social problems which were out of control. For Jencks, the reason was to be found in a contradiction between the architecture and the architectural codex of the social underclass to which its inhabitants belonged.

For Jencks, these are purely aesthetic questions. He works with semiological expression "codex" which became popular with French structuralism in the 1970s. "Codex" is used to criticize the "univalence" and "elitist reductionism" of modern architecture and to "enlarge the vocabulary of architecture in different directions – to include native (local), traditional and commercial jargon of the street." In the architecture of the Post-modern, Jencks sees a "radical eclecticism" in which different architectural languages make ironic comments and in this he sees a "double standard ... which appeals to the elite as well as to the man on the street." He bases the development of his theses on examples which mostly come either from England or the USA, and he asserts: "The buildings of today are ugly, brutal and too big." He criticizes the "univalent form" of Mies van der Rohe's buildings and the way in which their "universal grammar" represents a "universal disregard for place and function" in which everything is interchangeable. He also criticizes machine aesthetics of the architecture of the 1960s (Team X, A. and P. Smithson) and the belief in a *zeitgeist* determined by machines and technology.

Jencks claims that modern architecture developed from the interests of large corporations and because of progress in building technology. The aesthetic of factory and engineering buildings was then transferred to the construction of houses. Jencks agrees with the Nazis' criticism of the

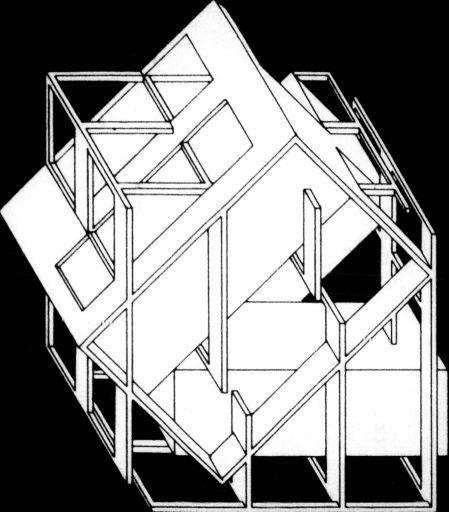

1927 Weissenhof housing estate in Stuttgart. Post-war architecture was only a reflection of the economic triumph of the consumer society in the West and of bureaucratic state capitalism in the East.

In Part II, Jencks examines "types of architectural communication." He asserts that "While there were once laws governing architectural grammar … nowadays there is only confusion and disagreement." Jencks tries to analyse architecture as a semantic system. First there is the metaphor as an architectural form. Man always looks at a building as a metaphor which he can relate to his experiences in life and his surroundings. The metaphors for Modernist buildings are cardboard boxes and checked paper. Metaphorical observation is always polyvalent. Jencks analyses the development of late Modernism, which uses polyvalency as a means of design. He refers to Robert Venturi's distinction between the iconic (the "duck") and the building covered in pictures (the "decorated shed"); he defines the one as iconic sign and the other as symbolic sign and opines: the more metaphors architecture triggers, the greater the dramatic effect: yet the more those metaphors remain mere suggestions, the greater the semiotic ignorance. He critically exemplifies this with the Sydney Opera House (1957–1974) and the Saarinen's TWA Terminal (1962). For him the most successful use of not-so-obvious metaphors is Le Corbusier's Ronchamp (1955).

Secondly, the architectural language of form is made up of words. This includes established motifs and elements like the column and the pitched roof. Words, which are traditional and familiar forms, have been disposed of by modern architecture's fundamentalist belief in progress. He names the reconstruction by the inhabitants of Le Corbusier's houses in Pessac as a basis for criticism of the Modern Movement. That the inhabitants of commercial houses in the United States were able to choose the style of the façade themselves is a legitimate means of satisfying the need for identification; however in the case of Pessac, the thoroughgoing modernity is an expression of elitist posture. Modern architecture is obsessed purely with the syntax of its architectural language, i. e. the rules and methods for designing buildings as a whole.

By semantics, Jencks means style in the sense used by the theory of art. A style is never eternally valid. That is why the claim of modern architecture to have created the style of the 20th century has become a banal consumer product. Jencks claims that architects should once again employ an explicit system of semantic order and he goes on to postulate a mixture of styles. In Part III of his book, Jencks deals with "Post-modern architecture." He detects its beginnings in trends in this direction since the 1950s: the Baroque paraphrases of Paolo Portoghesi in Italy and the "semi-historians," as he calls them, in the United States (Minoru Yama-

saki, Eero Saarinen). He considers Philip Johnson to be the most talented and the most intelligent. He puts him as well as the Japanese Kenzo Tange, Kikutake and Kurokawa into the category of "half post-modern." He judges the early work of Robert Venturi and Charles Moore critically and from a distance. He considers the state architecture of fascism in Germany and Italy as well as Stalinist architecture and the reconstruction of Warsaw as well as the historicist inventions of holiday architecture like Port Grimaud (1965–1969) to be reference points for a new Revivalism. He describes the Pompeian copy of the Getty Museum in Malibu (1970–1975) as an "unintentional example of a Post-modern building."

According to Jencks, an important development in Post-modern architecture was the "reanimation of down-to-earth architecture," which he finds in decorative forms and building materials, in the reduced dimensions, and more or less Revivalist-style domestic architecture of Ralph Erskine in England, Theo Bosch in Holland and Martorell in Spain. His opinion on their "pseudo-traditionalism": "what they lose in authenticity, they gain in cheerfulness" – a typical Jencks' bonmot.

Applying the equation "adhoc + urban = context", Jencks was enthused by the "beautiful pluralism" of Erskines "Byker Wall" in Newcastle, England (1974) and by Lucien Kroll's chaotic and seemingly improvisational buildings in Belgium (1969–1974). Modernism is also responsible for the decay of our cities. Post-modern oriented itself once again, he said, to urban planning in line with Camillo Sitte's programme of enclosed urban space. Jencks refers to Colin Rowe ("Collage City") and to the principles of the "contextualist" composition of city and large buildings from self-contained units which appear together in a single context but not in the context of one total order (Oswald Mathias Ungers). Jencks praises Post-modern architecture for returning to an explicit rather that an implicit system of metaphors. Jencks dedicates the last chapter to "Post-modern space," treating in detail the mathematical structures of Peter Eisenman and the "ironic unmasking of the public area" in Charles Moore's Kresge College.

In the conclusion to his book, Jencks notes a tendency in Post-modern architecture toward "the mysterious, ambiguous and lustful" and toward a "radical eclecticism" as the "naturally developed response to a culture of choice" of "different codices", He recognizes the dialectic of two codices: one which is "popular, traditional and evolves slowly, like a living language, full of clichés and rooted in family life, and one which is modern, full of new images and fast changes in technology, art and fashion." Post-modern architecture combines them both to a "double codex". For him, the most valid and creative example of this is Charles Moore's Piazza d'Italia in New Orleans (1976).   JP

1 | **Minoru Yamasaki, Pruitt-Igoe Housing, St. Louis (1952–1955)**
The building was demolished on July 15, 1972. For Jencks, this is
a symbolic date marking the end of modern architecture.
P. 9

2 | **Sydney Opera House by Jørn Utzon**
Example of metaphoric architecture with ambivalent symbolism.
P. 43

3 | **Caricature of the Sydney Opera House**
The caricature was presented by Australian students of architecture as
Queen Elisabeth II officially inaugurated the opera house.
P. 43. Drawing

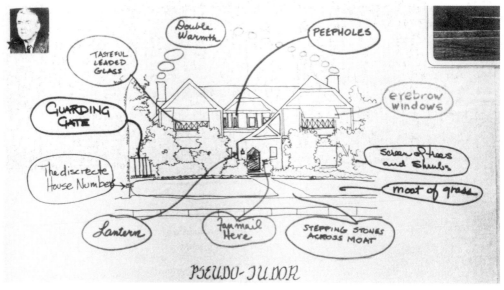

4 | **Jimmy Stewart's house, Beverly Hills** (ca. 1940)
The narrative eclecticism of a typical film star's house
and the ironic explanation of its semantic messages.
P. 65. Drawing and Photo

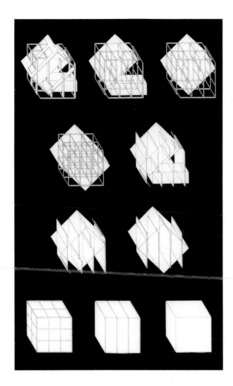

5 | **Peter Eisenman, Building III for Robert Miller** (1971)
The creation of a structure through the overlapping
of two orthogonal grids at a 45° angle.
P. 73. Drawing

6 | **Ralph Erskine, residential structure, "Byker Wall" in Newcastle, England** (1974)
Example of the use of different building materials in order to diminish
the optic volume of a structure.
P. 91. Photo

Rem Koolhaas (b. 1944)

Delirious New York:
A Retroactive Manifesto for Manhattan

NEW YORK, 1978

S, M, L, XL

ROTTERDAM, 1995

As the name suggests, Rem Koolhaas' Office for Metropolitan Architecture (OMA) busies itself with finding globally applicable strategies and solutions which give a new definition to the form and function of contemporary metropolitan development. His models for the development of metropolitan structures are based on a new approach to late modern functional analyses for a contemporary society of mass consumption and ever faster communication. Rem Koolhaas founded his office in 1975 with Zoe and Elia Zenghelis and Madeleine Vriesendorp. He is one of the most charismatic but also controversial figures in the contemporary architectural scene and has drawn attention to himself not only through his designs, but also through numerous publications. With *Delirious New York* from 1978 and the collection *S, M, L, XL*, a compendium of articles which appeared in 1995, Koolhaas made it into the ranks of bestsellers and became one of the most influential theorists of a new and critical modern style within contemporary architectural discourse.

Koolhaas was born in Rotterdam in 1944, and after working as a journalist from 1968 to 1972 he graduated from the London Architectural Association. With his future founders of the OMA, Koolhaas mounted the project "Exodus, or the Voluntary Prisoners of Architecture" in 1972. With its irony, quotations, fiction and a view of the functionalist modern city which was both polemic and fascinated, it anticipated the most important characteristics of Koolhaas' future

themes. In spite of its post-modern reflective style, it clearly distances itself from the formal retrospection of Post-modern. After years of mostly theoretical work in London and New York, in 1984 the OMA moved to Rotterdam. Since the mid-1980s, the group has consistently distinguished itself through spectacular building projects which, like the Dutch Theatre of Dance in The Hague (1981–1987), the Art Gallery in Rotterdam (1987–1992) and the masterplan and realization of individual buildings within the larger Euralille project in Lille (1988–1995) are among the most striking examples of a new and radical modern style.

Delirious New York: A Retroactive Manifesto for Manhattan, Rem Koolhaas' first book, was conceived, as the name implies, as an *ex post* manifesto for a specific urban culture which Koolhaas attached to Manhattan. Koolhaas called the superimposition of different life styles, ideologies and functions within a narrow space, which determine the character of the city environment, a "culture of congestion." This idea became the main theme of his reflexions. Using historical illustrations, cartoons and presentations of his own projects, Koolhaas tells a history of the city of New York in five illustrated chapters. Some of these texts, such as "The City of the Captive Globe" had been devised earlier as independent articles. He adduces observations about the amusement park, Coney Island, and general reflexions on the building style of New York skyscrapers, and puts great weight on an analysis of the Rockefeller Center as well as examinations of the "Eu-

ropean view" of New York. In the final chapter, the historical observations lead to fictional OMA projects which transpose the findings into model studies. According to Koolhaas, high density is the result of a neutral grid plan which is what largely characterizes Manhattan and is the prerequisite for timeless and flexible urbanism. The neutrality of the grid plan explains, on the one hand, a fundamental detachment from historical commitments and, on the other hand, it creates the conditions for demarcation and individuality. Like countless islands in the city, the Manhattan skyscrapers are an archipelago of possibilities which is subject to permanent change. The adaptability of the construction of the buildings is based, according to Koolhaas, on various conditions: the monument-like self-referentiality of construction, the independence of exterior from interior design as well as the vertical overlapping of different functions within the same larger structure. For Koolhaas, the "automonument" of a block is best represented by the large size of a skyscraper, because its exterior design stresses the sculptural quality of the object. Through a separation of this design from the transforming internal functions by what Koolhaas describes as "a lobotomy," the required flexibility of the block remains intact. A further contribution is made by the possibility of vertical functional differentiation, which Koolhaas calls "schism." In this way, Koolhaas clearly distances himself from the Modernist dogma about the relationship between form and func-

tion. At the same time, he provides a theory which bids farewell to all types of functionalist formalism. As a result, he believes he can create a basis for planning which matches the speed, flexibility and adaptability of modern civilization. The grid plan of Manhattan and in the assembly of autonomous high-rise monuments prefigures this concept of density and adaptability, which serves as the basis for Koolhaas' "retroactive manifesto". Each block has the potential to become a self-contained and highly flexible world unto itself; the metropolis becomes the "city of the captive globe … which is devoted to the artificial conception and accelerated birth of theories, interpretations, mental constructions, proposals and their infliction on the world. … The changes in this ideological skyline will be rapid and continuous: a rich spectacle of ethical joy, moral fever or intellectual masturbation." Koolhaas' strategy of storytelling proves to be an entertaining combination of historical observations, theoretical reflexions and fictional, occasionally ironic, episodes. The tone of the book alternates between objective commentary and expressive lyricism, some passages even resembling hymns, to emphasize the manifesto-like character and ambitious literary pretensions of the text.

S, M, L, XL, which appeared in 1995, is not, unlike *Delirious in New York*, a continuous text, but rather a collection of independent articles which is divided into chapters entitled "S" (small), "M" (medium), "L" (large), and "XL"

Fig. p. 557
1 | **Office for Metropolitan Architecture,
Hotel "Sphinx" project at Times Square**
P. 298

(extra large). The authors, Koolhaas and Bruce Mau, structured the book so that the letters refer to the size of the object in question. The concluding chapter, "XL," deals with Koolhaas' chief theme, namely, planning in megastructure format. The extravagant design of this opulent book is remarkable. It uses superimposed pictures and numerous text/picture collages and in 1997, the work was awarded the Book Award of the American Institute of Architecture. Just as complex as the design is the way in which different kinds of texts are strung together. These include passages of an abstract and theoretical character, epigram-like sequences, specially prepared comic strips and fictional and subjectively related essays. The text "Less is More" unexpectedly tells the story of Mies van der Rohe's Barcelona Pavilion (1929). After its demolition, the story continues as fiction and ends with the alleged "reconstruction" of this Modernist *incunabulum* by the OMA at the Triennale in Milan in 1986, the year in which the pavilion was, in fact, rebuilt on its original site in Barcelona. Other texts deal with the office's numerous plans and building projects; for example, a fundamental analysis of the development of spatial planning in Holland in the chapter "Puntstad – Zuidstad." Other themes include the Bibliothèque Nationale in Paris and the Centre for Art and Media Technology in Karlsruhe. One of the book's central texts goes into "The Generic City": as its name suggests, a city without any individual characteristics. In this piece, Koolhaas summarizes his observations about urbanism in the age of globalization and global urbanization. A central question posed in this work is that of which form of urbanism and urban identity to choose in the light of factors like worldwide analogous phenomena in late capitalist land use, architectural corporate identity by global players, global tourism as well as the loss of historical identity. Koolhaas' analyses are critical and polemic, his strategies for solutions are consciously reserved, and he rejects dogmatic affirmations concerning historical urban structures, saying that they are too restrictive and ultimately ahistorical. The city without characteristics, by contrast, is the result of liberation from historical patterns of identity; it is without limitations but at the same time available and open. The periphery, free of historical implications, with its identical structures of urban sprawls, becomes the distinguishing mark of the global city.

In a polemic honing of words, Koolhaas refers to the infrastructural junctions of modern civilization; namely, the megaprojects like giant airports and railway stations for international high speed trains, which are the manifestation of the identity of a global society and which still remain as design tasks for planners and architects. As provocative as the text seems – it positively invites disagreement – it is equally clear that the position of the author is less a manifesto of anti-urbanism than a sober analysis of current urban developments. Behind the seemingly radical and cynical polemic is the challenging question of the potential and limitations of contemporary urbanism.   PS

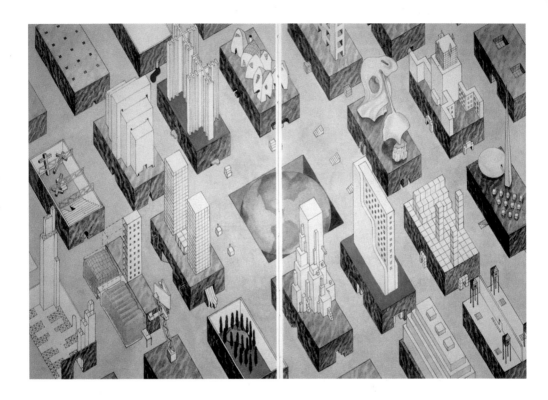

2 | Office for Metropolitan Architecture, The City of the Captive Globe (1972)
P. 295

3 | Office for Metropolitan Architecture, Project study for
"New Welfare Island." Axonometric projection and caption.
P. 302

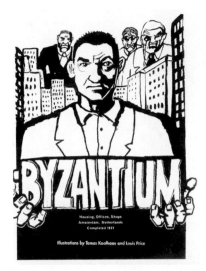

Bigness
or
the problem of Large

Beyond a certain scale, architecture acquires the properties of Bigness. The best reason to broach Bigness is the one given by climbers of Mount Everest: "because it is there." Bigness is ultimate architecture.

4 | Office for Metropolitan Architecture/Rem Koolhaas with Tomas Koolhaas and Louis Price, Cartoon
P. 354/55

5 | Office for Metropolitan Architecture/Rem Koolhaas and Bruce Mau, Illustration for the chapter "Bigness"
P. 494/95

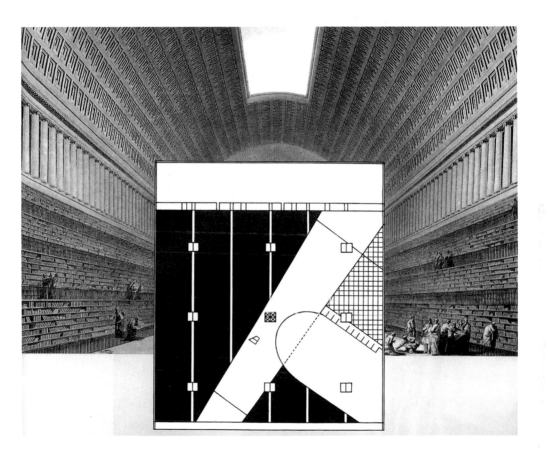

6 | Office for Metropolitan Architecture/Rem Koolhaas, Design for Bibliothèque
Nationale, Paris, ground plan, Level 4
P. 623

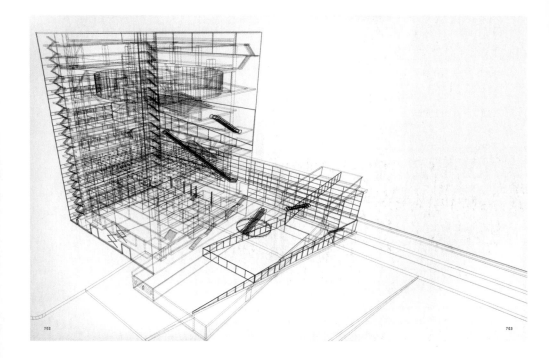

7 | Office for Metropolitan Architecture/Rem Koolhaas, Design
for the Centre for Art and Media Technology, Karlsruhe
P. 702/03

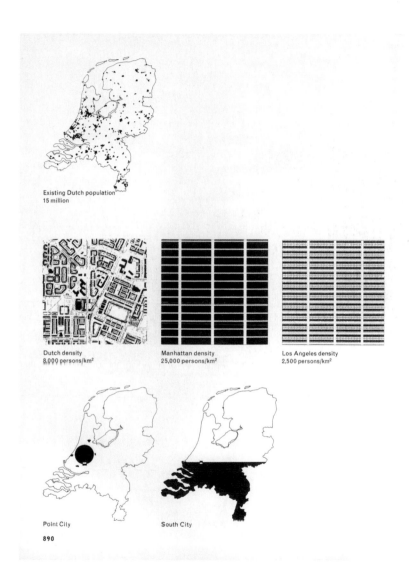

Existing Dutch population
15 million

Dutch density
8,000 persons/km²

Manhattan density
25,000 persons/km²

Los Angeles density
2,500 persons/km²

Point City

South City

890

8 | Office for Metropolitan Architecture/Rem Koolhaas,
Illustration for the text "Puntstad – Zuidstad"
P. 890

Appendix

Index

Acknowledgements/Photo Credits

The publisher wishes to thank the Director of the Kunstbibliothek Berlin, Bernd Evers, for the realisation of this project, and the staff of the library for their active support.

The publisher has made every effort to ensure that all copyrights were respected for the works illustrated and that the necessary permission was obtained from the artists, their heirs, representatives or estates. This was not possible in every case, in spite of intensive research. Should any claims remain outstanding, the copyright holders or their representatives are requested to contact the publisher.